Understanding the Leitmotif

The musical leitmotif, having  particular forcefulness in the music of Richa.   ligits   remained a popular
compositional device up to the   .y. In this book, Matthew
Bribitzer-Stull explores the bac   und and development of the
leitmotif, from Wagner to the ł ilywood adaptations of *The Lord
of the Rings* and the *Harry P*   eries. Analyzing both concert
music and film music, Bribitze   explains what the leitmotif is
and establishes it as the union o   .spects: the thematic and the
associative. He goes on to show ι . *Vagner's Ring* cycle provides a
leitmotivic paradigm, a model from which we can learn to better
understand the leitmotif across style periods. Arguing for a renewed
interest in the artistic merit of the leitmotif, Bribitzer-Stull reveals
how uniting meaning, memory, and emotion in music can lead to a
richer listening experience and a better understanding of dramatic
music's enduring appeal.

MATTHEW BRIBITZER-STULL is Associate Professor of Music
Theory at the University of Minnesota. He has presented and published widely on Wagner, nineteenth-century chromatic tonality,
musical association, and music-theory pedagogy. His articles appear
in *Music Theory Spectrum*, *Journal of Music Theory*, *Music Analysis*,
Intégral, *Journal of Schenkerian Studies*, *Journal of Musicological
Research*, *Journal of Music Theory Pedagogy*, *The Cambridge Wagner
Encyclopedia*, and *The Legacy of Richard Wagner*, among others. He
is author of the *Anthology for Performance and Analysis* (2013) and
co-editor of *Richard Wagner for the New Millennium: Essays on
Music and Culture* (with Alex Lubet and Gottfried Wagner (great-
grandson of the composer), 2007). The winner of the Society for
Music Theory Emerging Scholar Award, he has also received a
number of teaching awards.

30109 02766953 3

Understanding the Leitmotif

From Wagner to Hollywood Film Music

MATTHEW BRIBITZER-STULL

CAMBRIDGE
UNIVERSITY PRESS

782·
101
BRI

CAMBRIDGE
UNIVERSITY PRESS

University Printing House, Cambridge CB2 8BS, United Kingdom

One Liberty Plaza, 20th Floor, New York, NY 10006, USA

477 Williamstown Road, Port Melbourne, VIC 3207, Australia

4843/24, 2nd Floor, Ansari Road, Daryaganj, Delhi - 110002, India

79 Anson Road, #06-04/06, Singapore 079906

Cambridge University Press is part of the University of Cambridge.

It furthers the University's mission by disseminating knowledge in the pursuit of education, learning and research at the highest international levels of excellence.

www.cambridge.org
Information on this title: www.cambridge.org/9781107485464

© Matthew Bribitzer-Stull 2015

This publication is in copyright. Subject to statutory exception
and to the provisions of relevant collective licensing agreements,
no reproduction of any part may take place without the written
permission of Cambridge University Press.

First published 2015
First paperback edition 2017

A catalogue record for this publication is available from the British Library

Library of Congress Cataloging in Publication data
Bribitzer-Stull, Matthew, 1972–
Understanding the leitmotif : from Wagner to Hollywood film music /
Matthew Bribitzer-Stull.
        pages   cm
Includes index.
ISBN 978-1-107-09839-8 (Hardback)
1. Leitmotif.   2. Wagner, Richard, 1813–1883. Operas.   3. Motion picture
music–History and criticism.   4. Program music.   I. Title.
ML1700.B796 2015
781.8′2-dc23   2014043069

ISBN 978-1-107-09839-8 Hardback
ISBN 978-1-107-48546-4 Paperback

Cambridge University Press has no responsibility for the persistence or
accuracy of URLs for external or third-party internet websites referred to in
this publication, and does not guarantee that any content on such websites is,
or will remain, accurate or appropriate.

For Warren Darcy and Robert Gauldin,
whose teaching and scholarship inspired me
to study music theory and to study Wagner.

Contents

Music examples

Tables

Preface

"Understanding," the first word of this book's title, implies that we have not yet fully grasped the concept of the leitmotif. Certainly, past decades bear testament to a history of leitmotivic *deconstruction* – that is, subverting the musico-philosophical significance of the leitmotif to expose its fundamental assumptions and inconsistencies – and we must admit that the days of its facile usage in music scholarship are long past.[1] While it would be an exaggeration to assert its *destruction*, it is fair to say that the leitmotif concept has suffered considerable damage and abuse over the past century. Not only have critics disparaged its effectiveness and value as a compositional device, but also leitmotivic analysis has been attacked as a puerile, descriptive mania akin to collecting. Moreover, the very meaning of the word "leitmotif" itself has splintered; a cursory glance at the scholarly literature on the topic reveals an object imperfectly apprehended, as though viewed from different angles through a refracting lens.

Certainly, an entire book could be devoted to the history of leitmotivic analysis, criticism, and reception. I am less interested, though, in sifting through the detritus left in the wake of the previous century's leitmotivic de-(con)struction than I am in resuscitating the idea of leitmotif as a valuable component of musical understanding. To that end I attempt to establish the twofold importance of the leitmotif: first as a theme – a component of musical structure – and second as an associative entity – a component of musical meaning. In so doing, I engage largely, but not exclusively, with dramatic Western art music of the later nineteenth century and Hollywood film music post-1970. Among Western, functionally tonal musics, these repertories comprise what is arguably some of the most emotionally evocative music still widely enjoyed by modern man. In the pages that follow, I hope to show that both the accessibility and the subtlety of this music rest in no small part on the leitmotif.

Perhaps it is best to admit now that I find Wagner's thematic technique of singular importance to the history of Western dramatic music, hence the

---

[1] See Krims 1998 for a serviceable overview of the intersection between music analysis and deconstruction.

inspiration for this book. It is all too easy to perpetuate Wagner's self-aggrandizing teleologies and his followers' essentialist viewpoints regarding the nature of his compositional practice and of German art – something I have tried to avoid. That said, Wagner scholarship is, in my opinion, plagued with a critical *sine qua non* that one finds rarely – if at all – in the analytic work on other composers' music. There are many who argue, implicitly or explicitly, that *any* positive appraisal of Wagner's artistry *must* be counter-balanced by criticism of his deeply problematic philosophies, self-appraisals, and legacy; failure to do so is irresponsible, a thoughtless acceptance of Wagnerian hagiography. Because the darker side of Wagner and Bayreuth is well documented in the scholarly literature (including within an anthology I co-edited with Gottfried Wagner, great-grandson of the composer), it is my hope that readers will understand that I find it unnecessary to weave it into my narrative on leitmotif here.[2] Rather, I wish to argue, unapologetically, that Wagner's thematic technique not only admirably served his dramatic aims in *The Ring*, but also provided a paradigm adopted by countless later composers across a wide variety of genres. Illustrating said claim comprises the content of the final three chapters of this book.

My approach embraces what some will consider artificial separations – musical materials from musical meanings, and soundtrack from filmic whole. While I agree that such epistemological divorces necessarily impoverish and misrepresent the items under consideration, the criticism leveled against them really indicts analysis itself, an act that, by definition, separates complex objects into their constituent parts.[3] An analyst at heart, I must confess that I find the benefits of analysis outweigh its faults, and that I have no interest in pursuing a lengthy scholarly defense of it here. Such arguments are worth having, but readers familiar with the English-language musicological literature will know that these arguments have been made at length (and will doubtless continue) in more fitting places than the preface to a book about leitmotifs.

And that brings me to my final point – a point any writer of prefaces knows all too well – a pre-emptive disclaimer of what this book does not do. Because leitmotif is a complex topic, doing *it* justice means that I can't do full justice to the many topics it intersects – in my attempt to serve

[2] For those to whom this literature is unfamiliar, I suggest beginning with the writings of Paul Lawrence Rose and Gottfried Wagner. See Rose 1992 and 1990; Wagner 1999; and these men's essays in Bribitzer-Stull 2007.

[3] See Chion 2009: xi for just such a critique.

many audiences, I run the real risk of satisfying none. Wagnerians will long for more detailed insights into Wagner's prose, Wagnerian reception history, and modern-day opera productions; card-carrying music theorists may find the analytic content of the book too light; historical musicologists will likely feel an imagined rush of wind as we race through topics in the history of Western music that beg for deeper study; students of musical meaning will doubtless find the material in Chapters Four and Five synoptic (though I hope some of my thoughts on associativity are both new and deserving of further consideration); and film-music scholars will search in vain for probing new insights into the history of film music, or the analysis thereof.

That said, certain readers will likely experience opposite problems. Wagnerians may find their eyes glazing over when perusing the details of the Peircian trichotomies; musicologists might lament that the clutter of film music, semiotics, and thematic theory burdens what could have been a good book on the history of the Wagnerian leitmotif; readers without technical training in music may find *too much* analysis ("What do I do with these Schenker graphs?!"); and students of film might tire of the copious "classical" music citations. In my defense against dilettantism on the one hand and inscrutable specialization on the other, I can only plead that I have attempted to write a book that I would want to read – one that, in its discursiveness, affirms my command of certain bailiwicks, while challenging me to grow in others.

This goal will, I hope, explain why this book steers clear of a standard chapter arrangement. I eschew the formula of "literature review," followed by "theory," closing with "analysis," in favor of chapters peppered with all of these things united to explain a certain aspect of the leitmotif. Since I take Wagner's *Ring* as paradigmatic of leitmotivic practice, his thoughts feature prominently in the pages that follow (though I juxtapose them with those of numerous other musical thinkers). That said, Wagnerian citations are not confined to one section in a compilation or summary along the lines of what so many previous scholars have already accomplished, but are rather aired in service of the topic at hand.[4] Thus, it is my hope that readers of this book will trace a variety of *Leitfaden* (to borrow a Wagnerian metaphor) to help them make sense of a wide-ranging study much the way listeners continue to use the leitmotif to make sense of multi-media art forms like opera and film.

---

[4] For one lightly glossed collection of Wagner quotations on themes and expression, see Kirby 2004: 11–16.

A note on film-music excerpts

Many chapters of this book engage film music. Since the film soundtrack is often "team composed" under the direction of the lead composer, and is also subject to editors' and directors' input, it does not usually reflect one composer's musical conception or intention the way we assume most recent art music does.[5] (It is important to remember that film, including the soundtrack, in the period from 1970 to the present is largely the *director's* medium.) Thus, the analysis and transcription in this study relies on the full score *as heard* in the DVD release of the motion picture (director's cut, if available), rather than music or information presented in scores or soundtrack releases. Soundtrack releases often include suites, music cut from the theatric release of the film, and music played over the credits – that is, music catering to the needs of the composer or to a listener experiencing the music divorced from image, rather than the needs of someone engaged with the filmic experience as a whole.

Pedal points, atmospheric timbral effects, dialogue, and non-musical (though sometimes pitched) sound effects are all part of the film sound-track, often occurring simultaneously with the music. This, coupled with large orchestral forces, makes it difficult, if not impossible, to achieve a definitive transcription of any given musical passage. Since access to many film scores is difficult, if not impossible, the transcriptions in the pages that follow present only what is most salient *dramatically*. First and foremost this will comprise melodic content.[6] It may also include a prose description of the texture and orchestral colors and, when appropriate, the harmonic support presented as one or more of the following: a bass or other contrapuntal line, an accompanying chord progression, figured-bass nota-tion, or Roman numerals. These last are included only if they seem to accurately represent the tonal implications of the harmonies.

Finally, unless otherwise indicated, theme names are my own and rely on my judgment of the theme's associative role in the drama, rather than the name of the scene or cue used to identify tracks on CD soundtrack releases.[7]

---

[5] For an entertaining look behind the scenes at the frenetic process of team composition, see Raskin 1989.

[6] Danny Elfman believes it is *melody* that lodges in the memory after watching a film (see Halfyard 2004: 60).

[7] The practice of naming themes is a problematic one, though I believe the benefits outweigh the pitfalls. For some thoughts on the practice, see the discussion on pp. 18, 27, and 63–64 in this volume, as well as Bribitzer-Stull 2007; Thorau 2003: 138–44; and Monelle 2000: 41–42.

Acknowledgments

It is a persistent irony that the first sections of a book – the dedication, the acknowledgments, and the preface – are finished last. To frame a project, of course, requires clarity only hindsight can grant. Looking back over the journey that brought me to this point, it is with both a palpable sense of nostalgia and a deep feeling of gratitude that I celebrate the assistance I had along the way.

I would be remiss to thank anyone before my parents, who, in an age of decreased interest in arts-and-humanities education supported me financially and emotionally in my pursuit of music. Recognition is also due my teachers; they include: Earl Benson, my high-school band director, who introduced me to Wagner through a wind-band transcription of "Elsa's Procession to the Cathedral" from *Lohengrin*, and whose demand for excellence (captured so concisely with the banner stretching across our classroom that read "Results, not Alibis") instilled in me a lasting desire to reach toward excellence whatever the circumstances; Charles McDonald, my first horn teacher, who inspired me with his deep love of music, and encouraged me to start thinking about how music means things; Sylvan Suskin, who introduced me to Wagner's *Die Walküre* in his Music History 101 class at Oberlin; and Warren Darcy, another Oberlin professor, whose *Ring* course inspired me in ways that words cannot express, and who honored me in May 2014 with an invitation to present my work as part of his retirement celebration. I am indebted as well to my mentors at Eastman: Matthew Brown for numerous thought-provoking discussions on music and on making a living in the academy; and Robert Gauldin, for sharing his seemingly boundless knowledge of the repertory with me, a level of knowledge I aspire – in all likelihood fruitlessly – to attain.

My position at the University of Minnesota has not only allowed me the time and resources necessary to complete this project, but has also enabled me to make contact with many fine minds across the spectrum of musical thought. Anyone who enjoys conversations with passionate and intelligent people can imagine how much these contribute to one's own intellectual development and productivity, and what a rare blessing it is to lead a life as professor. The University and its College of Liberal Arts also supported this book in a more direct fashion, seeing fit to grant me a Single-Semester Leave, two Summer Research Fellowships, and a McKnight Fellowship to conduct research.

Of course, writing this acknowledgment would have been moot without a publisher. From my first inquiry to the completion of the manuscript, Vicki Cooper exhibited unflagging enthusiasm for the nature of my project. I hope the good men and women at Cambridge University Press recognize their great fortune in having her as a colleague. In my case, Vicki's editorship was a two-for-one deal: Vicki's husband, leading Wagner scholar John Deathridge, generously agreed to give the final manuscript a once-over before it went to press.

Various portions of this book passed through the hands of many other thinkers along the way. I find that I respect their judgment and advice all the more now that I can see how much they improved the end product. These include: family (Jason Bribitzer-Stull and Emily Stull), friends (David Philip Norris), students (Tim Brock), colleagues (Michael Cherlin, Sumanth Gopinath, Richard Leppert, Scott Lipscomb, and David Neumeyer), and, naturally, the anonymous readers for Cambridge who provided copious and helpful comments on my prospectus. The errors and shortcomings that remain are mine alone.

Finally, I wish to admit my debt of gratitude to those closest to my heart. To my sister, Emily: thank you for traveling to New York City with me in 2000 to join me for my first live *Ring*-cycle performance; a moment from our experience there finds its way into Chapter 4. And to my husband, Jason: I may never be able to fully repay your love, understanding, tolerance, and support. May the next twenty years put the last twenty to shame.

1 | Introduction: the leitmotif problem

> Both rings were round, and there the resemblance ceases.
>
> J.R.R. Tolkien[1]

With the statement above, the author of *The Lord of the Rings* defended the originality of his work against Richard Wagner's earlier *Der Ring des Nibelungen*. While we might argue with Tolkien about the amount of resemblance – both his Ring tale and Wagner's were epic structures heavily based on Norse mythologies – we can accept Tolkien's contention that he was not directly influenced by Wagner. The same distance from Wagner cannot be asserted, however, of Peter Jackson and Howard Shore's cinematic *The Lord of the Rings* adaptation. In fact, it's hard to imagine any Western musico-dramatic genre of the last 130 years – be it film, musical theater, programme symphony, or opera – that hasn't felt the long shadow of Richard Wagner in one way or another. And on no other topic does this shadow fall with such seductive suggestiveness and such maddening obscurity than on the leitmotif.

The opening of a book that purports to explain how to understand the leitmotif is a natural point at which to define it. This is, however, a task easier said than done. For that reason I begin not with a definition, but rather with a pair of examples, musical excerpts from Wagner's *Ring* and Shore's *The Lord of the Rings* that most listeners, I imagine, would agree are leitmotifs of one kind or another. If we can grasp the commonalities of form and function between these musico-dramatic constructs separated by genre, cultural context, and over a century in time, we can better frame the challenges that face us in defining, and in ultimately understanding, the leitmotif.

Example 1 presents two themes from Richard Wagner's *Der Ring des Nibelungen*. Both are associated with Fafner, the first in his incarnation as a giant (i.e., "Giants"), the second after his transformation into the dragon

---

[1] See Tolkien's letter of February 23, 1961 to his publisher, Allen & Unwin, on remarks made by Åke Ohlmarks, the Swedish translator of Tolkien's *Lord of the Rings* (Tolkien 1981: 306).

(a)

(b)

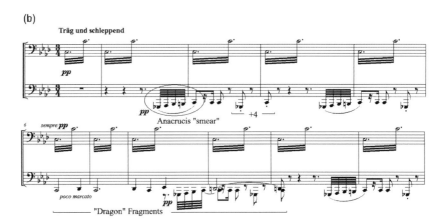

Example 1.1 Comparison of "Giants" and "Fafner as Dragon" in Wagner's *Ring*

a. "Giants," Rg/68/1/1ff.
b. "Fafner as Dragon," Sg/185/4/3ff.

(i.e., "Fafner as Dragon").[2] It is not necessary to know the story of Wagner's *Ring* to recognize the musical effectiveness of these themes and their relationship to one another. In "Giants" (Example 1.1a), the dotted rhythms and

---

[2] A note on methodology: All leitmotifs appear within quotation marks (e.g., "Spear") to distinguish them from the objects, characters, events, and moods represented by the same word. I name each theme from Wagner's *Ring* using Darcy's nomenclature (see Warren Darcy's (2001) unpublished guides to the themes of *The Ring* provided in the appendix to Bribitzer-Stull 2001). All references to Wagner's opera scores are as follows: music drama/page/system/ measure and refer to the Schirmer Vocal Score (e.g., Sg/184/3/1 = *Siegfried*, page 184, third system, first measure). The abbreviations for the music dramas are as follows: Rg = *Das Rheingold*, Wk = *Die Walküre*, Sg = *Siegfried*, and Gd = *Götterdämmerung*.

scoring for brass and timpani strongly suggest a march topic; the low register, minor mode, and *Sehr wichtig und zurückhaltend im Zeitmass* tempo further suggest a funeral march.[3] Clearly, this music reinforces the emotions surrounding the corresponding scene: the ominous and plodding approach of Fafner and his brother, Fasolt. The dramatic efficacy of "Giants" is thus predicated upon a blending of denotative and connotative associations; the affect of the specific scene on stage and the more generalized, culturally established funeral march topic reinforce one another.

Much later in *The Ring* drama Fafner transforms from a giant to a dragon. In Example 1.1b we see a theme associated with his latter incarnation, "Fafner as Dragon."[4] The musical relationship between this theme and "Giants" parallels the dramatic relationship between Fafner's two identities. The F minor tonality, register, dotted rhythms, falling fourth, and anacrusis smear are common to both statements, appropriate musical markers for the brutish nature Fafner retains in both guises. But the temporal changes – a slower, *Träg und schleppend* tempo, and interpolated rests – of the second theme lend it a ponderous quality compared to "Giants," and the fragments of the "Dragon" theme from *Das Rheingold* are an obvious reference to Fafner's new form.[5] The heart of this transformation, however, is the intervallic corruption from perfect fourth to augmented fourth (labeled "+4" on the example). This descending tritone is a local marker for Fafner's physical and moral corruption, distinguishing between the two themes; but Wagner also grants it global importance, for it later becomes both the sonic representation of Fafner's voice and the tonal structure of an entire scene.[6]

Of crucial importance in these examples is that the musical development from "Giants" to "Fafner as Dragon" parallels the dramatic developments of Fafner's character. In Wagner's mature dramas, such developments

---

[3] Musical topics, or *topoi*, have been operative in Western art music for centuries. Only recently, though, have scholars approached them formally, first describing and cataloging them (Ratner 1980), then analyzing the role they play in tonal structures and musical meaning (Agawu 1991; Hatten 1994). *Topoi* naturally bear an intimate relationship to the leitmotif, a topic taken up more thoroughly in Chapter 5.

[4] Since this transformation happens offstage sometime between the first and third dramas, and this theme's initial presentation is during the *Vorspiel* to *Siegfried* Act II (Sg/136/1/2ff.), first-time listeners might not yet understand its dramatic significance. Later in the act, during Siegfried's confrontation with the dragon, this significance becomes clear (Sg/185/4/3ff.).

[5] The "Dragon" theme first appeared during Alberich's transformation in Scene 3 of *Das Rheingold* (Rg/150/3/1ff).

[6] Most of Fafner's lines in *Siegfried* are sung to tritones. See, for example, Sg/154–56 and 185–88. Moreover, *Siegfried* Act II, Scene 1 features a bi-polar tonal arrangement that fluctuates between B minor and F minor.

Example 1.2 Thematic mutation of "Ring" theme in Jackson/Shore *The Lord of the Rings*

a. "Ring" during Galadriel's opening narration
b. "Ring" as Frodo enters the Cracks of Doom

become omnipresent, layering one upon the other. This environment allows for the possibility of *accumulative association* in which music, like language, becomes capable of modifiers – elements that qualify the meaning of an associative theme. With each re-statement of a theme there exists the possibility that added perspective will color the emotional associations we have with it, much like the experience of revisiting childhood haunts as an adult. This evolving associative capacity is what so inspired composers' continued use of leitmotif technique after Wagner.

Example 1.2 presents another theme from an epic musico-dramatic work about a ring of power. The "Ring" theme from Howard Shore's score to *The Lord of the Rings* films, shown in Example 1.2a, sounds at the opening of the first movie when Galadriel narrates the Ring's tortured history. On screen, audiences see *The Lord of the Rings* title frame followed by scenes depicting the forging of the great Rings of Power. Galadriel's narration implies that these rings exploited the baser drives of men and dwarves, leading to their eventual corruption. The narration, camera angles, and dark Tim Burton-esque cinematography all help construct the ancient, tenebrous history that undergirds the epic tale about to unfold.

Like Wagner's "Giants," Shore's "Ring" theme relies in part upon time-honored cultural tropes for its affect. The most prevalent of these is the

descending half-step, a musical figure bearing a long association with grief
and anguish. Echoes of this figure can be heard in the $\hat{6}$–$\hat{5}$, C–B in the bar 1
melody, the harmonic succession of F to E minor triads in bar 1, and the
feeling of half-step transposition from bars 1–2 to bars 3–4. Simultaneous
half-step dissonances between moving lines, and the underlying harmony
(e.g., the beat 1 melody note in bars 1–2 and the beat 4 horn note in bars
1 and 3) increase the poignancy of the affect. Other figures contribute an
air of static uncertainty to the "Ring" theme: The repeated rhythmic figure,
melodic turn figure (ultimately going nowhere), and recurring harmonic
successions contribute to the feeling of inertia, while the half-bar alternation of moving vs. long notes, the lack of clear tonic, the registral and
textural disjunction between melody and harmony, and the closing motion
from G minor to E♭ minor all lend the theme an aura of arcane ambiguity.[7]

That *The Lord of the Rings* begins with the "Ring" theme is only fitting –
the essential plot thread of the trilogy follows the forces of good as they
strive desperately to destroy the Ring, an accomplishment that will bring
down the Dark Lord, Sauron, whose forces teeter on the brink of overwhelming Middle Earth. Audiences hear the "Ring" theme a number of
times throughout the trilogy, but among these many iterations, one near
the climax of the final film stands out: it is a brief fragment sounded just as
Frodo enters the Cracks of Doom – a volcano that lies within the Dark
Lord's realm and the only place in which Sauron's Ring of Power can be
unmade (see Example 1.2b).

There can be no question that this is a variant of the "Ring" theme; the
melodic turn figure (an exact transposition of the first eight notes of "Ring")
over static harmony resembles no other musical materials in Shore's score.
But it is hardly the same thing we heard at the opening of the first film. The
obvious changes are the major-mode implications of this setting and its

[7] While the music cited in Example 2a is tonal in the broadest sense and is triadically based, it is
difficult to posit a tonic key for the excerpt. The beat 3 arrival of the melody on the B–E fifth
supported by E minor harmony is the most tonally confirming gesture. Rather than being
construed through a sense of prolongation or harmonic function, though, this is a tonality that is
merely *asserted*, one of the weaker senses of tonic as described by Daniel Harrison in his analysis
of *Ein Heldenleben* (see Harrison 2002: 143–45).

Bars 3 and 4 have a feeling of being transposed a half-step lower, to E♭ minor, even though these
measures are not an exact transposition of bars 1–2. In fact, an E♭ minor triad is reached only
after the G minor $^6_4$ that concludes the excerpt shown in Example 2a. (This juxtaposition of two
minor triads whose roots lie a major third apart bears a special Wagnerian tonal and
associational significance and comprises the subject of Chapter 6.)

Buhler 2006 describes the "Ring" theme as lugubrious owing to the attraction of the melodic
embellishments about $\hat{5}$ and to the weight of its burden conjured up by the slow tempo, initial
pause, emphasis on $\hat{6}$ and quick melodic descent to tonic.

extreme brevity. In short, the original "Ring" theme has been truncated and redeemed from minor into major. The falling half-step root progressions and melodic tendencies of the original are gone, replaced with a stable harmonic backdrop and a half-step dissonance (G♯ to A or ♯$\hat{4}$ to $\hat{5}$ in D major) whose tendency is to *rise* rather than fall.[8] Thus, the connotations are now of wonder and optimism – connotations abetted by the registral unity, heroic brass orchestration, and added human timbral element of non-texted chorus. Comparing this to the emotional evocation of the original "Ring" statement, we find that Shore, like Wagner, alters the musical materials of his themes to fit (and to help create) new dramatic environments.

If, as the brief analyses above suggest, leitmotivic emotional associations contribute in large part to the sense of drama in multi-media works like opera and film, then leitmotifs' relevance to the audience can hardly be denied.[9] This relevance is equally palpable from the composer's point of view; composers' remarks indicate that leitmotifs form a crucial component of the compositional process itself.[10] In addition to confirming the importance of the leitmotif, though, these two thematic comparisons also raise crucial questions. 1) "What part of thematic meaning derives from specific dramatic context and what part from generic, pre-existing cultural tropes?" The analyses above blended these, but their intersection remains unexplained. 2) "How do we determine theme names, thematic identity, and thematic relationships?" This is a natural question for those who noticed the name change in the first example pair ("Giants" became "Fafner as Dragon") and the name retention ("Ring") in the second. And, 3) "Why are these musical excerpts granted leitmotivic status when hundreds of bars of music from both Wagner's *Ring* and Shore's film score don't achieve such distinction?" In short we can boil down these inquiries to this: "What is a leitmotif, and how does it function?"

---

[8] The transposition to D major and the prevalence of ♯$\hat{4}$ are aspects of this thematic statement that have long-range connections to music throughout the *Lord of the Rings* trilogy. See the end of Chapter 9 for a full discussion.
    Note also the difference in effect between the tritone in this thematic presentation vs. that in "Fafner as Dragon." In the "Ring" variant the tritone is part of an [0137] tetrachord whose imbricated [016] trichord is often used cinematographically to evoke wonder (see Murphy 2006), while in "Fafner as Dragon" the tritone is a destabilizing force, a corruption of the F–C perfect fourth at the heart of the earlier "Giants" theme.

[9] See Ross 2003 for an argument concerning the continued relevancy of leitmotifs to today's audiences. His article also makes some comparisons between Wagner's *Ring* and Shore's film score that mirror claims in this book.

[10] See, for instance, Danny Elfman's comments during his interviews in Columbia Pictures, Inc. 2002 and 2004 in which he stipulates that developing themes is the most difficult portion of constructing a film score and the point at which he often begins to work in earnest.

What is a leitmotif?

We begin by considering the name of the entity we hope to understand – "leitmotif." When translated into English, it is often rendered as "leading motive." But the weak semantic sense of this phrase has conditioned English speakers to prefer the original German. "Leitmotif," however, has strong Wagnerian connotations that are not always appropriate to works both before and after Wagner. Moreover, "leitmotif" implies that the "motive" is the typical form these musical statements take. This is problematic in English-speaking communities where "motive" indicates an incomplete musical thought, a small piece of a larger musical whole. In actuality, the idea of the *theme*, a more-or-less complete musical thought and its concomitant developmental connotations, is more akin to what we are trying to describe. Despite these problems, "leitmotif" remains a valuable term when used with precision. Developmental associative themes that comprise an integral part of the surrounding musical context both in Wagner's works and in later musics should qualify. Generic musical-associative constructs, though (previously known as leitmotifs, reminiscence themes, *idées fixes*, and the like), are better known collectively as "associative themes." The distinction is found even within Wagner's works, both early and mature, which include various forms of associative musical statements, from static blocks that intrude upon the musical texture – reminiscence themes, that is – to plastic themes and motives highly integrated into a transformative network that parallels the vagaries of the drama. Thus, much of the subsequent material in this book is directed toward understanding what distinguishes the leitmotif from other associative themes.

Defining the leitmotif is not a novel pursuit. From 1860 to the present day, commentators have made the attempt; their solutions range from the elegant-but-oversimplified:

'Leitmotif' may be defined as a recurrent musical idea which has been invested by its composer with semantic content.[11]

to painful attempts at completeness that rival Wagner's prose for their prolixity:

[Leitmotifs] consist of figures, or short passages of melody of marked character which illustrate, or as it were label, certain personages, situations, or abstract ideas

---

[11] Darcy 1993: 45.

which occur prominently in the course of a story or drama of which the music is the counterpart; and when these situations recur, or the personages come forward in the course of the action, or even when the personage or idea is implied or referred to, the figure which constitutes the leit-motif is heard.[12]

A leitmotif is a short, uncomplicated musical phrase or theme, usually one to three measures, which is employed, and reused, by the composer when he deems it important to the composition. In the case of Wagner and his *Ring*, the leitmotif became a musical theme representative of a figure, an event, an emotion, a thought, an idea, or a concept in the drama, which theme he repeated, often in subtle but distinct, varying, and often tempered pitch, tone, and/or intensity according to the interpretive demands of his dramatic argument.[13]

Scholars like Thomas Grey get at important components of leitmotif – memory and recontextualization:

Leitmotif, then, is not just a musical labeling of people and things (or the verbal labeling of motives); it is also a matter of musical memory, of recalling things dimly remembered and seeing what sense we can make of them in a new context.[14]

It is, however, difficult to do justice to their rich complexity within only a few sentences.

Nor are Wagner's own writings a panacea. Numerous and at times inconsistent, they are both prescriptive (especially those written during his long period of retheorizing musical drama in the late 1840s) and reflective (like the essays and open letters written post-factum to enhance understanding and to steer reception history of his completed works). Moreover, all of them tell us something about what a leitmotif *does*, but little about what it *is*.[15] The excerpt below, from "Opera and Drama" (1850–51) is typical:

A musical motive (*Motiv*) can produce a definite impression on the Feeling, inciting it to a function akin to Thought, only when the emotion uttered in that motive has been definitely conditioned by a definite object, and proclaimed by a definite individual before our very eyes. The omission of these conditionments sets a musical motive before the Feeling in a most indefinite light; and an indefinite thing may return in the same garment as often as one pleases, yet it will remain a mere recurrence of the Indefinite, and we shall neither be in a position to justify it by any felt necessity of its appearance, nor, therefore, to associate it with anything else.—But a musical motive into which the thought-filled Wordverse of a dramatic performer has poured itself—so to say, before our eyes—is a thing conditioned by

---

[12] Parry 1889.   [13] Cord 1995: 133.   [14] Grey 2008: 114.

[15] Kirby 2004, 11–16 summarizes Wagner's theories of the leitmotif. Therein Kirby also comes to define the prototypic leitmotif and how it is different from other types of themes, motives, and associative entities.

Necessity: with its return a *definite* emotion is discernibly conveyed to us, and conveyed to *us* through the physical agency of the Orchestra, albeit now unspoken by the performer; for the latter *now* feels driven to give voice to a fresh emotion, derived in turn from that earlier one. Wherefore the concurrent sounding of such a motive unites for us the conditioning, the non-present emotion with the emotion conditioned thereby and coming at this instant into voice; and inasmuch as we thus make our Feeling a living witness to the organic growth of one definite emotion from out another, we give to it the faculty of thinking: nay, we here give it a faculty of higher rank than Thinking, to wit, the instinctive *knowledge* of a thought made real in Emotion.[16]

We sample much of Wagner's prose in the chapters ahead. For the time being, we might note that what sets his apart from most other leitmotif commentaries is the centrality of *emotion*, a topic to which we shall return at some length in Chapter 4.

Just as Wagner was not the only one to describe leitmotivic practice, neither was he the only one to compose recurring themes associated with the drama. And the appropriation of this technique in the works of other composers reveals the same disparity of understanding that the commentaries do. This, in short, is the leitmotif problem – because leitmotif admits to multiple practices and multiple interpretations throughout its reception history, it remains misunderstood.

Despite decades of explanatory vagueness and complexity, and scores of competing kinds of thematic recall in dramatic music of the last two hundred years, audiences remain enamored of the technique. Surely this is at least in part because we delight in repetition (more on this in Chapter 2) and easily recognize repeated themes when we hear them, realizing that they contribute to both a work's form and its sense of meaning.[17] Moreover, we recognize not only thematic *recall*, but also thematic *instantiation*.[18] How is this possible? As McClatchie put it:

How does a listener, hearing a work for the first time in the theatre, know that a particular musical gesture is significant and will recur? And how is conceptual

---

[16] Wagner 1966b: 329–30.

[17] If we agree with Wagner, they are one and the same: "dramatic Form is the conglomeration of plastic moments of feeling ... content is present in expression and expression presents the content" (see Wagner 1966b: 347–49).

[18] Dahlhaus notes this importance. Among his requirements for a functioning leitmotif is an extra-musical sense of recognizable identity to the audience (see Dahlhaus 1979: 107). Another of his requirements – that the music exhibit incompleteness stemming from harmonic and/or metric irregularity – is not, I think, mandatory. We will address this point at greater length in Chapter 2.

content then attached to these figures? With the exception of Lorenz, this matter is rarely discussed anywhere in the vast literature surrounding Wagner and his works.[19]

Answering these questions comprises the main thrust of this book. In so doing, I intend not only to *define* "leitmotif" in relation to the broader practice of generic thematic recall, but also to *resuscitate* its conceptual value, using an approach informed by past authors. I begin by culling from the leitmotivic definitions above three central components that circumscribe the concept:[20]

1. Leitmotifs are bifurcated in nature, comprising both a musical physiognomy and an emotional association.
2. Leitmotifs are developmental in nature, evolving to reflect and create new musico-dramatic contexts.[21]
3. Leitmotifs contribute to and function within a larger musical structure.

Note that throughout the last 300-odd years composers have used a variety of musical statements for dramatic purposes, usually musical themes associated with the drama in some way or other. These include not only leitmotifs, but also reminiscence motives, *ideés fixes*, motto themes, *tintae*, cyclic processes, musical symbolism, musical characterization, and recall of overture music. Such devices can all rightly be called "associative themes" (i.e., themes associated with the drama). Among them, though, only the leitmotif exhibits the music-structural and developmental characteristics listed above.[22] That is, the leitmotif is a special kind of associative theme.[23]

[19] McClatchie 1998: 109.
[20] Despite my grousing about incorrect and incomplete definitions of leitmotif by earlier authors, I must admit that there are plenty of examples of those who get it right, and not only by Wagnerian music scholars like Warren Darcy, Thomas Grey, and Barry Millington. I was heartened to see Meadows (2008: 105–29, an Elgar dissertation) calling out the emotional and transformative nature of the Wagnerian leitmotif as central to its identity. *Ibid.*, 112 even notes specific types of developments and relationships, though without going as far as categorizing them along the lines of Chapter 7 in this book.
[21] Warrack (2001: 391–96) distinguishes the leitmotif from the earlier reminiscence motive (found in operas of Spohr, Méhul, and Weber) by its symphonic nature, specifically Wagner's turning to the sonata-form development sections of the German symphonic heritage (Beethoven, in particular) for inspiration in generating the webs of motives and their concomitant developments he used for dramatic purposes.
[22] I am far from alone in using such a rubric to separate leitmotif from other similar entities. See the distinction made in Kirby (2004: 5–11) between leitmotifs and reminiscence themes.
[23] Readers familiar with my earlier work will notice that this is a reversal from my established practice. Over the years I have studied this topic, I have come to believe that the term "leitmotif" does have value, particularly in distinguishing a form of developmental and music-structural associative theme first found in Wagner's works and used in a variety of later genres.

Exploration of its defining characteristics and presentation of examples comprises the subsequent chapters of this book, with this first chapter serving to introduce these characteristics and some of the questions they engender.

Leitmotifs are bifurcated in nature

That the leitmotif (or any associative theme, for that matter) has a twofold nature – both musical and associative – seems almost too obvious to mention.[24] But the nuances of this conglomeration are often overlooked. How, for instance, does a musical figure acquire an extra-musical association? Is this accomplished purely in coincidence with a dramatic setting, or must the music itself carry some intrinsic emotional value? If the latter, are such values native to the musical figure in an absolute way or are they purely culturally conditioned? Moreover, regarding the extra-musical meaning itself, is it representational in nature? Narrative in nature? Expressive? Semiotic? At the present, it will suffice to accept that the leitmotif is a bifurcated entity, a conceptual blend of the musical and the associative; one can't really be considered without the other.[25] While such conceptual blendings are not new to either music or music theory, recent scholarship presents us with a manner in which to model this twofold nature: the Conceptual Integration Network (CIN).[26]

The model shown in Example 1.3a invokes a spatial metaphor. The Generic Space in the top circle is a blank template that allows for mappings between entities, types of development, and contexts. In Example 1.3b, Musical Space embraces entities like themes and motives; the forms of musical development these entities undergo; and the tonal, formal, and textural contexts in which they exist. Likewise, Emotional Space comprises

"Associative theme" thus strikes me as a more generic term appropriate to collective discussion of all musico-dramatic statements.

[24] Some might object to my approach here, arguing that musical materials and musical meaning are ontologically *inseparable*. This is an argument I consider in Chapter 4, though I will state here that *association* seems by its very definition to be a kind of meaning that stands apart from the musical sounds themselves.

[25] Wagner himself suggested this relationship when he stated that it was as great an injustice to separate his orchestration from his harmony as it was to separate his music from his text. See his letter to Theodor Uhlig of May 31, 1852 in Spencer and Millington 1987: 261.

[26] See Zbikowski 2002: 77–94, who discusses such conceptual blends, and adapts Turner and Fauconnier's CIN to musical concepts. Like many recent works in music, Zbikowski borrows a model developed for another field, in this case linguistics. For more on the linguistic, rhetorical, and grammatical underpinnings of the CIN see *ibid.*: 78, n. 28.

(a)

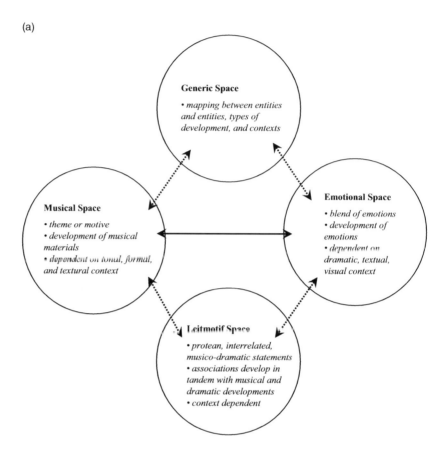

Example 1.3 Leitmotivic Conceptual Integration Network (CIN) Model

a. General model
b. Leitmotivic CIN for "Indy's Feelings for Marion" from *Raiders of the Lost Ark*
c. "Indy's Feelings for Marion" theme

emotions as entities; their potential for nuanced development; and their dramatic, textual, and visual contexts in a theatrical work. When blended, these two spaces map onto one another to form Leitmotif Space in which musically developing themes serve as vessels for emotional associations that parallel dramatic developments within a specific musico-dramatic context.[27]

As an example of its appropriateness for understanding the leitmotif, we can apply this CIN model to music from John Williams's score to Steven Spielberg's *Raiders of the Lost Ark*. The "Generic Space" bubble of the CIN

---

[27] Note that Buhler 2010: 36 also understands the leitmotif (at least its usage in silent film accompaniment) to be a conceptual integration, but one between music and narrative rather than music and emotion.

(b)

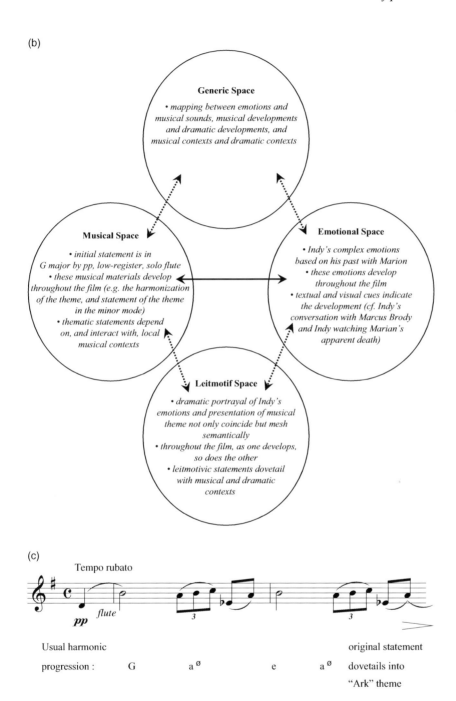

(c)

Tempo rubato

Usual harmonic

progression :   G   a ᵒ̸   e   a ᵒ̸   original statement
                                                                   dovetails into
                                                                   "Ark" theme

Example 1.3 (*cont.*)

indicates that we are mapping between entities (musical sounds and emotions), types of development (musical and dramatic), and types of contexts (musical and dramatic). The "Musical Space" bubble summarizes the musical materials of the "Indy's Feelings for Marion" theme and how these materials develop (see Example 1.3c for a musical representation of this theme). The original, purely melodic theme statement is later harmonized (during a thematic medley that accompanies the depiction of Indy's and Marion's flight to Egypt) and is also presented in the minor mode (when Indy watches the destruction of the truck onto which he believes Marion's captors have loaded her). The "Emotional Space" bubble makes clear that Indy's emotions concerning Marion are complex and based on a past history with her. It also indicates that Indy's feelings for Marion continue to develop throughout *Raiders* and that these developments are indicated in part by visual and textual cues in the film. The bottom bubble, "Leitmotif Space" shows how the specific mapping of emotions and musical materials creates the leitmotif, "Indy's Feelings for Marion." The dramatic moment and musical theme not only coincide temporally, but also fit semantically (for topical reasons discussed at greater length in Chapter 5). Both drama and music develop in tandem throughout the film. And, specific statements of the leitmotif dovetail with later local musico-dramatic contexts. For example, we hear "Indy's Feelings for Marion" during the couple's flight from Mongolia to Egypt. Musically, "Indy's Feelings for Marion" follows a fragment of the "Heroism" theme and bleeds into iconic Middle Eastern music. Full orchestral texture persists throughout this miniature suite of themes. Dramatically, the juxtaposition of "Indy's Feelings for Marion" with the other music in this suite captures various facets of the drama – not least among them, the sense of adventure – during this transitional scene.

Leitmotifs are developmental in nature

[N]either a mere play of counterpoint, nor the most fantastic art of figuration and most inventive harmonizing, either could or should transform a theme so characteristically, and present it with such manifold and entirely changed expression – yet leaving it always recognizable – as true dramatic art can do quite naturally.[28]

As this citation from an essay published shortly after the premiere of *The Ring* cycle makes clear, Wagner understood leitmotifs as mutable, musical

---

[28] Wagner 1966g: 188.

ideas motivated by dramatic impetus to develop. Other commentators, including those outside of Germany, also recognized the protean nature of the leitmotif. French scholar J.M. Bailbé, for instance, says that:

the leitmotif as conceived by Wagner . . . is not only a melody or melodic fragment that recurs, unchanging, throughout a work. Rather it is more like a mutable theme from a sonata form, inherently dramatic in nature. In essence, the musical design manifests in Wagner's works each time that the emotion it represents arises. If the emotion is not modified, the leitmotif recurs in its original form. If it is, then the leitmotif exhibits various rhythmic or melodic developments that suggest the dramatic influence it has been subjected to.[29]

For every scholar who correctly cites the leitmotif's plastic nature, conventional wisdom seems to sprout – hydra-like – two mischaracterizations of the concept. Moreover, the dramatic impact of the *kinds of musical developments* themes undergo has been almost completely overlooked.[30] Some thematic developments are patently motivated by changes in dramatic context, such as Examples 1 and 2 described at the opening of this chapter. Others are modified simply to fit a new musical context. The distinction is easy to see in Berlioz's *Symphonie Fantastique*. The main musico-dramatic idea, or *idée fixe* (like the leitmotif, a form of associative theme), is presented in the first movement (see Example 1.4a). Violins and flutes play an expansive melodic line meant to evoke the protagonist's unrequited love. The accompaniment punctuates the melody with rhythms suggestive of an increasingly elevated heart rate. The *idée fixe* recurs in each of the remaining four movements, but it recurs in different ways. In the second (waltz) movement, the theme is reworked to fit a triple meter and F major context (see mm. 120ff.). While the use of a waltz is part of Berlioz's larger programme, the thematic developments themselves here are not essentially motivated by the drama. Rather, the theme is simply restated, *mutatis*

---

[29] This quotation appears in Kelkel 1984: 279: "le leitmotif, tel qu'il sera conçu par Wagner [. . .] n'est pas uniquement une mélodie ou un fragment mélodique qui réapparaitrait immuable à divers endroits de l'œuvre. Les thèmes cycliques de la forme sonate avec leur valeur dramatique, peuvent en donner une idée. Car en fait, ce dessin musical se manifeste dans l'œuvre wagnérienne chaque fois que le sentiment représenté est en jeu. Si le sentiment n'est pas modifié, le leitmotif reparait intégralement, sinon il est porteur de certaines modifications rythmiques ou mélodiques qui suggèrent l'influence subie." See also Kirby 2004: 9, who reiterates McCredie and Einstein in stating that as leitmotifs evolve musically their meanings may also evolve.

[30] My dissertation (Bribitzer-Stull 2001, esp. chapters 2–4) is the first study to suggest that the specific kinds of musical developments that themes undergo are intimately linked to changes in thematic meaning, a topic taken up at length in Chapter 7 of this book.

mutandis, to fit its new metric and tonal setting. The statement in the final movement (the witches' Sabbath) is another matter altogether. Here the thematic developments *comprise* the musical context (see Example 1.4b); the E♭ clarinet and piccolo make a mockery of the tune with their shrill timbre and grotesque ornamentations. The flip 6/8 setting, reed accompaniment,

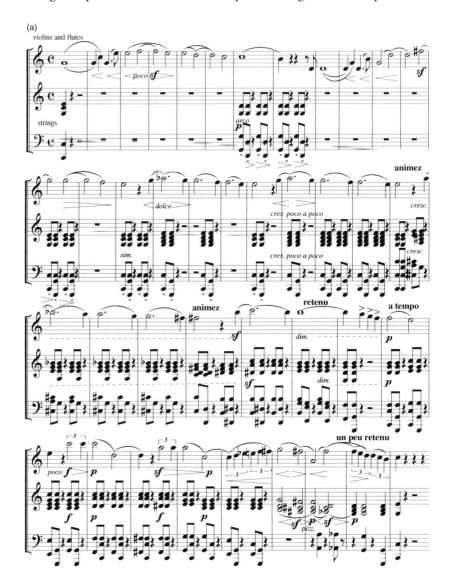

Example 1.4 Forms of the *idée fixe* in Berlioz's *Symphonie Fantastique*

a. Original statement, I, mm. 72–111
b. Witches' Sabbath statement, V, mm. 40–65

Example 1.4 (*cont.*)

and increasingly frenetic accompanimental texture accentuate the affect, as witches and goblins dance about the protagonist who, at this point in the story, finds himself in hell after slaying his beloved. Here, then, thematic development is inherently dramatic.[31]

---

[31] Liszt employs a similar compositional technique in his *Faust-Symphonie*, changing the texture of themes that first appear in Faust's movement when they later occur in Mephistopheles's movement.

Despite many leitmotifs exhibiting a constantly developing nature, we still wish to identify them by name, a seeming contradiction. How can we apply taxonomy to a moving target? This apparent conflict is a problem native to epistemology and one that long ago found a pragmatic solution in the creation of categories. Human cognition embraces labels that categorize like objects, accepting that our categorical approach will fit some objects better than others. This is true in music as well as many other fields of inquiry. As Zbikowski put it:

> categories are where our conceptualization of music starts. If to think is to think in terms of categories, then to think of music is to think in terms of musical categories.[32]

Categories, however, fit some of their constituents better than others. The category "fruit," for example, is one into which we have no problem placing "apple," a prototype of this category. Less-prototypical fruits – avocado or tomato for instance – are also category members, but don't fit quite as well. The leitmotif, like many musical concepts, also adheres to a categories-with-prototypes model.

Thematic categories can be conceived in two ways. First, we might imagine a prototypic form of a theme – a sort of Platonic ideal that may or may not actually exist in the music but that can be inferred from various statements of that theme. A prototype-and-variants concept is transformative in nature; each statement of a thematic category is slightly different, if not in content, then in context. A second kind of thematic category is a conception of theme families grouped by musical and dramatic relationships. Both types of thematic categorization imply growth and development of musical materials, leitmotif statements that, rather than interrupting musical syntax, work to create it. Since this notion is developed at length in Chapter 3, it will suffice for now to state that leitmotivic prototypes interact conceptually with categories that develop over time.

Leitmotifs participate in musical structure

The compositional problem Wagner faced in creating the music drama was that he needed to rethink old operatic forms for the sake of setting dialogue, while still achieving musical coherence (i.e., do away with the musical

---

[32] Zbikowski 2002: 58. *Ibid.*, 49–58 uses the *Leidensmotiv* from *Tristan* as an example of categorization of Wagnerian leitmotifs.

distinction between aria and recitative as much as possible).[33] Associative themes provided him with the solution – a solution that was markedly different from thematic techniques employed by earlier composers. In using them to achieve a sense of musical coherence across vast dramatic spans and changing tonalities and textures, though, he had to make them part of the larger musical structures in which they appeared. The riddle game that takes place in Act I, Scene 2 of *Siegfried* is a case in point. Structured as a pair of loose rondo or refrain forms, the contrasting episodes feature dramatically appropriate themes: "Nibelungs," "Giants," "Valhalla," "Volsung Race," and so forth appear at the ordained moments. Rather than simply being surface reiterations of these themes though, they structure the sense of refrain form, creating not only the contrasting themes, but also the contrasting keys of the form, keys dictated by these themes' associative tonalities.

We may seem to have strayed somewhat from our initial query – "What is a leitmotif?" – but by now it should be clear that the many threads involved in defining "leitmotif" must be untangled before attempting to justify a definition. A successful approach would provide a flexible definition of "motive" or "theme" while allowing for the multiplicity of ways that these can accrue meaning. In so doing, it would also admit to music's inherently plastic nature and, by extension, the ability of musical development to qualify associative meaning. It would also set up a methodology for describing a variety of meaningful musical-dramatic transformations. It would provide explanations for the manner in which leitmotifs interact with the surrounding musical context. And, finally, it would present examples of the leitmotif at work in the repertory of dramatic music.

This is, in short, what the remainder of this book attempts to do. Our main obstacle is the protean nature of leitmotifs themselves. Because their musical materials and extra-musical meanings evolve through time, leitmotifs have fuzzy musical and associative values, in effect customizable to form potentially limitless realizations of thematic prototypes. Moreover, it isn't always apparent where and how one might separate a leitmotif from its surrounding musical context. The frustration we feel in our attempt to define leitmotif echoes that of earlier writers. The difficulty they have had in agreeing upon a definition of "leitmotif" or even in agreeing upon one specific leitmotif's name, musical boundaries, or associative content parallel our own. These difficulties stem, in no small part, from the history of the leitmotif.

---

[33] Dahlhaus 1989: 109.

A brief history of the leitmotif and its reception

A detailed history of the leitmotif, both its development in Western music and its reception by Western culture, could easily exceed the confines of a book-length study. Fortunately, excellent work on this subject already exists, so our purpose here will be merely synoptic. In it, we follow Manfred Kelkel who divides the history of leitmotif scholarship into three streams:[34] 1) studies of leitmotif in pre-Wagnerian opera,[35] 2) semiotic approaches to leitmotif, and 3) leitmotif catalogues. We might add to this list a fourth stream: a recurring use of metaphor in leitmotivic exegesis.

The forerunners of the Wagnerian leitmotif – *topoi*, motivic linkage, and semantically endowed instances of thematic recall – appear in diverse musics, with notable examples coming from Italian madrigals, French opera, and German theatric melodrama. Examples are evident at least as early as the beginning of the seventeenth century in Monteverdi's recurrent use of proto-*topoi* in *Orfeo* that link a character to an obbligato instrument or a small group of instruments.[36] Another technique developing across the Baroque period was the rise of motivic linkage (*Fortspinnung*). Though

---

[34] Kelkel's objective, however, differs from ours in that he was attempting to expand the understanding of Wagnerian leitmotif and *Grundthema* to accommodate the use of reminiscence motives in the music of the naturalist and realist composers who followed Wagner. See Kelkel 1984: 279–82. Flotow's 1847 *Martha* makes use of a *Grundthema* of sorts, a three-note rising or falling motive that brings its own emotional associations to many other melodic utterances, not unlike what Wagner does with the falling-fourth-plus-ascending-step motive in *Meistersinger*. See Warrack 2001: 363–64.

[35] Much on this topic can be gleaned from Warrack 2001. This study marks the forerunners of the reminiscence motive in the late seventeenth-century operas of Johann Wolfgang Franck who used recurring rhythmic and melodic figures to identify characters (*ibid.*: 43). Reinhard Keiser, (another composer in Hamburg post-Peace of Westphalia) was also composing opera with a similar approach (*ibid.*: 54). Later composers used bona fide reminiscence motives, which Warrack defines as "the recall of music with a previous dramatic association." Among them, Nicolas Dalayrac used them to express new twists in the drama in his operas of the 1780s and 1790s (*ibid.*: 194). Weber, who praised Dalayrac's use of motive, also lauded a similar technique in Spohr's *Faust* of 1816, which employed a network of unifying themes associated with hell, love, and Faust's passionate nature (*ibid.*: 195). But it was the French opera composers Méhul and Cherubini more than any others who influenced Weber and the future course of German opera (*ibid.*: 197). Nineteenth-century German opera inherited its concepts of key association and motivic association from late eighteenth-century French opera, whose dramatic motives were often orchestral in nature, paralleling the development of the orchestral overture and orchestral interlude at the time (*ibid.*: 194–200, and 208). For other studies on pre-Wagnerian leitmotifs, see Goslich 1975: 413–16; McCredie 1985; and Wörner 1931–32.

[36] See McCredie 1985: 9. *Orfeo* is just one of Monteverdi's works showcasing this proto-topical aspect.

not explicitly associative, composers used it to achieve continuity, cohesion, and affective unity in their music. By the end of the eighteenth century, motivic recall of a patently associative nature appeared in the operatic works of French composers like Méhul, Cherubini, and Lemoyne.[37] Their German-speaking counterparts of the same period (ca. 1770–1830) – J.C. Bach, Mozart, and Schubert – included emergent leitmotifs in melodrama, opera, and singspiel. These early examples are often called "reminiscence themes," in the analytic literature, a moniker that distinguishes them from the mature Wagnerian leitmotif.[38] While reminiscence themes are bifurcated in nature – musical statements with dramatic associations – unlike leitmotifs they often come across as clunky and forced, musical stage props as it were, because they are rarely developed musically or dramatically, and because their relationship to the surrounding musical context often lacks subtlety, fluidity, or coherence.

A notable evolution in Germanic practice occurred in Carl Maria von Weber's use of thematic material in his operas – operas that Wagner knew well from conducting them. The timbral associations of horns with hunting and low registers (especially in the clarinet) with Samiel and Samiel's associative diminished seventh chord in *Der Freischütz*, for example, doubtless suggested the power of the associative technique to Wagner. Likewise, the transformation of the "Fairies" theme from the opening of *Oberon* (specifically the overture and first number) to later iterations (No. 2, the beginning of Act II and Rezia's aria in that act, No. 6), and the Harmonic Redemption of the ghost music in *Euryanthe* when the ghost is finally laid to rest suggested to Wagner the transformative potential of associative functions.[39]

Despite promising examples like Weber's, interest in these musico-dramatic constructs from both popular and scholarly communities was

---

[37] McCredie 1985: 12–13.

[38] See McCredie 1985: 24–25 for a more detailed distinction between reminiscence theme and leitmotif. See also Kirby 2004: 5–11, who summarizes earlier writing on this distinction. The essence of the distinction is that reminiscence themes are non-developmental statements that don't bear an intimate tonal, formal, or motivic relationship to their musical context. There are, of course, some exceptions; see, for instance, McCredie 1985: 7, 10–11, and 14–16 on J.C. Bach's use of motive in a developmental way in *Amadi*. See also Rushton 1971, who describes Lemoyne's use of associative themes in *Électre* in a manner that not only highlighted dramatic moments but also served to unify a surprisingly continuous musical fabric given eighteenth-century operatic idioms.

[39] The *Oberon* horn call is also developed from the overture (at the beginning of No. 1 and in the last number of Act III) through inversion, sequence, and so forth, but it's not really a leitmotif or even an associative theme; rather its developments play a music-structural role, fitting the overarching musical context at hand. We return in Chapter 8 to consider Weber in more detail.

low until the advent of Wagner's operas and music dramas. Among commentators, Wagner himself was the first great theorist of leitmotivic form and function; his description of a musical sign conditioned by verbal signs comprises a nascent semiotics, the beginning of another salient stream in the history of leitmotivic analysis. After the mid-twentieth century explosion of semiotics in francophone scholarship, scholars outside this tradition borrowed its concepts and methodology in approaching Wagner's work. Notable examples include Deryck Cooke's *I Saw the World End*, Eero Tarasti's *Myth and Music*, and Christian Thorau's *Semantisierte Sinnlichkeit*.[40] Thorau's is the most valuable to students of leitmotivic history, comprising an indispensable aid to tracing the reception history of leitmotivic semantics, and advocating a semiotic approach to semantic analysis.

The third stream, thematic cataloguing, is intimately tied to the term "leitmotif" itself. While the word is commonly associated with Hans von Wolzogen, the first commentator to publish a thematic catalogue for Wagner's *Ring*, it was historian and critic August Wilhelm Ambros who first coined "leitmotif" in 1860 to describe Wagner's operas as "symphonic poems with a libretto" and Liszt's symphonic poems as "Wagnerian operas without words."[41] Nevertheless, it was Wolzogen's 1876 *Thematischer Leitfaden* that popularized the term, and thus it was with the act of cataloguing that the leitmotif came to be associated. Scores of such catalogues were propagated in subsequent decades, their thematic taxonomies following a variety of methods.[42]

---

[40] See Cooke 1971, Tarasti 1993, and Thorau 2003. Cooke 1971 is not explicitly semiotic, but emerges from the same aesthetic as Cooke's earlier semiotic magnum opus, *The Language of Music*. See Cooke 1979.

[41] Grey 1998, 353. Wagner did not endorse the nineteenth-century German neologism *Leitmotif*. In *Oper und Drama*, Wagner preferred "*Melodie*" and later "*Motiv*." See Skelton 1991: 43. It is well known that the term *Leitmotif* was first used in relation to Wagner's *Ring* by Hans von Wolzogen in 1877 in an analysis based on Gottlieb Federlein's 1871–72 studies of *Das Rheingold*. It is perhaps less well known that *Leitmotif* appeared in the 1871 writings of Wilhelm Jähns in reference to themes of Weber, reinforcing the notion that leitmotif-as-concept pre-dated Wagner's experiments. See McCredie 1985: 3.

[42] See Kirby 2004: 29–37 for a serviceable overview of this literature. As examples of the various taxonomic types we might cite Cooke 1995 (grouping by musical relationships), Wolzogen 1876 (grouping by dramatic chronology), Donington, 1974 (grouping by Jungian psychological effect), and Kirby 2004 (grouping by topic). While each method brings out different relationships between themes while obscuring others, I find Kirby's to be the most bizarre. It is an amalgamation of *topoi*, emotions, and traditional musical types (like dance or song) grouped by analogic (i.e., onomatopoetic) vs. non-analogic themes further subdivided by how they express meaning.

In addition to popularizing both the term "leitmotif" and the catalogue approach to leitmotif exegesis, Wolzogen's study also participates in a long and prominent tradition of *Leitfaden* or "leading-thread" metaphors. The use of fabric or texture to describe associative thematic constructs appears in Wagner's own writings,[43] though the use of a leading-thread metaphor to describe the harmonic and melodic aspects of a musical work goes back centuries earlier.[44] With respect to Wagner and his themes, the image was adapted by Theodor Uhlig who coined the "red thread" (*rote Faden*) metaphor in response to *Lohengrin*: In order to compensate for the loss of operatic "number" structure in *Lohengrin*, Uhlig traced a sense of thematic continuity through the fabric of this work as the *rote Faden* repeatedly vanished into and emerged from the warp and weft of the musical texture.[45]

From this brief overview we see that there are a few central leitmotivic issues that have concerned scholars and commentators since the nineteenth century: the historical precursors of the leitmotif known from Wagner's *oeuvre*; the approach to leitmotif as meaning-filled sign; the desire to catalogue and name leitmotifs; and the metaphoric approach to leitmotivic commentary. Knowing these historical trends is fundamental to our continued study because it is precisely these trends that have led to the many misapprehensions of leitmotivic form and function – the continued obstacles facing musicians and commentators – that I group together into "the leitmotif problem."

The leitmotif problem

The title of this book, *Understanding the Leitmotif*, implies that the concept of leitmotif has been unintelligible or misunderstood. In fact, both are true, the latter having given rise to the former. The misguided approaches that brought this about are, in general, guilty of two common errors: first, they ignore or downplay the themes' musical attributes in favor of their dramatic ones;[46] and, second, they misunderstand how themes accrete meaning.

---

[43] Grey 1998: 352.

[44] These metaphors go back to the seventeenth century for harmonic aspects of music and to the eighteenth century for melodic aspects. *Ibid.*: 354.

[45] *Ibid.*: 355.

[46] The opposite also occurs. According to Abbate 1991: 37, in more recent scholarship the typical strategy for thematic appearances seemingly unrelated to the drama is to justify their presence on purely musical grounds.

These errors are attributable to a lack of distinction between the Wagnerian leitmotif and its unrefined, non-developmental forerunners. Deryck Cooke, criticizing Wolzogen, sums up the faults neatly:

1. The analysis fosters a "patchwork of short ideas" impression of musical works.
2. The word "leitmotif" is a misnomer.
3. The tally of themes is incomplete.
4. The interrelationships between themes are neglected in all but the most obvious cases.[47]

Of these faults, the first and fourth most clearly illustrate authors' tendencies to sacrifice the themes' musical aspects in favor of their dramatic ones. Because commentators uninterested in, or lacking training in, musical analysis neglect leitmotifs' tonal, formal, and thematic functions, leitmotifs are often treated as vessels for extra-musical meaning without being scrutinized as musical entities. Thousands of pages have been devoted to teasing apart the meanings and appropriate names of various musical figures as they relate to their dramatic texts or contexts, but relatively little attention has been paid to these figures qua music.[48]

Writers who do address musical considerations often over-simplify them. For instance, many cite concrete numbers of bars for a given theme, assuming each has an explicit beginning and end, and exists in one best form. If thematic boundaries were clean, we could expect most commentators to agree on them. Actually, the opposite is true. Table 1.1 provides a chart of the length for the "Giants" theme (cf. the music shown in Example 1.1a) as cited by a variety of authors.[49] While all begin at Rg/68/1/1, the

---

[47] Cooke 1979: 38–44. In fact, Cooke's perceptive response to Wolzogen – a theory of thematic family groupings based on dramatic and musical considerations – was itself overlooked in an unjustified critique that seems more appropriate to the misconceptions Cooke was trying to overcome than to his work itself. See Abbate and Parker 1989: 8–9, who describe Newman and Cooke as men who "accepted without hesitation the notion that finding, describing, and naming thematic fragments constituted a sufficient account of Wagner's musical language. Indeed, the process of deciphering alleged musical symbols mutated in their hands into an exercise with a momentum all its own, perused with comical doggedness."

[48] The exception that proves the rule is the work of Warren Darcy, whose theme guides published in the appendix to Bribitzer-Stull 2001 refine work done by Deryck Cooke in his groundbreaking book (Cooke 1979) and audio *discursus* on thematic families in Wagner's *Ring* (Cooke 1995).

[49] The works in which these thematic citations appear are as follows: Aldrich 1905; Darcy, unpublished guides (in the appendix to Bribitzer-Stull 2001); Donington 1974; Gauldin, *Analytical Studies in Wagner's Music* (unpublished manuscript); Holman 1996; Hutcheson 1940; Kobbé 1916; Lavignac 1926; Patterson 1896; Spencer *et al.* 1993; Wolzogen 1876; and

Table 1.1 Comparative lengths of "Giants" theme

Author	Theme name	Length
Aldritch	"Giants"	3 bars
Darcy	"Giants"	7 bars
Donington	"Brute Strength" and "Brutal Aspect of Parental Authority"	3 bars, repeated = bars 1–6 bars 7–10 10 bars total
Gauldin	"Giants"	1 bar
Holman	"Giants"	3 bars
Hutcheson	"Giants"	1 bar
Kobbé	"Giants"	3 bars
Lavignac	"Giants"	3 bars
Patterson	"Giants"	2 bars
Spencer *et al.*	"Fasolt & Fafner"	3 bars
Wolzogen	"Giants"	3 bars
Windsperger	"Giants"	8 bars

end-point is debatable. "Giants" is by no means an isolated example; many themes found in both film and art music exhibit open-ended boundaries that are elided with motivic *Fortspinnung* or another theme.

Examples of oversimplified leitmotivic analysis can be found in many thematic catalogues intended as listeners' guides for each of Wagner's music dramas. Often, these guides provide a melodic music example with a dramatically suggestive title and a brief plot synopsis, but ignore finer points of harmony, musical context, and thematic development.[50] Example 1.5 is from Newman's *The Wagner Operas*.[51]

Wagner himself critiqued Wolzogen for limiting his analyses to motif-naming:

Upon the new form of musical construction as applied to the Drama I have expressed myself sufficiently in earlier articles and essays, yet sufficiently merely in the sense that I imagined I had plainly pointed out the road on which a true, and alike a useful judgment of the musical forms now won from Drama by my own

---

Windsperger n.d. Since these thematic catalogues move chronologically through *The Ring*, page numbers are not cited. It will be a relatively simple matter for the reader to find the *Das Rheingold* Scene 2 "Giants" theme discussion in the works cited.

[50] In addition to Wolzogen 1876 there are many others ranging from nineteenth-century German works (Patterson 1896) to Newman's lengthy twentieth-century guide (Newman 1989). Newman's is an improvement over the average guide by virtue of the fact that it contains copious musicological references and occasional pitch classes listed beneath the melodic themes to illustrate a vague sense of harmonic support.

[51] Newman 1989: 497–98, ex 54.

Example 1.5 Stereotypical leitmotif guide excerpt

Declaring himself rested now he starts up and goes to the door, but at a word from her he halts; ill fate, he warns her, pursues him wherever he goes, and he would not bring unhappiness on her and her house by staying. He raises the latch, but at an impulsive cry from her of "Abide thou here! No ill fate canst thou bring where ill fate has made its home!" he looks searchingly into her face, and, reading what he does there as she lowers her eyes confusedly and sadly, he returns to her. The sorrow-laden motive of the Volsungs' Woe:

wells up in the orchestra, followed by that of Sieglinde's Pity (No. 51) and that of Siegmund (No. 50). "'Woeful', he says, is my own name for myself; Hunding here I will await." He leans against the hearth, looking intently at her with calm sympathy. She turns her gaze on him again, and during the long silence, during which the orchestra muses softly on the motives associated with the pair, they look into each other's eyes with an expression of deepest emotion.

artistic labours might be attained by others. To the best of my knowledge, that road has not been trodden yet, and I can remember nothing but the studies of one of my younger friends [Wolzogen] who has viewed the characteristics of what he calls my "Leitmotife" rather in the light of their dramatic significance, than in that of their bearing on musical construction.[52]

As is often the case, though, it was the analyst's and not the composer's thoughts that were absorbed by popular culture. Wolzogen's notion of the leitmotif became its popular definition and, in turn, spawned wrong-headed criticisms of Wagner's thematic technique.[53] Most of these over-generalize the themes as one-dimensional, static entities and include: Debussy and Stravinsky's joking references to "calling cards," Adorno's socio-philosophical exegesis describing the themes as mnemonic aides for a musically unenlightened and forgetful bourgeois audience, and Carolyn Abbate's recent description of Wagner's themes as "music's most familiar

---

[52] Wagner 1966g: 182–83.

[53] In their haste to correct Wolzogen's shallow approach though, scholars often overlook his insights into Wagner's music. His theories of tonality and form, for example, are rarely mentioned, and nuances of meaning he applied to naming the themes are often garbled in translation. See, for instance, Darcy 1994: 8. Wolzogen's title for the theme Darcy names "Glorification of Brünnhilde" can be translated into English in a variety of ways, but the one he intended was "Redemption *of* Love" (the preposition is often mis-translated as "through," "by," or "in"). "Glorification of Brünnhilde" was, according to Cosima, Wagner's own title.

and least interesting narrative competence."[54] These statements apply more accurately to other forms of associative themes like the reminiscence motive.

The practice of theme-naming has a long and almost omnipresent history, from guides to Wagner's operas that employ thematic titles like "the Death-Devoted Heart," or "the Wise Fool," to film soundtracks and interviews with modern-day film composers referring to their thematic materials with evocative tags.[55] Since themes develop both into variants of themselves and into entirely new themes, it is hard to imagine how to reflect such development in a brief thematic title. It seems that we would either need thousands of lengthy, detailed names reflecting every individual theme statement, or choose to abandon the practice of theme-naming altogether. Ultimately, names, despite their problems, are worth keeping – a brief title, however imprecise, coupled with a musical example can at least give an approximation of a commentator's understanding of the musico-dramatic fusion that constitutes a given associative theme, something impossible with either name or music alone.[56] From this compromise, a natural question arises: How do we determine whether thematic variants share the same name or bear a new title? (Again, cf. Example 1.1 and Example 1.2.) The degree and kind of thematic development must obviously serve as a guide in making this decision, but further exploration of this question must wait for Chapters 3 and 7.[57]

The second prevalent problem in writings on leitmotif is misunderstanding the semantic aspects of these themes. F.E. Kirby mentions that Wagner's leitmotifs have two functions: one is presentiment, the other is

to recall to the listeners a character who has previously appeared, a situation that has existed and continues to exist, an event that has taken place, a place, or a concept important in the drama.[58]

---

[54] See Deathridge and Dahlhaus 1984: 112; Adorno 1991: 31; and Abbate 1991: 86.

[55] See, for example, New Line Productions, Inc. 2001 in which Howard Shore refers to the "Fellowship" theme, citing its dramatic locations and musical transformations, and Columbia Pictures Industries, Inc. 2002 in which Danny Elfman mentions the "Goblin" theme by name and how he developed it by watching a clip of William Dafoe (the actor who played the Green Goblin in *Spider-Man*) talking to himself in the mirror.

[56] For a more thorough discussion of this topic situated within an apologia on the practice of theme naming, see Bribitzer-Stull 2007.

[57] Carl Dahlhaus divides thematic developments in *The Ring* into two types: those in which the musical relationship remains readily apparent and those in which a musical/dramatic relationship is constructed between two disparate themes. In both cases, these developments modify a theme's musical characteristics to suggest a change in meaning. See Dahlhaus 1979: 136–37. This topic is covered in greater detail in Chapter 7.

[58] Kirby 2004: 29. The bulk of this book is a laudable attempt at citing thematic appearances throughout *The Ring*, describing their musical materials, explaining their expressiveness vis-à-

Kirby, like many other commentators, misconstrues that associative themes recall *concrete things*. While it is true that Wagner will weave an associative theme into the orchestral texture when certain concrete things – objects, characters, events, and the like – are mentioned in the text, his dramatic-compositional intention is for thematic statements to recall *emotions*. If we return at this point to the Wagner quotation on pages 8 and 9, we see that he makes this emotional recollection clear. Unfortunately, the view of leitmotifs being stand-ins for objects is all too common. The largest drawback to such thinking is that it reinforces the static, reminiscence-theme view of leitmotif in which the musical ideas function more like stage props than part of a developing musical drama. Such thinking is not hard to find in the scholarly literature: Adele Katz, for instance, states that Wagner never genuinely developed his motives,[59] Adorno complained that associative themes fragmented the music, by virtue of their chronological and static nature;[60] and Hilda Meldrum Brown makes the questionable claim that leitmotifs rarely change, and when they do, they always remain recognizable.[61]

Even when addressing the dramatic aspects of associative themes, analysts often misunderstand the nature of their meanings. One widespread fault is concentrating on the *text* at the expense of the *drama*;[62] the text, like the music, serves in part to bring about the outcome of the drama,[63] and the leitmotif serves to capture the emotional essence of this drama. Such misunderstandings can lead to petty labeling disputes like the infamous "Love" vs. "Flight" debate cited by Deryck Cooke.[64] They can also lead to a characterization of thematic association being weakened by overly free usage. Jack Stein, for one, cites numerous examples within Wagner's *Ring* in which he feels the composer includes leitmotifs inappropriate to the

---

vis earlier music, *topoi*, and other culturally accepted bearers of musical meaning. There is, however, virtually no *analysis* of these materials.

[59] Katz 1972: 198. Katz does qualify this statement by allowing for some rhythmic diminution and augmentation of themes as well as the possibility of combining themes. We must also remember that Katz is comparing Wagner's development to Beethoven, and Wagner's themes are rarely "liquidated" in the ways characteristic of the Beethovenian sonata-form development section.

[60] Adorno also decried Strauss's decadence and film music's banality, both based on the Wagnerian leitmotif. See Holloway 1985: 14.

[61] Though this claim makes little sense in a musical setting, it may be more defensible in a *theatrical* sense. See Brown 1991: 59–60.

[62] Cooke 1979: 37.   [63] Dahlhaus 1979: 54–55.

[64] See Cooke 1979: 48–56. Stokes summarizes the continuation of the "Love" vs. "Flight" debate involving other commentators in his dissertation. See Stokes 1984: 20–53.

dramatic moment at hand.[65] Carolyn Abbate's characterization of the leitmotif is the most recent of these misconceptions. She asserts that the associative function of Wagner's themes tends to break down as they become increasingly musical (rather than dramatic) entities across the span of a given work. More than in any other of his operas, Abbate says, Wagner expends energy in *The Ring* to prevent this from happening, "suspending the themes against musical gravity" as it were. Nevertheless, she tends to hear leitmotivic origins only at "exceptional and solemn moments," most of which quickly dissipate, allowing the themes to become pure music.[66]

Our goal in the chapters that follow will be to construct an image of the leitmotif that allows for a subtlety, complexity, and artistry to leitmotivic composition missing in the writings of earlier commentators. If this smacks of teleology and essentialism – a compositional evolution inexorably leading to the ideal of thematic craft in Wagner's *Ring* and its later diaspora – I must admit some guilt in its construction. It is true that previous composers' thematic practice no more pointed toward a Wagnerian pinnacle than did sixteenth- and seventeenth-century composers point toward tonality, but there is a sense in which history looks back at both the Wagnerian leitmotif and at tonality as points of arrival because they are practices we still value as artistic consumers and creators today. It is in that sense only – of the leitmotif's lasting relevance to contemporary society – that I contextualize the historical narratives and musical analyses in this study.

* * *

All artists face challenges when embarking upon a new work. Their solutions, be they simple or complex, elegant or crude, in turn create fresh problems for their audiences – problems that raise questions about meaning, form, and artistic unity. In Western musico-dramatic works of the past two centuries, it is difficult to imagine a more richly textured exemplar of these solutions and problems than the leitmotif. In the pages that follow, our discussions of musical relationships and extra-musical associations will continue to evolve hand-in-hand as we construct our understanding of the leitmotif, illustrating its artistic merits by elucidating its forms and functions.

---

[65] See Bribitzer-Stull 2001: 20–22 for a summary of Stein's criticisms and some possible explanations for the seemingly misplaced leitmotifs. Other, similar criticisms are legion, and most, like those above, suffer from misreadings. See Bribitzer-Stull 2001: 22–23 for some examples.

[66] See Abbate 1991: 45 and 168.

In his book *Wagner's Musical Prose*, Thomas Grey invokes an extended metaphor for leitmotifs in *The Ring*, referring to the concept as "the beast at the center of the labyrinth."[67] It is likely that anyone who has written at length on this topic would find the metaphor apt. Given the scope of this study, the warren of passageways we face is considerably larger and more tortuous than the one earlier writers encountered; not only must we traverse the winding corridors of Wagner's *Gesamtkunstwerk*, but we must also consider the other genres that comprise our catacombs – opera, lieder, film, and so forth. Further complicating matters are the construction and detritus of intervening decades – the artists who have carved out their own routes, and the mislabeled junctions and faulty maps left behind by the musical thinkers who have undertaken the quest before us. Thus far we have only skirted the edges of the maze, examining memoirs of past explorers and plotting our own course toward understanding. But to accomplish our goal we must venture into the labyrinth ourselves and confront the beast. Now, then, is the time to put away the charts and guides, to pack our bags of analytic tools, and to begin the journey.

[67] Grey 1995: 372.

PART I

Musical themes

2 | Motive, phrase, melody, and theme

> My Trio is finished. I only need the themes for it.
>
> Maurice Ravel[1]

Who doesn't love a good theme? Themes are our first avenue into a piece of music and what we carry away from it. The composers who craft themes well rightly earn our admiration: We praise Mozart for his profligate thematic extravagance; we savor Beethoven for his dramatic thematic developments; and, we ponder Wagner for his profound thematic meanings – meanings that have inspired dozens of leitmotif guides over the years. Everyone loves a good theme, but it seems that no one can agree on what one is. To paraphrase Justice Potter Stewart's notorious definition of pornography: (as far as themes go) we know them when we hear them.[2] Since themes are what listeners often take away from a musical experience, it makes sense that commentary references them regularly. Hardly confined to scholarly analysis of so-called art music (or "classical" music), writing about musical themes inhabits a variety of contexts, and treats a host of musical genres. In almost all cases, though, this thematic exegesis assumes the meaning of "theme" to be self-evident. As Rudolph Reti put it:

Thus "thematic structure" has become an almost fundamental *term* in music, yet its full meaning and content have never been realized concretely. No real attempt has ever been made to comprehend in a systematic analysis the working of this most essential process of musical composition.[3]

As an example, take one excerpt among many that could be cited, Fred Karlin's list of five "themes" found in the score to *Close Encounters of the Third Kind* (1977): 1) the mountain motif, 2) the tensions motif, 3) the "high sustained string texture," 4) the Baroque action theme, and 5) the communication motif (the familiar five-note series now immediately recognizable by almost anyone invested at all in American popular culture).[4] A casual reading of Karlin's prose poses no difficulties with his use

---

[1] Stuckenschmidt 1969: 149.   [2] Jacobellis v. Ohio, 878 U.S. 184 (1964).   [3] Reti 1978: 3.
[4] Karlin 1994: 133–36.

of the word "theme," but a closer look raises questions: First, two of the "themes" are designated as "motifs" (or "motives"). Second, one of Karlin's themes appears to comprise nothing more than a musical texture, while another has as its identifying characteristic its status as pastiche of Baroque-era music. Third, the last theme on Karlin's list – the so-called "communication theme" – lies closest to what many musicians would consider a theme, though its brevity, monophonic texture, and lack of meter and rhythmic distinctiveness are hardly typical; it is, after all, little more than a series of equal-duration pitches, far from complete, developmental, or distinct enough to fulfill a traditional theoretic definition of "theme." Musical thinkers like Schoenberg, Wallace Berry, and William Caplin, for instance, all require something more substantial – a small musical form – for a passage to qualify as a theme. Over the course of this chapter and the next, I steer away from rigid definitions like these – definitions largely derived from an understanding of themes as small forms comprising or related to sentence and period structures in common-practice German instrumental music – in favor of a fuzzier, prototype model.[5]

Among the questions raised by Karlin's observations, we must include the following: What is the difference between theme and motive? Do themes require melodies? Are themes phrases or something else? What kinds of formal units do themes comprise? Are their functions even formal at all? Before considering these queries further, let us begin by taking Karlin's unexceptional usage of "theme" – one little different from many others in countless essays on music – at face value. Can "theme" in this context be defined? Clearly, it means *something*. But what? It seems, first and foremost, that in order to identify and list it, a theme – any theme – must be recognizable. That is, it must be heard as a unique entity, differentiated from its musical context, and significant enough to elicit notice. To do so, a theme must employ (and retain) a variety of identifiable musical parameters. These may include, but are not limited to: contour, rhythmic content, pitch content, length, orchestration, texture, register, tempo, harmonic progression, harmonic function, and contrapuntal framework.

Of all parameters, though, the one that establishes significance the most forcefully is *repetition*.[6] Karlin's list – one of *recurring* musical

---

[5] See Schoenberg 1967: 20–81; Berry 1966: 14–30 (whose discussion centers on *phrase* rather than *theme*, but nevertheless represents a link in the connection of thought from Schoenberg to Caplin); and Caplin 1998: 35–70 and 97–123.

[6] Margulis 2014 is a thoughtful treatment of musical repetition grounded in cognition and perception. The author notes, *passim*, that repetition is central to all musical cultures, and distinguishes music from language and other modes of communication. See also Lidov 2005:

materials – is hardly alone in this regard; musicians have long cited repetition as a necessary component of thematic identity.[7] Wagner scholar F.E. Kirby (speaking of Wagner's *Ring*), explains it simply: "It is in their recurrence that the significance of the themes becomes really meaningful."[8] Put another way, despite various musical means to establish thematic recognizability and significance, thematic salience only becomes *meaning-ful* under *repetition*. Others put a finer point on it: for *fin de siècle* Viennese theorist Heinrich Schenker, repetition is the *only* imperative for thematic content.[9] Likewise, modern-day film scholar Claudia Gorbman defines a theme in film music as anything heard more than once.[10]

Following Schenker, Anglo-American university-level instruction in musical form largely presents thematic repetition as a striking and distinctive formal characteristic, depicting thematic and motivic materials as musical objects – building blocks of phrases, rondos, sonatas, and so forth. In stark opposition, Wagner argued that thematic repetition *with-out variation or change of context* was an inorganic necessity ("crutch" might be a better word) devolved from absolute music.[11] Alfred Lorenz, whose analyses of Wagner's mature music dramas achieved notoriety in the mid- and late twentieth century, qualifies the repetition requirement by stating that the first principle in establishing a theme is repetition, *literal or varied* (and often immediate).[12] In truth, musical repetition is rarely exact, though this is not always for dramatic reasons. Certainly, this is a truth that extends to music well outside of Wagner's. Striving to balance homogeneity, continuity, and coherence with variety in the kinds and contexts of thematic statements is a concern that lies at the heart of

Chapter 2, for a discussion of musical repetition in the context of signification. Lidov divides repetition into three functions: formal, focal, and textural. For the purposes of establishing thematic identity, it is the focal that is of primary importance to our understanding, though, of course, having a formal function is one requirement for making an associative theme an actual leitmotif.

[7] See, for example, Dennison 1985: 33.

[8] Kirby 2004: 4. Because *repetition* reinforces memory (see Hoeckner and Nusbaum 2013: 242), it is a crucial technique for forming *meaning-filled associations*, a topic we explore in Chapters 4 and 5.

[9] Rothgeb 1983: 39. Rothgeb discusses Schenker's assertion that thematic repetition arose historically from imitative counterpoint.

[10] Gorbman 1987: 26.

[11] Korsyn 1993: 107–08. Korsyn compares Wagner's and Schenker's differing views on musical repetition here, and cites Wagner's criticism of Beethoven's *Leonore Overture 3* in his essays "Über Franz Liszts Symphonische Dichtungen" and "Über die Anwendung der Musik auf das Drama" as evidence.

[12] See McClatchie 1998: 109–13.

many composers' creative processes.[13] Rudolph Reti, describing the Brahmsian ideal of his teacher, Arnold Schoenberg, explains the compositional process as one preoccupied with the recombination of thematic components whose identity nevertheless remains clear because they are unified around a flexible *Grundgestalt* (fundamental shape).[14] In other words, composers present thematic statements under varied repetitions by keeping the components of the theme closely related to a central shape or form. Since no two repetitions will ever be perceived in exactly the same way (because, at the very least, they will occupy different temporal locations), context is everything. So long as repetition is *perceived*, however (rather than existing merely in an acoustic or notational sense), the effect functions.

While Reti's approach celebrates a Schoenbergian analytic value system, a brief look at the historical precedents of nineteenth- and twentieth-century western European thematic practice corroborates this fascination with repetition – it has, in fact, been a guiding compositional principle since the Middle Ages (and most likely earlier). Avoided in much early chant repertory, repetition-as-praxis was widely applied in fourteenth-century isorhythmic motets. The practice of isorhythm not only embraced repetition, it also defined which elements of music were to be repeated, namely pitch (in the *color*, a series of repeated pitches) and rhythm (in the *talea*, a series of repeated note lengths). Because the *color* and *talea* rarely synchronized (that is, the *talea* would begin a second iteration before the *color* had completed a first, or vice versa), such repetitions were not obvious on the musical surface, and probably escaped the notice of casual listeners, as they continue to do today. Their importance in compositional planning, however, is difficult to overestimate.

Medieval Europe also witnessed the rise of another practice of repeated pitch and rhythmic relations: imitation. Early imitative forms like the caccia and round comprised two or more voices stating the same melodic material at different times (i.e., imitation at the unison). As imitative and contrapuntal practice developed, imitation occurred at different pitch intervals (such as the fifth and octave). Various forms of canon, and later, ricercar and fugue, written by musicians throughout the Renaissance and

---

[13] According to Reti 1978: 13, that is. I am inclined to agree, at least for repertories influenced by eighteenth- and nineteenth-century tonal music of central Europe.

[14] Reti 1978: 177. The notion of the *Grundgestalt* is one Reti borrows from Arnold Schoenberg. See Carpenter 1983: 15–18 for a serviceable overview of Schoenberg's ideas on this topic.

Baroque eras – musicians like Ockeghem, Frescobaldi, and J.S. Bach – showcased celebrity composers' technical abilities at manipulating imitation (i.e., thematic repetition).

In time, imitation penetrated the binary dance forms of the suite. In many of Bach's two-reprise forms, for instance, the same material that opens a dance recurs at another tonal level just after the double bar. Classic-era composers like Haydn and Mozart began commonly locating the thematic repetition near the *end* of the second reprise and *in the tonic key*, a thematic practice designated as "rounding" (as in "rounded binary"), and one central to the emergent sonata principle. Compared to the modest rounded binary form, the sonata's expanded physiognomy featured a central section devoted to thematic *development*, with thematic instability mirroring a concomitant tonal instability.[15]

Sonata-form thematic developments were markedly different from the kinds of thematic modifications composers tended to make in earlier works; the intervallic augmentations and melodic inversions of a Bach invention or fugue and the extravagant repetitions (even in different keys) of a Vivaldi concerto no longer sufficed. As it evolved, sonata-form practice required that *thematic identity itself be dismantled through development and then re-established through recapitulation in the tonic key*. This new thematic treatment arguably reached a point in Beethoven's middle-period works where it served a dramatic and/or expressive purpose, as well as providing the composer a special formal space in which to explore compositional techniques and to display the originality of his technical and expressive ideas.[16] Wagner apparently found Beethoven singular in this regard; according to Cosima's diaries, Wagner said to Richter on December 7, 1870 "before Beethoven, no one knew anything about *repetition*" (emphasis in original).[17] Despite the sonata's formal origins as a *two-part tonal* plan (e.g., the many so-called "monothematic" sonata forms of Joseph Haydn), the melodic content of the form came to dominate the musical surface and listening experience to such an extent, especially in something like a Beethovenian development

---

[15] Hepokoski and Darcy 2006 describe five types of sonata-form categories in their seminal work on the topic. Not all of them (i.e., Type 1 and Type 2) have a development section, per se.

[16] The notion of music, and Beethoven's music in particular, being dramatic is nothing new. Music as a vehicle for personal expression and the musical theme as a protagonist – even a synecdoche for the composer himself – bolster the idea of Beethoven's music enacting a live drama. For more on these topics, see Maus 1988 and Burnham 1995.

[17] Wagner 1994: 82.

section, that audiences began to think of the sonata as a *three-part thematic* plan. The tension between these two approaches to sonata form remains palpable today.[18]

There is a simple elegance to understanding theme simply as any repeated musical material. But, risking the slash of Ockham's razor, theme as it evolved over hundreds of years of musical practice in western Europe demands a definition that is more complex; repetition alone will not suffice. Why not? Because "theme" connotes a musical idea that is not only repeated, but one that is also repeated in such a way as to demand its musical salience. It is central to the identity of the piece it inhabits (or some would say, begets). It is a musical idea that, without identification, would make discussion of its attendant music nigh well impossible. Usage by theorists and analysts seems to concur. The term "theme," as we understand it, first appeared in Zarlino's 1558 treatise, *Le istitutione harmoniche*, where he defined it as a repeated melody subject to variation (and in that regard distinct from a *soggeto* or cantus firmus). By the seventeenth and early eighteenth centuries, terminological specificity had loosened, and "theme" appeared interchangeably with "subject" and "invention" in prose of the time. Modern-day usage coalesced in the mid-nineteenth century when themes were understood to emerge throughout a piece (not just at its beginning), were relatively complete musical statements, and comprised recognizable entities that could be used to identify a work.[19]

Having reached the nineteenth century in this whirlwind tour, we see that the themes in question have not only been recognizable and repeated, but have also played a crucial role in local and global musical form. They have largely comprised melodies – single lines of pitch-rhythmic content. This is not to say that other parameters (text, texture, harmonic support, and orchestration among them) didn't matter to the thematic identity in these works, but themes were, first and foremost, melodies. Thus, the definition and understanding of "theme" from a historical perspective is more specific than Karlin's and Gorbman's "as long as it's repeated, it's a theme" condition.

---

[18] Rosen 1980 (especially 16–26) lays out the binary and ternary historical antecedents for sonata form. While most scholars admit to the sonata exhibiting both binary and ternary traits, the tension between two-part and three-part interpretations persists. See, for instance, Hepokoski and Darcy 2006: 14–16 who come down on the side of binary form (an interpretation favored by contemporary eighteenth-century theorists and by more recent Schenkerian analyses) and Caplin 1998: 195 who favors a ternary understanding.

[19] The preceding paragraph draws heavily on Drabkin n.d.

A better summary is Paul Reale's:

Generally speaking, a theme is a musical event; it is a central, complete, musical idea from which the building blocks of a piece are generated. Although it may not necessarily have a vocal or singable contour, *it has an unmistakable musical identity.*[20]

Better, at least, on the face of it, but upon closer examination, this definition leaves much unanswered. The issue of what comprises a musical theme is exceedingly more complex than the preceding quotation suggests. How long is a theme and where are its boundaries? What differentiates "theme" from related terms like "motive," "melody," or "phrase?" How much must a theme interact with a work's construction of tonality and musical form? How many of a theme's parameters can be changed before it is perceived as a new entity altogether? Most of us would agree that we know a theme when we hear one (recalling Justice Potter Stewart), and yet we remain unable to formulate a cogent definition. Even Schenker – the architect of our most powerful theory of tonality – doesn't propose or imply a theory of thematic construction or relations.[21]

As good a place to begin as any is by distinguishing our emergent understanding of "theme" from other related musical concepts. Themes are often understood to subsume smaller musical objects (melodies, motives, pitches, etc.) and to be, in turn, subsumed by larger ones (phrases, periods, sections, movements, etc.). The role of the theme is somewhat analogous to the role of the clause in prose. Just as clauses include phonemes and words and are in turn included in sentences, paragraphs, scenes, chapters, and acts, so too do themes occupy something of a midpoint in the continuum of musical entity lengths. Coming to grips with these mid-length entities is central to artistic understanding since they most often provide our first and easiest access to a new work. Put another way, themes identify a perceptual/psychological "sweet spot." They are salient in part because they are long enough to be meaningful and short enough to be comprehended as salient musical entities – even by a musical novice – upon first listening, with a sense of immediacy in the present moment. In music, the extremely small (notes) and extremely large (pieces) levels are rarely difficult to discern. Anything in between, though, is fair game for interpretation. The fuzzy definitions understood by today's musicians for these mid-length entities overlap one another. In many contexts this terminological freedom would be unproblematic. Here,

---

[20] Reale 1970: 6 (emphasis mine).   [21] See Rothgeb 1983: 38.

however, I argue for a theme and its attendant piece-specificity as the prototype for both the notion of "associative theme" and the more specific "leitmotif." We take up prototypes, associativity, and piece-specificity in the next three chapters. To prepare for these later discussions, we attempt an understanding of "theme" that distinguishes it from other common terms for musical ideas like "phrase," "melody," and "motive."

Phrase and theme

While defining both "phrase" and "theme" are difficulties oft lamented in the scholarly literature on music, distinguishing "phrase" *from* "theme" is far less problematic. True, the two terms both describe mid-level musical entities, but virtually every definition of "theme" relies on salience and recurrence. A chunk of music need be neither salient nor recurrent to qualify as a phrase. In the opening of his book on phrase rhythm, William Rothstein admits to the difficulty in nailing down a cogent definition of "phrase."[22] At the heart of his understanding of the term, though, is the notion that phrases embody tonal motion. To over-generalize Rothstein, phrases are directed tonal motions that end with (real or implied) cadences.

Considered from a thematic point of view, phrases (and a related musical concept – the sentence) are usually tightly knit musical shapes that begin with piece-specific gestures and move toward style-generic ones.[23] The same is true of our earlier literary metaphor: clauses embody piece-specific content but end with style-generic punctuation. This parallelism likely exists in large part due to the practices established when setting text to music; verbal clauses and musical phrases often line up. In Example 2.1, for instance, lines of text conclude at points of tonal punctuation: the half cadence on F♯ at *Kind* tonicizes B, and the deceptive motion to F♯ at *Stolz* suggests the key of A.[24] In fact, this excerpt is but a small part

---

[22] Rothstein 1989: 3–5.

[23] The idea of the phrase being "tightly knit" is one I borrow from Caplin 1998 (see especially 35–70), though I don't subscribe to a rigorous division between sentence and period structures – and the concomitant necessity for "hybrid" structures – when describing the larger musical units in which phrases occur. Nor do I understand these small forms to be themes themselves. In this, my understanding is somewhat less formal, along the lines of Hepokoski and Darcy 2006: 69, n. 10, who define a phrase as "a more or less complete musical thought involving motion to a cadence," a definition itself heavily reliant on Rothstein 1989: 5ff.

[24] Formally, Wagner favored a poetic verse and melody to be followed immediately by an answering unit that resembled and complemented the first, thus linking the form of the text to a crude musical period construction. See Stein 1973: 94.

Example 2.1 Text phrase and musical phrase in concert; Wagner's *Die Walküre*, Act II, Scene 4 290/2/1–3/4

of a larger section of Wagner's *Die Walküre* in which the composer regularly pairs text and musical phrases; lines of text are set to regular four-bar phrases, alternating *recitativo* textures with more lyrical, melodic writing. It is clear, throughout, that points of articulation in the music confirm points of articulation in the text.

Of course, only some texted or thematic music exhibits such a clear relationship to phraseology. Not all phrases begin with themes, nor do all themes fit neatly within a phrase. Rather, themes and phrases rely on completely different kinds of musical understanding. A phrase (likewise, a sentence) is a manner of hearing tonal, melodic and (hyper)metric organization. It is a unit of musical form. A theme is a musical idea, a central argument in a musical thesis, if you will. As such, themes often comprise the bulk of a phrase, but some themes are less than a phrase, and others occupy a period or other multi-phrase shape. That is, thematic and phrase organization are related, but neither is dependent upon the other.

Melody and theme

Given the historical overview earlier in this chapter, it would be natural to state that themes are repeated melodies. Or, that melodies, once repeated in a given work, take on thematic importance. Wagner implies as much when he argues for "endless melody," a practice in which stock formulae like cadences and madrigalisms are to be avoided in favor of continuously relevant thematic content. And he is not the only one to link melodic repetition to thematic identity. Halfyard, for one, states, "Very often it is melody that lodges in the memory both during and after watching a film, with the result that music lacking an obvious melody is less likely to be recalled after the film has finished."[25] Likewise, Stravinsky: "In writing variations, my method is to remain faithful to the theme as melody – never mind the rest! I regard the theme as a melodic skeleton, and am very strict in exposing it in the variations."[26]

But melody and theme are not the same. The modern-day understanding of melody has a whiff of musical purity, of essentialism, to it that "theme" does not, as if melody somehow embodies the very soul of what we consider to be music.[27] This is because definitions of melody throughout Western history engage fundamental aspects of musical identity, among others: harmony, rhythm, music as cultural icon, scale, form, musical motion, and musical perception. The questions that previous musical thinkers raised are legion, and engage these topics. Does melody grow out of harmony as Rameau and Hegel suggest, or is it autonomous, as Rousseau would have it? Does melody as a pitched phenomenon stand in opposition to rhythm in the way we often separate sung music from dance music? Rousseau argued that the best melodies, simple and periodic, idealized vocal manifestations of a populist musical mind. Do we agree? If melody is a folk-derived cultural currency, does it draw from existing scale structures within a musical practice, or rather does it *provide* the raw material from which theorists derive such scales? What is the nature and importance of internal melodic form (i.e., periodicity and motivic repetition) and how do melodies contribute to larger formal units? Does melody create a sense of motion in music (Kurth and Helmholtz argue that it does)? Is melodic identity, rather than being acoustic or notational, constructed by the mind as it *perceives* melody, and how do melodic

---

[25] Halfyard 2004: 60.   [26] Nelson 1962: 327.

[27] This connotation emerged from ancient Greek poetic-musical usage and came to be the provenance of pure music in the European Middle Ages. See Ringer n.d.

structures color our experience of expectation and grouping in music?[28]
I raise these questions here not to answer them – an undertaking that lies
well outside the scope of this book – but rather to suggest that the issues
bound up in our concept of "melody" are not the same as those for
"theme."

Melody also has implications of *voice* (recalling Rousseau), or at least of
a single line. Early melodies in Western music – that is, chant and narrative
recitation – were strikingly athematic; they often scrupulously avoided
motivic repetition. Even in later music, athematic melody is most often
the province of a vocal (or solo instrumental) line. The "Christe eleison"
from the Kyrie of Mozart's C Minor Mass, for instance, is a pure unfurling
of melody, a soprano line whose two words fill over four minutes of music
largely unburdened by thematic or motivic repetition and the formal
functions thematic materials fulfill. However, *thematic* music has connotations of the instrumental and multi-part about it. Imitation, of course,
requires multiple parts, and the most intensely thematic works in the
canon of Western music are instrumental – think Beethoven's Fifth
Symphony. This is not to say that there is little to no thematic vocal
music – perish the thought! – or that all instrumental music is thematic
(it isn't); rather, that melody and theme, though they often overlap, arise
from disparate traditions and still carry implications that differ from one
another.

Thematic or not, for most Western listeners, melody is probably the most
accessible thing about music. Melodies are what we sing in the shower,
whistle while we work, and imbue with texts. There have been thousands of
studies on melody, but the customary tools for tonal music analysis are
nowhere near as sophisticated for melody as they are for harmony,
counterpoint, or form.[29] A definition of "melody," like "theme," remains a
chimera; Stravinsky's definition – "Melody is . . . the musical singing of a
cadenced phrase"[30] – is both simple and technical, but also remains mad-
deningly vague. Schoenberg's definition is likewise explicit but still leaves us
wanting. For him melodic identity is dependent on an understanding of
theme as a connection of motivic transformations linked together into
phrases. Melody is *a particular kind of theme*, slow and sparing in
development, with a concentration of all events in a single voice, indications
of figuration, and frequent repetition of slightly varied phrases.[31]

---

[28] The foregoing list of questions are all raised in Ringer n.d., a first stop for anyone interested in
the history of melodic practice and the definition of melody.
[29] Solie 1977: 2–3.   [30] Stravinsky 1970: 40.   [31] See Schoenberg 1995: 181.

Ruth Solie's dissertation, devoted entirely to the analysis of melody, refuses to define it altogether.[32] Solie finds it more useful to adumbrate a satisfactory *theory* (rather than *definition*) of melody. First, such a theory should deal with melodies as foreground events.[33] Second, this theory must view melody as a *Gestalt* whole.[34] Third, the theory should deal with phenomenal reality, or what is actually heard.[35] Fourth, it should encompass musical time and a sense of melodic motion.[36] Solie also raises the question of how to differentiate melody from theme and motive, but leaves us without a clear-cut answer.

Jack Stein posits an understanding of melody that echoes our original qualification for thematic status – repetition:

Melody can impress itself forcefully on the hearing only if it contains a repetition of certain melodic elements in a certain rhythm.[37]

As with "theme" one finds that reading these authors brings us closer to an understanding of "melody" without being able to state a concise definition. And, as with "theme" and "phrase," it is almost as if we must identify these things by triangulation, the direct method proving impossible or involving at the very least a formal, thesis-length study built up from Boretzian first principles.[38]

Of them all, Stravinsky's definition appeals because it invokes singing; a melody is a line that one can imagine being sung. Melody also implies textural importance – monophony or homophony being the natural implications – in that melody is not only a singable line, but also a *prominent* singable line. Certainly, melodies can be combined polyphonically (or elaborated simultaneously in a heterophonic texture), but the idea of

[32] Solie 1977: 3–4.

[33] *Ibid.* Solie outlines these four qualifications at the beginning of her thesis (15) and explores their implications later on. She prefers Tovey's melodic analyses – they focus on the musical surface – to the overly "reductive" methods of Schenker and Reti. That is, Solie is more interested in the hunt for individuation of melodies rather than similarities between them (39 and 143).

[34] *Ibid.*: 34–35. Here, Solie relies on psychological models in the writings of P.E. Vernon. She stipulates that a sense of contour and gesture must be retained in a good melody, causing it to be easily remembered as a unit, or *Gestalt* whole.

[35] We begin to get a sense of Solie's theory as perceptually based. The concentration on the musical surface, the mind's grasping of the melody as a *Gestalt* unit, and the basis for melody in terms of phenomenology all indicate that melody, for Solie, exists in the mind of the listener.

[36] That is, the perception of melody not as an object, but rather as a dynamic time span.

[37] Stein 1973: 88.

[38] See Boretz 1969–73 for the ambitious project – one now widely regarded as laudable but impractical – of creating a new language for discussing music construed from musical fundamentals and their interactions.

melody is one that implies focus, a line that draws the ear. In that way, it is much like theme: it is noticeable. Yet, if we are to criticize the thematic definitions of those like Karlin and Gorbman mentioned earlier in this chapter as too promiscuous, theme-as-melody seems too restrictive. Melodies can be themes and themes can be melodies, but there is more to it than that. Schoenberg, perhaps, articulates the clearest distinction, one based on *profundity of musical function*:

> Every succession of tones produces unrest, conflict, problems. One single tone is not problematic because the ear defines it as a tonic, a point of repose. Every added tone makes this determination questionable. Every musical form can be considered as an attempt to treat this unrest either by halting or limiting it, or by solving the problem. A melody re-establishes repose through balance. A theme solves the problem by carrying out its consequences. The unrest in a melody need not reach below the surface, while the problem of a theme may penetrate to the profoundest depths.[39]

In short, melodic problems work themselves out on the musical surface through melodic and harmonic closure, and motivic completion. Thematic problems, however, have far-reaching consequences and may be the very problems of the piece itself. In sum, then, what this musing upon melody has led us to is not a preferred definition of the term, but rather an understanding of how it differs from *theme*. It is at once broader – theme communicates the essence of a single work, whereas melody communicates the essence of music itself – and more narrow, in that the concept of theme embraces a host of musical parameters like orchestration and texture that melody – with its emphasis on pitch, rhythm, and contour alone – is free to jettison in favor of the purity of idealized unilinear musical utterance.[40]

Motive and theme

Of all musical terms, the one that comes closest to theme is "motive." Unlike our comparison of theme to phrase, or to melody, the comparison

---

[39] Schoenberg 1967: 102. See also *ibid.*:101–04, where he devotes himself to explaining the difference between melody and theme.

[40] This is what Busoni 1957: 33 implies in his definition: "[Melody comprises] . . . a row of repeated (1) ascending and descending (2) intervals which (3) organized and moving rhythmically (4) contains in itself a latent harmony and (5) which gives back a certain atmosphere of feeling; which can and does exist (6) independent of accompanying voices for form; and in the performance of which (7) the choice of pitch (8) and of instrument (9) exercise no change over its essence."

of theme and motive uncovers a similar function. Both are repeated, both are central to musical identity, and both often develop throughout a piece of music. But whereas the concept of theme intersects with various tonal levels, themes themselves are conceptually surface-level entities. Varied repetitions of motives, however, may occur on deep structural levels, helping to unify the surface of the music with its tonal background.[41]

That said, this Schenkerian understanding of motive is not the only viable approach. Many motivic processes function purely on the musical surface, adorning it while also providing continuity or coherence. Late Baroque-era music often exhibits such usage, where simple, faceless, note-against-note contrapuntal patterns, once adorned with repeated motives, assume the guise of individuated "real music" (see Example 2.2). These surface-level repetitions frequently smooth over some kind of musical seam, juncture, or rupture, a technique sometimes referred to as "motivic linkage," and one abundant in Baroque-era counterpoint. In Example 2.3, fragments of Bach's fugue subject and countersubject are employed to provide musical unity from fugue subject to episode.[42]

Motives on the surface may also echo deeper-level patterns in ways not described by Schenkerian analysis.[43] Following McCreless, who defines Wagner's use of the E/F dyad in *Parsifal* as "motivic," or Anson-Cartwright, who hears the augmented triad as a motive in Wagner's *Siegfried Idyll*, we might allow within a definition of "motive" any musical object that provides coherence and continuity through cross-reference and development on multiple structural levels.[44] These are motives of a tonal and/or referential type, rather than Schenkerian recursive patterns of voice-leading models.[45] Like the "Tristan chord," such motives would be: 1) usually untransposed; 2)

[41] See Burkhart 1978: 151. Burkhart defines a "pattern" as the first appearance of motive, a "copy" as a later appearance (in the same, or on a deeper structural level) and "variation" as a variation form of the pattern with the same harmonic rhythm on the same structural level.

[42] Fragmentation is somewhat different from the English term "liquidation," which appears in the translation of Schoenberg 1995: 53ff and 382. For Schoenberg, this is a motivic procedure characteristic of developing variation technique in which a recognizable *Grundgestalt* is broken down into smaller, less characteristic fragments. These fragments, which may not bear obvious relationships to the parent theme, serve to unify the surface level of a composition.

[43] The issue of Schenker and motive is complex. For a thorough discussion of motive and tonality in Schenker's theory, see the second chapter of Marvin 2001.

[44] For examples, see Anson-Cartwright 1996 and McCreless 1990.

[45] That is, tonal/referential patterns of keys or harmonies may recur without recursively exhibiting the same *Auskomonierung* spans. For examples of this sort of motivic repetition on multiple levels of tonal structure, see Anson-Cartwright 1996, Bribitzer-Stull 2006b, Gauldin 1991, and Marvin 2007, among many others.

Example 2.2 From note-against-note framework to elaborated music by addition of motives (from Gauldin 2013: 147, ex. 12.9b and c)

tonally ambiguous; 3) capable of resolution to a number of structural keys; and 4) heavily weighted with symbolic meaning.[46]

    The last category, symbolic meaning, brings the conception of motive back to its psychological origins. Its original usage in musical parlance developed out of an eighteenth-century understanding of psychological "motives"; by the mid-nineteenth century, the term had broadened to include appearances in diverse contexts, simply meaning "leading idea or emotional purpose."[47] Residue of this etymology remains in place today. As evidence of this, we need only observe how many authors commandeer

[46] McCreless 1990.   [47] McCredie 1985: 4.

(a)

(b)

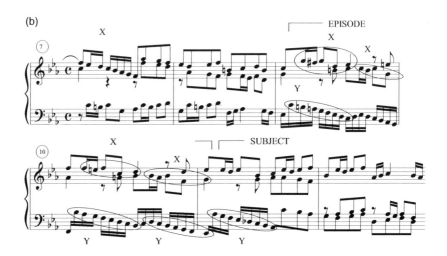

Example 2.3 Motivic linkage in fugue #2 in C minor, *Das Wohltemperierte Klavier I* BWV 847, mm. 1–3 and 7–12

Gestalt psychology to describe chunks of music. Charles Osborne, for instance, reiterates our earlier requirements of repetition and salience when he states that motives comprise a *Gestalt* if there is more than one statement of the motive and it bears a striking interval, interval progression, rhythm, and/or rhythmic progression. Osborne continues by describing larger musical units – *Grundgestalten* (themes?) – that also occur repeatedly within a whole piece, and that are the sources to which derived motivic *Gestalten* can be traced.[48] According to these parameters, the passages in Example 2.4 would all qualify as motives.

In many of these works, rhythm, instrumentation, and contour carry as much of the weight of motivic identity as does pitch.

It is not mere coincidence that the motives in Example 2.4 all inhabit minor-mode contexts. From the eighteenth century onward, minor was

---

[48] Osborne 1993: 169.

(a)

(b)

Allegro con brio

(c)

(d)

Allegretto

Example 2.4 Some examples of motives

a. Schubert, "Erlkönig," mm. 1–2
b. Beethoven, Symphony No. 5 in C Minor, I, mm. 1–2
c. Tchaikovsky, Symphony No. 4 in F Minor, I, mm. 1–3
d. Beethoven, Bagatelle in G Minor, Op. 119, No. 1, mm. 1–3
e. Joseph Haydn, String Quartet in D Minor, Op. 76, No. 2, I, mm. 1–2
f. Wagner, "Nibelungs" motive from *Das Rheingold*, 114/1/1

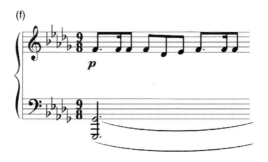

Example 2.4 (*cont.*)

expressively marked relative to major, and motivic repetition was often expressively marked, especially in minor keys where it implies obsession or the overwhelming omnipresence of a negative state of mind.[49] This is certainly true of the "Nibelungs" motive from *The Ring*, the "Erlkönig" motive, and the opening of the Beethoven and Tchaikovsky symphonies. The Beethoven bagatelle and the "Quinten" quartet motives are perhaps less specifically expressive but they (like the "Erlkönig" motive") play central roles on deeper levels of tonal structure, shaping the expressive force of their respective works on middleground levels.[50]

Motives, however, are rarely linked with an *explicit* extra-musical dramatic narrative with the same force or richness one finds in themes – particularly themes of an associative type like those in Wagner's *Ring*. This is, perhaps, largely a result of motives' relative brevity in comparison to themes, a facet of motivic identity remarked upon frequently in the

---

[49] Hatten 1994: 36.   [50] See Stein 1989, Cadwallader 1988, and Agawu 1991: 100–09.

analytic literature. For Schoenberg, "*Motive* is at any one time the smallest part of a piece or section of a piece that, despite change and variation, is recognizable as present throughout,"[51] that is, a subset of theme or melody, which is a more complete musical thought. Also, "The features of the motive are intervals and rhythms, with harmonic implications which combine to produce a memorable shape or contour."[52] The present musical definition is perhaps most succinctly stated by Stokes:

A motive, then, may best be thought of as a particular point of dramatic culmination or intensity on a line of musical development, as a special fixing of otherwise fluid and perhaps even commonplace musical material.[53]

A motive is one point of fixed musical focus – occupying no more than the psychological "now," – whereas a theme extends beyond this singularity. Motives comprise this "special fixing" or recognizability in the same ways that themes do. Schenker says there are four elements that determine a motive: melody, rhythm, counterpoint, and harmony.[54] We could say the same of theme.

And, of course, the length of motives is flexible. It would be nonsensical to bar any given musical idea from the designation of "motive" or "theme" based solely on its length.[55] Arnold Schoenberg contends that some motives comprise a (tonally closed) Classical period construction, some a phrase, some a sub-phrase, and some a simply striking harmony or progression. Regardless, motives must be musically flexible:

In general, motifs represent pithy musical gestures that lend themselves to subsequent modification – symphonic development.[56]

But how much development is too much? Variations must keep something of the original in order to be recognizable.[57] Most often, this "something" is the melodic contour of the idea. Stokes, however, suggests that contour alone is too permissive a feature to define motivic identity:

---

[51] Schoenberg 1995: 169.   [52] Schoenberg 1967: 8.   [53] Stokes 1984: 64.

[54] See Hooper 2011: 41 in which he discusses Schenker's unpublished essay, "The Path to Resemblance." See also the Oster Collection at the New York Public Library, manuscripts 83/2–43, and 83/10ff.

[55] Kirby 2004: 198 does just this, saying that a number of recurring themes in *The Ring* aren't leitmotifs at all because they are too long to be *motives*. By his own categorization system he is oddly forced into calling them reminiscence *motives* instead, keeping the "motive" designation despite the claim of excessive length.

[56] Schoenberg 1995: 169–71.

[57] For Rothstein, this is a defining characteristic of the associative theme: "leitmotifs do not readily lose their individuality by being fragmented, spun out, or otherwise 'developed.' They tend to be recognized as distinct subphrases in most contexts." Rothstein 1989: 279–80.

Motive is the "smallest part of a piece or section of a piece that, despite change and variation, is recognizable as present throughout." Motives have features which mark them (pitch, intervals, rhythm, harmony, contrapuntal combination, stress, dynamics, *and* expression, character, mood, color, movement, sonority, etc.).[58]

In addition to their *functional* distinctions, we can admit to only partial success in differentiating "motive" from "theme" in terms of *content*, remarking simply that themes are relatively more complete statements than motives. The perceptual distinction implied by Stokes – that motives occupy a psychological now whereas themes by definition extend beyond that horizon – says much the same thing: themes have a beginning, a middle, and an end (often a cadence); motives do not. Rigorous formulae here won't serve any better to distinguish the two than experienced musical judgment in terms of content. But what of function? We have seen that themes have a greater degree or richness of surface-level extra-musical meaning; is there more to it than that?

Thematic function

Thematic function is a diffuse topic. A wide variety of themes serve a wide variety of functions. We see this in the act of composition where composers may treat themes as alpha or omega – a point of inspiration or a necessity for completion. Thus, Tchaikovsky can write, "The Introduction is the *kernel* of the whole symphony, without question its main idea" (emphasis in original) while Ravel states, "My *Trio* is finished. I only need the themes for it."[59] Wagner seems to have done it both ways, beginning with thematic sketches and later tinkering with texts and musical contexts to make room for themes not originally present. Existing texts and music were altered so themes could fit them, and themes were modified to serve in a given context. Wagner's sketches suggest that some themes pre-existed any conception of tonal structure. The "Fafner as Dragon" and "Woodbird" themes for *Der junge Siegfried* were penned in June 1851 well before the music in *Siegfried* that included them.[60] And, the characteristic Valkyries' music was also written early in the process, crafted especially to

---

[58] Stokes 1984: 54 (emphasis in original).

[59] The Tchaikovsky quotation can be found in Weiss and Taruskin 1984, 398. The kernel to which Tchaikovsky refers is the same idea from the fourth symphony presented in Example 2.4C. The Ravel quotation appears in Stuckenschmidt 1969: 149.

[60] Bailey 1972.

capture the essence of the warrior maids; B minor, ♭II, the "riding" rhythm (♪. ♪ ♪), and the modulation to III all coalesced before the text for *Sieg-fried's Tod*. When it came time to unite words and music, Wagner altered the *text* (by adding the Valkyries' "hojotoho"), rather than the *music*, to fit the "Valkyries" theme, demonstrating that thematic concerns can overrule textual ones.[61] Nevertheless, while Wagner typically began compositional sketches with the vocal line (often thematic in nature) and a sort of shorthand for other aspects of the musical fabric, he also inserted, deleted, transposed, or moved themes according to the demands of the text and drama.[62] Many times, these thematic alterations remained in the music even if the dramatic forces that caused them had been dispelled.[63]

Regardless of when they emerge in the creative process, themes, like motives, function to provide piece-specific continuity and coherence; this coherence may be formal, expressive, or both. The letter scene from Tchaikovsky's *Eugene Onegin* is one example of the formal type. While the repeated theme in this scene accrues the dramatic sense of the stage action, its overarching purpose is to bind the scene together musically.[64] Likewise, themes in Howard Shore's *The Lord of the Rings* score often function as scenic unifiers, though their sense of expressive or dramatic associativity also remains strong. Examples include: the "Shire" theme as the refrain in a loose rondo form that unites the opening Shire scenes, the "Machinations" theme that spans Gandalf's dark pondering in Bilbo's hobbit hole until Frodo's departure, the "Rivendell" theme throughout the Rivendell scene, the "Rohan" theme that unites the confrontation between Gandalf, Aragorn, Gimli, Legolas, and Théoden in Meduseld, and the "Gondor" refrain throughout the flashback scene when Boromir conquers Osgiliath. Much of this thematic practice devolves from Wagner's *Ring* where certain leit-motifs arise primarily as form-defining themes, only later returning for largely expressive purposes. Many examples come to mind, though a

---

[61] Bailey 1968: 464–67.

[62] Bailey 1972: 241. See also Darcy 1993: 65–68 for one of many discussions concerning Wagner's tampering with his sketches.

[63] In early drafts of *Siegfried's Tod*, Bailey finds vocal motives that had been musically adapted to fit the text. In the mature *Ring*, however, these same motives remain in adapted forms even when they appear in purely instrumental contexts: Bailey 1968.

[64] Gorbman 1987: 29, notes similar thematic functions in film music: "In many cases, the theme's designation is so diffused that to call it a leitmotif contradicts Wagner's intention." Whether or not the neologism of "leitmotif" contradicted Wagner's intention is a complex topic; one discussed at some length in Chapter 1. Gorbman's sense is correct, however; themes in film – as in art music – may serve purely music-formal purposes, fostering continuity and coherence without expressivity playing a prominent role.

particularly clear one is the nested bar forms that arise from Wagner's statements of the "Fate" and "Annunciation of Death" themes in the Sieg-mund/Brünnhilde duet that comprises Scene 4 of *Die Walküre* Act II.

Both concert and film, however, music introduce themes that are primar-ily expressive – rather than formal – in nature. The best example in Wagner's *Ring* is the theme Sieglinde sings to Brünnhilde near the end of *Die Walküre*, Act III, Scene 1, upon learning that she carries the scion of the Wolsung race in her womb. Comprising an unbounded outpouring of melody, this theme – often called "Glorification of Brünnhilde" – punctuates this dramatic moment for expressive purposes and serves no scene-binding or form-structuring role at all. In fact, it is only heard one other time in the entire cycle: at the end of *Götterdämmerung* when Brünnhilde redeems the world from the Ring's curse, her destiny fulfilled. A similar moment from film music occurs with the statement of the "Mummy's Ring" theme in the score to *The Vengeance of Egypt* (1912). The strange music for this theme suggests its expressive importance even though it does not formally unite the scene in which it is first heard. It is only upon its later repetition that we recognize the theme's associative significance and narrative usage: it sounds each time the ring is passed on to curse a new victim.[65]

Nowhere is this ambiguity in thematic function more acutely felt than in the relationship between theme and tonal syntax. Most Schenkerians, among others, would have us believe that themes arise from tonal structure rather than determining it.[66] But themes affect our perception of tonal syntax even if they are "merely" surface-level phenomena. Theme state-ments tend to shape phrases and, when aligned with key statements, our conception of form.[67] In fact, Dahlhaus's major addition to Wagner literature was the idea that associative themes of varying lengths destroyed regular phrase rhythm, resulting in "musical prose." Such themes tend to shape form in a way that the more traditional themes of, say, Mozart, do not.[68] Surely, then, an accurate conception of theme must be flexible enough to span different composers' uses of tonality.[69]

---

[65] See Buhler 2010: 33, who quotes Clarence Sinn on this film score.

[66] See Schenker's argument against the practice of determining form by theme rather than tonal structure, Schenker 1979: 133. See also Cadwallader 1988: 8–11, who describes how an "apparent fourth" surface motive grows out of a harmonic motion that clarifies the tune as a third plus a step and how this surface-level theme is really an echo of deep levels of structure.

[67] This is true of both *Formenlehre* and other approaches. For instance, see McClatchie 1998: 109–13 for a discussion of the role themes play in the Lorenzian poetic-musical-period.

[68] Deathridge and Dahlhaus 1984: 152.

[69] In fact, Weisel, 1978: 81 suggests that deficiencies in thematic analyses often arise from misinterpreted musical structures or an inadequate awareness of the vocabulary of each particular composer or era.

Having come this far, we have raised a number of questions but have provided precious few answers, and our attempt at a definition remains vague: Themes are relatively complete musical entities, often melodic in nature, by definition repeated, more complete than motives, often beginning and comprising the better part of one or more phrases, and exhibiting various relationships to tonal syntax. But themes seem to exhibit a curious ambiguity in relation to the pieces that contain them. On the one hand, they are dependent on rhythm, instrumentation, harmonization, register, dynamics, embellishments and a host of other surface-level phenomena for their specific characters. On the other hand, they stand apart from the pieces that contain them; we can sing a theme and hear the implied harmonization even when it isn't present; and we can introduce a theme into an entirely different musical context (as in thematic development, or musical quotation) without destroying its identity. Perhaps most problematic is that themes *develop*; their quintessence is protean, be it in regard to content or to function. Rather than admitting defeat in providing an airtight definition, we are perhaps better served by embracing an understanding of both theme-as-concept and of specific musical themes themselves as fuzzy, mutable entities. We follow this line of thinking in the next chapter, proposing that the heart of thematic identity lies in the concept of the prototype.

Thematic development, thematic identity: musical themes and the prototype model

> The musical coherence [of the Wagnerian leitmotif] is there, to be sure –
> but . . . the "theme" [is] more important than its development.
>
> Roger Sessions[1]

Roger Sessions was wrong; in Wagner's *Ring*, the developments are more important than the themes.[2] And – according to Danny Elfman – they are also more fun to compose.[3] Of course, neither Sessions nor Elfman directly broaches the ontological question of *which* musical statements are developments and which are the themes, though both men imply that such a distinction is necessary. Wagnerian opera and film music are, of course, just a pair of genres among many whose thematic structure raises such questions. Considering two – "How do we determine what constitutes thematic identity?" and "What constitutes a developmental relationship vs. a new order-of-thematic being?" – leads us to this chapter's central topic: a prototype approach to understanding thematic identity.

Thematic development

Themes themselves can be lovely, powerful, heart-wrenching, or foreboding, but it is only in their development that we experience a sense of progress through musico-dramatic (or musico-narrative) time. Take, for instance, Nicolai Rimsky-Korsakov's *Scheherazade*. The opening of the first movement pits the menacing forcefulness of the Sultan, Shahriar's, theme against the alluring arabesques of Scheherazade's (see Example 3.1a). This

---

[1] Sessions 1979: 47. This quotation comes from a more extended passage in which Sessions argues that individual musical details assumed greater importance in nineteenth-century music than they did in earlier repertories.

[2] Like Adorno, I hear thematic developments and thematic becoming bearing greater importance than thematic materials or thematic identity. See Adorno 1982: 179.

[3] See the bonus features on the *Spiderman 2* DVD in which Elfman confesses during an interview that he prefers doing sequels because he doesn't have to come up with new thematic material (an act of composing he dislikes) but, rather, gets to work with variations.

presentation is evocative, but it is the subsequent development of the musical materials that grants this work its expressive power. Shahriar's and Scheherazade's music serves a framing, introductory function at the beginning of the piece rather than comprising its core. Scheherazade's tales are, after all, about Sindbad, the Khalandar Prince, and other fabulous,

(a)

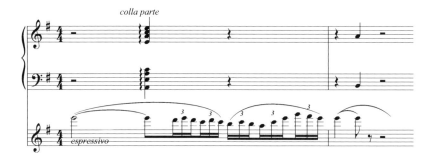

(b)

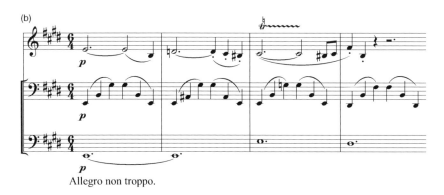

Allegro non troppo.

Example 3.1 Scheherazade's and Shahriar's themes from Rimsky-Korsakov's *Scheherazade*

a. Initial presentation in the first movement
   1. Shahriar's theme, mm. 1–4
   2. Scheherazade's theme, m. 14ff.
b. Principal theme from first movement (based on Shahriar's theme), mm. 20–23
c. Secondary theme from first movement (devolves from Scheherazade's triplet figure), m. 94ff.
d. Fanfare theme from second movement (devolves from Shahriar's theme), mm. 132–35

(c)

(d)

Example 3.1 (*cont.*)

semi-mythic characters, not about the Sultan and herself. Yet while Scheherazade and the Sultan stand outside the narrative of any one tale, they are the central characters in the overarching storyline of *One Thousand and One Nights*, and, arguably, of Rimsky-Korsakov's musical rendering as well. Consequently, their musical materials pervade each of the four movements (see Example 3.1b–d), and ultimately unite at the end of the fourth, which serves both to recapitulate themes from the previous three movements and to signal the union of Scheherazade and the Sultan.[4] These musical materials aren't leitmotifs, per se; they are more akin to *idées fixes*, thematic reminders of a dramatic connection serving to link separate movements together. Nevertheless, they demonstrate the expressive power of thematic development.

The description above assumes that listeners to *Scheherazade* can tell that material from Scheherazade's and the Sultan's themes develops across the entirety of the four-movement work. But how, specifically, do we as listeners know that two themes are related? Answering this question relies largely on an appraisal of the themes' constituent musical components, among them: linear motion, rhythm, harmony, linear function, structural

[4] The manner in which these two themes pervade later music is not always obvious. Take, for instance, the *piano* chord progression immediately following Shahriar's theme: the voice leading crosses instruments, but the same whole-tone descending tetrachord that Shahriar's theme outlines guides the chord progression as well (in an upper voice instead of in a theme that sounds like a bass line).

Example 3.2 Thematic relationships

a. Two themes that are not structurally related
b. Two themes that are structurally related

location, meter, tempo, tonality, texture, instrumentation, articulation, phrasing, and dynamics. A relationship between two themes exists when some of these components are shared or related. In most thematic analysis, the impact of meter, tempo, tonality, texture, instrumentation, articulation, phrasing, and dynamics on thematic relationships is sufficiently small to be ignored in terms of a *structural* thematic relationship, unless supported by another parameter.[5] (Of course these parameters can be quite powerful *associatively*, and link two disparate themes together in that manner. For more on this topic, see Chapters 4 and 5.) Typically, when we speak of structural relationships between themes, we speak of related rhythmic, intervallic, and/or contour cells of material. Thus, two D major themes that are both legato, in slow 3/8 meter, and written for flute don't exhibit enough similarities from this information alone to support drawing meaningful relationships between them. Two cadential themes, however, related by inversion – themes that both feature syncopated rhythms composing

---

[5] Weisel 1978: 82.

out $\hat{2}$ with neighbor motions – would exhibit a structural thematic relationship (see Example 3.2).

But not all structural thematic relationships are so patent as Example 3.2b. Thematic relationships need to strike a balance to be effective. On the one hand, developed themes must be altered enough that they are heard as distinct from the original. On the other hand, the themes must share a unifying idea that is *central to the themes' identities*. Thus, the intensity of a relationship between two themes is in direct proportion to the degree to which the unifying idea shared between the two reflects the characteristic qualities of each.[6] This prevents trivial relationships such as stipulating that two themes are related because they embellish triadic motion. But it also makes it difficult – if not impossible – to formalize the nature or degree of thematic relationship. Substantive concepts like "sharing," "relatedness," and "central idea" lie more in the realm of experienced judgment than algorithmic proof.

Wagner himself thought of thematic relationships in terms of shared materials, relationships, and central ideas. In fact, he noted the core motive of the entire *Ring* cycle – the $\hat{6}$–$\hat{5}$ falling step of the Rhinedaughters' paean, "Rhinegold! Rhinegold!" – in his prose, and urged listeners to trace its many variants throughout the entire cycle as a means for understanding how his thematic technique differed from the earlier Classic-era practice of variation.[7] Like Wagner, film composers often link a number of disparate themes by means of one central musical idea or *Urmotiv*. A few examples from the past thirty-five years include: tritones and chromatic double-neighbors around $\hat{5}$ in John Williams's scores to the first three *Harry Potter* films, the descending tetrachord in Danny Elfman's scores to the *Spiderman* films, the use of $\sharp\hat{4}$ throughout Howard Shore's *Lord of the Rings* scores (further explored in Chapter 9), the *Dies Irae* allusions in Danny Elfman's score to *The Nightmare Before Christmas*, and the perfect fifth interval throughout Williams's score to *E.T.* (said interval also appearing diegetically when E.T.'s heart glows).[8]

Like many other aspects of thematic analysis, establishing relationships between two thematic statements is not an exact science. Musical judgment must be invoked in all cases, and the analyst's decision should be supported by empiric evidence. In addition, this judgment is made by the

---

[6] *Ibid.*: 87.   [7] Wagner 1966g: 187.

[8] Film composers often highlight *Urmotive* and central thematic ideas by moving them from the realm of the non-diegetic to the diegetic. Hagrid, for instance, plays the "Harry Potter" tune on his flute in *Harry Potter and the Sorcerer's Stone*. Likewise, Jack Nicholson, as the Devil, whistles the central "Devil's Tune" featured in John Williams's score to *The Witches of Eastwick* in the ice-cream shop scene near the end of the film.

listener (analyst) and is not necessarily an attempt to describe the composer's intent or conscious knowledge with regard to thematic relationships. There is, however, some wisdom in focusing only on thematic
relationships a composer makes explicit in the music. Otherwise we open
ourselves up to the valueless analytic ability to draw a relationship between
any two themes.[9]

To reiterate: determining *if* two themes are related requires making a
judgment as to the relatedness of their musical materials. Determining *how*
two themes are related is a separate, though related, question, one that relies
on knowledge of compositional technique. Across large spans, both temporal and geographic, composers of Western music have relied largely on a
few stock devices when developing thematic materials.[10] Romantic-era
composers had two primary thematic traditions upon which to draw. The
first comprised Renaissance and Baroque contrapuntal techniques. These
included imitation, retrograde, inversion, rhythmic or intervallic augmentation and diminution, and the like. The second comprised the eighteenth-
century practices of variation and figuration, in which treatment of an
underlying harmonic pattern, and abundant use of melodic non-harmonic
tones, were of primary interest.[11] In both traditions, composers retained
at least a vestige of the original theme within each alteration, thereby (as we
noted in Chapter 2) establishing variation as a form of repetition.[12]

Continuing to consider Romantic-era composers, we find that
Beethoven's and Liszt's thematic techniques resemble Wagner's. This
should come as no surprise. But a comparison of Brahms's thematic
developments to Wagner's is also illuminating, suggesting a common
thematic practice in nineteenth-century Europe. Given their differences
in musical ideology, one might expect the two men to handle thematic
development differently. Dennison suggests as much when he revisits
Schoenberg's two methods of extending a theme: Brahms's developing
variation (in which tonality is of paramount importance and may
necessitate thematic development that disguises the relationship between
prototype and variant) and Wagner's sequential extension (in which the

---

[9] See Newcomb 1981: 48 n. 19, who makes this case for Wagner.
[10] Legion are the catalogs of thematic developments. Among some of the more rigorous are Reale
1970, who subdivides them into melodic, rhythmic, and harmonic developments; Anderson
1977, who subdivides them into melodic, temporal, and contribution (essentially musical
context); and Reti 1978, who eschews a formal approach to thematic developments in favor of
copious examples intended to demonstrate how pervasive thematic relations are in common-
practice concert music.
[11] Reti 1978: 56–65.   [12] Schoenberg 1995: 227–29.

hegemony of motive over tonality insures that thematic developments remain recognizable).[13] Yet a thematic study by Ann Scott devoted to Brahms's thematic techniques looks suspiciously like a list of devices one hears frequently in *The Ring*. The author avoids the typical thematic developments listed above, preferring instead techniques such as: "culminating thematic recall" (of themes from earlier movements near the end of a final movement), "motivic unification" (constructing diverse themes with a small number of motives), "developing variation" (gradually transforming themes through subtle changes in each statement arriving at incremental generation of new themes from old), using abstract pitch patterns to govern harmonic and thematic structures (e.g., using $\hat{6}$ and vi in the same movement (chord as motive)), "linkage" (dovetailing or overlapping thematic material from one section into or across the boundary of the next or previous section), and finally, retention or anticipation of an accompanimental pattern as a backdrop for contrasting themes.[14]

Another approach to classifying thematic developmental types is the one taken by Carl Dahlhaus, who avoids lengthy discussion of exact developmental techniques, and instead divides thematic developments (in *The Ring*) into two categories: those in which the musical relationship remains readily apparent and those in which a musical/dramatic relationship is constructed between two disparate themes.[15] In both cases, these developments modify a theme's musical characteristics to suggest a change in meaning. The techniques Wagner employs in this regard, while decidedly musical, are subtle and flexible enough to rival language's semantic nuances. In Gauldin's words:

> The way in which he [Wagner] adapts each thematic recurrence to the dramatic needs of the event at hand, while still managing to maintain its aural identity, is often nothing short of sheer magic.[16]

Gauldin likens variants of associative themes to letters from a single person – the author remains the same but the content changes,[17] a process of thematic diversification Wagner termed *Entwicklung* (development or evolution).[18] Such diversifications comprise a vast continuum of degrees of intensity. Analysts walk a fine line when distinguishing between modified statements of the same theme and musical relationships between distinct themes. This line, however, is made explicit by the use of theme labels – labels force any

---

[13] Dennison 1985: 35.   [14] Scott 1995: 179–82.   [15] Dahlhaus 1979: 136–37.

[16] Gauldin, *Analytical Studies in Wagner's Music* (unpublished manuscript), chapter 14: 7.

[17] The metaphor is made in distinction to the caricature of the themes as "calling cards." See Gauldin, *Analytical Studies in Wagner's Music* (unpublished manuscript), chapter 36: 3–4.

[18] See Wagner's 1857 open letter on Liszt's symphonic poems: Wagner 1966d, *passim*.

thematic reference to identify with a previous theme by virtue of their shared name, or to distinguish between the two as objects of a different order: different names signal different themes.

Borrowing from Heinrich Schenker, we might invoke an evolutionary metaphor to clarify this distinction.[19] The relatively less-intense thematic transformations and concomitant dramatic colorations they imply can be referred to as "mutations" in which a given theme is musically developed without radically altering its associational significance, just as slight genetic mutations affect the DNA but not the species classification of the life form involved. In most cases, this process involves only slight modifications, changing one or two musical parameters while retaining the others. But some developments engage another order of magnitude. In *The Ring* for instance, distinct-but-related themes often evolve out of shared musical materials just as distinct-but-related species evolve out of shared genetic materials. Each theme has an independent dramatic association, however, and a large number of musical discrepancies between themes can help distinguish this relationship from thematic mutation. Thus, while thematic mutation concerns itself with musical-dramatic differences between variations of the same theme, thematic *evolution* seeks to find musical-dramatic similarities between different themes as witnessed in "Giants" and "Fafner as Dragon" at the beginning of Chapter 1, related themes given two different names.

The problem with names

If each theme has such fuzzy musical (and associative) parameters, in effect customizable to form potentially limitless realizations of a thematic prototype, the whole act of naming the themes seems questionable. We would either need thousands of names to reflect every individual thematic statement, or, perhaps, none at all.[20] Avoiding names altogether is especially attractive in Wagnerian exegesis, given that many of the popular theme names in works like *The Ring* identify objects or characters (e.g., "Gold," "Sword," "Valhalla," "Loge," "Giants," etc.) while the themes themselves capture emotions, not object identifications. Wagner expressed his thoughts about this practice on a number of occasions. In Cosima's diaries, for instance, we find the following:

---

[19] Schenker 1906: 6/6 employs this metaphor.

[20] I have written at greater length on theme naming elsewhere. I urge readers wishing for a more protracted discussion than the abbreviated comments here to examine Bribitzer-Stull 2007.

I play excerpts from *Götterdämmerung*, arranged for piano duet, with Loldi. R. says he is pleased with the work. Unfortunately, in this edition, there are a lot of markings such as 'wanderlust motive,' 'disaster motive,' etc. R. says, 'And perhaps people will think all this nonsense is done at my request!'[21]

It is an unfortunate truth that the leitmotif became a piece of reception-history currency intimately tied up with understanding and interpretation – a "middle-brow" way into Wagner's dense and problematic works that allowed audiences to feel they had some knowledge of the musical materials without requiring them to engage in, or understand, technical musical analysis.[22] Even for Hans von Wolzogen, though – the most abused of Wagnerian theme collectors – the linguistic tags that identify each theme reflect the inner essence, idea, or representation of the music, not the object itself.[23] Wolzogen heard music as inherently expressive; themes only become associative when conjoined with the poem, similar emotions being captured by similar music.[24] Thus it seems only right to give them a tag that reflects the drama that gives rise to the emotional association. Moreover, it is worth considering not only naming themes, but also supplanting the earlier notion of a "definitive" thematic statement with a thematic "prototype" instead.[25] Why? *Because it is the idealized concept of a theme we name, not any one particular iteration on the musical surface, no matter how definitive.* Names then imply that various surface-level thematic statements are instantiations of a specific prototype or idealized thematic construct.[26] This, of course, raises the question of what exactly constitutes a prototype.

The prototype

Because thematic identities, like species classifications, arise from observations of many individuals with similar features, thematic identity can be understood as comprising a musical-dramatic prototype, an idealized

---

[21] Wagner 1994: 435 (Monday, August 1, 1881).

[22] See Thorau 2003, which states this among its central arguments.

[23] *Ibid*.: 62. This grew out of Wolzogen's Schopenhauerian belief in melody as expression of the will and thus influenced Wolzogen toward *melodic* analysis of Wagner's music.

[24] *Ibid*.: 62–63. We explore the topic of associativity at length in Chapters 4 and 5.

[25] Cooke 1995 was the first to define "definitive" and "embryonic" forms of themes. These notions are similar in spirit to my "prototypic statement" and "proto-theme."

[26] In fact, Wagner's associative themes are virtually never stated in exactly the same way twice.

mental construct that may or may not appear on the actual surface of the music. In theory, the listener, hearing multiple repetitions and variations of a theme, forms an abstract prototype of it. By way of analogy we might picture the prototypic bird. While this image will be slightly different for each individual, most people will picture an animal that is small and colorful; has two wings, a beak, and feathers; lives in trees; flies; and sings pretty, high-pitched songs; in sum, something not unlike Siegfried's wood bird. The vast majority of birds do not fit all these categories, and some, like the penguin, fit fewer than half. The category is fuzzy. The prototypic bird exists only in the imagination. Objects can be compared against the prototype to determine their relative bird-ness – high but not perfect for an owl, much lower for a Valkyrie (they fly, but are their high-pitched songs pretty?), and practically non-existent for a Nibelung.

Steven Pinker explores the notion of prototype in his 1999 book, *Words and Rules*:

People think in categories, like "furniture," "vegetable," "grandmother," and "turtle." The categories underlie much of our vocabulary – such as the words *turtle* and *furniture* – and they underlie much of our reasoning. We are not dumbfounded by every new turtle we see; we categorize it as a "turtle" and expect it to have certain traits, like being slower than a hare and withdrawing into its shell when frightened. This means that beforehand we did not mindlessly record every turtle we had seen, like a video camera; we must have abstracted what turtles have in common. To understand mental categories is to understand much of human nature.

. . . the members of a category are not created equal, which is what one would expect if they were admitted into the category by meeting the definition. Everyone agrees that a blue jay is somehow a better example of a bird than a chicken or a penguin . . . the best member of all is called the prototype, such as the sparrow for "bird" and a wrench for "tool."

. . . the categories of the mind have fuzzy borders. People aren't quite sure whether garlic, parsley, seaweed, or edible flowers should count as vegetables . . .

. . . categories have stereotyped features: traits that everyone associates with the category, even if they have nothing to do with the criteria for membership. When people think of grandmother, they think of gray hair and chicken soup, not of a node in a genealogical tree.[27]

---

[27] Pinker 1999: 270ff. Though Pinker works in this book to establish a sort of Chomskyan generative grammar underlying language acquisition, I am *not* arguing for a similar understanding of thematic relationships. Rather than a set of transformative rules undergirding thematic relationships, I imagine instead a cloud of musically and dramatically related themes with the prototype (the best or ideal member of the category) situated near the center of the cloud and standing as exemplar for an entire class of objects. Unlike generative grammar, which

The notion of prototype appears, too, in music scholarship, often explicitly borrowed from cognition and perception research. Matthew Brown, for one, mentions that, because cognitive scientists find certain concepts impossible to define by "necessary and sufficient conditions," researchers tend instead to define these concepts by appealing to the notion of prototypes – idealized versions of an entire class of individual things.[28] In recent years, however, prototype thinking in music theory has largely fallen out of the mainstream in favor of conceptual-model thinking (i.e., category- and schema-based thinking) – a move implicit in the Pinker quotations above.[29] In his book, Lawrence Zbikowski moves from prototypes toward categories, explaining how the former comprise a cognitive construct around which we organize the latter. Zbikowski's discussion necessarily broaches epistemology, defining a preferred basic level of category that sits at the intersection of the "efficiency principle" and the "informativeness principle." For example, we often prefer referring to "musical instruments, fruit, and furniture" when naming objects in a house rather than the too-specific "horn, apple, table" and the unspecific "things." (For musical discourse, Zbikowski argues that it is the motive that occupies this conceptual "sweet spot," though theme and phrase are probably not far off the mark.) Since each category is a graded structure, members exhibit different degrees of fit. Sparrows and penguins are both birds, but sparrows fit the category better. The reason for this becomes clear when we understand that we weigh features of a category differently with regard to specific prototypes. Locomotion (flight vs. swimming), for instance, carries a great deal of weight for the "bird" category.[30]

Despite this recent turn away from the prototype in music theory, it still remains an attractive model. Unlike categories – which function on weighted, shared attributes – or schemata – which function on descriptions of a shared underlying or adumbrated structure – the prototype model elevates the prototype, an actual individual thing – albeit an abstract thing – in the perceiving mind. Thus, the prototype model fits well with our concept of theme. There is often one statement (usually the first) that comes closest

---

forces binary distinctions, a prototype model allows for a given thematic statement to sit, for example, on the edge of two different "clouds," related, as it were, to two different thematic prototypes simultaneously (and perhaps equally).

[28] Brown 2005: 5–6. For a brief summary of the many music psychologists who have made use of the notion of prototype see *ibid.*, 226. London 2007, 116–17 reiterates much of what Zbikowski and Brown have to say on the topic.

[29] See Zbikowski 2002 for an example of category-based thinking, and Gjerdingen 2007 for an example of schema-based thinking.

[30] See Zbikowski 2002: 31–49 for more detail.

to the thematic prototype, with other, later statements bearing greater or lesser resemblance to it. This is why thematic guides to all sorts of musical works so often present *a prototypical thematic statement* in music notation, something one would hear (or could imagine hearing) on the surface of the music, rather than, say, a list of weighted category attributes or a schemata-like adumbration of underlying thematic structure. That said, there are plenty of instances where the first thematic statement is not the prototype.[31] Howard Shore refers to one such instance when he dubs a specific musical statement "the *fully-formed* 'Fellowship' theme" (which sounds when Elrond announces the "Fellowship of the Ring" about two hours into the film of the same name). Earlier versions, at least to the mind of the composer, were somehow not yet complete. Shore also notes that the heroic version of this theme never occurs after Gandalf (a member of the fellowship) is lost, implying a dramatic rationale for the disappearance of prototype statements in favor of developed statements.[32]

Much the same thing occurs in Wagner's *Ring*. The composer rarely states leitmotifs in exactly the same way twice, but we, the audience, understand these varied thematic iterations as related to an idealized prototype that may or may not appear on the surface of the music. The "Sword" theme, as described in John Edward Jenkins's dissertation, exhibits a prototypic mode (fifty-five of the eighty-seven appearances are in major), a prototypic tonic key (thirty-three of the fifty-five major-key appearances are in C with the next most frequent key appearing only five times) and a prototypic instrumentation (prominently featuring the solo trumpet). Jenkins obtains similar results for articulation, "mood," time signature, tempo, dynamic, coordination with other motives, and medium (voice, orchestra, or both).[33] Statements that exhibit all of these characteristics simultaneously, however, are few and far between. Thus, Jenkins's research suggests that motives have fuzzy values for determining associative keys, instrumentation, harmony, tempo, meter, and other musical parameters. Each parameter has a prototypic value; when all are combined conceptually, they form a prototype of the theme even if such a combination rarely or never actually occurs in the music per se.

---

[31] Deathridge and Dahlhaus 1984 warn against assuming the first thematic statement to always be the most definitive.

[32] See the interview with Howard Shore on the appendices DVD included with the *The Fellowship of the Ring* DVD, a four-disc special extended edition from New Line Home Video, 2001.

[33] Jenkins 1978: appendix A, 141–45.

The prototype model fits not only the identity of specific themes themselves, but also the notion of *theme* as concept. In Chapter 2, we noted the difficulty in codifying a clear-cut definition of theme, preferring instead a looser definition. Wagner's leitmotifs in *The Ring* are a case in point: they can be melodic and/or harmonic entities of variable length, not necessarily a "theme" or a "motive."[34] As Grey put it:

> This plurality aptly, though not in any systematic sense, reflects the spectrum of his practice: his "leitmotifs" come in many shapes and sizes – some are themes or melodies, some are motives, some are "fundamental," "principal," or "natural," some are not.[35]

There is no ideal prototypical leitmotif that exists on the surface of the music. But there are parameters we value in labeling musical identities as such. For most commentators, the musical parameters would include, in decreasing order of importance: a clear melodic and rhythmic profile, a clear tonal and/or harmonic context, an identifiable timbre or orchestral color, and a sense of relative completeness balanced with an open-ended quality that can fit a variety of musical contexts. (We shall address leitmotifs' *associative* parameters in the next two chapters.) Thus, themes like "Renunciation of Love," "Curse," and "Hunding" fit the prototype better than "Scheming" (which lacks a clear rhythmic profile and a sense of completeness), "Resentment" (which lacks a clear melodic profile and a sense of completeness), or "Brünnhilde's Reproach" (whose tonal/harmonic context is often ambiguous, and which lacks an associated timbre) (see Example 3.3).

Many other scholars have addressed the fuzzy nature of leitmotivic identity without resorting to explicit invocation of prototype model. Some describe the transformative capacity of the themes, grouping them into families linked by both musical and dramatic connections.[36] Others admit to a wide variety of musical constructions as leitmotifs.[37] Many recognize the importance of harmony and counterpoint in the definition of an associative theme.[38] A few realize that not all thematic developments are

---

[34] Darcy 1993: 46.   [35] Grey 1995: 319.

[36] Cooke 1979: 43–46 addresses this problem. He presents his introduction to thematic transformation and thematic families, *ibid.*, and in Cooke 1995. Darcy's exhaustive study of the themes of *The Ring* in his four unpublished booklets relies heavily on Cooke (see the appendix to Bribitzer-Stull 2001).

[37] See Darcy in the appendix to Bribitzer-Stull 2001, who allows anything from a chord to a musical period as a theme; Anson-Cartwright 1996; and Lewin 1984. This last article, though primarily involved with a *Stufen*/function distinction, implies an associative function for pitch-classes and harmonies.

[38] Darcy cites harmonic considerations throughout his guides (see the appendix to Bribitzer-Stull 2001). Other studies such as Anson-Cartwright 1996 examine the manner in which salient component harmonies of associative themes are composed out on deeper levels. He follows

(a)

(b)

(c)

Example 3.3 More and less prototypic leitmotifs in *The Ring*

a. "Renunciation of Love," Rg/43/1/1–2/1
b. "Curse," Rg/175/2/4–3/2
c. "Hunding," Wk/16/2/3–4
d. "Scheming," Sg/1/1/4–6
e. "Resentment," Rg/174/4/3
f. "Brünnhilde's Reproach," Wk/265/4/1–7

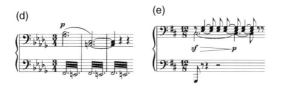

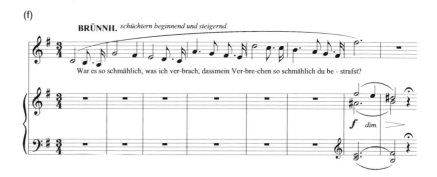

Example 3.3 (*cont.*)

created equal – thematic variation in one music drama may function quite differently from similar techniques in another.[39] Schenkerian approaches describe the impact that associativity has on large spans of music.[40] And finally, recent studies address the issue of listener perception and how musical parameters determine meaning in a context divorced from staged drama.[41]

One could even extrapolate the prototype model expounded above to the level of leitmotif-as-concept. Leitmotifs, and other associative themes, occur in a variety of works not only by Wagner, but also by other composers. The reason Wagner's *Ring* is most famous for their use is that

Morgan 1976 in allowing these prolonged sonorities to be dissonant. Though Anson-Cartwright's claim that the *Siegfried Idyll* composes out an augmented triad is problematic in Schenkerian terms, it is an important step toward realizing the multi-level power of harmony in the associative theme.

[39] Gauldin, *Analytical Studies in Wagner's Music* (unpublished manuscript), Chapter 34: 21 points to one such difference between the themes in *Parsifal* and those in *The Ring*. In *Parsifal* cases of "Harmonic Redemption" occur in which a chromatic theme becomes diatonic. One example is the theme representing Amfortas's wounds. The original form clearly outlines an augmented triad. With the healing of Amfortas's wounds and the return of the Grail in Act III, this theme becomes diatonic, outlining a major triad. In the pessimistic world of *The Ring*, the reverse is true; diatonic themes often become corrupted by chromaticism.

[40] See Brown 1989, who describes a situation in which a leitmotif is a tonal model for larger spans of music.

[41] See Deliège 1992; and Hacohen and Wagner 1997.

Table 3.1 The prototype model and the leitmotif

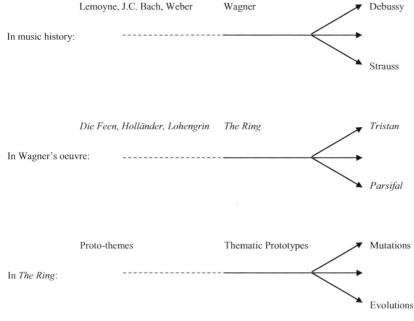

Forerunners	Prototypes	Variations

In music history: Lemoyne, J.C. Bach, Weber — Wagner → Debussy / Strauss

In Wagner's oeuvre: *Die Feen, Holländer, Lohengrin* — *The Ring* → *Tristan* / *Parsifal*

In *The Ring*: Proto-themes — Thematic Prototypes → Mutations / Evolutions

leitmotifs appear in their most *prototypic* form in this work. Within Wagner's compositional output, the prototype model holds as well. Out of the inchoate beginnings in the earlier operas, the associative theme reached prototypic status in *The Ring* and then ramified in the later operas.[42] Wagner's development of the leitmotif is not a history of a single technique – it varies from work to work – but *The Ring* is the yardstick against which all others are measured.[43] In fact, the prototype concept applies equally well to the historical development of the leitmotif, Wagner's development of the leitmotif, and the development of individual themes within *The Ring*. The list of attributes in the paragraphs above looks like category thinking, but as Table 3.1 points out, it is really the *prototype* we are considering. (This is why Chapter 7 concerns itself entirely with

[42] Of course the Wagnerian leitmotif was, in turn, adopted and subtly transformed by later composers. We cover this phenomenon in greater detail in Chapter 8.
[43] McCredie 1985: 2.

thematic development techniques in *The Ring*; it attempts to describe a *prototypical* practice rather than defining a category or depicting a schema.)

The manner in which associative themes developed in the history of art music and within Wagner's oeuvre also parallels the development of themes themselves within *The Ring*. Just as composers before Wagner hinted at his mature use of the associative theme, and Wagner operas before *The Ring* yielded similar inklings, so too do proto-themes presage the appearance of more-or-less definitive statements of themes in *The Ring*. Much less has been written about the pre-appearance of associative themes than of the themes themselves or restatements of them. A threefold appearance, however, of a rich musical idea from vague sentiment to apotheosis to reminiscence is a typical nineteenth-century gesture; in fact, Wagner's prose suggests that one of music's greatest abilities is to create expectation and longing in the listener and then fulfill that longing in a psychologically satisfying way.[44] The composer's original theory in *Oper und Drama* was to include in the new musical drama he imagined motives of both presentiment and reminiscence – devices serving equal and complementary functions.[45] In the process of composing, though, reminiscence motives became the more highly developed of the two; echoes of Wagner's theory of presentiment still sound in *The Ring* dramas, however.[46] These serve in the way intended: as a psychological or emotional *preparation* for what is to come, thus making the actual event a *fulfillment* of this preparation.[47] In short, leitmotivic genesis often occurs via adumbration or presentation of one or more of its characteristic musical elements. Repetition and transformation of these hazy, non-distinct utterances then morph into a recognizable musically and dramatically highlighted theme.[48] Wagner theorizes about this process in *emotional* terms, stating that the orchestra can imply something as yet unheard or unseen by the vague suggestion of an emotion – an emotion that is later clarified when it is brought into alignment with the drama.[49] Though Wagner's writings emphasize the emotional association of the themes, proto-themes have often been interpreted semiotically as a foreshadowing of objects or

---

[44] Drake 1985: 77.

[45] See Wagner 1966b: 330–48. We return to this topic near the end of Chapter 4.

[46] Stein 1973: 74.   [47] *Ibid.*: 77.   [48] Stokes 1984: 54–72.

[49] This was first suggested to me during course work with Warren Darcy. Hacohen and Wagner 1997 implies that the semantic connotations of the associative themes may be the vehicle for such emotional foreshadowings.

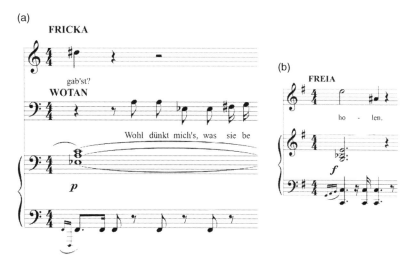

Example 3.4 Pre-statements of "Giants"

a. Rg/58/4/1
b. Rg/64/3/5

events yet to be introduced.[50] This, however, is something of an impossibility. Without the drama to give meaning to the sign, such foreshadowings can only convey the connotations of topics or word painting, suggesting the emotion that will eventually accompany the full thematic statement and priming the audience to make the eventual association.[51]

By way of a brief example, let us return to the "Giants" theme we investigated in Chapter 1. Previews of the march topic, orchestration, register, and characteristic grace-note anacrusis appear in dramatically suggestive locations, first in Rg/58/4/1 when Wotan considers the bargain he made with the giants, and later in Rg/64/3/5–64/4/1 during Freia's frantic warning that Fasolt is coming to take her away (see Example 3.4). The prototypic "Giants" theme begins in Rg/68/1/1. Example 1.1, discussed in Chapter 1, is the "Fafner as Dragon" theme, presented first during the *Vorspiel* of *Siegfried* Act II (Sg/136/1/2ff) and later during the Siegfried/Fafner confrontation (Sg/185/4/3ff). The musical relationship between it and "Giants" (the falling fourth, now augmented; dotted rhythm; low

---

[50] Darcy 1993: 46–47.

[51] Note that by foreshadowing with proto-themes, the orchestra takes on the role of narrator; it presumes the entire *Ring* drama as past tense, thus allowing the orchestra to allude to future events. See Abbate 1991: 169–70.

register; etc.) parallels the dramatic relationship between Fafner in his role as giant and, later, as dragon. As such, it represents thematic evolution. Here it illustrates a post-prototypic theme-statement variation.

While proto-themes presage the appearance of more or less "definitive" statements of themes in *The Ring*, these definitive statements are hard to nail down. Proto-themes are often motivic in nature, and not articulated clearly as discrete entities in the musical fabric. And thematic restatements remind the audience of music they have already heard. But defining the point at which the theme crystallizes into a definitive statement is tricky. It is critical to pause here and reiterate the distinction between *definitive* and *prototypical* thematic statements. Neither is necessarily easy (or even possible) to identify on the musical surface, and each is different from the other, conceptually speaking. Return, for a moment, to Examples 3.3a–c, among the more prototypical leitmotifs in *The Ring*. Each excerpt is a candidate for the *definitive* statement of each theme (i.e., the first complete, or mature, statement). But these might not be good candidates for the *prototype* of each of their attendant themes. This is because in Wagner's theories (and often in practice), leitmotifs arise in the vocal line and later recur in the orchestral texture. Definitive statements tend to be more or less complete. That is, the themes are often longer than proto-themes or thematic restatements and they often fill out complete phrases or periods. Also, these main statements are usually prominent musically, demanding the attention of the listener while proto-themes and restatements are more likely to be subtly woven into the musical texture. Finally, definitive statements are more likely to accompany salient and first-time dramatic occurrences. Wagner even suggested performing the types of themes differently. According to Porges, during rehearsals Wagner said:

When a motive is depicting an actual event it should be delivered in a grand style, slowly, and broadly, but when serving as a reminiscence . . . it should be slightly faster and with accents less pointed.[52]

Something resembling a thematic prototype, however, may occur later. These statements often feature thicker or more forceful orchestration and texture, richer or more arresting harmonic support, and/or more convincing motion toward cadential or concluding gestures. Though they are not the first complete statements of these themes, they are probably – at least to some listeners – better *exemplars* of the ideal natures of these themes.

---

[52] Porges 1983: 12.

For those seeking simple definitions, it is natural to reach the end of these two chapters on thematic identity with a sense of disappointment; our extended reflections have yielded more fuzziness and questions than clarity and answers. If nothing else, though, we have reaffirmed one crucial insight: *we know the very nature of the leitmotif to be developmental.* Completely static entities – even those with important formal or associative functions – are not true leitmotifs. Thus, the mutability of both music and meaning must be central to our understanding of this concept. Having considered music and musical (i.e., thematic) materials at some length, the task that remains is to explore extra-musical associations; specifically, how they become established and how they develop over time.

PART II

Musical association

4 | The phenomenon of musical association

> They stood there full of meaning, and yet there was no saying what
> they meant.
>
> Ursula K. LeGuin[1]

Dvořák's *Zlatý Kolovrat* (*The Golden Spinning Wheel*) opens with an
F major horn theme (eee Example 4.1). This music recurs a number of
times, but only once – at the very end of the work – in a clear A major
tonic.[2] For a listener versed in Western music but unfamiliar with this
piece, and unaware of its programme (say, listening to it on the radio during
the morning commute), it's likely that this horn music would call attention
to itself as *thematic* in nature, a salient and relatively complete repeated
musical idea. Given its stylized horn calls, our theoretical listener would
probably also detect an air of pastoral nobility.[3] And, the theme's repetition
would cement for the listener its importance relative to the identity of this
particular symphonic poem. Furthermore, our hypothetical listener might
attend to the specific play of themes (there are many others) and textures,
along with the work's unusual form, to conclude that the music suggests a
story. Beyond that, however, she would have little idea of the story's
specifics, the narrative significance of the F major horn theme, or why this
theme occurs in A major only at the end of the work.[4] In fact she might
even feel compelled to *create* a story to explain the music; like the standing
stones in Ursula LeGuin's *The Earthsea Trilogy*, the work suggests deep

---

[1] This is an excerpt from LeGuin 1975: 15 in which the author describes the nine ancient standing
stones that comprise the Tombs of Atuan.

[2] A major is the key associated throughout the work with the love between the king and Dornička
(established at *Larghetto*, thirteen bars before rehearsal 6, the point in the story when the king
asks for Dornička's hand). There are fragments of the theme in A major at *Allegro, ma non
troppo* (just after reh. 6). They quickly move through A minor back to F, however, when the king
departs Dornička's cottage for the first time, optimistic that he will have her as his wife.

[3] Pastoral nobility devolves from a high-style blending of the three topics treated in Monelle 2006:
hunt (specifically the use of horns), military (specifically the fanfare-like melodic/rhythmic cells),
and pastoral (F major, slow harmonic rhythm, bass pedal points, and so forth).

[4] Here I use the term "narrative" informally, in the spirit of Maus 1991, rather than alluding to the
more focused definitions of narrative in music proposed by Carolyn Abbate and others.

Example 4.1 The F major opening theme from Dvořák's *Zlatý Kolovrat*, mm. 9–22

meaning without revealing what it is.[5] With knowledge of the fairy tale upon which Dvořák's work was based, however, it is likely that our listener would form associations between the storyline and the sounds in the piece: In fact, after associating the horn theme with the king (the tale's protagonist) and A major with his love for Dornička, the powerfully meaningful reason for these two elements to unite at the end of the piece becomes clear: after many missteps, the tale concludes with the nascent love story finally realized.

---

[5] Note that music's ability to *create a story* is very different from its ability to *represent*, a point made clear throughout Kivy 1984, who very much accepts the latter and rejects the former. Kivy 1990 goes on to argue that, even when representational, music may be considered qua music (i.e., as an object of human cognition); its sonic presence in the human mind can be considered and analyzed apart from its meaning.

Composers have used aberrations from stylistic norms for centuries to depict, color, or suggest a particularly dramatic or emotional scene. Thus, it is understandable, if not excusable, that listeners are inclined to add a program to apparently "absolute" music when its formal, textural, harmonic, or thematic physiognomy is unusual. See Maus 1991: 18 for a brief overview of the pitfalls associated with this assumption, and the concomitant problematic division between absolute and programmatic musical logic.

Note also that imagined programs can provide the mind with *imagined* visual stimuli that aid in association. See Walton 1997 and the section on associativity at the end of this chapter for more on this point.

There are countless examples of musical works that serve as presentations of pre-existing prose. Composers take it for granted that audiences familiar with the story (or presented with the story in programme notes (think Berlioz's *Symphonie Fantastique*) or narration (think Prokofiev's *Peter and the Wolf*)) will perform the requisite mapping of prose narrative to sound. But how does this work? How can something as abstract as organized sound communicate the specificity of meaning necessary to recount a certain series of events? And how does musical meaning go beyond representation, to embrace less tangible things like emotions? The question of musical meaning has fascinated mankind for thousands of years. It has a rich and complex history, most recently engaging scholarship on expression, representation, semiotics, referentiality, topic theory, and subjectivity, among others. These concepts are capacious, with various commentators reading them in distinct and overlapping ways. Moreover, they are all bound up with another, relatively unexplored, vehicle for musical meaning – association, which comprises the focus of this chapter.

Associations range from the personal to the widely cultural and lie behind many of the cultural competencies Western listeners evoke in a variety of musical experiences, as in the thematic and tonal associations adduced in our hypothetical reading of Dvořák's *Zlatý Kolovrat*. These experiences need not be in a concert hall, or even at a musical performance, but rather make use of musical association as a currency of communication, a portion of the vast number of shared memes that unite and – in part – define a culture or community. In fact, we invoke them every day, often without conscious realization of the communal storehouse we access and expect others to access as well.

Two examples from my own life will illustrate this point. The first comes from my days as an undergraduate: A friend of mine and I were sitting in a café on the main drag of our small college town, and one of the Conservatory deans rode by on her bicycle. As she did, my friend and I exchanged a glance and – without a word – immediately started singing the "Wicked Witch of the West" music from *The Wizard of Oz*. This was, predictably, followed by our shared, uncontrollable laughter.

The second anecdote occurred more recently: A family member told me about a website entitled "Benny Hill This!" – a site that will stream any YouTube clip at double speed while overdubbing it with the Benny Hill theme music (Boots Randolph's "Yakety Sax").[6] When I shared it with a

---

[6] I wish to thank my brother-in-law's sister, Laurie Richardson, for showing me this website.

friend and asked him what he thought might be an amusingly incongruous video to select, he suggested the trailer to the movie *Schindler's List*. Mere seconds after we had "Benny Hill'ed" it, I gasped, horrified. Rather than experiencing John Williams's poignant violin melody as a backdrop to somber images of European Jews being corralled onto trains, we saw the trailer's figures racing around to the irreverent strains of caterwauling saxophones. Surely an afterlife of eternal damnation awaited two souls who had even contemplated such an unholy union of images and music.

Both events were predicated on shared associations. It was only upon later reflection, however, that I came to two realizations: 1) the association of music with drama works in both directions; and 2) association's power is as great in settings where the media are incongruent as when they are congruent. We usually think of musical associations calling to mind things outside of music, as in the Dvořák example adumbrated above. But once the association is formed, it works in the other direction as well: Returning to the first anecdote, the image of an adult female authority figure riding a bicycle instantly called to mind – seemingly without the intermediary step of the filmic image of Elvira Gulch – the "Wicked Witch of the West" music. And in the second anecdote, while "Yakety Sax" evoked the antics of a British comedian, the images of *Schindler's List* recalled the quiet dignity of Williams's score. Blending the two was shocking.

Both occurrences involved memory, emotion, meaning, and music. More specifically – even though one was humorous and the other egregious – both functioned on the phenomenon of *association*. In much writing on musical meaning, the words "association(s)" and "associated with" occur frequently (though usually without the author feeling a need to define "associativity" per se). Lawrence Kramer's 2002 book, *Musical Meaning: Toward a Critical History*, is but one example. As Kramer puts it, the central problem with musical meaning stems from music's inherent ambiguity – it occupies a space between autonomy and contingency.[7] That is, music has an internal coherence of pure sound while simultaneously *associating* with ideas and things outside itself. This, of course, raises the question of whether or not music can have an unmediated, meaningful effect on a listener, without relying on metaphor or some other medium.[8] I'm not about to argue, *pace* Treitler, that music *never* has an unmediated effect, but in the case of leitmotif, it seems obvious that music's meaning is

---

[7] Kramer 2002: 1–9.

[8] Treitler 1997 takes as its premise that music can't have an unmediated, meaningful effect on a listener.

mediated at the very least by the attendant drama. I take it as my task in the pages ahead to investigate this phenomenon, and to frame associativity as a valuable way of understanding musical meaning that intersects with other thinkers' understandings of expression, signification, referentiality, topic theory, and subjectivity.

Expression

Wagner once advised Cosima that: "music always expresses the direct present."[9] The spirit of his statement engages music's ability to function dramatically – that is, as a series of actions occurring in *real, present time* (rather than, say, evoking a narrative of something that happened *in the past*).[10] While it is clear how the drama of human gestures, denotative language, and performance rhetoric of speech all found in theater (not to mention everyday life) expresses thoughts and feelings, it's not at all clear how – or even if – music expresses anything.[11] Is the music expressing the emotions of the performers as they play the piece? The emotions of the composer at the time of composition? The audience's emotional state as they listen? We might find a way to rationalize a naïve "yes" to answer any of these questions, but in most cases when people speak of expressive music, they mean that it is *the music itself* that is expressing something. And *what* is it expressing? Considered opinion differs on this point. In the second half of the eighteenth century, musicians and poets advocated for music's ability to express things that composers or performers really felt at the moment of performance.[12] Recent experiments, however, confirm the suspicion that many of us (Raymond Monelle included) share; namely, that what a performer is trying to express – emotionally speaking – isn't necessarily what any given listener hears being expressed.[13]

---

[9] Wagner 1978: 418 (cited in Daverio 1993: 166).

[10] Or, at least a narrative in some way removed from the narrator (as in sportscasters, who narrate in the present, but stand apart from the action they narrate; likewise prophets who may narrate the future). See Maus 1991: 22.

[11] Monelle 1992: 274–303 argues that expressive statements in language rely not on the words used, but rather on the performative manner of their speech (how it is intoned), which is something music can mimic. See also Kivy 1980, for a monograph-length consideration of music and expression.

[12] See, for instance, Bach 1949: 152, who urges that a musician must feel the emotions he means to express as he expresses them. See also the similar sentiments in Herder 2006: 254–55, 268, etc.

[13] For one, see Gabrielson and Juslin 1996. Monelle 1992: 203–04 argues that music is not expressive because one does not learn something about a performer's present condition from

Music's very nature – sounding abstraction unfolding in real time –
makes it a natural metaphor for that most abstract of human real-time
experience: feelings. But, if music isn't a mode of communication for
directly expressing emotion from one person to another, then what *is* it
expressing? One answer is that music expresses *itself* – merely sound and
nothing else. Another way of putting it, by Peter Kivy, the most volumin-
ous writer on musical expression, is that music expresses *nothing*.[14] Rather,
we anthropomorphize music in creating, performing, and hearing it,
allowing it to suggest emotional states we as human beings are familiar
with. Just as the face of a St. Bernard dog (to borrow one of Kivy's
examples) may *suggest* sadness because of its droopy features, this
expression of sorrow is mapped on to the canine physiognomy by human
observers; the dog itself is not necessarily sad, nor is it trying to communicate sadness to a human audience. What it does, however, is *resemble*
signals we're used to seeing humans exhibit when they are sad. Likewise, a
rush of themes piling up one atop the other could be said to be expressive
of hysteria because it *resembles* the familiar emotional state of being
overwhelmed by a simultaneity of mental and emotional signals.[15]

It's all too easy, however, for listeners to accept as axiomatic the expressive force of these culturally defined anthropomorphisms. We've been
doing it for millennia. From Plato's description of the essential nature (in
expressive terms) of Dorian and Phrygian music,[16] to Thomas Tallis's
citations of the expressive content of the eight church modes,[17] to a
2009 session at the Society for Music Theory entitled "Sounds of Sadness,"
we tend to essentialize musical expression. That is, music has for humans a
forceful immediacy (recalling Wagner's remark to Cosima) that we hear as
expressing something directly, even if that something is communicated on
an abstract, emotional level. If it didn't, Peter Kivy would hardly have
spilled so much ink cautioning listeners against such a widespread, and
apparently natural, behavior.

---

hearing him play; that is, contra the eighteenth-century view, music's emotional content is
inherent, not communicative.

[14] Kivy 1980 makes this point throughout, distinguishing between *expressing* something and being
expressive of something. The latter does not require an agent actually feeling the expressed
emotion.

[15] See Hyer 2006 for a detailed description of musical hysteria in *Parsifal* grounded in
contemporary medical and psychological writings of the later nineteenth century. *Ibid.*: 297–99
Hyer stresses the role of *memory* in Parsifal's hysteria and how leitmotif may connect past to
present.

[16] This comes from Plato's *Republic*, cited in Weiss and Taruskin 1984: 8–9.

[17] Ellinwood 1962: xi–xii.

"Expression," of course, is also used as a generalized synonym for "meaning." F.E. Kirby's typologies of expression among Wagner's leit-motifs divides expression into what Kirby calls iconic and analogic types (those that accrete meaning through mimesis or onomatopoeia) versus a variety of themes he calls "associative," which indicates themes grounded in some topical meaning.[18] (I prefer a different, though also broad, notion of associativity, which should be clear by the time we reach this chapter's end. Iconic/analogic and topical meaning will also be revisited in the pages ahead.) That said, we see here in Kirby's work an understanding of expression as a broad space that contains more circumscribed kinds of meaning.

Going one step further, we find that music's abstract nature has even encouraged the embracing of "expression" without expressive content. Think of the so-called *Empfindsamer stile* of the mid-eighteenth century, or of pervasive comments about certain pieces or performances being particularly "expressive." Expressive of what? It seems not to matter. As long as there is a sense of strong emotional content, we don't always mind if we don't know what that content is. Like LeGuin's standing stones, we are content to gaze upon objects that strike us as strong expressive vessels even if the freight they carry remains obscured. Expression can even serve as the meaningful significance of last resort. As Claudia Gorbman argues in reference to Wagner, if a given motive doesn't *refer* to a specific *object* then it can't be referential, merely *expressive* (italics mine).[19] That is, lacking reference to something *concrete*, music can still express something *abstract*. This is an extraordinary statement, and one that approaches a definition of a certain kind of human experience we call "artistic:" the ability to evoke in people meaningful contemplation without concrete signification. The only other arena in which humans regularly engage in such activity is religion (or, more specifically, the mystical side of religious or spiritual experience).

Art and religion have, of course, been paired throughout history, sup-porting one another and spawning more than a few philosophical compari-sons of their similarities.[20] But our task here is not to continue musing upon aesthetics or spirituality, for expression is not the same as association. Both are bound up in musical meaning, but association implies a pairing made through some kind of coincidence, a connection or juxtaposition that is

---

[18] Kirby 2004: 29–37.   [19] Gorbman 1987: 29.

[20] Among them, of course, is Wagner's essay, "Art and Religion." See Wagner 1966h.

forged for an individual just as it is for a community, whereas expression carries with it more than a whiff of both essentialism and universality.[21]

Signification and referentiality

Wagner's essay, *Zukunftsmusik*, aims to capture the sense of music's significance-without-specification when the author states that musical utterances raise for us (as do all "impressive phenomena") the question "Why?" without satisfying our need for an answer; or, more correctly, requiring the aid of poetry and drama to supply an answer.[22] Of course, there are many counter-examples of musical meaning that *do* point to something specific. In such cases, music functions as a denotative sign or referent. It signifies or refers to something else concretely. Of course, not all signs are purely denotative. They are "signifiers" rather than "referents." For some, such a fine distinction may be academic, but others strongly prefer it, with the former indicating music's ability to refer to real-world objects and the latter indicating music's ability to function as a sign that substitutes for an idea.[23] Put another way, we could say that referentiality is lexical – defining musical ideas that are universal – while signification is hermeneutic (or interpretive) in nature.[24] Both signification and referentiality evoke signs. We note here a generalizable difference with the literature on expression because the study of signs, or "semiotics," moves away from describing the direct communication of emotionality toward an understanding of *how* music points to something other than itself.

Given the volumes of prose in recent years devoted to musical semiology, we can't possibly rehearse it all here. Music scholarship available in the English language stems mainly from the writings of Deryck Cooke and Jean-Jacques Nattiez (in translation).[25] Earlier work in semiotics – before its adoption by music scholars – fell largely into two camps: linguistics and

---

[21] Adorno suggests as much when he complains that leitmotifs are mere gestures, repeated rather than developed, thus creating a disjunct musical form and failing to express *emotions*. Rather, the expression of leitmotifs for Adorno is the expression *of themselves* as "particles of congealed meaning," an allegory in which the signifier and the signified are one and the same. See Adorno 1991: 28–42, 44–46, and 57. It follows, for Adorno, that film music would embrace a positivistic interpretation of leitmotivic meaning and appropriate these themes to orient audiences to a new and disjunct medium.

[22] Wagner 1966e: 320.   [23] See, for instance, Monelle 2006: 20–22.   [24] *Ibid.*: 30–31.

[25] Cooke 1990; Nattiez 1990.

structuralist criticism (largely Russian (Jakobson and Propp) and franco-phone (Saussure, Lévi-Strauss, and Barthes), with American Charles W. Morris the exception) and logic, of which American scholar Charles S. Peirce is the main source.[26] At this point, we are best served by narrowing our exploration of semiotics to Peirce (we return to other semiotic considerations in Chapter 5). This is because his ideas avoid the Procrustean bed of music-as-language invited by use of linguistic semiot-ics.[27] Rather than engaging syntactic deep structures and generative-grammar models developed for understanding language, Peirce conceives of signs as epistemologically prior to language, an advantage when describ-ing non-linguistic semiotic effects like those in music.[28] Thus, we will find them helpful as we return to consider association and leitmotivic meaning throughout the remainder of this book.

Peirce's notion of semiotics is overwhelmingly tri-partite, devolving from his threefold theory of categories.[29] To begin with, it requires a sign (the signifier), an object (the signified), and an interpretant (the mental construct of signification). The signs and sign-object-interpretant relations are themselves organized into three groups of three, with each trichotomy embodying the principles of potential, real, and category (see Table 4.1 for a graphic arrangement of the concepts described below).

The first, fundamental trichotomy is potential in nature, a pre-ontological grouping that concerns essence and nature. Within it, though, is an exemplar of each of the three categories: 1) Potential: the Qualisign, an abstract quality or elemental property that is a sign – like the quality of redness for danger; 2) Real: the Sinsign, a single occurrence of a sign (the red of an individual stop sign); and 3) Category: the Legisign, a law which

---

[26] For a serviceable overview of structuralist criticism as applied to music, see McCreless 1991: 148–53. Original sources include: Barthes 1974, Barthes 1977, Chomsky 1957, Jakobson 1959, Jakobson 1973, Lévi-Strauss 1963, Propp 1968, Saussure 1959.

[27] See Keiler 1978a: 176–94 for one explanation (in the context of reviewing Eugene Narmour's *Beyond Schenkerism*) of why one cannot simply appropriate linguistic generative grammar, *mutatis mutandis*, to explain tonal music. See also Keiler 1978b: 197–203 and 206–12 (in the context of Keiler's critique of Bernstein's Norton lectures).

[28] Peirce is not much discussed in recent literature dealing with musical semiotics, though see Nattiez 1990: 5–6 for a brief overview of Peirce in relation to Saussure, and Lidov 2005: chapter 7. (*Ibid.*: chapter 5 also presents a brief overview of Nattiez's thoughts on signification.) In music studies, the best-known advocate for Peircian semiotics is Thomas Turino. For a thoughtful, comprehensible, and more detailed overview of the Peircian trichotomies and their application to musical meaning than I provide here, see Turino 1999.

[29] The following paragraphs summarize Peirce 1960: 142ff. Note that Peirce was active in the later nineteenth and early twentieth centuries, but it was not until the mid-twentieth century that fellow scholars recognized the profundity of his thought and published his papers.

Table 4.1 Ideal arrangement of the Peircian trichotomy of signs

	Potentiality of being a sign	Actual occurrence	Law-like generalization
Essential (a sign itself)	Qualisign	Sinsign	Legisign
Experiential/Practical (sign to object)	Icon	Index	Symbol
Abstract Category (sign to interpretant)	Rheme	Dicent	Argument

is a sign (like the *concept* of "stop sign," which encompasses all individual stop signs and the quality of redness they all share). Note that the legisign is not an actual occurrence of an individual sign; it is closer to the notion of the Platonic ideal, not unlike the concept of "prototype" adumbrated in Chapter 3. In terms of Wagnerian leitmotifs, we could return to our Chapter 1 example and say that the quality of "Giantness" (low, slow, minor-mode sounds with dotted rhythms and anacrusis smears) is a quali-sign, any one statement of the "Giants" theme is a sinsign, and the concept of a group of individual musical statements, all of which are similar enough to create the mental construct of an idealized "Giants" theme, is a legisign.

The second trichotomy is real in nature, experiential and practical. It includes: 1) the Icon, a type of meaning relying on a sign's resemblance to its object (as in mimesis or onomatopoeia); 2) the Index, a type of meaning predicated on cause-and-effect or correlation, that is, the object is linked to the sign itself (like a pink hand imprint on a face being a sign for a recent slap); and 3) the Symbol, a type of legisign that involves an index of a peculiar kind and comprises an association of general ideas or a general type or law; that is, it is a culturally agreed referent that derives meaning by convention, as in a car alarm, whose meaning emerges from cause-and-effect (something strikes the car to bring the sign into existence) and is a culturally agreed referent that could be a symbol of a car-jacking, but is more often understood as a symbol of exasperated annoyance by the listener who knows it is likely that this sign is a false alarm. In short, symbols are arbitrary (most words are Peircian symbols), whereas icons derive meaning from the very identity of an object, and indices derive meaning from causal and/or coincidental relationships.

Turning again to the Wagnerian leitmotif, of Peirce's second-trichotomy concepts all apply, but the index is the most crucial. Leitmotifs may be icons, as in the "Nibelungs" theme, which derives from the actual sound of hammering on anvils (though the rhythm of that hammering is, of course, highly stylized).[30] And the proliferation of theme guides points to the symbolic nature of many leitmotifs (their meanings are arbitrary and must be explained by language). Ideally, though, all leitmotif legisigns are index-ical because for an association to form, music must be correlated with drama at some point.

The third trichotomy is categorical and abstract in nature, including: 1) the Rheme, a sign of qualitative possibility, like a dog barking, which may indicate alarm, distress, exuberant joy, or something else – in short, it has the potential for meaning; 2) the Dicent, a sign of actual existence, as in any declarative sentence, it conveys information rather than requiring it be inferred; and 3) the Argument, a sign of law, which requires the cooper-ation of the sign's interpreter to function. The street musician's hat on the ground is an example; it is a law-like acculturated generalization meant to signal a place to donate money and, as such, is a legisign. But it also interacts with the interpretant, who may or may not opt to toss a dollar bill into it.

Using Peirce's terminology, we might say that wrong-headed commen-tators have historically characterized associative themes as dicent in nature – dicent because they are statements of objective truth the music makes about the drama (e.g., Siegfried's theme sounds to indicate that the character has appeared on stage). The reality of the matter is more compli-cated. Again, in Peircian terms, a better characterization might be to say that associative themes *may be dicent*, but are *more often rhematic* because sinsigns of a legisign comprise developments and transformations (rather than merely a repeated appearance) motivated by the drama that *have the potential to signify something*. The larger legisign itself is *associative* because *a given sinsign* (often the first heard in the opera) *has an indexical property* – it occurred in correlation with a meaningful element of the drama.[31]

Ideally, any sign would manifest one member of each trichotomy in the three-by-three arrangement presented in Table 4.1. (From twenty-seven possibilities, Peirce selected ten that actually occur, though he later modi-fied this categorization.) An example would be a given thermometer reading. It is a dicent–indexical–sinsign. It is dicent because the infor-mation it conveys is taken as unmediated truth – a measurement of the ambient temperature. It is indexical because the information it conveys

---

[30] Monelle 2000: 77 makes the case for the "Nibelungs" themes as icon.

[31] This is a distinction pointed to by Floros 1983: 9 when he indicates that the "Siegfried" theme in *The Ring* symbolizes not the person Siegfried but rather the idea of heroism.

bears a causal relationship with the said information (the air temperature affects the sign). And it is a sinsign because it is an individual reading (rather than the category of all thermometers, a legisign, or the essence of temperature-measuring, which is the qualisign for all such devices).

Musical signs could be understood similarly. Of course much music derives its meaning from pre-existing cultural tropes along the lines of those imported from the Italian madrigal into early opera. These include rhematic–symbolic–legisigns like the lament bass (found, for example, in Monteverdi's *Lamento della Ninfa*). This is rhematic because it has the *potential to mean something*, symbolic because its meaning is arbitrary (though established indexically through correlation with madrigalists' texts) and a legisign because it embraces all instances of lament bass. A specific instance of *stilo concitato* (a technique that morphed into the dramatic tremolo) in Monteverdi's *Il Combattimento di Tancredi et Clorinda*, however, might be understood as a dicent–iconic–sinsign. The fast repeated notes mime the physiological corollaries of action and emotional distress, the meaning is meant to be lexical (or nearly so), and the sign is a specific instantiation of the quality of excitedness.

There is a complicating factor with the Monteverdi examples just mentioned: they both include language, signs that are not musical in nature. The same is true of many leitmotifs – they arise in conjunction with a sung text. For some – like the Rhinedaughters' "Rheingold!" cry – this matters little (see Example 4.2). The dicent–symbolic–sinsign "Rheingold!" (the word) indicates what the Rhinedaughters are excited about, but the associated leitmotif, a rhematic–indexical–legisign, emerges because the emotional outburst of the Rhinedaughters caused the sign to come into existence, calling attention to the object that instantiated it.[32] The word itself, however, does not affect how the theme means something. The Rhinedaughters could just as easily have been shouting "Vodka!" In this case, the theme's name would change, but the manner in which it accrued meaning would remain the same. As far as the music is concerned, the word the Rhinedaughters sing is merely a placeholder for the expression of exuberance.[33]

Most of the time, though, the text signs *do* affect how the musical signs accrue meaning. As Thomas Grey puts it, verbal signs condition a network

[32] See Pierce 1960: 147.

[33] In fact, there is an argument to be made that even when accompanied by text, the emotional content or association of the music is of primary importance. Certainly Wagner thought so. In his open letter, "A Communication to My Friends," he makes reference throughout to feeling, emotion, and love with respect to how music communicates and how art (drama) communicates. See Wagner 1966c, esp. 364.

Example 4.2 "Rhinedaughters' Joy in the Gold," a rhematic indexical sinsign,
Rg/33/2/1–2

of musical signs with which they align.[34] Despite Wagner's characterization of leitmotifs as "melodic moments of feeling" rather than representa-
tions of objects, leitmotifs can still be a variety of Peircian signs, just not
dicent ones. Rather, when conditioned by text, they are Peircian symbols –
their meaning is arbitrarily established through language. Of course, their
meaning is also indexical, conditioned by the dramatic context (whether
there is sung text or not). So, too, are their transformations predicated on
dramatic context, suggesting an "indexical" nature of all leitmotivic sinsigns, whatever the larger legisign may be, since the theme's transformed
iterations are "caused" by the drama.

We see here that musical association can be understood as a kind of
semiotic function or, more accurately, as a conglomeration of simultaneous

---

[34] Grey 1998: 352.

semiotic functions. Of course, a stricter reading of the term *signification* puts it squarely in Peirce's dicent category, stating, as it were, that leit-motifs act almost like nouns. The Wagnerian ideal, though it has been characterized as such, is *not* a technique of this limited kind of definite, dicent *signification*, something I reserve for the *evolution* of signs, not the signs themselves. (We explore this in Chapter 7.) The distinction between leitmotivic music being *associated* with emotions arising from drama versus *signifying* something definite is a critical one. Association *calls to mind* rather than *indicates*. It is a technique predicated on *connection* rather than *reference* or *substitution*.

Topic theory

Topic theory lies somewhat between association and dicent signification. Its three major English-language proponents – Leonard Ratner, Robert Hatten, and Raymond Monelle – explain how topics comprise *genres* of meaning, a rather broader object than most work on signification imagines.[35] That is, certain musical conventions of almost every imagin-able parameter (meter, texture, harmony, orchestration, dynamics, melodic profile, rhythmic profile, and so forth) working in concert can evoke for the culturally conditioned audience a sense of a genre, a setting, context, or coloration that enables the music to call forth impressions – for example – of the hunt, the military, or the pastoral.[36]

Such expressive genres, as Hatten calls them, are not iconic; they don't attempt to mime or represent things.[37] Nor are they dicent substitutes, stand-ins for other things. Rather, they are cultural constructs that evoke other constructs. The musical pastoral does not accurately present bird songs, the sounds of wind through leaves or rushing water, and so forth, but rather calls forth the western European cultural construct of the pastoral. Topics are, at their heart, an artificial code for evoking another artificial code. In that regard they approach to the Peircian notion of

---

[35] See Ratner 1980, Hatten 1994, Hatten 2004, Monelle 2000, and Monelle 2006. Interesting studies inspired by these authors have proliferated in the field of music theory in recent years. Among them, Agawu 1991 and Klein 2004 are particularly worth investigating.

[36] These are the three topics Monelle 2006 asserts are the greatest because they capture through-going cultural themes.

[37] This is not to say that music cannot represent things other than itself; Kivy 1984 provides a list of ways in which this happens. Though I have not devoted a separate section to representation, it should be clear that it, too, is distinct from association.

argument. Moreover, topics often comprise various signs, like the pervasive, falling-step "sigh" motive or a military fanfare, but they are almost
always more vague and layered – one might say Peircian legisigns that
point to qualisigns – than directly denotative, as a dicent sinsign would be.

Wagnerian-style leitmotifs often rely on topics for the forcefulness of
their presentation; a leitmotif intended to recall for a listener the emotions
surrounding Siegfried's self-reflection while meditating in the forest is
going to be more effective if it engages with pastoral and spiritual expressive genres.[38] Likewise, Wagnerian strophic, or refrain-oriented, song
forms (e.g., Senta's ballade in *Der fliegende Holländer* or Siegfried's forging
song in *Siegfried*) can tap into a sense of age-old ritual solemnity by
evoking myth-as-topic; that is, old forms in the context of Wagnerian
opera construct an expressive genre in and of themselves.[39] But the specific
associative themes of any type inhabit a *specific piece of music,* whereas
topics belong to a wider cultural repository.[40] By extension, one might
posit that association is an element of meaning *separable* from the music it
connects with, while topical meaning is *inherent,* inseparable from the
music itself. In the next chapter, we shall parse this distinction further,
examining its origins in linguistics and structural criticism (including how
piece-specific associations evolve into wider culturally accepted tropes).
For the time being, though, it is enough to understand that leitmotivic
associativity is more localized than is topical associativity.

Subjectivity

On the other end of the spectrum from topical association, we find
association as a component of subjectivity. Subjectivity intersects with
association on a *personal* level and gives the lie to the trite, oft-repeated
aphorism that music is a "universal" language. For sure, certain aspects of

---

[38] In fact this is what happens. The softly oscillating string figuration of the "Forest Murmurs"
was, by the time of Wagner's *Siegfried,* already an old nature trope. It emerged from sixteenth-
century madrigals as a form of metonymy (see Taruskin 2010: 229) and featured prominently
in the music of the nineteenth century. See Cherlin 2012 for a full treatment of this texture in
the later nineteenth and early twentieth centuries as a moonlight topic.

[39] This is an observation I borrow from Monelle 2000: 77–78.

[40] Monelle 2000: 41–80 comprises a chapter purportedly on topic and leitmotif. After mentioning
a few of Wagner's leitmotifs (largely from *The Ring*) and how they embody both Classic-era
(hunting and military), Romantic-era (chromaticism), and earlier music topics (like the pianto),
Monelle devolves into a lengthy tangent on horse topics in support of his reading of the
Valkyries' music from *Die Walküre.*

the human condition make it natural to speak of musical universals (higher pulse rates resulting from excited or physically active states make faster tempi more "exciting"). We have just seen, however, that the bulk of musical meaning devolves from cultural competencies. Or does it? It may be more accurate to say that the bulk of musical meaning devolves from cultural competencies filtered through individual experiences. Lawrence Kramer puts it well:

musical meaning consists of a specific, mutual interplay between musical experience and its contexts; the form taken by this process is the production of modes or models of subjectivity carried by the music into the listener's sense of self; and the dynamics of this production consist of a renegotiation of the subject's position(s) between the historically contingent forms of the experience and the experience of a transcendental perspective that claims to subsume (but is actually subsumed by) them.[41]

As Naomi Cumming demonstrates in her narrated experience of Bach's *Erbarme dich*, an individual's life experience (strongly conditioned by demographics such as race, gender, religious affiliation, and so forth) features prominently in how music means something.[42] The same music might very well speak of young love to one person and corporate drudgery to another, depending on whether said individual heard it once during a magical prom night or every day on the office musak playlist. Likewise, film music can create autobiographical memories – via frightening films viewed during childhood, or romantic films viewed early in a relationship.[43] These are all associations, to be sure – meanings cemented onto music colored with emotion from past experience – but they're not the meanings scholars (or composers, for that matter) usually concern themselves with when making claims about musical meaning. Unless there is a compelling reason to accept one individual's lived musical experience as particularly worthwhile to another's (or to an entire society's), subjective associations usually remain too specific to be useful to many besides the individual who experiences them.

Certainly there are exceptions, as when audiences desire to hear music the way the composer of that music heard it. Then Beethoven's *Muß es sein? Es muß sein!* of the Op. 135 quartet, or Messaien's church windows, become valuable and enter the repository of cultural competencies. Can we

---

[41] Kramer 2002: 8.

[42] Cumming 1999. See also Cumming 2000 for another take on subjectivity, grounded in Peircian semiotics.

[43] Hoeckner and Nusbaum 2013: 242.

say the same, however, of Wagner's comment to Cosima about the curious links in memory between themes and the places they came to him? Do we need to know that a certain theme from *Die Walküre* recalled for him a walk in Zurich?[44] Such examples illustrate exactly the point: the kind of association most of us care about is *shared association* (even if that association arose as a subjectivity). These are the kinds of musical meanings that unite and define a culture; they are the places where minds can meet, the spaces music constructs that allow for meaningful connection with other human beings.

As much as we may enjoy creating or consuming music alone, music's origins and its current manifestation rests on its status as social praxis, whether it be in its composition, its execution, its commodification or, yes, its meaning. So, while association functions on a continuum from individual to universal, there is a piece-specific "sweet spot" of associativity for the leitmotif, one that often engages topical associativity, but that carries a more detailed association of drama and emotion from the context of a given work.

It is hardly an exaggeration to say that all of these kinds of musical meaning – expressive, referential, signifying, topical, and subjective – have been applied to leitmotifs by prior commentators. In fact, F.E. Kirby catalogues Wagner's themes in *The Ring* by divisions such as these.[45] This is, to my mind, the wrong way to think about them. While Wagnerian leitmotifs may be, at times, exemplars of these various forms of musical meaning, the one factor that binds them all together – that, in fact, makes them *associative* themes – is their *associativity*. By making manifest the emotions that surrounded a certain dramatic moment of the past, they allow the composer to inject this experience into a new musico-dramatic context. As such, leitmotivic association sits at the intersection of emotion, memory, and meaning.

Associative themes: emotion, memory, and meaning

There is an extraordinary moment in the first act of Wagner's *Götterdämmerung*. At the beginning of Scene 3, Brünnhilde sits alone on her mountaintop gazing at the ring on her hand, Siegfried's parting love-

---

[44] See Wagner 1994: 128 in the entry for Monday, Feb. 26, 1872.

[45] See Kirby 2004: 29–37. *Ibid.*: 5 refers to diegetic themes as "iconic" and onomatopoetic themes as "analogic." *Ibid.*: 74–75 makes the questionable claim that there is only one iconic theme in *The Ring*: the Nibelungs' hammering. Others, like "Siegfried's Horn Call" or "Wood Bird," Kirby calls analogic, implying that they are not diegetic (though they clearly are).

Dritte Scene.

Der Vorhang wird wieder aufgezogen.
Die Felsenhöhe wie im Vorspiel.
(Brünnhilde sitzt am Eingange des Steingemaches in stummem
Sinnen Siegfrieds Ring betrachtend.)

Example 4.3 *Götterdämmerung*, Act I, Scene 3 (Gd/89/5/1–90/4/1)

gift. As she does, we hear a variety of leitmotifs: "Magic Potion," "World Treasure," and "Valkyries" (see Example 4.3). In terms of chronological audience experience, the "Magic Potion" is a theme we have heard for the first time in the previous scene – while it sounded, Siegfried's memory of Brünnhilde vanished, allowing him to fall in love with Gutrune. The "World Treasure" is a theme we know from the end of *Siegfried*; there it accompanied the burgeoning feelings of love that Brünnhilde had for Siegfried. And the "Valkyries" theme has embodied the energy of Brünnhilde and her warrior sisters from Act II of *Die Walküre* onward.

Without memory of these earlier thematic statements *or* the visual stimulus of the stage action, these would likely strike a listener as musical standing stones: meaning-filled but ultimately mute. When paired with their earlier associations and the association of the present moment, however, they come to mean something incredibly poignant. They suggest the filmic technique of continuity-cutting between two simultaneous scenes; that is, just as Brünnhilde sits atop the mountain gazing at the Ring remembering Siegfried, Siegfried stands in the Hall of the Gibichungs gazing at Gutrune and forgetting his past with Brünnhilde. The nullity of the enigmatic "Magic Potion" progression contrasts with the warmth and tenderness of the "World Treasure" theme. Fragments of the "Valkyries" theme interrupt Brünnhilde's halcyon reveries as the demands of the musical present (the frantic approach of Brünnhilde's sister Valkyrie, Waltraute) intrude onto our savoring with Brünnhilde the idyllic musical past. This is association at its best – a complex and powerful blend of memory, emotion, and meaning. And it requires all three elements; the meaning is dependent upon both memory and emotion.

Association requires memory of course, since the emotion must first be forged and then *recalled* at a later point in time. And memory seems to work best when it evokes a moment of strong emotion or taps into the profundity of myth and the subconscious.[46] (This is, perhaps, why comic operas and films have fewer moments of associative thematic import.) Before exploring how this works, it is important to pause for a moment to consider the difference between history and memory. While the former is *recorded* and aims at (or at least makes claims toward) objective truths, the latter is ineffable and susceptible to all sorts of errors and reconfigurations predicated on subjectivity. Memory, in other words, cannot be divorced from meaning and emotion. Each of us remembers things best when they caused in us strong emotional reactions, and when that memory continues to be meaningful and relevant to us in the present. In fact, there is evidence that prodigious savants often use memory fueled by emotion and a kind of associative synesthesia to achieve their remarkable feats.

Daniel Tammet, whose abilities were featured in the documentary *Brainman* and in his book *Born on a Blue Day*, is one such example. He associates numbers and mathematical operations with synesthetic qualities, sensations, and emotions (four is shy and quiet, nine is tall and enormous,

---

[46] Hoeckner and Nusbaum 2013: 244 suggest that autobiographical memory is more easily accessed when cued by a song that moved a subject emotionally: "memory was positively correlated with the emotional salience of a song."

eighty-nine evokes falling snow, multiplying by eleven feels like numbers tumbling down inside his head, etc.). Scientists studying Tammet find that his remarkable mathematic abilities (like performing division to 100 decimal places almost instantaneously, or reciting *pi* to 22,500 decimal places) is a feat of memory, not of computation per se.[47] Tammet's abilities rely heavily on subjectivity; his associations are unlikely to be shared by anyone else. The same is true of memory. While history strives for objectivity – a collective memory, if you will, that everyone can agree upon – memory is subjective.

Milan Kundera's novels (the most famous being *The Unbearable Lightness of Being*) play on this foible of human intelligence; his tales are predicated on various characters misremembering the same event in different ways.[48] In this regard, his books resemble Carolyn Abbate's observation that Wagnerian music can lie (or subjectively "misremember" along with the characters).[49] Wagner, of course, was far from the first or last musician to play in the medium of sound – as Kundera does in the medium of prose – with the nature of human memory. Perhaps, as in so many other things musical, Wagner was inspired by Beethoven, whose song cycle *An die Ferne Geliebte* features at the end of the final song a return of the melody from the first (see Example 4.4). Note that the original presentation of this music speaks of gazing out into the distance toward the place where the musical protagonist met his beloved. The musical recollection at the cycle's close speaks of regaining that which was lost in lonely hours (i.e, the intervening songs). Is this a recapitulatory gesture or an associative gesture? Probably both, but more the latter than the former, since the first song, "Auf dem Hügel sitz ich, spähend," and the last, "Nimm sie hin denn, diese Lieder," are the only two that refer directly to the musical protagonist's singing. Thus, the melodic return recalls for the listener the emotional/dramatic state of the first song, providing not only a formal/recapitulatory conclusion but also a *dramatic* conclusion as the protagonist's music reaches (and is reiterated by) the beloved.

One might speculate that the rise of such so-called "cyclic" multi-movement works (in which opening-movement materials return at the close of the last movement) comprise a defining genre of romanticism. From Schubert's famed *Wanderer Fantasy* to Berlioz's *Harold in Italy*, to Dvořák's D minor *Serenade for Winds*, not to mention Wagner's entire *Ring* cycle itself, the principle of return proved to be not only of *formal* value, but also of *emotional* value, a way for music to tap into the

[47] See Bernstein 2007.   [48] See Kundera 1984.   [49] Abbate 1991: 19.

Example 4.4 Melodic return in Beethoven's *An die ferne Geliebte*, Op. 98: "Nimm sie hin denn, diese Lieder," mm. 40–48 (cf. "Auf dem Hügel sitz ich, spähend," mm. 1–9)

emotional power and experience of memory. This technique reached something of an apex in the works of Ravel and Proust, fading from prominence later in the twentieth century as the modernist drive toward the future replaced the *fin de siècle* penchant for gazing backwards.[50] In

---

[50] See Puri 2011: 15–51. Puri's aim in his book is to describe how *the music itself* can remember
things. While this is an issue raised by associativity (particularly in works like Wagner's *Ring*

one sense, then, Wagner merely participated in the arch-Romantic fascination with the emotional power of memory and association. As Thomas Grey put it:

Leitmotif, then, is not just a musical labeling of people and things (or the verbal labeling of motives); it is also a matter of musical memory, of recalling things dimly remembered and seeing what sense we can make of them in a new context.[51]

Associativity is, however, something more complex than simple recollection – or at least more complex than the one-time, cyclic recollection of music just discussed. To conceptualize it, we must understand how associations form, and how they are later reactivated.

Associativity

Associativity is, in short, the forging of a connection between two separate ideas such that one may evoke or recall the other.[52] It is predicated on two necessary criteria: temporal correlation and topical resonance. As we already noted, associativity functions on a continuum from the intensely personal to the widely cultural. It can be vague, as it often is in "absolute" music when topics and the associativity of such things like keys, themes, progressions, textures and so forth comprise important formal and/or expressive components of the music.[53] In the present context, however, we are more concerned with *explicit* associations between drama and music: "any characteristic musical idea that occurs in more than one scene and that acquires an explicit referential function in the drama through its consistent association with an extra-musical element."[54]

Once established, such associations can be difficult to maintain. Constantin Floros notes as much when he explains that *Beziehungszauber*

---

where one senses that the orchestra – or at least the music it plays – is capable of memory), it is an uncommon one and entangles us in questions of how a musical past tense presents itself, who is remembering it (i.e., agency), and what it means.

[51] Grey 2008: 114.

[52] Cohen 2013 summarizes the history of the development of progressively more complex Congruence-Association Models in association with film music; we will return to engage this in Chapter 9.

[53] For examples of this kind of associativity, see McCreless 1990.

[54] This is a quotation from Perle 1980: 94. His use of the word "referential" is problematic in light of our earlier discussion, but the main thrust of his point remains a functional summary. For Perle, many themes he cites in Berg's *Wozzeck* are literary, accompanying repetitions of the same text (i.e., Wozzeck's "Wir arme Leut!"). See *ibid.*: 93–117 for an overview of what Perle calls "leitmotifs" as well as their transformations.

(usually translated as "the magic of association") is evanescent; music has a tendency toward the absolute and away from the programmatic, pulling away from drama as it were, even though we as listeners, composers, and performers try to hold them together.[55] Likewise, Carolyn Abbate mentions Wagner's directed efforts to suspend themes in *The Ring* against "musical gravity," expending much compositional energy to as it were prevent them from reverting to pure music.[56] We shall return to this point shortly. Let us begin, however, with what happens *before* association is established.

Presentiment

Because association depends on memory for its effectiveness, it follows that memorable music is ripe for associativity. One way composers make music memorable is by repeating it; specifically, by ensuring that the music playing during the critical moment when the association is formed is itself a repetition.[57] Thus we find Wagner, and others, "previewing" (or, more accurately, "prehearing") associative music in advance of the dramatic moment of feeling needed to form the association.[58] We saw an example of this sort of thing in Chapter 2 with the "Giants" theme.[59] Let us turn to film music for another. In *Star Wars Episode IV: A New Hope*, the audience hears the "Force" theme a number of times before the scene of dramatic association when Ben Kenobi explains the Force to Luke. Before this moment the music is like LeGuin's standing stones; we *know* this theme has great meaning, especially given its presentation alongside the striking image of Luke standing on a sand dune staring out at the setting of Tatooine's two suns, but it is only later that our vague presentiment coalesces into a clear association. John Williams seems particularly fond

---

[55] Floros 1983: 8 makes this observation.   [56] Abbate 1991: 168.

[57] This point echoes Hoeckner and Nusbaum 2013: 242 and Burkholder 2006: 82 who posit that audiences like to hear music they've heard before because it is more *meaningful* (my italics) to them.

[58] Wagner explicitly states that this is a useful technique in *Opera and Drama*. See Wagner 1966b: 330–31 in which he outlines music's capacity to express foreboding (Ashton Ellis's translation of what I'm calling "presentiment") of a (333–34) definite emotion expressed by gesture and word-verse. *Ibid.*: 335–48 *passim*, Wagner designates the orchestra as an organ of feeling capable of foreboding and reminiscence.

[59] Hoeckner and Nusbaum 2013: 251 combine what they call *episodic* and *semantic* memory into a larger category of *declarative* or *explicit* memory, which involves conscious recall of facts or events. This contrasts with *implicit* memory, which is subconscious in nature, what composers appear to be activating when they utilize underscoring and/or presentiment of themes.

of this technique – one finds it as well with fragmentary presentiments of the "Yoda" theme in *The Empire Strikes Back* and with presentiments of the "Grail" theme in *Indiana Jones and the Last Crusade* before the association of music and Christian icon is forged.[60] Thus, even before associational meaning becomes clear, both emotion and memory can be primed by musical premonitions.

Another vessel for priming association through presentiment is the use of the operatic overture (or, in film, the title music). This convention of opening with a compilation of "coming attractions" (thematically speaking) serves a number of purposes: it announces to the audience that they have a short time span in which to get settled before the action begins; it sets the scene, emotionally (largely through the evocation of topics); and it primes the audience's memory for the later establishment of associations with the thematic material presented. In most cases, these works present themes *before* any dramatic association can be formed, the exceptions being when filmic titles roll over visual drama of some kind or when directors add staging to operatic overtures (a questionable practice as far as associativity is concerned). The music in all cases is often a presentation of two contrasting themes and/or textures, setting up a drama of topical opposition, not unlike that of the nineteenth-century reading of masculine vs. feminine forces in the sonata form.[61] What all this means for association and the later establishment of associative themes is largely dependent on the particular piece.

It goes without saying that before an association can be remembered, of course, it must be formed. This formation comprises two necessary components, temporal coincidence and topical resonance. Coincidence – two things happening at the same time (or nearly the same time) – is a *temporal* correlation, and topical resonance – the music "fitting" the dramatic scene at hand – is a *meaning-filled* correlation.[62] Hoeckner and Nusbaum's recent study of music and memory in multi-media implies the importance of these two components in their definitions of *episodic* (i.e., temporal, cued by concurrent events) and *semantic* (i.e., content based, cued by topical literacy) memory.[63] In their own words, "powerful

---

[60] The "Yoda" leitmotivic premonitions occur when the befuddled, hobo-like green guy (who is – unbeknownst to Luke or a first-time viewer – in fact Yoda) helps Luke look for the great jedi master.

[61] See McClary 1991: 13–16.

[62] See Iwamiya 2013: 141, who distinguishes between formal (i.e., temporal) and semantic (i.e., affective) congruency in film.

[63] Hoeckner and Nusbaum 2013: 243.

combinations of music and image, especially when viewed for the first time, tend to form a lasting impression and create persistent associations for music."[64] We will examine each in turn.

Coincidence

When scientists caution that correlation does not imply causation, they do so because it is such a natural reaction. Composers, of course, know this and can exploit music's associative power by setting up these correlations. In film (and one might assume in opera, too), the simpler the visual and audio stimuli, the more powerful is the alignment effect; as these stimuli become more complex, however, association becomes more important than alignment.[65] Thus, a very simple example, like "Mickey Mousing" – when music directly mimes the motions of a visible figure – requires precise correlation to be effective.[66] (This would be an example of a Peircian icon.) Something considerably more complex, like the Brünnhilde ring-gazing scene from *Götterdämmerung*, allows for a large offset in temporal placement, which is why it can function even though in the staged diegesis Siegfried visibly drinks the magic potion many minutes before the music of the Brünnhilde scene. Scott Lipscomb's recent study of this effect finds that there seems to be a range of "tolerance bands" for the temporal correlation necessary for association based on the complexity of the visual and aural stimuli and the sophistication of the listener.[67]

Must there be a coincident visual stimulus for association to occur? Wagner seemed to think so, since he argued that the visual component of associating an emotion with music emerged from the gestures of onstage actors, clarifying that thought and memory – one and the same to Wagner – are conditioned by emotion, and that that which is visible makes distinct the emotion.[68] The oft-cited crisis he had with whether or not Wotan should hold a sword aloft at the end of *Das Rheingold* for the first

---

[64] *Ibid.*: 246.   [65] Lipscomb 2013: 200 and 206.

[66] Iwamiya 2013: 142 found the strongest correlation in such simple examples between pitch and vertical location, size and loudness, and shape and timbre.

[67] Lipscomb 2013: 202 finds that association is strongest if music and visuals align exactly, or if the visuals slightly precede the music. *Ibid.*: 205 suggests that listeners are aware of synchronization being off, without it radically disturbing the formation of the audio-visual associations.

[68] See Wagner 1966b: 317–30. McGuire 2002: 86 concurs by stating that leitmotifs are difficult to establish in oratorio, because they require a visual element to cement meaning.

presentation of the "Sword" theme provides further evidence of the composer's view on the matter. Most clearly, he said in an 1851 letter to Theodor Uhlig:

I realized from this [a passage in *Lohengrin*] that the themes that I write always originate in the context of, and according to the character of, some visual phenomenon on stage.[69]

There is an element of truth to this statement; human beings are, after all, overwhelmingly visually oriented creatures. That said, my thinking lies more along the lines of Kendall Walton, who argues that music produces *experiences* we can *use as props* in imagined mind games.[70] That is, music is not representational, and does not require representation-as-visual-image to form associations, but rather that the *visualizable* is what is required to form association. Thus, works of music that lack a staged drama may still develop associations if the listener is able to *imagine* a staged drama of sorts. Certainly this is what happens when listening to symphonic poems or works like Berlioz's *Symphonie Fantastique*. Put in Peircian terms, as long as a theme can be *indexed* to a dramatic event, *real or imagined*, its meaning can be established.

Resonance

Chapters 2 and 3 of this book explored the nature of thematic identity: the kind of fixity that a theme communicates to a listener, "Sit up and listen; this is important!" That discussion now comes to bear upon the current subject of association. Themes are so often associated with things in part because they are memorable and because they recur. At the moment of thematic focus, the music tells us that something important is happening. It follows that, in programme and dramatic music, moments of thematic clarity are often moments of dramatic intensity. One need only turn to film music to see the truth of this statement. In many films, underscoring during dialogue is typically athematic (though often heavily motivic), not unlike recitative in opera; the music tells us by its athematic nature to pay attention to the flow of events and information in the action and dialogue. Like arias in opera, thematic statements commonly sound during moments-out-of-time – moments of emotional and dramatic intensity. And, as in opera, thematic transformations effectively accompany and communicate moments of transition.

---

[69] See Spencer and Millington 1987, 259.   [70] See Walton 1997.

By way of example, I beg the reader's indulgence for one more personal anecdote; namely, my experience of taking my sister to see *The Ring* cycle at the Metropolitan Opera. My sister was neither familiar with the operas nor a trained musician. Leaving the theater, however, after *Die Walküre*, she asked me, "What was that beautiful music Sieglinde sang just before she left?" From four-and-a-half hours of music, this was what made the firmest impression upon her mind. The theme in question is one of the very few Wagner named; he called it *Verherrlichung Brünnhildens* ("Glorification of Brünnhilde").[71] It recurs at only one other point in the cycle: the very end of *Götterdämmerung*. In order for its associative power to function, it would have to be highly memorable to withstand ten hours of intervening music before returning. And if my sister's reaction is any indication, it is. It is an ineffable moment of thematic lyricism; the clarity of the musical content providing an appropriate partner for the emotional content of the drama at that moment, and fixing in the mind of the listener a powerful association.[72]

There is much in recent film-music scholarship to corroborate this view. For instance, Hoeckner and Nusbaum suggest that music from films with memorable scores would be remembered the same way as music in opera.[73] More specifically, "We encode memories of music narratively, similarly to discourse. We remember the organization of meaningful groups of events dictated by narrative relevance rather than remembering things as an undifferentiated stream."[74] Danny Elfman suggests much the same from a composer's point of view in an interview he gave about his work on the score for *Spiderman 2*. In that interview, Elfman states that when he begins work on a new film project, he always starts with *dramatic, emotional* scenes rather than action scenes to begin creating his materials.[75] Music provides a strong component of both emotion and memory in film,[76] and

---

[71] The title occurs in an unpublished letter from Cosima Wagner to Edmund von Lippman. See Deathridge 1981: 84.

[72] *Why* this moment is so striking rests on a number of factors: the soprano line – itself an endless-sounding G embellished with neighbor notes and a dramatic leap down a seventh – doubled by high strings, the slow harmonic rhythm, the use of "juicy" half-diminished seventh harmonies, and so forth have much to do with it. Equally important, however, are the musical and dramatic contexts: dramatically, this is a turning point – Sieglinde has decided she has a reason to live; musically it serves as a foil to the tedium of the lengthy parlando/recitative section that precedes it.

[73] Hoeckner and Nusbaum 2013: 235–36.   [74] *Ibid.*: 239–40.

[75] See the interview with Danny Elfman on the *Spiderman 2* DVD.

[76] Hoeckner and Nusbaum 2013: 252 state this and reinforce it throughout their entire article. See also the interview with Peter Jackson included on the *Two Towers* DVD. In it, Jackson explains that the music ties in very closely to the emotion of the film. While working with the composer,

musical memory appears to be tied to emotion in particular,[77] but it may be *texture*, rather than *melody*, that accomplishes this.[78]

Thematicism itself – whether melodic, rhythmic, textural, or what have you – is not enough, however. If the music at the moment of Sieglinde's departure sounded like the "Dragon" theme from Scene 3 of *Das Rheingold*, its effect would be utterly vitiated. Topical resonance – the similarity of an associative theme to topics native to the culture at hand – is also necessary to make the associative connection a strong one.[79] In this case, the slow harmonic rhythm, major mode, soaring soprano melody line, and orchestral color all mesh with nineteenth-century tropes of heroism, adulation, and strong emotionality, exactly what is happening onstage with Sieglinde's brief paean to Brünnhilde when she learns from the valkyrie that she has a reason to live: Siegmund's unborn child, whom she carries.[80] This is not to say that a topical or semantic mismatch between music and drama can't produce a powerful effect (one, irony,

Howard Shore, Jackson often spoke in emotional terms, asking Shore to make the music more sad and so forth.

[77] A recent experiment reported finding that with regard to listeners hearing familiar film scores, they recall *feelings* (rather than specifics like images or dialogue) *most quickly* while *accuracy of specific details* is recalled *more slowly* (and better if a visual stimulus is supplied). See Hoeckner and Nusbaum 2013: 257. Kendall and Lipscomb 2013: 49 corroborate these findings, stating that music trumps visual elements in communicated meaning.

[78] As Howard Shore mentions, "Orchestral color in film is even more important than in concert music because it evokes specific emotional responses, thereby becoming powerfully integrated with the character or texture of the film." See Karlin and Wright 2004: 297.
See also Darrow 2006. *Ibid.*: 9–10, between groups with hearing loss and groups without, interestingly, it was single-line melodies that were perceived most alike in terms of emotional content, implying that texture is a large factor in acculturated emotional content. *Ibid.*: 11, perception of emotion in music depends on neurological processes active when listening. Individuals with sensorineural hearing loss (i.e., not completely deaf) do not perceive music in the same way as members of the same culture without that loss. This is largely attributable to deaf individuals not being acculturated to music as much – or in the same way – as hearing individuals.

[79] Hoeckner and Nusbaum 2013: 248. It is also important to recall that memory is culturally conditioned; people remember things better when those things fit with and reinforce their cultural experience. Film is able to construct these culturally situated narrative relevancies and thus create powerful memories.

[80] *Ibid.*: 248, citing an earlier study: "The authors argued that film and television music uses a well-established stock of musical stereotypes that evoke more or less well-defined sets of verbal and visual associations. As these associations shape the understanding of visual content, the continuing circulation of musical stereotypes in multimedia reinforce not only a broad network of existing associations, but also form new ones." Of course, both these and piece-specific themes are open to the same kinds of criticisms leveled at hackneyed thematic treatment in film. For one, see Butler 2013: 170–72, who criticizes composer Murray Gold's use of Rose's theme *without development* in different dramatic contexts of the new *Doctor Who* television series.

we explore in Chapter 7), but rather that such pairings are the exception to the rule, especially at an association's first establishment.[81]

Such topical resonance, of course, does not rely just on expressive genres. It can also arise from a listener's knowledge of formal structures native to a given style, mimesis ("Mickey Mousing"), arbitrary references (think the reference to the duck in *Peter and the Wolf* made by the oboe), iconic referentiality relying on processes like tone painting or onomato-poeia, and intra-referentiality of already established, work-specific associa-tive material.[82] Regardless of how it is formed, however, association is meaningless without recollection.

Recollection

Once the association has been formed, its later power rests on synecdoche; a piece (just the music) of a whole (multi-media, visual, dramatic, musical synthesis) returns, standing in for the whole and pulling along with it all the other pieces.[83] It is interesting to note that music functions so well in such arrangements. Apparently, its mnemonic encoding is different from other stimuli, and it is more easily remembered. Humanity has recognized this for centuries: nearly anyone will be familiar with music as a mnemonic for text; from the Christian liturgy (and before) to the alphabet, such pairings of music with text as aid to recall have happened for millennia.[84]

Associative themes, then, straddle the past and the present.[85] As phe-nomena, they unfold with the limits of a psychological present – just as Wagner's aforementioned observation to Cosima suggests.[86] Thought,

---

[81] Lipscomb 2013: 206. Note that in Lipscomb's study, highly trained listeners were more sensitive than untrained listeners when presented with "dissonant" combinations (i.e., combinations that had a semantic mismatch rather than those that were simply asynchronous).

[82] Kendall and Lipscomb 2013: 51–53 provide this list, based on their reading of Leonard Meyer. Note that "Mickey Mousing" (what *ibid.*: 55 define as "syntactical relations" (iconic and referential)) can be more cognitively complex than its moniker suggests. While something like the "Alberich's Aggressiveness" theme when Alberich scrabbles over slippery rocks in the first scene of *Das Rheingold* provides a simplistic example of how music and visual image may align, *ibid.*: 56 cites the "Cool" scene of *West Side Story* as another in which Bernstein's polyphony matches with the visual spectacle of more complex dance choreography onstage.

[83] Synecdoche is one of the four master tropes (or figures of speech) proposed in Burke 1945: 503–17 as the basic rhetorical structures by which we make sense of experience. I also mention irony and metonymy, two others, in this and later chapters. Harold Bloom expands Burke's four tropes to six and reimagines them. See Bloom 1973 and Bloom 1975, esp. 84 (chart).

[84] In fact, many medieval compositional models may have emerged from the exigencies of mnemonic oral practice. See Berger 2005.

[85] Wolzogen, too, remarks upon this. See Wolzogen 1897: 324.

[86] For more on Wagnerian themes and the psychological present, see Hacohen and Wagner 1997: 448.

however, enables us to access the past by *recalling* emotions that we feel in the present. Wagner once eloquently stated, "Thought grasps the absent, feeling the present."[87] While existing in the present, repetitions of associative themes remind audiences not just of past events but also of elapsed time, serving as Wagnerian sonic manifestations of memory and self-awareness.[88] These recollections exist in their own present-moment context and, as such, open themselves up to additional associations, overlaying the previous ones.[89] Associative themes may also function in a wider associative context than merely the work in which they first appear – they may come to inform associations in later music as well. How this works, including a close reading of one specific example, comprises the material of our next two chapters.

[87] Wagner 1966b: 349.
[88] See Abbate 1991: 55 and Corse 1990: 50, who note Wagner's Hegelian/Feuerbachian understanding of thematic recall in terms of memory and self. In *The Ring*, this effect, coupled with the sheer number of themes and their transformations, establishes the epic proportions of the cycle.
[89] Floros 1983: 9 mentions that themes develop musically to fit new dramatic circumstances, a topic we shall address at length in Chapter 7. See also Hoeckner and Nusbaum 2013: 245, 246, and 247, who explain that associations can change over time (usually with a layering rather than with a replacement effect; sometimes the result of intertextuality); and Kendall and Lipscomb 2013: 50, who cite various other studies on association as a learned behavior, noting its ability to change the meaning of a given visual scene or to imprint on the memory of a viewer.

5 | Piece specifics, cultural generics, and associative layering

> Study Bach! There you will find everything.
>
> Johannes Brahms[1]

Sometime in the late 1980s, I heard Bach's "Air on the G String" in a most unusual setting. Visiting friends of my parents, I found myself watching a television show about a mad scientist. In it, the scientist captured a young woman with the intention of transplanting her brain into his ailing daughter. During the macabre basement laboratory scene in which the scientist prepped himself and his patients for surgery – the young woman sedated and about to die – there was no dialogue; rather, the "Air on the G String" provided an eerie backdrop to the visual spectacle. I had heard Bach's "Air" before, of course, but in this context it haunted me. For days, I couldn't get the combination of scene and sound out of my mind.

In retrospect, it was the power of the multi-media, associative irony that struck me. A work I had long paired with feelings of serenity and sentimentality (as had others – e.g., the Cleveland Orchestra plays the "Air" as a eulogy when one of its members or alumni dies) was set to a scene of absolute horror. Of course, in another sense, perhaps the choice of music fits the scene: Its portrayal of the scientist's state-of-mind was appropriate given that he was finally about to achieve a goal ultimately motivated by love for his daughter. Sadly, in the years since seeing the show, I have been unable to relocate it; I remain unsure to this day whether it was a movie, an episode of a series, or something else. But my drive to find it attests to the power it had over me. That power came from the cultural associations I already had with Bach's "Air" (and, for that matter, mad scientists). But it also came from the extremity of cognitive dissonance I experienced in this ironic setting – the perspective on perspectives the pairing of sound and image made, perspectives that forged this specific combination into a

---

[1] "Johann Sebastian Bach." *Encyclopedia of World Biography* 2004. *Encyclopedia.com*. (April 16, 2014). www.encyclopedia.com/doc/1G2-3404700366.html.

powerful personal association I continue to experience whenever I hear the "Air" to this day.[2]

And that, in short, is what this chapter is all about: the evolution of associativity and associative layering. In the previous chapter, we largely steered clear of these topics, rather attempting to situate associativity in relation to other kinds of musical meaning and to investigate how it functions relative to memory and emotion. This work was necessary to explain associativity, to my mind an under-theorized concept. That is not to say, however, that associativity is completely *un*theorized. At least one example of previous work on the subject folds the notion of associative layering into the very definition of the phenomenon. I refer here to an article by J. Peter Burkholder – namely his model for deriving associative meaning from music, which he summarizes as a five-step process. It comprises:

1. Recognizing familiar elements.
2. Recalling other music or schemata that make use of those elements.
3. Perceiving the associations that follow from the primary associations.
4. Noticing what is new and how familiar elements are changed.
5. Interpreting what all this means.[3]

According to Burkholder, these steps may occur in any order and with any degree (or lack) of rapidity, including simultaneity.[4] In some ways – memory and meaning being fundamental – Burkholder's model echoes our discussion in the previous chapter. In other ways it differs. Among the most obvious differences is that Burkholder does not specifically address the *formation* of association. He does, however, consider the potential for *associative layering* as a fundamental aspect of associative musical meaning. For Burkholder, this layering occurs when cultural associations – the "familiar elements" and "schemata" in his five steps (and the kinds of associations composers are usually most interested in exploiting) – mix with piece-specific, or even personal, associations.[5] Though he doesn't refer to it as such, Burkholder mentions another kind of layering in his

---

[2] See Burke 1945: 512. In his discussion of the "four master tropes," he refers to irony as a "perspective of perspectives."
Note that there is a literature of sorts on Bach's music forming part of a horror trope. See Brown 2002, Cenciarelli 2012, and Gopinath 2013: 89–90.

[3] Burkholder 2006: 79.   [4] *Ibid.*: 80.

[5] *Ibid.*: 82. For understandable reasons, scholars rarely mention personal associations to support arguments of musical meaning. Recent work on subjectivity stands as an obvious exception.

article in intertextuality.[6] In the pages that follow, we shall consider both piece-specific-plus-cultural-generic and intertextual associative layering in turn. Before this, though, it will be helpful to briefly reconsider semiotics, signification, and topic theory; specifically what these fields of inquiry have to say about how cultural associations function.

Semiotics revisited

We noted in Chapter 4 that semiotics has enjoyed a recent flourishing in music scholarship, and that it concerns itself with meaning-filled relationships involving signs. Our summary leaned heavily toward the logical-philosophical treatment of Charles Peirce, largely neglecting semiotics's strong linguistic thread. The time has come to rectify this neglect by exploring linguistic semiotics in some greater depth. One discerns within linguistic semiotics three broad categories of meaning: semantics (the relationship of a signifier to a sign), syntactics (the relationship of a signifier to other signifiers), and pragmatics (the relationship of a signifier to an interpretant).[7] While these relationships require little by way of explanation, they all include the notion of a "signifier," an idea whose function does bear explanation.

Linguist Charles Morris provides us with an easily digestible categorization of a signifier's five modes of operation. They include three primary (or pragmasemantic) modes – designative (statements), appraisive (valuations), and prescriptive (imperatives) – and two secondary ones – identificative (locators in time and space) and formative (contextual functions such as conjunctions, quantifiers, and other function words, and punctuation marks).[8] For our purposes, Morris's modes themselves are relatively uninteresting. His understanding of *ascription* – how language may signify in more than one mode at a time – however, is germane; most musicians would agree that this ability belongs among the more promising characteristics that music shares with language. An ascriptive example of language is the statement, "This is a group of brilliant scholars in this room." The statement signifies both in the *identificative* mode ("group of scholars") and in the *appraisive* mode ("brilliant scholars").[9] Music can do something similar.

---

[6] *Ibid.*: 99.   [7] See Noske 1994: 35–36.
[8] See Morris 1946 and the discussion in Rodman 2011a.
[9] I am indebted to Rodman 2011a for the understanding of this material.

Consider, for a moment, almost any popular television theme song. Among recent examples, we might turn to Ramin Djawadi's music for the hit HBO series, *Game of Thrones*. The theme identifies the particular show through week-to-week association of the theme with the show itself, that is, a *piece-specific* association. In this case, for listeners familiar with it, it will likely recall the visually stunning, award-winning title sequence and the ethos of the world of Westeros. It also connotes excitement and obsession (via the driving percussion riffs and repeated rising-third lines), and perhaps a sense of melancholy (via the natural minor scale and focus on the subtonic harmony). These are, however, *cultural-generic* associations that the music would manifest even if played out of context for a first-time listener. So, while the *modes of signification* may not be isomorphic to those of music, both media share the *potential for ascription* – signifying in multiple modes simultaneously. Put in Peircian terms, this title music functions both indexically and symbolically.

A similar distinction lies at the heart of the work by French semiologist Ferdinand de Saussure. Also working from a linguistic perspective, Saussure – like Morris – defines *associative* relations in language as a category distinct from what he calls *syntagmatic* relations.[10] These associative relations are predicated on similarity to one another based on a shared cultural storehouse possessed by members of a culture (e.g., brooms and black cats share an associative relation by virtue of their shared association with witches). Saussure's idea of associativity – a cultural-generic relationship – differs categorically from the treatment of associativity in the tradition of structural criticism by thinkers like Jakobsen, Lévi-Strauss, Barthes, and Propp.[11] Though these other men also rely on systemic (i.e., cultural-generic) associations, they were largely interested in associations *within* a work (i.e., piece-specific). Saussurian systemic associative relations, however, are analogues to topics and other culturally accepted meaning-filled signs.

Another important distinction is that Saussure limits himself to smaller units of language – basic sounds (phonemes), words, and sentences – while Jakobsen *et al.* are interested in associative relations of larger structures. We might extend this metaphorically to music to say that themes are analogous to Saussure's smaller structures whereas form sections would be of similar length to the linguistic units considered by structuralist criticism. All of this is not to say that various linguistic approaches to associativity are incompatible; quite the opposite, rather – they are

[10] Saussure 1959: 123–26. Much of the following derives from the discussion in McCreless 1991.
[11] See Jakobson 1959 and 1973, Lévi-Strauss 1963, Propp 1968, and Barthes 1974 and 1977.

complementary. Smaller structures combine to form larger structures, and we can understand larger structures as groupings of smaller units. Likewise, piece-specific associations can grow to become culturally accepted associations, and culturally accepted associations can inform how we understand piece-specific associations. It is instructive to consider this complementarity in the context of Wagner's *Ring*.

The semiotics of Wagner's leitmotivic process is not really new; it relies – as did earlier associative music – upon a tendency already important to musical literacy: topical association (e.g., scoring for trumpets to signify honor, strength, integrity, or battle).[12] Connotations applicable to absolute music – specifically, those connotative aspects of Wagner's music whose meanings had been established by earlier musics – would have been apprehended by most audience members topically. *The Ring* includes both topics previously in place as culturally accepted musical icons and musical elements that grew to assume topical status over the course of the entire cycle and later musics.[13] These comprise almost every aspect of music imaginable, including, but not limited to: harmony, especially diminished seventh and Neapolitan chords;[14] harmonic progression;[15] dissonance;[16] rhythm;[17]

---

[12] Corse 1990: 58.

[13] Hacohen and Wagner 1997: 447. One of the more famous of Wagner's progressions that assumed topical status in later music is the harmonic motion from i to ♭vi in the "Tarnhelm" theme (Rg/117/2/6ff). See Chapter 6.

[14] Patterson calls root position vii^{o7} "the pure harmonic essence of danger and disaster." See Patterson 1896: 288. Gauldin, *Analytical Studies in Wagner's Music* (unpublished manuscript), chapter 15: 14 suggests that vii^{o7} is one of three devices Wagner used in the treatment of dark, sinister forces in *The Ring*. See also Darcy's statement that "melodic descent and the Neapolitan harmony fuse into a musical analog of impending doom and dissolution," in Darcy 1994: 10. Deathridge and Dahlhaus 1984: 150 assert that musical meaning in Wagner is linked to harmony, especially the use of the Neapolitan. Finally, Abbate suggests that a simple verbal-musical device ubiquitous in Wagner's music is the use of a harmonic quirk in coincidence with a specific text reference. See Abbate 1989b: 53.

[15] Lerdahl posits that Wagner moved through harmonic regions (like those described by Gottfried Weber and Arnold Schoenberg) to associate music with drama. In *Parsifal*, for instance, the direction of harmonic motion on the harmonic region map below is associative as follows: up = ascent and heaven, down = descent to mortal realm, right = good, left = evil.

vii° V iii

ii I vi

vi IV ii

See Lerdahl 1994.

[16] In Wagner, musical tension is equated with moving into "regions of dissonance" while the return to consonance equals relaxation. See Dennison 1985: 41. This intriguing notion is unfortunately marred by Dennison's conflating chromaticism with dissonance.

[17] Two of the three *Ring topoi* Noske identifies have to do with rhythm. They are: rhythmically repeated block chords = ritual; and sixteenth- or thirty-second-notes followed by eighth-notes = death. See Noske 1994: 35–36. Of course, manipulations of the dotted-eighth–sixteenth–eighth

conventional operatic style;[18] metric consonance and dissonance;[19] metric regularity;[20] key;[21] melodic fragments;[22] melodic contour;[23] texture;[24] form;[25] and orchestration.[26] Moreover, each parameter in and of itself may accrue layered associative meanings.[27]

This may all sound very much like a description of *thematic* (rather than *topical*) identity. It is important to remember, though, that topics and themes are not the same. Rather, as noted in Chapter 2, themes are

division of one compound-meter beat are legion in *The Ring*, often associated with riding, battle, heroism, and such.

[18] The "diurnal, exterior-oriented" characters in Wagner's music dramas tend to adhere to or fall back on operatic tradition, thus emphasizing the reflective and inward-focused nature of the characters whose music is not stereotyped. See Dahlhaus 1979: 15.

[19] Direct metrical dissonance often illustrates conflict while indirect dissonance (changing meter signatures), a new dramatic environment. See Krebs 1988. Krebs also hears metrical dissonance as associative: 2 vs. 3 is used for the anvil chorus and the clumsiness of the toad's hopping (11). Metrical consonance is used to show that all is well or that a character thinks all is well (8–9).

[20] Robert Gauldin suggests that hypermetric irregularities at the beginning of the Ride of the Valkyries symbolize their gathering. The hypermeter does not become normative until they are all there. See Gauldin, *Analytical Studies in Wagner's Music* (unpublished manuscript), chapter 19: 5. One of Dahlhaus's major additions to Wagner literature was the idea that leitmotifs of varying lengths destroyed metric/harmonic periodicity, resulting in "musical prose." This occurs mainly in monologues rich with a variety of motives. Spans representing physical activity (the Ride of the Valkyries, Siegfried's forging, etc.) are more often strongly periodic. See Murray 1978: 218–19 (cf. Gauldin on rhythmic regularity in the Ride of the Valkyries).

[21] Associative keys in Wagner's oeuvre are well documented in the scholarly literature. For more on this topic, see Chapter 7 in this book.

[22] Among the three *Ring* topics Noske defines is the descending tetrachord, equated with sorrow. See Noske 1994: 35–36. According to Gauldin, *Analytical Studies in Wagner's Music* (unpublished manuscript), chapter 15: 2, the C–F♯ tritone stands among Wagner's principal treatments of dark, sinister forces in *The Ring*. (In fact, Gauldin locates over 200 allusions to this interval on the musical surface throughout the cycle.)

[23] In *The Ring*, ascending melodic motion often symbolizes progress, while descending motion indicates decline. See Deathridge and Dahlhaus 1984: 150. The implication is that inversion of a musical gesture renders its meaning opposite, a concept explored in Chapter 7 of this book.

[24] The sheer number of associative themes appearing at any given moment can itself be associative. See Millington 1992a: 211, who describes the "bewildering and breathtaking profusion" of motives in *The Ring* after Act II of *Siegfried* in a Schoenbergian sense (i.e., in *Erwartung*) as a depiction of the psychological tension of the drama.

[25] Wagner consciously avoided traditional phrase lengths of four and eight bars in the Norns' scene in favor of tripartite formal and phrase divisions. See Bailey 1968: 471. The symbolism here for the three sisters is unmistakable.

[26] The kettledrums suggesting death is a meaning based on instrumentation. See Noske 1994: 36. According to Corse 1990: 65, orchestration can strengthen the "linguistic" meanings of Wagner's music. Orchestration can also take on an associative reference even when actual themes aren't present (e.g., muted horns suggesting "Tarnhelm" and upper woodwinds, "Loge"). See Gauldin, *Analytical Studies in Wagner's Music* (unpublished manuscript), chapter 13: 39–40.

[27] See Dennison 1985: 33.

repeated, piece-specific musical entities that tend to embody specific rhythmic and intervallic shapes, whereas topics usually evoke more gener- alized musical parameters (e.g., rhythm and orchestration for the march *topos*) and bear extra-musical associations of a more universal kind.[28] And, while it is certainly possible to blend topics, they are not subject to the same sorts of developmental procedures that themes are.[29] Put another way, themes are mutable musical individuals that may embrace generalized topical stereotypes. Associative themes are at their most powerful when they invoke topical resonance (as described in Chapter 4) to cement a piece-specific meaning.

Ideally, topical meaning is iconic or indexical in the Peircian sense. For modern-day listeners, though, many meanings have become Peircian sym- bols – meanings that must be established through scholarly explanation because the objects to which they are iconically associated (say, the rhythm of a danced gavotte) or indexically associated (say, the horn calls used during a hunt) are no longer part of the lived experience of many modern- day people. Leitmotif guides and books on musical meaning include these explanations among their central aims; that is, they serve to establish arbitrarily – through prose – what might to another culture signify without the need for explanation.

Two examples of topics appear below, one illustrating march style and the other French overture style (see Example 5.1). Note that general features of texture, rhythm, meter, melodic contour, figuration, and expres- sive markings (e.g., the rapid conjunct motion and double-dotted rhythms of the French overture), *not* specific pitch and interval content, allow the listener to recognize these excerpts as examples of more generalized topics. In this regard, topics participate in a broader code of meaning, a space that discrete works access – and in which they interact intertextually.[30]

While topical resonance in *The Ring* (and other works) contributes to musical meaning in a largely unproblematic way, it is not clear that this is enough to establish the meaning of certain leitmotifs. Fritz Noske, for one, argues that a scholarly level of music literacy is necessary to understand the *denotative* meanings of Wagner's signs.[31] His view provides one

---

[28] Ratner 1980: chapter 2 presents a full exposition of topics (*Topoi*) in Classic-era music.

[29] Hatten 1994: x, mentions the possibility of combining *topoi*, an explanatory model he turns to throughout the remainder of his book. See also *ibid.*: 74–75 for a concise summary of Ratner's discussion of *Topoi* cited above.

[30] Here I echo Klein 2005: chapter 3 (51–76) who situates topics within codes, which are themselves intertexts.

[31] Noske 1994: 35–36.

(a)

(b)

Example 5.1 Two topics (Ratner 1980: 16 (Ex. 2-17) and 20 (Ex. 2-22).

a. March type. Christmann, *Elementarbuch*, 1782, examples, p. 24
b. French overture style. Mozart, Symphony in E♭ Major, K. 543, 1788, introduction

explanation for the proliferation of thematic guides to *The Ring* – they continue to fill the consumer demand for a crash course in Wagnerian signs (a sort of leitmotivic *Hooked on Phonics*, if you will). By definition, such a thing would not be necessary for topical meanings. All signs must be learned, since they are not inherently bearers of meaning, but culturally accepted signs are ones learned mainly during childhood, at least for natives of a given culture; their cultural currency is a large part of what makes them topical. Signs particular to a specific opera, however, gain meaning from that work (or even from motive-tables); one isn't prepared by cultural immersion to hear, in an unfamiliar work, things like "Wotan's Frustration," "The Purpose of the Sword," or "Decision to Love," the way one would recognize a musical topic in the same context.

Even when not as specific as, say, "Wotan's Frustration," association needs to have *some* focus; without it, the entire concept of the leitmotif falls apart.[32] In Peircian terms, music can achieve associative focus by imitating the sound of something (iconic), by correlating with something (indexical), or by agreement (symbolic). It is the second and third that are problematic and create the need for thematic guides; if all words were onomatopoeic, we would likewise have little use for dictionaries.[33] Even when correlation or agreement occur, leitmotivic association – meant to recall a certain emotion – can be exceptionally difficult to define in words because it

[32] Gorbman 1987: 29 makes this point in film music, stating that, "In many cases, the theme's designation is so diffused that to call it a Leitmotif contradicts Wagner's intention."
[33] Kivy 1989: 29.

doesn't always relate directly to events or objects on stage. One need only consider some of the recurring material in Wagner's *Tristan* to recognize music's ability to associate with complex and nuanced "inner dramas" grounded in philosophy or unexpressed emotion. Put in Peircian terms, the indexical relationship may be so subtle that listeners don't understand what the music correlates with. Why, then, don't we reject these works along with so-called "absolute" music, as meaningless? In part it is because musical ideas can also be associated *with each other* through shared use of musical materials and compositional techniques. Even if meaning is not clear, as long as themes relate to one another musically, some sense of unity for the listener can be achieved. That unity, however, is not leitmotivic in nature – it lies closer to the autonomous than the contextual. That is one reason why *The Ring*, and not *Tristan*, is the touchstone of leitmotivic technique: by and large, thematic associations are obvious, and moreover Wagner employs as an aide to musical comprehension only a small number of individual motivically related thematic families.[34] From these, themes develop as motivated by the drama:

> In *Das Rheingold*, I at once set out along the new path where the first thing I was to find was the plastic nature motifs, which shaped themselves, as they developed in ever more individual ways, into the vehicles for the promptings of the passions motivating the much-ramified action and the characters that expressed themselves in it.[35]

Thus, unlike teleological music driven towards a thematic and/or tonal goal (e.g., the typical Classic-era sonata recapitulation, or many of Beethoven's codas), Wagner's music embodies a constantly "waxing past" that informs our hearing of new or altered themes as variants of – or contrasts to – previous ones.[36] Evolution for Wagner trumps structure and teleology, at least in theory.

---

[34] Cooke 1995 explores in detail his concept of thematic families in the *Introduction to* The Ring. Robert Gauldin follows a similar tactic, grouping themes in each of Wagner's operas from *Holländer* onward via relationships to prototypes he calls *Grundthema*. See Gauldin, unpublished manuscript. See also Dahlhaus 1979: 116–17. Dahlhaus's three essential ingredients of leitmotivic intelligibility are based on semiotic principles: He states themes must be recognizable (i.e., distinct from other signs and recognized *as a sign*), they must be dramatically motivated (imbued with a semantic content), and there must be a small enough number of *Urmotive* to be able to remember them all, but these must be varied enough to avoid monotony (facilitating interpretation).

[35] This quotation comes from Wagner's *Epilogischer Bericht* (1871). See Deathridge and Dahlhaus 1984: 149.

[36] Dahlhaus 1992: 305–06.

Music as symbolic

By now, we are well aware that accepting leitmotifs (and associative themes, in general) simply as musical dicent signs – even developmental ones – doesn't entirely capture the sense of how they function. In much of Wagner's (not to mention later composers') output, music operates less precisely than signs like words do; its meaning is often vague and difficult to articulate. It short, it is closer to symbolism than denotation. My use of "symbolic" and "symbolism" here is *not* an extension of the Peircian "symbol" – an arbitrary relationship of meaning established through language and/or cultural agreement. Rather, I use here the more colloquial meaning of the term. For clarity's sake, herein "symbol" will be a Peircian term and "symbolic" or "symbolism" will be the more familiar, widely used concepts.

Take, for instance, the song that Cinderella sings from time to time ("Una volta c'era un re") throughout Rossini's *La Cenerentola*. This isn't a leitmotif, nor even an associative theme; rather, it is symbolic of Cinderella's character, her aspirations beyond her life as a drudge. Some of its meaning devolves from the text, which describes a king choosing a kind-hearted and true wife from among three possibilities. But its meaning also rests on its function: Cinderella sings it at times of depression and boredom as she goes about her housework, dreaming of a better life.[37] Another example of symbolic music – one closer to leitmotif – is the citation of Marguerite's melody from her aria "Le roi de Thulé" later (at the beginning of Scene 13) in Berlioz's *La damnation de Faust* (see Example 5.2). Subsequent composers of operetta and Broadway-style musical found this citation of music from a character's first appearance to be a useful technique for re-introducing the character during later entrances. Unlike the leitmotif, which captures the emotion of a dramatic moment and repackages it in a developmental way to inflect a later moment, reminiscences like Cinderella's song and Marguerite's aria melody function symbolically.

But what exactly do we mean by "symbolically?" What is musical symbolism? Is it different from leitmotivic association? While leitmotif and musical symbolism both employ sound for extra-musical communication, musical symbolism reaches more toward the ineffable. Directed toward the

---

[37] In as much as the story of Cinderella's song reflects the story of Rossini's opera, we could cite this as an example of Carolyn Abbate's "reflexive narrative," though the connection to the rest of the opera is entirely bound up in the plot; there are no *musical* connections between "Una volta c'era un re" and the rest of *La Cenerentola* the way there are, say, between Senta's ballad and the rest of Wagner's *Der fliegende Holländer*. See Abbate 1991: 85–87.

Example 5.2 Recollection of material from Marguerite's "Le roi de Thulé" used symbolically in Berlioz's *La damnation de Faust*, Scene 13, mm. 5–10

subconscious, it is thus a natural vessel for composers wishing to engage the intangible. Where leitmotifs function on *association* to capture, recall, and recontextualize *emotions*, musical symbolism strives to capture the *essence* of something and communicate it on a level of understanding that bypasses language and rejects denotative specificity in favor of a direct, indescribable conception.[38] Symbolism, of course, appears in a variety of contexts, not just musical ones, and defining symbolism using language – regardless of its medium – tends to be messy work, largely incompatible with semiotics (relegated, for instance, to the intensely rhematic in a Peircian sense).[39]

Given this characterization of symbols as inscrutable mental constructs, it should come as no surprise that they fascinate students of psychology. Christopher Wintle, for one, claims that sonic events in Wagner's music stand as metaphors for psychological states or processes, tracing Freudian and Jungian aspects of these and their musical expression. His approach to musical meaning advocates music analysis borrowing from psychoanalysis the way literary theory does. That is, musical symbolism acts metaphorically to unlock composers' understanding of their characters' psyches.[40] Substitute, "music" for "myths" in the passage below, and we approach an understanding of how musical symbolism works:

[38] See, for example, Tarasti 1979: 93–94, who hears the rising sixth as a "heroic mythic isotope." Like many attempts at describing musical symbolism, though, this one falls short, ignoring important aspects of *context*: major vs. minor sixths, sixths as adjacent vs. boundary intervals in a melodic line, and the harmonic or melodic function of the pitches involved.

[39] See McCredie 1985: 20–21 who cites Wörner on five symbolic functions – symbols of psychic content, symbols of supernatural powers, symbols of primary poetic forces in the plot, symbols of factors in the external plot, and symbols of objects – and four symbolic purposes – reappearance of emotional or conceptual entity, memorable presentation of an entity, appearance of an entity without dialogue, and indirect reference to an entity. One senses in the clumsiness of categorization here the difficulty of circumscribing symbolic content and function using language.

[40] Wintle 1992.

Managed news, with its "photo opportunities" and "sound bites'" is presented as factual but is really manipulated and often deceptive story telling. In contrast, myths [music], with no claim to factuality, tell[s] us the truth the way dreams do – in the language of metaphor and symbol.[41]

All this emphasis on the ineffability of symbolism, however, doesn't mean that we stop trying to explain symbols using language. Donington is a prime example. In his interpretation of the "Giants" theme from *Das Rheingold* (Example 1.1A), he uses symbolic thinking to explain leitmotivic meaning. We noted in Chapter 1 the funeral-march topical resonance of this music. This cultural-generic association reinforces the piece-specific emotions associated with the ominous and plodding approach of the giants. Donington's description of meaning in the "Giants" music cites the "brutal aspect of parental authority"; for him, the music is symbolic of a psychological effect any human being should find familiar (if only subconsciously).[42]

But must every listener concur? Thematic exegesis is, at its heart, interpretation, and we use the imperfect mechanism of language to explain and communicate our understandings. That is, discussions of musical meaning invoke a second network of signs (words) to interact with the first (music). This is the point at which the Peircian symbol re-enters the picture – using language to establish arbitrary meaning. When scholars argue about the meaning of a given theme, we don't argue about the musical sounds themselves, but rather the translation of music into meaning; disputes are resolved not by composing "refutation" music, but by comparing the persuasiveness of language between the two accounts.[43] This does not mean such interpretation cannot be *empiric* (i.e., based on evidence) – the most persuasive accounts usually are – but claims to *positivism* in interpretation are clearly oxymoronic. Translating musical signs into verbal ones will always rely in part on perception and intuition; the appeal of such work lies in its potential for multiple interpretations.

Interpretation of music overlays one network of signs – words – on another, music. In that sense, any music that needs to be explained to achieve a sense of meaning puts it squarely in the realm of the Peircian symbol. Of course, the same can be said of texted music itself: two systems of signs exist simultaneously, allowing for the possibility of interaction between them. Wagner knew this well and exploited it in his operas. The most celebrated instance of semantic mismatch between words and music

---

[41] Bolen 1992: x.   [42] Donington 1974: 296.   [43] White 1988: 21.

in *The Ring* occurs in *Siegfried* Act II. Tasting the dragon's blood has allowed Siegfried to detect Mime's evil intentions in his words. The music Mime sings, however, signifies the falsely reassuring words he thinks he is saying rather than those Siegfried (and the audience) hears. One system of signs (text as Peircian dicent symbol) contradicts the other (music having an indexical – i.e., coincidental – relationship to the text), creating layers of meaning.[44] The same happens without text when layered musical meanings intersect, for music is rarely singular in meaning or association.

From piece specifics to cultural generics

There are plenty of musical ideas that mean something, but not in an *associative* way. Think for instance of the iconic flowing-brook texture arpeggiated in the piano throughout Schubert's song cycle *Die Schöne Müllerin* (see Example 5.3). It's not meant to be *associated* with anything, but rather to create a musically stylized *representation* of water. Likewise, there are plenty of associative objects that aren't themes.[45] Here, we can cite the *Jaws* motive. Anyone even slightly familiar with later twentieth-century American pop culture will hear a low-register rising half-step of a certain duration and recall the horror of an impending shark attack, especially if the sonic gesture occurs in some kind of aquatic context.[46]

By and large, musical meanings, whether thematic, associative, both, or neither, rely heavily on their context and on listener familiarity to function. Conveniently, so long as listener familiarity remains, context can change. This is how culturally accepted topics inform the meaning of piece-specific themes, and how piece-specific themes can become generalized cultural topics (as with the *Jaws* motive). It is also the point at which Peircian semiotics loses its value for the purposes of our investigation. We're no longer concerned with *how* things achieve a sense of meaning, but rather *in what context* they do so.

From this wide variety of meaningful musical gestures, Wagner explicitly preferred some over others. He particularly eschewed word painting and pre-fabricated gestures with highly specific extra-musical associations.

---

[44] Weiner 1997: 76–77. This scene stands as evidence supporting Abbate's claim that music in *The Ring* can lie. See Abbate 1991: 156–57.

[45] Anson-Cartwright 1996 suggests that a chord itself (in this case, the augmented triad) can be an associative motive on both the musical surface and at deeper structural levels.

[46] See Rodman 2006: 124 for a description of both denotation and connotation in what he calls the "shark leitmotif" from *Jaws*.

Example 5.3 The brook texture from Schubert's *Die Schöne Müllerin*

a. "Wohin?," mm. 1–6
b. "Der Müller und der Bach," mm. 78–82

But it would be a mistake to naively take him at his word, arguing that leitmotivic meaning is arbitrary in nature and completely piece-specific; in effect, stating that associations rely on intrinsic qualities of the music they are associated with. Even a passing knowledge of topic theory shows this to be patently false in almost every case, even Wagner's. As much as Wagner might have wished his themes to be invested with meaning through the drama alone, many adopt culturally accepted topics to cement their meanings, like the falling half-step *pianto* madrigalism that comprises the "Anguish" and "Servitude" themes in *The Ring*, or the funeral march topos for the "Giants" noted previously.[47] Equally untenable, of course, is the opposite argument: that piece-specific contexts matter little to musical meaning.[48]

The truth of these wholly piece-specific vs. wholly cultural-generic arguments for musical meaning, as in so many cases, lies in the middle.[49] Even today, composers continue to craft themes specific to a given work, *and* to rely on generalized associations. Topics continue to persist and evolve throughout the twentieth century, even in so-called "post-tonal" music and in popular genres like film.[50] Film-music associations, in particular, provide convincing evidence for the blended associations of musical materials, relying heavily on both piece-specific themes and topical resonance inherited not only from so-called "art music," but also from prior filmic practice. Iconic movies like *2001: A Space Odyssey* inform later musical choices such that the use of Strauss's *Also Sprach Zarathustra* in Kubrick's film created a connotative category of major-mode brass fanfares to accompany the opening credits of later space-themed movies (think, for example, of the *Star Wars* and *Star Trek* films, which, like *2001*, feature panoramic visual images of deep space).[51] While the brass fanfare draws upon earlier associations with heroism and battle, in this new context it becomes strongly wedded not only to visual imagery of space, but also to the idea of *epic, filmic beginning*. Thus, we see that associations need not be necessarily made with specific *dramatic contexts* (as in Wagner) but may even signal *stage or filmic techniques* like curtain-opening, transition, fade out, flash back, and so forth.[52]

What we're speaking of here is a move from a specific musical statement, with a specific association and context, to a more generalized

---

[47] Rieger 2010: 133–38 provides a number of examples of what, specifically, Wagner drew upon from the earlier language of musical affects when constructing his leitmotifs. Included are specific intervals, collections, instrumentation, and so forth.

[48] Corse 1990: 60, for instance, argues that Wagner's themes derive their meanings not from association with text and drama, but with thoughts or categories already present in the audience's mind.

[49] Gorbman 1987: 27–28 notes that themes accumulate meaning both through association and through cultural reference (as topics).

[50] See Narum 2013 for more on the twentieth-century topic.   [51] Burkholder 2006: 102.

[52] See Leydon 2001 for a study of continuity and disjunction in Debussy's music read in terms of contemporaneous silent-film editing techniques.

musical quality that can function in a variety of settings. In later twentieth-century film music, for instance, there had come to be a virtual playbook of culturally accepted, meaning-filled gestures that included the rising major sixth for love themes, the rising perfect fifth for heroism and adventure, tritones for magic and the supernatural, chromatic double neighbors around $\hat{5}$ for menacing or ominous scenes, and so forth.[53] Many of these arose not out of one iconic filmic usage (as in *2001*'s *Also Sprach Zarathustra*) but rather a collective re-usage of similar gestures by a variety of composers in a variety of films.[54] Particularly striking, popular, and/or influential piece-specific associations can become part of the larger cultural currency. Their piece-specific associations may be the original reason for their use in another context, but eventually these piece-specific associations soften and become broader cultural-generic associations. What starts out as quotation relaxes into allusion, and eventually becomes topical – a process that illustrates the power of intertextuality.

Intertextuality

Intertextuality is a simple concept with far-reaching interpretive reper-cussions. Originally coined by Julia Kristeva, the term is one she developed from Bakhtin's notion that authors structure texts in relation to other texts, and that texts take into account the past, present, and future lives of other similar-type texts.[55] Later critical theorists found a variety of uses for this notion: structuralists use intertextuality to locate and cement meaning; post-structuralists use it to deconstruct a text; and so on. According to Allen:

Texts, whether they be literary or non-literary, are viewed by modern theorists as lacking in any kind of independent meaning. They are what theorists now call intertextual. The act of reading, theorists claim, plunges us into a network of textual relations. To interpret a text, to discover its meaning, or meanings, is to trace those

---

[53] For a formalized catalogue of such associative progressions, see Murphy 2000.

[54] Others, though, remain specific to certain composers or certain films. Danny Elfman, for instance, seems to have his own topical code for instrumentation. The harpsichord is a sonority he uses for sinister calculation, evil, and amorality; the celesta with memory, mystery, and the otherworldly (broader associations that hail from the nineteenth century, perhaps Tchaikovsky's *Nutcracker*), children's choir with dangerous alien or supernatural creatures; and all-male choir with foreboding or threatening emotions. Halfyard 2004: 32 adumbrates these associations.

[55] Allen 2000: 30–35.

relations. Reading thus becomes a process of moving between a text and all the other texts to which it refers and relates, moving out from the independent text into a network of textual relations. The text becomes the intertext.[56]

Most recently, Michael Klein articulated the many ways we might under-stand music in terms of intertextuality – Is it a text? A space between texts? The force of influence itself? Something else entirely? – and what's at stake in such understanding.[57] In the present context, while we lack the space to investigate the nature of intertextuality in any satisfying way, it would be irresponsible not to mention the breadth of the concept since our focus will rest on but two of its tangible manifestations: *quotation* and *allusion*.

In the history of Western music, intertextuality goes back to the dawn of musical notation (and almost certainly before, if one accepts a non-literate musical tradition as capable of construing texts); musical practice, by its very nature, borrowed and reused material from earlier works, thus con-structing a conceptual space between texts. It was in the Renaissance, though, that such things began to take on the meaning we now associate with them, and, more specifically to our purposes, *allusion* and *quotation* came to bear reference not only to specific works, but also to specific composers, often in homage (as in Obrecht's reworking of lines from Ockeghem's *Missa 'Mi-mi'* in the former's *Missa 'Sicut spina rosam'*). We assume both quotation – recognizable, pre-existing music appearing within another text – and allusion – newly composed music that strongly resem-bles earlier work – to be intentional on the part of the composer, though with allusion one can't always be certain. Separating the two is something of an arbitrary binarism since they exist on a continuum that stretches from exact quotation including the same pitches, rhythms, timbres and other parameters of the original to vague allusion that obviates the neces-sity of *any* material repeated verbatim. These concepts are fascinating in their own right, and worthy of further study in musical practice, but it is not our purpose to accomplish that here.[58] Rather, we seek to understand what function allusion and quotation play in the larger concept of intertextuality, and how they affect associative meaning.

We begin by examining a couple of examples of associative layering in film that employ obvious – but not exact – quotation. Many film scores quote pre-existing melodies, their ready-made associations layered with the new musical and filmic context. This layering often creates an aura of

---

[56] *Ibid.*: 1.   [57] See Klein 2005: 1–4 and 11–21.
[58] See, especially, Part III of Joe and Gilman 2010. See also Orosz 2013.

Example 5.4 Pre-existing tunes recontextualized to create associative layering

a. "Dixieland" in the score to *Gone with the Wind*
b. "There's No Place Like Home" in the score to *The Wizard of Oz*

distance, as in uncertainty or memory (see, for instance, the two excerpts in Example 5.4). In the first, a choral (later obbligato fiddle) version of "Dixieland" in Max Steiner's score to *Gone with the Wind* sounds just after the opening credits when the first verses of the novel scroll on screen over scenes of the Old South. At the movie's premier, this folksong spoke to members of the audience with a strong sense of cultural resonance. (Despite the passage of time, it still does, evoking patriotism for lovers of the Old South, or derision from those who hear it as a glorification of oppression.) Its setting here, however, is "composed" rather than sung, folk-style. The use of harmonies and bass lines native to "art music" suggest the patina of elapsed time, a nostalgic look back at the storybook, antebellum days of Dixie. That is, we know by its setting that we're hearing the song "quoted" out-of-time and out-of-context, as it were, as a reference within one text to another. Something similar happens to the melodic phrase accompanying the words, "Be it ever so humble" from the song "There's No Place Like Home" in *The Wizard of Oz* (see Example 5.4b). Here the music underscores Glinda's instructions when Dorothy clicks her heels to return to Kansas. The fragmentary quotation, reharmonized with ambiguous and dissonant hallmarks of Romantic-era tonality, speaks to the audience with a sense of self-awareness, the new context functioning like quotation marks to set the moment apart from the rest of the text.

Thematic intertextuality often creates cognitive dissonance between the original material and its new context – dissonance that serves humorous purposes well. Thus it's unsurprising that the technique appears frequently in comedy.[59] Explaining these musical jokes renders them largely inert, but for the purpose of analysis we must risk ruining the effect. Examples of comic intertextuality are particularly common in television and film: Comparing Mr. Burns in *The Simpsons* Season 6 (1999) episode "A Star is Burns" to the evil leaders of the Empire from George Lucas's *Star Wars* trilogy requires little more than the citation of the "Imperial March" theme for the first appearance of Mr. Burns in an episode about the residents of Springfield hosting a film festival. Also likely to get a laugh is Elsa Schneider's question, "Are you sure?" directed to Indiana Jones when Indy identifies a fresco of the Ark of the Covenant while the duo explores the rat-infested catacombs under a Venetian library in *Indiana Jones and the Last Crusade*. Indy answers "Pretty sure!" while the underscoring sounds the "Ark" music from the franchise's first film: *Raiders of the Lost Ark*. Similar humorous quotations of John Williams's music occur elsewhere, in both his own scores (one thinks of the "Yoda" music appearing in *E.T.* accompanying a trick-or-treating child in a Yoda costume) and those of others (like Dave Grusin's quotation of Williams's "Superman" fanfare in the score to *Goonies* when Sloth rips open his shirt to reveal the Superman insignia on his undershirt).

Of course, such things had been happening for well over a hundred years before the advent of film or television. One imagines that audiences

---

[59] It serves other purposes as well. In the first *Star Trek* film, for example, Jerry Goldsmith weaves the TV series' theme into the underscoring for the opening "Captain's Log" monologue. This is not comedy, but rather an unspoken appeal for continuity and audience loyalty in translating the beloved characters and storylines of the television series to a filmic context.

in the know chuckled over Mozart's quotations of Soler's *Una cosa rara*, Sarti's *Fra i due litiganti il terzo gode* and Mozart's own *Marriage of Figaro* in the dinner scene near the end of *Don Giovanni*, not to mention Wagner's quotation of the *Tristan* prelude when Eva refers to that "famous pair of lovers" in the third act of *Die Meistersinger von Nürnberg*. Nor did such examples comprise only self-quotation. Like John Williams today, Wagner enjoyed an iconic status, one that made him a favorite target for parody. Richard Strauss, for one, seems to have structured an entire opera on lampooning Wagner.[60] And, Wagnerian comedic intertextuality also functioned side-by-side with other thematic techniques. Act II of Benjamin Britten's *Albert Herring* provides an excellent example. The arpeggiated horn theme that opens the act recurs throughout as a Wagnerian-style formal unifier, though without any clear extra-musical association; the rising chromatic line that accompanies any mention of the spiked rum is an obvious (and hackneyed) form of associative theme, and the citation of *Tristan und Isolde*'s opening phrase pits the deep Germanic philosophizing of Wagner's sound world against the playful silliness of Britten's.

If we return to quotation in film music for a moment, an example from the recent *Spiderman* franchise introduces another consideration into our investigation of intertextuality. At one point in the film *Spiderman 2*, a street violinist plays the "Spiderman" theme from the 1970s animated television show. Like many instances of musical quotation, this one is diegetic, a fact that highlights its self-aware referentiality, much like the reharmonization of "There's No Place Like Home" in *The Wizard of Oz*. Normally associated with film (less so with opera), the idea that some music belongs to the story and is heard by the characters (i.e., is diegetic, part of the narrative or plot) and the rest (usually the bulk) of the music is for the audience's benefit alone applies to any music with an explicit drama – ballet, programme symphonies, or lieder for example. Composers play with this boundary, bringing diegetic music into the non-diegetic realm and vice versa, and when they do, they create a certain type of intertextuality, an importation of music from the text as experienced by the characters to the text as experienced by the audience (or vice versa).[61] This, too, is ripe for associative layering.

---

[60] In his *Feuersnot*, Strauss parodies the "Giants" theme, the "Magic Fire" music, "Valhalla," and music from *Tristan und Isolde*.

[61] See Neumeyer 1997 and 2000, which explore film-makers' early blurrings of the diegetic/ non-diegetic boundary and proposes that this is just one among a number of interacting binary distinctions applied to descriptions of music in film. Moreover, Neumeyer 2000 argues

One thinks of instances like Mel Brooks's *High Anxiety* when foreboding music suddenly begins during a scene in which characters investigating a mystery drive down the highway. At first this music strikes us, the audience, as non-diegetic, its mystery topic an appropriate association for the setting. The characters themselves, however, also notice the music and are subsequently passed by a bus transporting performing symphonic musicians who, it turns out, are the music's source. Suspense becomes comedy. This diegetic/non-diegetic distinction, however, is not always so clear. Claudia Gorbman describes as "metadiegetic" a filmic technique in which a character's (rather than the audience's) remembrance brings forth earlier music to take over the narrative discourse.[62] Carolyn Abbate notes the same thing in Wagner's *Tannhäuser*: the title character's Rome narrative *creates* its narrative voice by blurring the diegetic/non-diegetic boundary in the act of performance; music remembered by the character infuses the symphonic texture heard by the audience, creating for us a musical past tense.[63]

Anahid Kassabian points to yet another kind of diegetic blurring, citing the medal ceremony at the end of *Star Wars*. The music during that scene can be heard as part of the diegetic ceremony, or as non-diegetic music for the audience's benefit.[64] There is a subtlety to this example – one not mentioned by Kassabian – worth noting: the minor-mode ceremonial march that accompanies Luke, Han, and Chewbacca is actually the "Force" theme from earlier in the movie. Here it has reached a development that reflects the dramatic development of Luke's character from callow brat to his status now as seasoned hero. This is not intertextuality per se, but it *is* a use of associative layering in a deliciously ambiguous way with regard to diegesis. Do the characters themselves now hear the transformed leitmotif the audience has enjoyed for the past ninety minutes?

* * *

against prioritizing symphonic, non-diegetic music as higher in quality and more worthy of analytic investigation than other genres.

[62] Gorbman 1987: 22–23.

[63] Abbate 1991: 98–118. *Tannhäuser* brings up another interesting case of intertextuality: that caused when composers revise early works using compositional techniques of their later works. The "Paris" versions of *Tannhäuser* have more than a whiff of *Tristan* to them (notably in the Act I motion from the overture to the Venusburg music); that is, a new musical idiom mixes with the old. Something similar happens in reverse in John Williams's scores to *Star Wars* episodes I, II, and III, which import music from the original trilogy into a new musical and filmic context.

[64] Kassabian 1994: 75–76.

In closing, let us mention that at least one author has cast the associative layering between piece-specific and cultural-generic associations as another kind of binary – that between private and public.[65] Most works of music we preserve as part of our cultural heritage were composed for a well-defined venue, a specific time and place. Even for those that weren't – say Mozart's last three symphonies – it's hard to imagine them being written simply for posterity's sake, at least before the (Beethovenian) myth of the deathless masterwork rose to prominence in the nineteenth century. Another way to say this is that composers write music with an audience in mind; musical meaning therefore, must be – at least in part – public, part of the cultural currency of a time and place. To be sure, there is a great deal of difference between the audience that attended the intimate settings in which, say, sixteenth-century madrigals of Orlando di Lasso were performed versus, say, the considerably wider public embraced at the premiere of a Mahler symphony.

At some point in Western history, around the time of Beethoven's life, meaning in music turned inward in a way that had little to do with the size or nature of the audience: musical ideas within the same piece exhibited a rich and nuanced connectivity that would fall apart should they be taken out of context. Even so, some of these inward-facing, piece-specific meanings did manage to spawn cultural-generic associations. They achieved this in two ways: first, by repeated performances of a work continuing until the work itself became so well known as to become cultural currency itself (one thinks of the opening of Beethoven's fifth symphony), or, second, by other composers imitating successful techniques over and over in a large number of discrete pieces. By and large, it is the latter that happened most often; musicians heard something that "worked" in another's composition and then "borrowed" it for use in their own. When this practice reached a tipping point for a given idea, formerly piece-specific meanings known only to a few became public – widely shared across a culture, and contributing to the musical lexicon as it were. It is a worthwhile exercise for anyone striving to understand associativity to trace just how musical gestures originally intrinsic to a specific piece approach universality and become part of a larger cultural literacy. That is the aim of our next chapter.

---

[65] I borrow this binary from Taruskin 2010: 528–40 and 680–82, who summarizes Classic-era musical meaning as a blending of *extroversive* and *introversive* semiotics (separable only in theory) which, in the music of Beethoven's Ninth, evolved into two sets of meanings, one public, the other private – a set of meanings that depends on the context of the music in which it appears.

6 | From Nibelheim to Hollywood: the associativity of harmonic progression

> It will be generally admitted that Beethoven's Fifth Symphony is the most sublime noise that has ever penetrated into the ear of man. All sorts and conditions are satisfied by it. Whether you are like Mrs. Munt, and tap surreptitiously when the tunes come – of course, not so as to disturb the others – ; or like Helen, who can see heroes and shipwrecks in the music's flood; or like Margaret, who can only see the music; or like Tibby, who is profoundly versed in counterpoint, and holds the full score open on his knee.[1]

The passage above, from E.M. Forster's novel *Howards End*, describes four modes of listening. While Tibby's elevated mode boasts the advantage of musical training, Helen's programmatic hearing is not without merit. Her heroes and shipwrecks exemplify a quintessentially romantic sense of drama that has comprised a powerful hermeneutic for the composition and consumption of music for nearly two hundred years. During these years, Western culture has retained both its fascination with the multi-media union of music and drama, and the problems of meaning and coherence this union engenders. Arguably, the most successful solutions to these problems, like Helen's imagination, evoke music's associative power. Many, like the nineteenth century's requisition of chromatic harmonies and musical themes for dramatic purposes, cut across genres and style periods, remaining effective in contemporary film scores.

The tonal-dramatic contexts posed by modern-day film music and nineteenth-century dramatic music thus provide a natural avenue into the topic of associative harmonic progression – the ability of a chord progression to accrue extra-musical significance. This chapter explores, for two reasons, the various associations borne by one specific chromatic progression in both concert and film music. First, it asserts that there exists a common solution to problems of musical coherence and meaning that cuts across the disparate forms and purposes of the genres in question. And second, it partners with earlier chapters in attempting to rectify, in

---

[1] This quotation from E.M. Forster's novel *Howards End* is cited in the epigraph to Kivy 1990.

small part, the neglect that the topic of associativity has suffered within the larger study of musical meaning.

The progression in question is the evocative combination of two minor triads whose roots lie a major third apart – perhaps best-known as the opening of Wagner's notorious "Tarnhelm" music. During the scene in *Das Rheingold* when this music first sounds, Mime, the dwarven smith, presents the mysterious Tarnhelm to his brother, Alberich, ruler of the benighted realm of Nibelheim. As Alberich activates the helm's dark magic, we learn of its powers: it enables the wearer to vanish into a grey mist, it transforms the wearer into any creature imaginable, and it transports the wearer vast distances almost instantaneously.

The effectiveness of the "Tarnhelm" music relies not only on the murky timbre of muted horns, the unusual harmonic progression, and the rarely used tonal center of g♯ minor, but also on its coincidence with the drama – its indexical nature, in Peircian terms.[2] In earlier chapters, we revisited the theories Wagner laid out in his treatises of the late 1840s and early 1850s[3] – theories that suggest that musical themes accrue the emotional residue of the scene they accompany.[4] We recall that these associative moments can be foreshadowed before the listener has formed the association, and reiterated later in the drama when the composer wishes to evoke the feeling of the original scene.[5] Wagner's theory presupposed that thematic association would operate in any number of specific dramatic situations. What he did not emphasize was that such associative themes were most effective when they relied not only on piece-specific cues linked to the drama at hand, but also on time-honored cultural tropes, to reinforce their meaning.[6]

Both cultural and piece-specific associations operate on the natural link between memory and emotion. Anyone who has experienced the stimulus

---

[2] See Bribitzer-Stull 2006a for an account of the origins of the Wagnerian associative theme and associative tonality in Wagner's first opera, *Die Feen*, and Bribitzer-Stull 2006b for a study of the connection between key associations and tonal structure in nineteenth-century music.

[3] See, especially, Wagner 1966b: 329–30ff.

[4] Or, cast in the language of the film critic: it [the associative theme] creates a kind of *memoire involontaire* and a sense of active expectation within the filmic context by linking characters and situations from the filmic past to those of the filmic present while also, at certain points, paving the way for the filmic future. A recent study by Annabel Cohen concerning the psychological effects of combining music with drama supports Wagner's theory: one of Cohen's described effects is association – things happen at the same time and, because of connotative overlap (as in metaphor), one can evoke the other even when only one appears. See Cohen 1990.

[5] Brown 1988: 201.

[6] See Ratner 1980: chapter 2 for a discussion of *topoi* in the context of eighteenth-century music and Hatten 1994 for the use of these *topoi* as meaning-filled signs in Beethoven. Refer to Chapters 4 and 5 in this volume for a more thorough discussion of this phenomenon.

of vague emotional arousal followed only later by a self-interrogation of why the arousal occurred will understand memory's associative link between emotion and experience. (Driving by "Val's Pie Shoppe" on the interstate, for example, may result in a vague, kneejerk emotional response: positive if Val recalls the name of a favorite third-grade girlfriend, negative if Val was the strict school librarian.) Evolutionarily speaking, it makes sense for human beings to associate emotion with experience and for memory to recall the emotion first and foremost since survival might depend on a snap judgment to repeat a positive experience or avoid a negative one. Recent research in neuroscience suggests this to be the case, with particularly strong or multi-faceted memories initiating a neuronal avalanche of emotions that cascade by in rapid succession.[7] Unexpectedly running into an old flame, for instance, could set off a neuronal avalanche and evoke a particularly strong mix of emotions, impressions, and memories, not unlike the effect Wagner strove for with the piling up of themes at the end of *Götterdämmerung*.

The human propensity for association extends, of course, to all sorts of situations, resulting in our assigning meaning to otherwise meaningless things. Magic numbers, lucky underwear, and the song that was playing during one's first kiss are all common examples. While the vast majority of these associations are personal in nature – meaningless to anyone else – some, like the owl's association with wisdom, achieve the status of cultural tropes. This phenomenon is well known in music, exemplified by the association of English horn and pastoral, E♭ major and heroism, or low register and darkness. Post-cadential plagal progressions, the minor mode, horn fifths, and so on all have well-established cultural associations for reasons ranging from the onomatopoeic to the arbitrary.

In the case of the "Tarnhelm," Wagner may have succeeded too well in his effort to establish an emotional association. This music not only remains dramatically effective throughout *The Ring*, but also its idiosyncratic harmonic progression – two minor triads a major third apart – came to exhibit a remarkable commonality of connotation throughout the later nineteenth century, frequently evoking the sinister, the eerie, and the eldritch.[8] Most recently, the "Tarnhelm" progression has achieved an

---

[7] See Beggs and Plenz 2004.

[8] Note that my definition of "associative harmonic progression" is categorically distinct from the use of "associative" in reference to pitch collections in the writings of previous scholars. In Babbitt 1961, Lewin 1962, Wintle 1976, Sobaskie 1985, and Sobaskie 1987, for instance, the term is used to indicate a referential or motivic sonority rather than one that has meaning-filled, extra-musical associations.

iconic role – one could even say a topical one – in music for science-fiction-, fantasy-, and horror-themed movies composed during the post-1975 renaissance of the orchestral film score.

This suggestion of leitmotif-as-topic is not to say that every leitmotif becomes topical in later music. In fact, the situation is quite a bit more complicated than that. Some leitmotifs engage with Ratner's eighteenth-century topics,[9] others invoke topics newly emergent in the nineteenth century, and still others hark back to more ancient tropes. Many leitmotifs are not topical at all, and those that are reach out beyond the confines of the score.[10] As Raymond Monelle states:

it is not enough to identify a motive, give it a label, and then move on to the next. Each topic may signify a large semantic world, connected to aspects of contemporary society, literary themes, and older traditions.[11]

As Monelle explores the "riding" or "horse" topic in Wagner's *Ring* and its resonance with "contemporary society, literary themes, and older traditions," this chapter attempts a thorough-going exploration of the "Tarnhelm" music and how it begat a new topic that has now become commonplace in later art and film music.

Before examining some of these later examples, though, let us first consider what it is that makes the "Tarnhelm" progression itself so special. Turning to Example 6.1, we will investigate its structure from a variety of vantage points. The sketch in Example 6.1a suggests hearing the "Tarnhelm" music as the expansion of a melodic upper-neighbor gesture. The g♯ minor tonic is prolonged by the soprano half-step from D♯ to E both in mm. 1–4 and over the entirety of the theme, creating an internal motivic parallelism of sorts.[12] While the Roman numerals below the score indicate that the harmonic support for 6̂ is the chromatically altered minor submediant, the analysis stresses the contrapuntal upper-voice neighbor tonic prolongation over the harmonic progression.

Example 6.1b, a presentation of three early Tarnhelm progressions in *Das Rheingold*, reverses this emphasis; parsimonious voice-leading implies counterpoint but it is triadic transformation that comes to the fore. In David Kopp's recent monograph, *Chromatic Transformations in Nineteenth-Century Music*, triadic third progressions such as these, in which one common tone is retained and the other voices move by step,

[9] See Ratner 1980.   [10] See Monelle 2000: 41–80.   [11] Monelle 2000: 79.
[12] Buvkhart 1978 lays out the classic treatment of such parallelisms in Schenkerian thought is laid out in Burkhart 1978.

A.

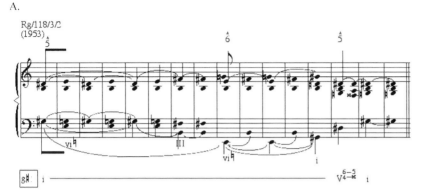

B.

"Tarnhelm"	"Tarnhelm"	"Tarnhelm" music
Surface Level	Deeper Level	interrupts half
Motions	Motions	cadence in c
Rg/118/3/2–4	Rg/118/3/2–4/8	Rg/118/2/5–3/2

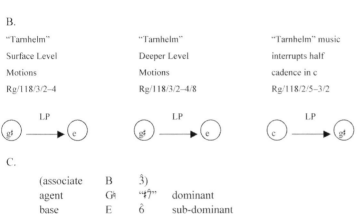

C.

(associate	B	3̂)	
agent	G♮	"♯7̂"	dominant
base	E	6̂	sub-dominant

D.

•   The pentachordal collection of pitch-classes in the "Tarnhelm" progression, above (G♮, G♯, B, D♯, E or {3, 4, 7, 8, B}) comprises set class 5-21 [01458]

•   [01458] is also the set-class for the I – ♭VI progression often associated with a more benevolent otherworldliness (e.g., Schubert's "Nacht und Träume")

•   [01458] is the only pentachordal set class abstractly included in the "Magic" all-combinatorial E hexachord 6-20 [014589]

•   [014] is the most salient trichord in both SC 5-21 [01458] and SC 6-20 [014589], being abstractly included in both more times than any other trichord

Example 6.1 Wagner's "Tarnhelm" progression

a. Analytic sketch
b. Neo-Riemannian transformational parallelisms
c. Scale-degree functions
d. Set-theory observations

are called "chromatic," to distinguish them from the "diatonic" (two common tones) and the "disjunct" (no common tones).[13] The Neo-Riemannian L and P operations make explicit the two voice-leading moves, each operation indicating the stepwise motion of one note of the triad.[14] This LP progression in the music is immediately followed by a PL progression, effecting a harmonic oscillation between g♯ and e. While Example 6.1a points to the structural parallelism between tonic prolongation in mm. 1–4 and the entire theme, Example 6.1b suggests that the theme's harmonic progression – major third root motion between minor triads or keys – is the unifying force in this music.

A third vantage point arises from a discussion of the "Tarnhelm" music in a recent article by Kevin Swinden[15] (see Example 6.1c). Invoking Daniel Harrison's monograph of a decade before, Swinden points to the scale-degree constituency of the minor submediant triad to explain this chord's mixed functionality.[16] The triad includes not only the dominant-functioned, respelled leading-tone "agent," but also the subdominant-functioned "base," – the submediant – creating a delicious functional ambiguity perfectly suited to the dramatic moment at hand. The ambiguity created by this oscillation of sonorities in the "Tarnhelm" theme thus has a tonality-abrogating effect, one reason why it is well suited to association with things dark and unknown.[17]

Example 6.1d displays the set class constituency of the "Tarnhelm" progression. Of interest here is the associative similarity with the progression of two *major* triads whose roots lie a major third apart – another nineteenth-century trope commonly associated with the benevolent aspects of magic, mystery, and otherworldliness.[18] Moreover, this [01458] pentachord is the

---

[13] See Kopp 2002: 10–11.

[14] For a fully formal exposition of the L and P operations see (among others) Hyer 1995. I use L and P here rather than Kopp's M in order to explicitly show the two voice-leading moves involved. This usage, however, is not intended to imply that the "Tarnhelm" progression never achieves a direct or unary character.

[15] Swinden 2005: 249–50.

[16] Harrison 1994, especially 43–72, presents a scale-degree-based theory of harmonic function.

[17] Note that Tovey 1949 lists ♭vi in relation to a minor tonic as neither direct nor indirect in his catalogue of key relationships. (It is thus listed as "ambiguous" in Brown et al. 1997: 161 who provide a summary table of Tovey's observations.) Smith 1986: 122–23, however, includes ♭vi, along with a host of other sonorities containing ♯2̂, in a group of chromatic dominant chords that arose in later nineteenth-century music.

[18] A recent example in film music is the [01458] juxtaposition of A and F major triads associated with the magical haven of Rivendell in Howard Shore's score to *The Fellowship of the Ring*. There are certainly many other harmonic progressions that carry extra-musical associations in both art and film music. Richard Cohn's recent study (Cohn 2004) of the "uncanny"

sole five-note set class in the so-called "Magic" all-combinatorial hexachord [014589], a set class that has come to be almost *de rigueur* for panoramic space scenes and lush, fantastic landscapes in modern film music.[19] And the [014] trichord, whose associations are closely linked with those of the "Tarnhelm" in music ranging from Schoenberg's *Pierrot Lunaire* (especially "Nacht") to John Williams's score for *Harry Potter and the Chamber of Secrets* (to be discussed shortly), is the most salient trichord in both the [01458] pentachord and the [014589] hexachord.

The interpretive potential of the "Tarnhelm" music, both associative and structural, should now be apparent. But choosing these few bars from Wagner's *Ring* as the instantiation of a persistent associative trend smacks of arbitrariness – surely this progression must occur in earlier music. Surprisingly, apart from a handful of Gesualdo madrigal excerpts, the "Tarnhelm" progression is virtually non-existent as any kind of salient dramatic gesture before the nineteenth century.[20] I find it suggestive that the few examples I have found in music prior to *Das Rheingold* (1853) occur almost universally in settings that suggest elements of mystery, dark magic, the unknown, or the otherworldly.[21] (Perhaps the rise of the "Tarnhelm" progression shortly after the "Gothic" literary period that saw the birth of such works as Mary Wollstonecraft Shelley's *Frankenstein* (1818) and Edgar Allen Poe's "The Raven" (1845) is not a coincidence, given that a fascination with the supernatural is one defining component of Western romanticism.)[22]

associations with hexatonic poles (a minor triad and a major triad with root a major third above the root of the minor triad, e.g., C minor and E major, or PLP-related chords) is a good example of the former, a progression closely related to the "Tarnhelm" progression, but not one I treat in this study. Murphy 2000 identifies a number of such progressions and their associations in modern-day film music.

[19] Another common choice for such scenes is the combination of two major triads a tritone apart [013679]. See Murphy 2006.

[20] See the madrigals of Gesualdo, Book 4, No. 4, "Invan dunque o crudele," m. 6;. Book 5, No. 8, "Se vi duol il mio duolo," mm. 48–49; and Book 5, No. 11, "Mercè grido piangendo," mm. 13–14, 16–17.

[21] Though not a Tarnhelm progression, Méhul's *Mélidore et Phrosine* includes a passage for four stopped horns, using three different crooks, playing an A♭ chord near the end of the Act I Finale (*Allegro Moderato*). This occurs after Méliodore strikes down Aimar in the darkness. See Warrack 2001: 198.

[22] That said, program music had enjoyed a topic of sorts, known as ombra, long before the advent of the nineteenth century. The ombra tradition – one predicated on discontinuity (thematically, tonally, harmonically, texturally, metrically, etc.) – tapped into music as the source of the sublime and ineffable. Dissonance, chromaticism, stile antico, moderate and slow tempi, use of tremolo and sighing figures, dotted rhythms, syncopation, rarer flat minor keys, and pallid or ethereal textures were all markers of this topic; many are audible in the Tarnhelm music. See McClelland 2012 for an in-depth study of ombra in Western art music.

The "Tarnhelm" progression, mm. 35-37

b → g

Der Wegweiser (final stanza)	The Signpost (trans. Arthur Rishi)
Einen Weiser seh' ich stehen	One signpost stands before me,
Unverrückt vor meinem Blick;	Remains fixed before my gaze.
Eine Straße muß ich gehen,	**One road I must take,**
Die noch keiner ging zurück.	**From which no one has ever returned.**

Example 6.2 Sketch of Schubert's "Der Wegweiser" from *Winterreise*, mm. 1–39

An early "Tarnhelm" progression occurs in Schubert's 1827 Lied, "Der Wegweiser," the twentieth song of the *Winterreise* cycle (see Example 6.2). While the "Tarnhelm" progression (shown below the graph) does not play a deep-level structural role, the direct tonal motion from B minor to G minor (here a local submediant within the prolongation of B) has a striking phenomenological effect: It highlights the text's eerie sense of alienation in which the protagonist speaks of avoiding the [tonal?] paths

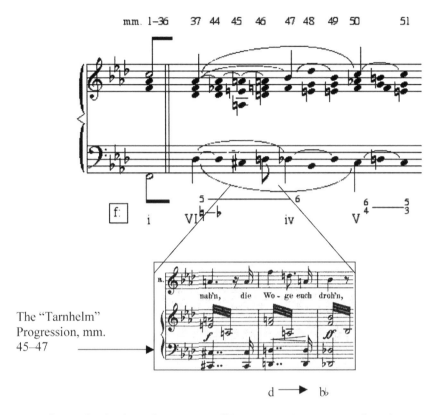

Example 6.3 Sketch of Rezia's Act III aria, "Traure, mein Herz, um verschwindenes Glück" from Weber's *Oberon*, mm. 37–51

that other travelers favor (leading, eventually, in the poem to the protagonist's desire to travel the road from which there is no return, i.e., death). Another pre-*Rheingold* example occurs in Weber's *Oberon*, completed in 1826 (see Example 6.3). In her Act III aria, Rezia, once royalty and now a slave, bemoans her fate. The motion from D minor to B♭ minor shown beneath the graph occurs just after her words, "and picture a future of darkness and wreck," a dark augury of what she believes will befall her.

A few other examples from this time period stand out. They, too, occur in the expected dramatic contexts: the Wolf's Glen scene from Weber's *Der Freischütz*, or the dark church chorus from Berlioz's *La Damnation de Faust*, for example.[23] Some reproduce the tonality-abrogating *oscillation* of

---

[23] See mm. 146–47 of the Act II Finale of *Der Freischütz* when the owls fan the flames of Caspar's fire, and m. 46 of No. 5 ("Chant de la Fête de Pâques") in *La Damnation* along with the words "burning arrows of adversity."

two minor triads whose roots lie a major third apart, but others present only the singular *progression* of root motion down by major third that opens the "Tarnhelm" theme, or the return gesture of root motion up a major third. Moreover, these progressions may involve tonic (e.g., i–♭vi, i–iii♭), or not (e.g., vi–iv♭), or be tonally indeterminate. Given this variety of functional contexts, I will continue to refer to these collectively simply as "Tarnhelm" progressions in order to highlight the shared *dramatic* association.[24]

Thus far, the early nineteenth-century "Tarnhelm" progressions we have examined have comprised chromatic moments, isolated foreground events that had a dramatic effect but that played no role on deeper levels of tonal structure. While Wagner knew, and was influenced by, these earlier works, his "Tarnhelm" music is the first example I have found that *thematicizes* the progression. Its minor triads and functional ambiguity may have appealed to a number of Romantic-era composers for dark dramatic effects, thus laying the foundations for a common association throughout western European music, but Wagner was the first to harness these nascent associations and create a lasting topical resonance out of dramatic coincidence, one that persists into contemporary film music.[25]

Conventional wisdom holds that the tonal-dramatic musical language of nineteenth-century Europe – especially Wagner's – is alive and well in the modern-day film score. While this view is erroneous (more on this in Chapter 9), the two genres do share the emancipation of isolated themes and uncommon or unusual harmonic progressions for expressive purposes.[26] Film music, like opera, lieder, and programme music, is an explicitly dramatic genre, but unlike its predecessors, it bears the onus of providing continuity to a disjunct medium. The brevity of film scenes and the quick jumps in time and space common to filmic narrative necessitate recurring music comprising concise, pithy gestures – a sort of makeshift programme symphony that both contextualizes the interpretation of coincidental drama

[24] Despite the variety of function and context, the vast majority of "Tarnhelm" progressions also feature semitonal, neighbor-note voice-leading in at least one voice. For an overarching look at the associations of several harmonic progressions featuring chromatic neighbor notes in twentieth-century film music, see Murphy 2000.

[25] Refer to Chapter 5 for a discussion of how piece-specific associations become elevated to culturally accepted topics.

[26] It is erroneous for two reasons: first, the demands of the film medium vitiate functional monotonality, and second, music serves a wide variety of functions in film, many of which are foreign to most concert music. For an overview, see Prendergast 1992: 213–26.

in film and conjoins its disjunct segments.[27] Given the brevity of filmic musical gestures, it is only natural that the associativity of harmony and the use of harmony-as-theme escalate in this medium.[28] Audiences since the inception of film music have understood these musical gestures because they draw upon associative topics established in Romantic-era dramatic music; often borrowing directly from extant music.[29]

In the 1970s, John Williams revived the orchestral, leitmotivic film scoring techniques of mid-twentieth-century composers like Erich Korngold and Max Steiner, in part at the behest of George Lucas.[30] Korngold and Steiner, as well as the composers whose music I surveyed for this study – John Williams, Jerry Goldsmith, James Horner, Danny Elfman, and Howard Shore – trace their musical heritage back to nineteenth-century Europe, and to Wagner in particular, often comparing the artistic demands of the multi-media *Gesamtkunstwerk* with those of film.[31] References to leitmotifs in writing about film music are pandemic. Unfortunately, they suffer even more than does Wagner scholarship from

[27] See Cook 1998: 98–106, who lays out three possibilities for the combination of different media (e.g., film and sound): conformance, complementation (the most common), and contest. See also Nasta 1991.

[28] Frank Waxman speaks to the brevity of film music themes in Karlin 1994: 73: "Motifs should be characteristically brief, with sharp profiles. If they are easily recognizable, they permit repetition in varying forms and textures, and they help musical continuity." See also Karlin and Wright 2004: 223–78. The authors here erroneously refer to different types of harmony (*sic*) like modality, serialism, diatonicism, and chromaticism as having different associations. Within this discussion, however, they also mention the possibility of harmony-as-theme. Finally, see Dahlhaus 1974: 73, who states: "Some harmonic progressions and even some individual chords in Wagner have the same significance as a leitmotif."

[29] Huckvale 1988: 52. Adorno and Eisler 1994: xx–xxi note that a working knowledge of the classics formed the basis of the typical Hollywood composer's career and early composers often borrowed heavily from the classics in constructing their soundtracks. *Ibid.*, 99 also note that themes' characters come from the formal functions they imply (closing, developmental, expository, etc.) in common-practice music. Of course, many film scores also borrow directly from extant music (see Marshall and Cohen, 1988), a practice that evolved into thematic film scoring by the 1920s. See Altman 2007.

[30] See MacDonald 1998: 260–61 and Scheurer 1997. The leitmotivic score, despite its popularity in certain film genres over the past thirty years, is not the only, or even the most common, form of film score. Others, such as the monothematic, the developmental, and the atmospheric, are often favored in comedies, dramas, action films, and documentaries, to name but a few. See Prendergast 1992: 227–42.

[31] See, for example, MacDonald 1998: 261, Paulin 2000, Kaufman 2002, and Huckvale 1988. Howard Shore asserts that film music is essentially operatic in nature (Brown 1994: 336) and that the music for *The Lord of the Rings* was his opera (Karlin and Wright 2004: 141–42). He also mentions that he got into film music as a venue to get his concert music performed (Schelle 1999: 324). Finally, Shore makes the suggestive observation that the piano accompaniments in Schubert song cycles do what film music does. See Schelle 1999: 328.

the "calling-card mentality."[32] This is, in part, justified because the limited
length and disjunct narratives of most films encourage a simplistic thematic treatment. But some composers, especially in the context of epic film
cycles like *Star Wars* or *The Lord of the Rings*, transcend this stereotype
and develop their thematic materials to reflect changing dramatic contexts.[33] Fantasy, science-fiction, and horror films, much like Wagner's *Ring*
cycle, are particularly rich in mythic symbolism, suggesting music's ability
to evoke the Jungian unconscious mind, and so it was in these that
I searched for the "Tarnhelm" progression.[34]

An excellent example occurs at the climax of a long narrative by
Professor McGonagall in John Williams's score to *Harry Potter and the
Chamber of Secrets*. During this scene, the professor recites to her rapt
audience of students the history of Hogwarts and the legend of the
Chamber of Secrets – a hidden room that is home to a horrible monster.
Throughout the scene, the "Tarnhelm" progression serves as the harmonization of a repeated set-class [014] melodic motive that softly underscores
the dark history of the Chamber that McGonagall presents. This motive
comprises an ascending minor third followed by a descending major third
in equal note lengths. When McGonagall mentions that the Chamber is the
home of a monster, the motive comes to the forefront: an E minor chord
under a melodic E-to-G moves to an A♭ minor chord under a melodic E♭.
From this point forward, the [014] motive pervades the soundtrack as a
marker of the drama's dark mystery.[35]

A similar "Tarnhelm" motive grows out of the "Bubble, bubble, toil and
trouble" chorus that pervades Williams's score for the next film, *Harry*

[32] See, for example, Buhler 2000: 51–54, Cohen 2001: 258, Gorbman 1987: 29, and Leinberger
1996.
[33] For a detailed investigation of this phenomenon in Wagner's *Ring*, see Bribitzer-Stull 2001. For
film music, see Prendergast 1992: 231–33.
[34] See Huckvale 1988: 49 and 52, and Kulezik 1997. Danny Elfman watched many horror, sci-fi,
and fantasy films during his adolescence in Los Angeles and maintains that this experience
comprised his training in film music. See Halfyard 2004: 21.
[35] John Williams employs the [014] cell for the first time in *Harry Potter and the Sorcerer's Stone*
as the "Forbidden Treasure" motive sounded during the dark goblin-vault scene in Gringott's
Bank. Later in the same film, this motivic cell is associated with the Sorcerer's Stone (*the
forbidden treasure*) and is also worked into the cadence of the second phrase of the
"Voldemort" theme. There is even an arch evocation of this music when Hermione remarks
that as long as Dumbledore is around Harry can't be touched (i.e., he's the treasure that is being
guarded!).
Interested readers are encouraged to consult Morgan 2011 for further analysis of themes in this
film, particularly the author's assertion that themes associated with Harry (good) have musical
and dramatic connections to one another, as do themes associated with Voldemort and the
forbidden treasure (evil).

Table 6.1 "Tarnhelm" progression formal functions

	Function	Time period	Description
I	Dramatic moment	1820s onward (e.g., Schubert's "Wegweiser")	Isolated surface-level progression highlights one dramatic movement
II	Thematic focal point	1850s onward (e.g., Wagner's "Tarnhelm" theme in *Das Rheingold*)	Part of recurring (associative) theme
III	Motivic backdrop	Twentieth-century (e.g., [014] motive in Williams's *Chamber of Secrets*)	Recurs frequently as a psychological or background gesture

Potter and the Prisoner of Azkaban.[36] The original "Something wicked this way comes" cadence that ends the chorus is a perfect authentic progression in D minor with a $\hat{1}$–#$\hat{7}$–$\hat{1}$ melodic line and a running bass. Throughout the remainder of the film, this cadential gesture is abbreviated and harmonically darkened such that the "Tarnhelm" progression (D minor to B♭ minor) underlies the melodic $\hat{1}$–#$\hat{7}$ motion. It effectively serves as a musical-psychological motive throughout the remainder of the film. In its first appearance it punctuates Headmaster Dumbledore's beginning-of-the-year speech in which he states, "Happiness can be found even in the darkest of times, if one only remembers to turn on the light," while simultaneously extinguishing and reigniting a candle flame by magic.

The examples thus far from both concert and film music suggest three formal-dramatic roles for the "Tarnhelm" progression (see Table 6.1). In works from the 1820s to the present day, it may function as a dramatic moment – an isolated chromatic color that punctuates the drama, as in Schubert's "Wegweiser." From the mid-nineteenth century onward, beginning with *Das Rheingold*, the progression can be thematicized to form the harmonic basis of an important associative theme. Such themes, like the "Tarnhelm" theme itself, comprise clear statements that stand out from their musical surroundings. Finally, in the twentieth century, the progression often functions motivically, undergirding an entire work

---

[36] Incidentally, the fourth Harry Potter film, *Harry Potter and the Goblet of Fire*, also contains pervasive Tarnhelm progressions. Patrick Doyle rather than John Williams, the composer for the first three films, composed this music. As Doyle used virtually none of Williams's pre-existing thematic material, the net effect was of a great loss of musical narrative memory – as if Puccini, rather than Wagner, had written the music for *Götterdämmerung*, choosing, in the process, to jettison the thematic material from the previous three operas.

(or large sections thereof) to suggest pervasive associations of dark mystery.[37] Unlike thematic presentations, motivic usage of the "Tarnhelm" progression is not musically foregrounded, but rather serves as an omnipresent or regularly recurring, subcutaneous component of the musical texture.

"Tarnhelm" progression as dramatic moment

The dramatic "Tarnhelm" progression moments in music prior to *Das Rheingold* multiply both in concert music post-1850 and in film music.[38] Example 6.4 presents one such moment in the second stanza of Brahms's "Wie Melodien." The music in question appears just after the song's protagonist mentions how 'meaning' appears like a grey mist and then vanishes in a breath – a possible reference to the powers of Alberich's Tarnhelm. The Example 6.4 graph models the harmonic structure of the song's first two stanzas and illustrates that the "Tarnhelm" motion from F♯ minor to D minor is a relatively surface detail – the bass F♯ serves to prolong the bass D as its upper third; the bass D, in turn, provides the harmonic support for the large-scale upper neighbor to the *Urlinie* E, creating a plagal prolongation of tonic from the beginning of the second stanza (m. 14) to the beginning of the third (mm. 28, the final tonic shown on the graph).[39]

Richard Strauss also uses the "Tarnhelm" progression to great effect in his dramatic works. One example (C to A♭ minor) occurs at the beginning of his lied "Frühling" to highlight the opening text "in shadowy caverns" (see Example 6.5). Another "Tarnhelm" progression (F to A minor) accompanies the Page's eerie description of the moon as a dead woman at the

[37] The examples in this chapter seem to argue that the "Tarnhelm" progression *only* occurs in dramatic music linked to mystery, dark magic, the eldritch, and the otherworldly. While a surprisingly large percentage of the examples I have found do bear this association, there are certainly counter-examples. (The fourth movement of Berlioz's *Harold in Italy*, mm. 217–19 and 380–82, and John Williams's 2005 score to *Memoirs of a Geisha* are but two.)

[38] The third act of Berlioz's *Les Troyens* (1856–58) not only includes the "Tarnhelm" progression, but also a quartet of stopped horns (see mm. 119–20 during the appearance of Hector's ghost)!

[39] I wish to thank Bob Gauldin for showing me this example. Interested readers may wish to consult Laufer 1971 for another Schenkerian analysis of this song. My analysis differs from Laufer's in two important respects. First, I read the second stanza as a large I–IV–I expansion while Laufer reads it as I–vi–I. Second, Laufer reads the upper voice as a 3-line, I read it as a 5-line. Both upper-voice readings require invoking implied tones; Laufer's highlights many motivic thirds while mine highlights contrapuntal parallelisms between the opening and the second stanza; my reading also keeps the *Urlinie* somewhat "hidden" in the texture (cf. the text of the poem) until the end of the song.

The "Tarnhelm" progression, mm. 25–28 →

f♯ ⟶ d

Wie Melodien (second stanza)	Like Melodies (trans. Klaus Groth)
Doch kommt das Wort und faßt es und führt es vor das Aug', **wie Nebelgrau erblaßt es und schwindet wie ein Hauch.**	The word then comes and grasps it, and leads it before my eyes; **like mist it evanesces, and vanishes like a whiff.**

Example 6.4 Sketch of Brahms's "Wie Melodien," Op. 105/1, mm. 1–28

opening of *Salome* (see Example 6.6).[40] In both cases, these are isolated harmonic progressions used to highlight a specific textual/dramatic

[40] The same progression occurs a few measures earlier in *Salome*, when the Page says that the moon looks like a woman rising from a tomb, mm. 12–15. It also occurs near the end of the opera during Salome's Tanz, three and four bars before letter Q or bars 5 and 6 of *wieder erstes Zeitmass*.

Frühling (first stanza)   Spring (trans. Bribitzer-Stull)

In dämmrigen Grüften   **In dusky tombs**
träumte ich lang   I have long dreamt
von dein Bäumen und blauen Lüften,   of your trees and blue skies,
von deinem Duft und Vogelsang.   your fragrant airs and birdsong

Example 6.5 Opening of Richard Strauss's "Frühling" from *Vier letzte Lieder*

Example 6.6 Richard Strauss's *Salome*, mm. 23–26

moment; neither plays a long-range role of structural or motivic importance within the works cited.

Two notable examples of "Tarnhelm" moments in film accompany the
first appearance of ominous figures in black: *Marcato* B♭ and D minor
chords punctuate Vader's first appearance in *Star Wars*. While this harmonic relationship foreshadows the "Imperial March" to come in *The
Empire Strikes Back*, in the context of *Star Wars* it is simply an isolated
event.[41] Likewise, Batman's first appearance in Danny Elfman's score to
Tim Burton's gothic *Batman* film includes the "Tarnhelm" progression. In
this scene, a CGI Batman walks out onto a dark, stone ledge above a crime
scene. The tuba plays a fragment of the "Batman" theme supported by full
orchestra C and A♭ chords and punctuated by a cymbal crash. While there
is certainly a thematic link between this moment and much of the *Batman*
score, the "Batman" theme is usually not supported by the "Tarnhelm"
progression. Likewise, the use of isolated "Tarnhelm" progressions at other
dramatically appropriate points in the film lends the narrative a sense of
musical continuity without achieving a real motivic status due to differences in texture, orchestration, pitch content, and so forth.[42] Nevertheless,
these connections blur the boundary in this score between isolated "Tarnhelm" progressions and those that serve a more obvious thematic purpose.

---

[41] The appearance of Vader to an abrupt succession of B♭ and D minor triads is noteworthy in
that the harmonic succession continues to F♯ minor, thus completing the cycle of major thirds.

[42] See, for instance, the scene in which Bruce Wayne lays roses in the dark alley where his parents
died; the cadence to the Joker's circus music after he kills the mob boss, Carl Grissom; and the
scene in which the Batmobile destroys Axis Chemicals.

Example 6.7 Tchaikovsky's *Swan Lake*, Finale, *Allegro Agitato*, mm. 67–81

"Tarnhelm" progression as theme

Thematic presentations of the "Tarnhelm" progression remained comparatively rare in concert music after Wagner. One instance appears in
Example 6.7, the Finale to Tchaikovsky's *Swan Lake*. Here the original
melody associated with the mysterious swans is chromatically altered at
Odette's death. While the harmonic support for the melodic A♯ is not a
minor triad (rather a half-diminished seventh chord, a sonority with its
own history of functional ambiguity and extra-musical association),[43] the
melodic outline presents a strong case for hearing an implied B minor to
G minor "Tarnhelm" progression.

One of the best examples of a thematicized "Tarnhelm" progression in
nineteenth-century concert music occurs in Antonin Dvořák's tone poem
Polednice ("The Noon Witch"). Legend has it that the noon witch – a dry,
shriveled creature – comes to the houses of children who call upon her, and
then kills them by stealing away their souls. In Dvořák's musical portrayal
of the noon witch, the thematic material associated with her appearance is
rich with "Tarnhelm" progressions (see Example 6.8), comprising an
alternation between E♭ and B minor as well as the motion from C to
E minor a few bars later.

[43] See Bass 2001.

Example 6.8 Dvořák's *Polednice*, mm. 265–68, 274–75

Full orchestra, dominated by low brass and percussion

Example 6.9 Transcription of "Imperial March" from the *Star Wars* films (**N.B.** The grayed-out portions of the excerpt above comprise an incipit and tail not always included in the presentation of the theme.)

In distinction to concert music, film music frequently thematicizes the "Tarnhelm" progression. The most familiar example is the "Imperial March," presented in Example 6.9 as a marker for the "Dark side" of the Force in John Williams's scores to George Lucas's *Star Wars* movies.[44] One noteworthy instance of this theme accompanies the Emperor's arrival at the Death Star in *Return of the Jedi*. Another Williams score, to Spielberg's *E.T.*, features the "Tarnhelm" progression for the government agents (see Example 6.10). When this theme is first presented, government agents are

---

[44] Vis-à-vis the "Imperial March" theme, see Kalinak 1992: 194 who notes its tonal ambiguity, but in a different way, making the claim that the melody of the march is major, but the harmonization makes it sound minor. See also Buhler 2000: 49 who, in an Adornian turn, describes in this theme the "fetishization" of technology made manifest by the inexorable alteration of i and ♭vi, a claim that also applies to the Tarnhelm as "technology" of a sort in *The Ring*.

Bassoons, bass clarinet, and low strings

Example 6.10 Transcription of the "Menace of the Agents" theme from *E.T.*

English horn over low brass

Example 6.11 Transcription of the "Gollum" theme from *The Lord of the Rings* trilogy

patrolling dark woods, looking for the alien spaceship. The shots and camera angles imply that the filmic narrative at this moment is from E.T.'s point of view: even commonplace items like keys, flashlights, and trucks are made to appear menacing and otherworldly. Thus the use of the "Tarnhelm" progression is fitting, given the appearance these men must have to the alien. Moreover, Williams emphasizes the "Tarnhelm" progression in this scene by sequencing the "Menace of the Agents" theme through a series of minor keys related by major third: G–E♭–B. Finally, Howard Shore uses the "Tarnhelm" progression to great effect in Peter Jackson's *The Lord of the Rings* trilogy. Both Gollum's theme, shown in Example 6.11 and "Gollum's song," which plays over the end credits of *The Two Towers*, feature the "Tarnhelm" progression. As a twisted, inhuman creature whose very nature embraces deceit and treachery, the choice of progression is a natural one.

"Tarnhelm" progression as pervasive motive

The use of the "Tarnhelm" progression as a recurring psychological motive is a twentieth-century phenomenon. Many will be familiar with its implications in hexatonic contexts that feature the [014] trichord

Example 6.12 Opening of "Neptune" from Holst's *The Planets*

common in disturbing, expressionist music like Schoenberg's "Nacht" from *Pierrot Lunaire*. In more tonally oriented art music we hear Gustav Holst using the sound of this progression to evoke Neptune, "the Mystic" (see Example 6.12 in which the alternation of e and g♯ serves as a recurring musical icon that both opens and permeates the Neptune movement of Holst's suite, *The Planets*).

In film music we find a number of motivic "Tarnhelm" settings. In *Batman*, for instance, the progression undergirds the foreboding Gotham cathedral scene. It begins when Batman chases the Joker and Vicki Vale up a rickety wooden staircase in the gloomy stone edifice, and then continues throughout the cathedral scene, combining with a dark waltz topic to lend some continuity to a score punctuated by "Mickey Mousing" musical effects. Rather than highlighting an isolated dramatic moment as it did with Batman's first appearance, the progression now takes on the role of a recurring motive that binds together an extended scene. A similar treatment occurs in Shore's *The Lord of the Rings*, where the composer repeats the "Tarnhelm" progression as an obsessive gesture accompanying Frodo and Sam's stygian journey into Mordor; the progression is clearly audible in the final scene of *The Two Towers* as Gollum leads the hobbits toward the bleak land, the camera panning upward, over the mountains, to give the audience a preview of the hellish terrain featured in the final film. It then returns, as expected, in *The Return of the King* throughout Frodo and Sam's Mordor scenes. And, in Danny Elfman's scores to *Beetlejuice* (a farcical suburban ghost story) and *The Nightmare Before Christmas*, the "Tarnhelm" progression appears in enough separate moments to justify calling it a motive.[45] Even these often coincide with appropriate dramatic moments: while Goth teenager Lydia ventures to the attic and picks up the *Handbook for the Recently Deceased* in the former, and at the appearance of the opening title in the latter.

***

A while back, I was fortunate enough to have the opportunity to speak to Peter Kivy about associativity. When I mentioned that it was human nature to associate emotions, images, and memories with music, he grabbed my arm, stared me in the face, and said earnestly, "Resist it! Resist it!" I took this to mean that Kivy, like most connoisseurs of Western art music, abhors the practice of mapping external meanings onto absolute music – the "shipwrecks and floods" of Helen's hearing cited in the epigraph to this chapter. But explicitly dramatic music is another thing altogether, a work of multi-media that begs our understanding of how music and drama interact. Recognizing and celebrating associativity's multiple musical and dramatic functions allows for greater detail in style analysis of dramatic music. By applying music-analytic methodologies that elucidate the "Tarnhelm" progression's *Stufen*-centric, harmonic functions, its voice-leading transformations, and its various roles in establishing formal coherence, this chapter has suggested functional and semiotic ambiguities that shed light on the multiplicity of connections between harmonic progressions and the textual, programmatic, visual, narrative, and dramatic components of the works in which they appear. Ultimately, this comparison of recent film scores and Romantic-era art music argues for further research into the topic of associativity – a topic capable of significantly augmenting our understanding of musical meaning.

---

[45] Apart from the scene mentioned here, the "Tarnhelm" progression in *Beetlejuice* coincides with Beetlejuice discovering the Maitlands' obituary; the first appearance of Goth girl, Lydia; and numerous scenes involving the Maitland ghosts.

Appendix: Some other associative examples of the "Tarnhelm" progression

Art music

Berlioz	*La Damnation de Faust,* No. 5, in the church chorus at "burning arrows of adversity"; and just before Marguerite's "Folie!" ("What madness!") in mm. 51–52 of Scene XI *Harold in Italy* fourth movement, 217–19 and 380–82
Boulanger, Lili	*Faust et Hélène,* when Mephistopheles says "What madness!" seven bars after rehearsal 8 (cf. Berlioz, above)
Dvořák	*Vodník* ("The Water Goblin"), when the girl is trapped underwater as the wife of the water goblin (e.g., 351–52)
Elgar	*Scenes from the Saga of King Olav,* "The Wraith of Odin," mm. 35–48
Massenet	*Esclarmonde,* Act I when Parséis finds herself transported by Esclarmonde's magic to an unknown land; Act III opening when the Saracens besiege the city of Blois; Act IV
Moussorgsky	*Boris Godunov,* Prologue, Coronation Scene, at the opening of Boris's speech about evil presentiments
Penderecki	*Paradise Lost,* "Tarnhelm" progressions associated with Satan, evil, Hell's victory over Heaven, Eve's temptation of Adam, and the like
Rachmaninov	*Francesca da Rimini,* rehearsal 23 shortly after the tormented ghosts of the Second Circle of Hell pass by
Reger	*Die Todeninsel,* Op. 128/3, mm. 7–8, 12–13, and *passim*
Rimsky-Korsakov	Symphony No. 2 "Antar," opening "Tarnhelm" progressions represent Antar lost in the desert
Schoenberg	*Verklärte Nacht,* m. 251, the unseen is now revealed *Gurrelieder,* before and after reh. 108 in the Wood Dove's song
Schubert	*Schwanengesang,* "Kriegers Ahnung," mm. 52–53 ("hier fühlt die Brust sich ganz allein")
Sibelius	*The Swan of Tuonela,* mm. 8–9, 15–16
Strauss	*Elektra,* 22/5/4 right after "Reif von Purpur ist um deine Stirn, der speist sich aus des Hauptes offner Wunde" (part of the "Invocation of Agamemnon" theme)

	Die Frau ohne Schatten, Act III *Vorspiel* opening (the underground grotto)
Verdi	*Macbeth*, Act III apparition scene, at the appearance of the sixth king
Wagner	*Parsifal*, "Klingsor" music opening Act II, etc.

Film music[46]

Elfman	*Hulk*, when David Banner sees his old house (sinister memories)
	Men in Black II, "Mysteries in History" spooky music opens with "Tarnhelm" progression
	Spiderman 2, certain instances of the "Doc Ocks" theme, especially when he listens to his arms and decides to rebuild his fission machine
Goldsmith	*Star Trek*, when entering the sinister cloud near the end of the movie
	Star Trek Insurrection, when Captain Picard and Lieutenant Data discover a cloaked ship in the lake
	The Mummy, when the pharaoh slays his mistress, Anck Su Namun
Grusin	*The Goonies*, after the boys hear gunshots and prepare to enter the spooky, old restaurant
Horner	*Krull*, when the old one reveals the skull and approaches the Widow of the Web; also when the female changeling trying to seduce Colwyn reveals herself by letting her eyes turn black
	Star Trek: The Wrath of Kahn, when Kahn commands "Kill admiral Kirk!"
	Willow, at the opening of the film when the baby is being abandoned by being placed in a stream
Navarrete	*Pan's Labyrinth*, when Ofelia opens the door to the dining hall of the pallid man
Powell	*X-Men: The Last Stand*, for Dark Phoenix and her powers
Shore	*The Hobbit*: pervasive (including the coming of Smaug, the mysterious arrival of Gandalf and the dwarven visitors at the young Bilbo's house, and Bilbo's "Riddles in the Dark" scene with Gollum)

---

[46] In keeping with the film genres treated in the chapter proper, this list contains only references to science-fiction and fantasy films from the past forty years. There are certainly many older films whose scores make use of the Tarnhelm progression (Bernard Hermann's *Mysterious Island,* for one) but which I omitted to keep the analytic scope of the study within manageable limits. I wish to thank Scott Murphy for pointing me to the excerpts from Brahms, Moussorgsky, Penderecki, Rachmaninov, and Silvestri.

Silvestri	*The Mummy Returns*, pervasive
	Van Helsing, pervasive
Williams	*Raiders of the Lost Ark*, in the "Ark" theme, just after the opening tritone-related chords
	Indiana Jones and the Temple of Doom, the music for Pankat Palace
	A.I., when David's mother abandons him in the forest
	Star Wars Episode I: The Phantom Menace, Darth Maul's theme (see especially his entrance near the end of the film – a clear musical reference to the "Imperial March" from the original *Star Wars* trilogy)

PART III

Leitmotifs in context

7 | The paradigm of Wagner's *Ring*

My lord! How intolerable these men in helmets and animal skins
become by the fourth evening ... Remember they never appear unless
accompanied by their damnable leitmotif, and there are even those
who sing it! It's rather like those silly people who hand you their visiting
cards and then lyrically recite key information they contain. Most
annoying to hear everything twice!

Claude Debussy[1]

I have witnessed and greatly enjoyed the first act of everything which
Wagner created but the effect on me has always been so powerful that
one act was quite sufficient; whenever I have witnessed two acts I have
gone away physically exhausted; and whenever I have ventured an entire
opera the result has been the next thing to suicide.

Mark Twain[2]

The historical record is filled with extreme and ambivalent reactions to
Wagner; both the hagiographic and the execrable tend toward hyperbole.
Wagner's leitmotivic practice, for one, has been celebrated, imitated, belit-
tled, and consciously rejected since its inception, these contradictory viewpoints sometimes evinced by the same person. In Chapter 1 we saw that
Wagner's associative thematic practice was often oversimplified by his
detractors, which in turn produced conscious misinterpretations like
Debussy's calling-card metaphor above. While banal examples of thematic
recall certainly exist both in Wagner's music and elsewhere in the canon,
Wagner's mature technique is marked by a subtlety rarely acknowledged in
the critical or analytic literature. In short, Wagner develops his themes –in
terms of both their musical materials and their musico-dramatic contexts –
to fit the changing needs of the drama. In this chapter we explore the
specific developmental techniques he used in his leitmotivic magnum opus,
Der Ring des Nibelungen.

It is perhaps ironic that Wagner's *Ring* cycle had such a profound effect
on later Western music. Excepting his own explicit acknowledgment of

---

[1] This quotation appears in Debussy 1977: 203.   [2] Twain 1996: 18.

Beethoven, Wagner's early development as a composer was shaped mainly by predecessors whom history has deemed at best second-rate: Weber, Marschner, and Meyerbeer, among others.[3] From these unassuming models Wagner constructed an idiom that came to be the dominant musical influence on the leading musicians who succeeded him. Debussy was far from the only composer to develop a strong and multi-faceted reaction to Wagner; Brahms, Elgar, Chausson, Strauss, Mahler, Schoenberg, and many others all grappled with Wagner's musical influence and sought their own methods of reconciliation with it, resulting in a collection of leitmotivic ramifications that will be explored in the final two chapters of this book. And so, while it might be possible to argue that Wagner himself wasn't a first-rate composer,[4] no one can argue against the enormous impact he had on Western art and culture.

The force of this impact rests largely on the difficulty that audiences and other musicians had with Wagner's music – technically, formally, and, most importantly, interpretively. Thomas Grey suggests that these difficulties were the same ones Wagner addressed in the composition of *The Ring*, and all of them bear relation in some degree or other to what Grey calls the "beast at the center of the labyrinth" – the leitmotif. Although the beast rears its head in all of Wagner's operas, it was first explicitly confronted (and finally conquered?) during the thirty-odd years Wagner spent conceptualizing and composing *The Ring*. While Wagner's thematic technique developed throughout his career, *The Ring* marks an important point of articulation in his oeuvre: he composed it after a long period of theorizing

---

[3] Wagner himself implicitly acknowledges his debt to Beethoven's thematic developments in Wagner 1994: 79 and 142. It was the inspiration of Beethoven's thematic/dramatic developments in the Ninth Symphony that Wagner most revered. See Wagner 1966b: 108–10.

[4] Even an overview of Wagner criticism lies well outside the scope of this book. Within Germany alone, Wagner was attacked for a multitude of reasons: his stylistic break from tradition (by noted Viennese music critic Eduard Hanslick), his engagement with Schopenhauerian and Christian philosophies (by Friederich Nietzsche) and for his aesthetics and thes way they have shaped Western culture (Theodor Adorno) are but three of the best known.
Best known among music theorists are Schenker's criticisms. Schenker, a one-time proponent of Wagner's compositions, disparaged Wagner's music for lacking the strict contrapuntal infrastructure necessary for the unity characteristic of great music. Playing Beckmesser to Wagner's Walther, he articulated his primary criticism – that Wagner failed to coordinate multiple *Auskomponierung* spans and instead used pungent foreground flavours as cheap substitutes. The force of Schenker's reaction can be explained in part by his general hostility to texted and dramatic musics, or, more specifically, musics Schenker felt substituted a text or drama for true organic unity. See Schenker 1994: 29. Much of Schenker's anti-Wagner commentary is sprinkled throughout Schenker 1992, though some also appears in Schenker 1979: 106. For a synopsis of Schenker's views on Wagner, see the discussion in Marvin 2001: chapter 1.

on the nature of musical drama; it is the richest in terms of themes and
thematic developments; and, among Wagner's works, it has been the most
influential on the thematic practices of later composers. For these reasons,
I have selected *The Ring* as paradigmatic for this study. If, as Grey suggests,
the leitmotif is central to Wagner's oeuvre, we must also concede that *The
Ring* is central to the Wagnerian concept of leitmotif. But *The Ring* is
hardly the beginning of the story.

Wagner's thematic technique before *The Ring*

It is unfortunate that little attention has been paid to the thematic
components of Wagner's first three operas; these works, after all, comprise the birthplace of the Wagnerian associative theme. While Barry
Millington argues that *Das Liebesverbot* (1834–35) contains the first
appearance of leitmotifs per se, there is at least one important associative
theme, treated with some artistry, in Wagner's first complete opera, *Die
Feen* (1833–34).[5] Nevertheless, *Das Liebesverbot* does include the first
thematic idea to span Wagner's oeuvre – namely the "Dresden Amen," an
iconic tune that Wagner would have known from his childhood in
Dresden, and one that appears also in *Tannhäuser* ("Dresden" version,
1842–43) and *Parsifal* (completed 1881) (see Example 7.1). Even *Rienzi*
(1837–40), an opera largely lacking in pervasive thematic connections,
has proto-leitmotivic moments.[6] Common to these early leitmotivic
forerunners, however, is sporadic usage of the technique: comparatively
isolated events stand out occasionally rather than comprising the unified
networks of themes analysts have found so interesting in Wagner's
later works.

Robert Gauldin and Charles Osborne consider *Der fliegende Holländer*
to be the first of Wagner's operas to employ such a thematic network.[7]
Themes in *Holländer* roughly resemble those in a symphonic movement;
that is, they are clear, memorable, and small in number.[8] Unlike most

---

[5] Millington 1992: 143–47. Amazingly, Kirby 2004: 39 states that Wagner didn't make use of
   reminiscence themes in *Die Feen*. See Bribitzer-Stull 2006 for a contrary view comprising
   analysis and discussion of the "Transfiguration" theme in *Die Feen*.
[6] See Rothstein 1989: 254 for an associative thematic interruption in the three-part prayer in Act
   III that refers back to the emotions of the battle hymn immediately preceding it.
[7] Osborne 1993: 74. Gauldin, *Analytical Studies in Wagner's Music* (unpublished manuscript),
   chapter 2: 7ff.
[8] Müller and Wapnewski 1992: 451.

(a)

(b)

(c)

Example 7.1 The "Dresden Amen"

a. *Das Liebesverbot*, Act I, No. 3, "Duett"

b. *Tannhäuser*, Tn/278/1/1

c. *Parsifal*, Ps/4/4/2 (cf. this excerpt, from the Act I *Vorspiel*, with its corruption in the Act III *Vorspiel*, Ps/215/1/1–2)

symphonic themes though, *Holländer*'s are not, on the whole, significantly developed; isolated from their immediate musical environments, they comprise a set of musical stage props that serve more of a semantic than a formal or tonal-structural function.[9] There is a striking exception, however: the "Longing for Death" theme exhibits a transformative nature, emotional (rather than representational) associations, and a structural

---

[9] *Ibid.*: 419. That is, they stand apart from the musical structure rather than comprising it in the manner of a germinal motive in a Beethoven symphony. See also Dahlhaus 1979: 19 and Millington 1992: 161. In general, the themes are either cited in isolation or inserted from the outside into other musical structures (e.g., the "Helmsman's Song" liquidation in Act I of *Holländer*).

Example 7.2 **"Longing for Death"** variants; from Gauldin, unpublished manuscript, chapter 2: 10

a. Hd/4/2/1
b. Hd/101/4/1
c. Hd/107/3/1
d. Hd/176/3/3

relation to a number of musical contexts, foreshadowing Wagner's mature thematic technique in *The Ring* (see Example 7.2).[10]

Wagner himself argues for Senta's ballad being the emotional (and, by extension, thematic) core in his open letter, "A Communication to My Friends" (1879). Purportedly about his thematic technique in *Holländer*, it is perhaps better understood as a revisionist look at Wagner's earlier opera in light of where he knew he was heading with his *Ring* project:

I remember, before I set about the actual working-out of the *Flying Dutchman*, to have drafted first the Ballad of Senta in the second act, and completed both its verse and melody. In this piece, I unconsciously laid the thematic germ of the whole music of the opera: it was the picture *in petto* of the whole drama, such as it

---

[10] Gauldin, *Analytical Studies in Wagner's Music* (unpublished manuscript), chapter 2: 7–9.

stood before my soul; and when I was about to betitle the finished work, I felt strongly tempted to call it a "dramatic ballad." In the eventual composition of the music, the thematic picture, thus evoked, spread itself quite instinctively over the whole drama, as one continuous tissue; I had only, without further initiative, to take the various thematic germs included in the Ballad and develop them to their legitimate conclusions, and I had all the Chief-moods of the poem, quite of themselves, in definite thematic shapes before me.[11]

Like *Holländer*, themes in *Tannhäuser* are generally unrelated to one another musically and appear as extrinsic to the formal structures of the opera.[12] There are two main exceptions: 1) the E major motives associated with Venus – these comprise five or six interchangeable themes that are musically and dramatically related, serving to recall the emotional content of the Venusberg scene;[13] and, 2) the thematic development that occurs within the Act III Rome narrative. Here, thematic materials (particularly the Dresden Amen and the chromatic double neighbor around $\hat{5}$ that opens the narrative) are integral components of formal and tonal structure. Nevertheless, their musical importance is limited, failing to reach beyond the confines of the narrative itself (Tn/304/4/4–314/1/3). Themes in *Tannhäuser* also tend to be either strictly instrumental or vocal in nature, lacking the balance between vocal introduction and orchestral reiterative transformation Wagner sought to achieve in *The Ring*.[14] We might also note that tonality serves an associative function to a much greater degree in this opera than in its predecessors, anticipating the use of associative tonality so prominent in *The Ring*.

Returning to Wagner's "A Communication to My Friends," we find the composer admits to greater thematic development in *Lohengrin*. While it is tempting to eschew such teleologies, especially when expressed by Wagner

---

[11] Wagner 1966c: 370.

[12] Abbate 1988: 45–47 suggests that this may be because the themes in *Tannhäuser* serve as reminiscences of the title character rather than part of an omniscient, *Ring*-like orchestral narrative. The many choral numbers in *Tannhäuser* serve this narrative function instead, commenting on the drama as per the ancient Greek chorus.

[13] See Gauldin, *Analytical Studies in Wagner's Music* (unpublished manuscript), chapter 6: 12 and Dahlhaus 1979: 31–32.

[14] Dahlhaus 1979: 33–34. *Tannhäuser* was, of course, composed before Wagner's period of theorizing about the music drama in the late 1840s and early 1850s. See Wagner 1966b: 318–30 for his thoughts during this period on the association of music and emotion, specifically how definite associations with themes are created by dramatic context (words and gestures) and how these definite emotional associations can be later recalled by the orchestra without need of word or gesture.

about his own compositional technique, in this case I believe the composer's self-appraisal to be accurate:

Tannhäuser I treated in a similar fashion, and finally *Lohengrin*; only that I here had not a finished musical piece before me in advance, such as that Ballad, but from the aspect of the scenes and their organic growth out of one another I first created the picture itself on which the thematic rays should all converge, and then let them fall in changeful play *wherever* necessary for the understanding of the main situations. Moreover my treatment gained a more definite artistic form, especially in *Lohengrin*, through a continual re-modelling of the thematic material to fit the character of the passing situation, and thus the music won a greater variety of appearance than was the case, for instance, in the *Flying Dutchman*, where the reappearance of a Theme has often the mere character of an absolute Reminiscence – a device that had already been employed, before myself, by other composers.[15]

Upon reaching *Lohengrin*, we really do arrive at the work that provides the missing link between the earlier operas and *Der Ring des Nibelungen*; here associative themes are both musically and contextually developed leit-motifs, as it were. Ortrud's themes in particular are modified in a number of novel ways. Like the *Nibelungen* "Ring" theme, Ortrud's music is tonally unstable and fragmentary, marked by open-ended harmonic and melodic contours (see Example 7.3a–b). Consequently, this music is versatile and easy to implement in a variety of contexts. Moreover, "Ortrud" is motivically related (by falling fifth) and linked on the surface of the music (Lg/ 115/1/3–8) to the "Forbidden Question" theme (see Example 7.3c), prefiguring the types of thematic familial relationships common in *The Ring*.[16] The "Forbidden Question" itself is a forerunner of Wagner's ideal leitmotivic technique in that it originates in the vocal line and later appears in the orchestra in conjunction with related text as a sort of commentary on the action. This is not to say that *Lohengrin* approaches the thematic maturity of *The Ring*; the number of themes in *Lohengrin* is comparatively small and many are "stage props" like those in the earlier operas. Moreover, most of the principal themes ("Grail," "Elsa," "Lohengrin," and the "Forbidden Question") comprise closed periods, much less fluid constructions than the prototypically open-ended *Ring* themes. While there is markedly more thematic development in *Lohengrin* than in Wagner's earlier works, such development tends to be more a matter of context (tonal, orchestrational, or dramatic) rather than content.[17]

---

[15] Wagner 1966c: 370.   [16] Grey 1993: 30.

[17] Grey 1993: 29–30. Certain examples of Thematic Truncation are an exception to the mainly context-based development. See Dahlhaus 1979: 46.

(a)

falling fifth + rising third

(b)

vii°⁷/f♯

(c)

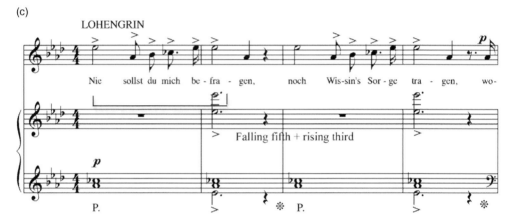

Example 7.3 Some themes in *Lohengrin*

a. "Ortrud" theme 1, Lg/115/1/3
b. "Ortrud" theme 2, Lg/115/2/4
c. "Forbidden Question," Lg/62/4/3

Thematic development in *The Ring*

Up through *Lohengrin*, Wagner's associative themes were mainly referential; in *The Ring*, they become structural, too, giving birth to the mature leitmotif. As Alfred Lorenz put it, the greatest thematic innovation in *The Ring* stems from thematic "double-function" in which themes' purely musical functions are identical to those in a symphony, but are also wedded to an associative/dramatic function.[18] Thus, the musical networks of related themes, their thematic role in phrases and larger formal units, and their role in surface-level unity, co-exist with the powerful emotional associations reinforced by various repetitions and their coincidence with the drama. In this regard, I am satisfied that Wagner achieved what he thought he did:

> Nevertheless, to be an artwork again qua music, the new form of dramatic music must have the unity of the symphonic movement; and this it attains by spreading itself over the whole drama, in the most intimate cohesion therewith, not merely over single small, arbitrarily selected parts. So that this Unity consists in a tissue of root-themes pervading all the drama, themes which contrast, complete, re-shape, divorce and intertwine with one another as in the symphonic movement; only that here the needs of the dramatic action dictate the laws of parting and combining, which were there originally borrowed from the motions of the dance.[19]

At the point he was writing it, Wagner approached most closely in *The Ring* his Beethovenian ideal of symphonic development and endless melody (though, arguably, *Tristan* and *Parsifal* surpass it). Ironically, *The Ring* also drew his compositional practice closer to Brahms's, whose technique of developing variations resembles Wagner's constant reworking of thematic material.[20] The abrupt contrasts provided by musical phenomena in traditional opera (recitative vs. aria for instance) are smoothed over by themes that are at once both dramatic and music-structural.[21]

There are many theories as to why Wagner made the thematic quantum leap in *The Ring*. One possible rationale for his evolved technique is narrative in nature: in order to bring an emotional believability to his story, Wagner required a consistently more nuanced thematic treatment.[22]

---

[18] See McClatchie 1998: 78 for a synopsis of this idea in English.   [19] Wagner 1966g: 183.

[20] Deathridge and Dahlhaus 1984: 98–99.   [21] Dahlhaus 1979: 27.

[22] See Abbate 1991: 166–67. Abbate contends that the first music composed for the Norns' scene in *Siegfrieds Tod* failed because Wagner didn't have the pregnant musical motives necessary to establish the emotional force of the narrative. In order to introduce these motives with the proper emotional association, Wagner needed to complete three more operas that prefigured

Another hypothesis is that the sheer length of the drama created the space necessary for increased thematic repetition. As we have seen in previous chapters, the process of leitmotivic "semanticization" entails a theme becoming saturated with ideas and associations that can be brought out over and over to convey messages. Each repetition can then be subjected to further transformations.[23] Though the listener may associate a given theme with a certain emotion or mood, it is the *repetition* of this theme, at an appropriately dramatic point, that cements its association and allows for future qualification of its meaning; in this regard the capacious fifteen hours of *The Ring* were preferable to the limited two or three of a stand-alone opera. A third reason may have been Wagner's growing artistic relationship with Franz Liszt. Liszt had shown a great interest in Wagner's music for years before the inception of *The Ring*. And, Liszt had already had a hand in the unveiling of another musical setting of the *Nibelungenlied*.[24] We do know that the "Magic Sleep" and "Wanderer" themes from *The Ring* were based on third progressions featured at the end of Liszt's *Orpheus* and *Faust-Symphonie*.[25] But, how much Liszt's influence might be responsible for Wagner's transformative, symphonic version of the leitmotif in general – as Wagner suggests in his open letter on Liszt's symphonic poems – may never be fully known. It is not unreasonable, however, to assume that Liszt's ideas had a profound impact not only on Wagner's music but also on the speculative theories he penned in the late 1840s on the *Gesamtkunstwerk*.[26]

Wagner's advances, however, seem not to have affected conventional wisdom; the typical approach toward identifying and naming leitmotifs began as, and has often remained, entity-centered – a one-dimensional mapping between music and meaning. Wagner himself, in response to Wolzogen's thematic catalogue, remarked that the real interest his themes provoked was the manner in which dramatic transformation "opened up a radical new way of developing musical material."[27] And so the remainder

---

Siegfrieds Tod. Seeing and hearing events on stage was a much more effective way to ensure belief in his myth than having them narrated by a third party. *Ibid.*: 160.

[23] Brown 1991: 49.

[24] See Warrack 2001: 372–73 who explains how the composer Heinrich Dorn wrote his own *Die Nibelungen* in 1853. Dorn's use of leitmotif was mainly limited to French-style reminiscence motives; the few that undergo Lisztian-style transformations suggest that Liszt (who conducted the premier of Dorn's opera in January 1854) may have had a hand in its composition.

[25] See Grey 1992: 87.

[26] For a summary of Wagner's theorizing on leitmotif, see Kirby 2004: 11–16 who also provides a take on transformational categories that is radically different from mine.

[27] Cooke 1979: 45. Millington 1992: 213–18 suggests heeding Wagner's admonition to examine thematic development in *The Ring*, offering a brief sample of the power of transforming just

of this chapter takes Wagner's words to heart, adopting a transformative approach in which *the methods of thematic developments themselves* function as a hermeneutic for reflecting upon the drama. This approach allows for recognition of accumulative association – a phenomenon in music that, like language, allows for modifiers, elements that qualify the meaning of a leitmotif. We follow here Werner Breig who suggests that:

The main prerequisite for commentaries on Wagner's works is that they should enable listeners to follow *musical processes* rather than seduce them into merely labeling the motifs.[28]

The thematic transformative techniques I describe below are not new to musical commentary and analysis, but the transformations' topical commonality of associations and how they become part of the emotional impact of Wagner's music remains unexplained. To resuscitate our discussion of Peircian semiotics from Chapter 4, it can be put thus: Leitmotifs, as opposed to other kinds of associative themes, are not dicent signs, musical nouns as it were. But the *types of thematic developments* they undergo *can* be understood as dicent; in fact, that is the essence of my argument, that the ways in which Wagner transforms his themes have something concrete and definite to say about their musico-dramatic contexts.

Before addressing specific thematic developments, we may generalize as follows. Thematic developments in *The Ring* fall into two types: those in which the musical relationship remains readily apparent, and those in which a musical/dramatic relationship is constructed between two disparate themes;[29] both are described by what Wagner termed *Entwicklung* (development, or evolution).[30] Individual themes vary greatly in their frequency and intensity of development.[31] The "Curse," for instance, is almost never developed, while the protean "Valhalla" theme appears in a

one gesture, the falling half-step vs. falling whole-step, a gesture Wagner himself suggested analysts trace through the cycle. See Wagner 1966b: 187–88.

[28] Breig 1992: 451 (emphasis mine).   [29] Dahlhaus 1979: 136–37.

[30] Wagner 1966e: 237–54. I prefer the translation of *Entwicklung* in this context as "development" rather than "variation," "transformation," or a host of other possibilities so as to evoke the symphonic developmental techniques of Wagner's role model, Beethoven.

[31] Put in Schoenbergian terms, some themes (prototypic statements and static themes) tend more toward stable formations, motivic forms that vividly present the main tendency of the *Grundgestalt*. Others (developments of dynamic themes) tend more toward dissolution in which motives paralyze the tendency of the *Grundgestalt*, harmony strikes away from tonic, and the musical surface begins to let go of characteristic thematic elements. Most themes exist somewhere on a continuum between fully concentric (tending toward stability and away from development) and fully eccentric (vice versa). See Schoenberg 1995: 253.

multitude of guises. This distinction, in and of itself, suggests a dramatic significance: developed themes represent mutable, dynamic aspects of the drama, while those that retain a firm identity imply static or fixed elements in the story.[32]

Thematic Mutation

I discuss the relatively mild musical transformations and the dramatic colorations they imply under the rubric "Thematic Mutation." Thematic Mutation occurs when a given theme is musically developed without radically altering its associational significance. In most cases, this process involves only slight modifications, changing one or two musical parameters while retaining the others. Given my use of the term "mutation," we might invoke an analogy based on biological definition: Singular genetic mutations affect the DNA but not the species classification of a given life form; just as there are almost infinite possibilities for genetic mutation, a seemingly limitless variety of musical techniques can effect Thematic Mutations. While no two transformations will ever be *identical*, recent scholarship explored in Chapter 3 suggested that there are common transformative strategies used by a wide array of Western art composers. For the purposes of this discussion, I have selected five examples for presentation and analysis.

Change of Mode

Thematic modal shifts are a common, almost trivial, occurrence in Western art music, but they remain powerful, nonetheless.[33] In his recent study of chromatic music, Dan Harrison asserts that major-versus-minor is the primary duality of the tonal system. Even in late nineteenth-century examples rife with mixture, Harrison asserts that major and minor coexist "like oil and water," not fully integrated until the music of Schoenberg.[34]

---

[32] Holloway 1985: 14.

[33] For an example, consider second-theme statements in the recapitulation of Classic-era minor-mode sonatas. They are routinely transposed from III to the minor tonic, but can we really ignore the dramatic effects of these modal shifts? I, for one, hear the second theme in the recapitulation of the first movement of Mozart's Symphony 25 in G minor as markedly bleak for the simple fact that it once existed in major.

[34] Harrison 1994: 19–20. Note that this duality exists mainly between *parallel* keys, unlike the fluid shifting between *relative* keys one often hears in Baroque music. *Contra*, Harrison, Bailey and

Example 7.4 W.A. Mozart, Horn Concerto, K. 447, I, mm. 79–85

There is, however, a distinction to be made between the ways in which modal shifts were used in Classic- and Romantic-era music. In the eighteenth century, the Change of Mode from major to parallel minor was a device often used to initiate chromatic modulation, as in Example 7.4 from the development of Mozart's Horn Concerto, K. 447.

In nineteenth-century music, the same modal shift was often used for coloristic, dramatic, or extra-musical effects. For a relatively subtle example, see the excerpt below (Example 7.5) from "Die Liebe Farbe," the sixteenth song of Schubert's cycle *Die schöne Müllerin*. On the initial statement of the words "*Mein Schatz hat's Grün (Jagen) so gern*," the mode is major. An immediate repetition of these words causes a shift to the parallel minor key. These mode changes are meant to reflect the young man's initial joy at understanding the color green and hunting as symbolic of the woman he loves, and his immediate reinterpretation of these icons as markers of despair that remind him of the hunter for whom the young woman has fallen. (The falling bass half-step, D♯–D♮, is the most obvious marker of this shift and obtains a motivic importance in the song due, in part, to its role as such.)

McCreless play down modal distinction in nineteenth-century analyses, favoring instead a "fully chromatic" twelve-key system. See Bailey 1985: 116.

mein   Schatz hat's Grün so   gern,   mein   Schatz hat's   Grün — so   gern.

pp

Example 7.5 Schubert, "Die Liebe Farbe," mm. 10–13

Though Change of Mode reflects the nineteenth century's most trivial musical-dramatic association – joy, light, goodness, and truth with the major mode versus sorrow, darkness, evil, and corruption with the minor – this associative duality reflects a central thread in Wagner's *Ring*: tension between elements of the pure or natural and those of the corrupt or degenerate – a tension first manifest in Alberich's theft of the gold in Scene 1 of *Das Rheingold*. This associative valuation explains why Wagner seemingly goes out of his way to stress a given modality for theme prototypes and crucial sections of *The Ring*.[35] It also explains why the pitch-class alterations that result in a Change of Mode from one thematic statement to another almost always transform major to parallel minor (or some transposition thereof) rather than vice versa.[36] The musical development is most often predicated upon a dramatic presentation or qualification that suggests a darkening of the theme's original meaning. While both mode changes and bleak dramatic developments occur frequently in *The Ring*, only when they occur simultaneously is Change of Mode an effective explanation for them.

---

[35] Gauldin, *Analytical Studies in Wagner's Music* (unpublished manuscript), chapter 13: 3–4.

[36] This predilection for major-to-minor shifts is found throughout Wagner's oeuvre. However, Gauldin, *Analytical Studies in Wagner's Music* (unpublished manuscript), chapter 33: 25 mentions two cases in which the opposite (minor-to-major) occurs: In *Parsifal*, the B minor tonality of the "Lance" shifts to B major when restored to the Grail Knights (Ps/231/4/3–4). Additionally, the D minor of the "Pure Fool" theme changes to D major during the Good Friday music to signal Parsifal's maturity and success in his quest (Ps/248/2/4–253/1/6). There are exceptions even in *The Ring*, of course, though most of these are for purely musical reasons (e.g., a minor-mode theme occurring in a major-mode context or the diatonic sequencing of a theme). For an example, see the sequential repetition of "The Volsung Race" in B♭ major (Sg/67/4/2).

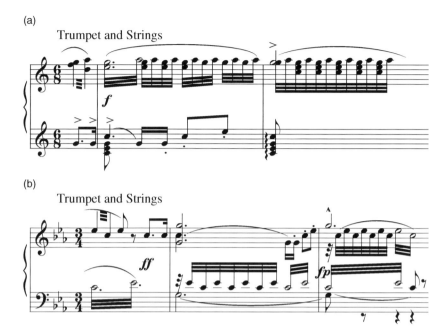

Example 7.6 "Gold" subjected to Change of Mode

a. Rg/32/3/2
b. Rg/50/1/4

Three excerpts will suffice to demonstrate Wagner's Change of Mode technique. An early example in the cycle occurs with the "Gold" theme (Rg/50/1/4–2/1) (see Example 7.6). The appearance of "Gold" in C minor (as opposed to its prototypic major mode (Rg/31/1/4–2/1)) is a musical-dramatic marker of Alberich's theft and perversion of the gold. Just as the "Gold" theme's bright major mode darkens over into C minor, so too is the purpose of the gold perverted to craft the Ring of power.

Another example occurs in *Das Rheingold* Scene 2; near the end of the scene, Loge mocks the aging gods whose bodies, deprived of Freia's golden apples, begin to decay. The "Freia's Golden Apples" theme makes its first appearance in Rg/74/2/1–2 in its associative key of D major. At the end of the scene, however, it appears in a mournful E minor (Rg/103/4/2–3) (see Example 7.7).[37] The joy normally associated with the eternal youth gained

---

[37] Here, the move is not an immediate shift from major to *parallel* minor, but rather a recollection of a major-mode theme within the local tonal context (the key of E). Nevertheless, the Change of Mode operation and its attendant associations obtain.

Example 7.7 "Freia's Golden Apples" subjected to Change of Mode

a. Rg/74/2/1
b. Rg/103/4/2

from eating the apples is now absent, as the gods, having ransomed Freia to the giants, must watch the deleterious effects of the missing apples manifesting in their own bodies.

Example 7.8 depicts the "Sword" theme. Unlike "Freia's Golden Apples," the "Sword" theme appears frequently in the minor mode. Its prototype, however, is clearly major, as evinced by its first appearance near the end of *Das Rheingold* when Wotan is struck by his great idea to redeem the Ring (Rg/213/1/3–5). Near the end of the second act of *Die Walküre*, Wotan's spear shatters the sword, and the feelings of glory and grandeur usually associated with the weapon shade into Wotan's despair and Siegmund's defeat. The music portrays this with the depression of

(a)

(b)

Example 7.8 "Sword" subjected to Change of Mode

a. Rg/213/1/3
b. Wk/180/1/3

the "Sword" theme's usual associative key of C major to a statement in C minor (Wk/180/1/3).[38]

Harmonic Corruption

Change of Mode is really only the mildest form of pitch-class modification. Comparing Example 7.6 (above) with 7.9 (below), we see a chromatic twisting of the already darkened "Gold" theme. The theme's arpeggio, usually a consonant triad, now comprises a diminished seventh chord. I refer to this twisting of a diatonic theme into a chromatic variant as Harmonic Corruption.[39] The transformation represents an intensification

---

[38] The key of C minor has an association with the Renunciation of Love. Note also the concomitant beginning of the dramatically appropriate minor-mode "Spear" theme in the bass, further influencing the Change of Mode.

[39] See Hunt 2007 for a neo-Riemannian approach toward analyzing thematic corruption.

ALBERICH

Example 7.9 "Gold" subjected to Harmonic Corruption, Rg/50/2/1

of the musical-dramatic process occurring in Change of Mode. In Example 7.8, a simple shift to minor serves only as a first step in the musical expression of Alberich's hateful deed. In a Shavian sense, the audience witnesses the rape of the natural world to serve a greedy, materialistic purpose.[40] The perverted, chromatic "Gold" statement is necessary to portray the intense emotions this event triggers.

Change of Mode and Harmonic Corruption accomplish similar dramatic goals but they differ in intensity, suggesting that Wagner's musical language spans a dramatic continuum. Musical objects in major represent the pure, noble, and just aspects of their dramatic counterparts. Those in minor suggest a darkening of quality, and when chromaticized, a profound evil or perversion (see Example 7.10).[41] Such a harmonic-dramatic continuum is possible because harmonic function is a measure of similarity, not equivalence. That is, different harmonies can function similarly (e.g., V_5^6 and vii°^{7}) but differ in intensity due to the greater or lesser degree to which they are imbued with functionally charged scale degrees.[42]

Just as in Change of Mode, the drama of *The Ring* demands that motion along this continuum travel in one direction as the natural world slowly decays.[43]

[40] Bernard Shaw's socio-political reading of *The Ring* appears in Shaw 1898.
[41] Dahlhaus 1979: 152.
[42] Harrison 1994: 42. In general, minor-mode passages, which often feature altered $\hat{6}$ and $\hat{7}$, employ more charged scale degrees than major, while other passages of non-scalar chromaticism introduce an even greater number of functionally charged chromatic pitches.
[43] Gauldin, *Analytical Studies in Wagner's Music* (unpublished manuscript), chapter 34, points to a case in *Parsifal* for "Harmonic Redemption" in which a chromatic theme ("Amfortas's

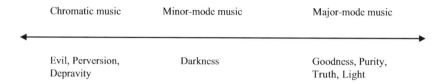

Chromatic music   Minor-mode music   Major-mode music

Evil, Perversion,   Darkness   Goodness, Purity,
Depravity   Truth, Light

Example 7.10 Harmonic-dramatic continuum

Harmonic Corruption, in particular, seems to be a favorite of Wagner's for suggesting stygian alterations in thematic association. Notable examples occur in all his operas after *Rienzi* in conjunction with a dramatic corruption of a theme's original meaning.[44] But it is in *The Ring* that we find the greatest number of examples.

The "Volsungs' Bond of Sympathy" originally occurs in Act I of *Die Walküre* (Wk/15/1/3). There it represents the strengthening bond between Siegmund and Sieglinde, growing out of motives from both of their themes. In *Siegfried*, the "Volsungs' Bond of Sympathy" appears in another guise when Mime recounts the tale of Siegfried's birth. The normally diatonic form of the theme mutates into a chromatic variant containing a prevalent tritone and augmented triad (Sg/37/4/1–4) (see Example 7.11).[45]

Much remains the same between the two versions of the "Volsungs' Bond of Sympathy." Register, contour, instrumentation, texture, and tempo (*Langsam*) are all nearly identical. The rhythm, apart from minor adjustments made to accommodate the shift from triple to duple meter, also remains recognizable. The harmonic support implied by the two themes, however, is markedly different. The rising sixth of the original form becomes a tritone in Mime's version. Likewise, the melodic triads immediately following it are twisted into an augmented triad and a diminished seventh chord respectively. The theme, repeated sequentially in both instances, remains tonal in the original version; the opening major sixth

---

Wounds") becomes diatonic. The original form of the theme clearly outlines an augmented triad. With the healing of Amfortas's wounds and the return of the Grail in Act III, this theme becomes diatonic, outlining a major triad. The dramatic connection is especially clear when considering Gauldin's comments on the role of chromaticism and diatonicism in the opera as a whole.

[44] See, for instance, the mutations of the "Sailor's Song" (Hd/43/2/1), "Elsa" (Lg/214/4/2), "Longing" (Tr/214/4/2), "Marking Song" (Ms/402/4/1), and "Grail" (Ps/104/4/1, upper staff).

[45] Gauldin, *Analytical Studies in Wagner's Music* (unpublished manuscript), chapter 15 traces the appearance of this same tritone throughout *The Ring*. According to his reading, the C–F♯ tritone represents the dark forces of Alberich's Curse.

(a)

Example 7.11 "Volsungs' Bond of Sympathy" subjected to Harmonic Corruption

a. Wk/15/1/3
b. Sg/37/4/1

becomes minor in the second iteration to preserve the D minor tonality. In Mime's version, the sequence is "real" instead of "tonal," denying the listener a tonal center.[46] Finally, the sequence in the original version moves up one diatonic step (T_1 in diatonic, mod7 pitch space).[47] The bass motion and harmonic progression conform to tonal models of progression from tonic to predominant.[48] The iterations in the corrupted version move

---

[46] See Proctor 1978: 181–200 for a discussion of the transposition operation in later nineteenth-century music.

[47] See Santa 1999 for definitions of various scale moduli. The motion up one diatonic scale degree in the Wagner example conforms to Santa's motion by step through mod 7^6.

[48] This progression leads within a few bars to a structural dominant that sets up an even more elaborate exposition of this theme in D major, interwoven with the "Love" theme.

down chromatically (T_{-3} in chromatic, mod12 pitch space) and suggest Phrygian half-cadences in two different keys. Rather than securing a tonal center, this excerpt denies one.[49] Even the differing directions of the transpositions in the two excerpts provide one last associative contrast by relying on the culturally accepted cliché distinction between ascending and descending motion.

The change in dramatic context between these two appearances of the theme is equally clear. The original bond of sympathy and compassion is meaningless to Mime. When recounting his tale of the gravid Sieglinde, he can think only of his possible benefit from the situation (*"aus Erbarmen allein barg ich dich hier: nun hab' ich lieblichen Lohn. Was verhofft' ich Thor mir auch Dank?"*).[50] Thus, the corruption of the theme accompanying his tale reflects Mime's perversion of the sentiment originally expressed by the "Volsungs' Bond of Sympathy."

While the examples above all represent a generic twisting of the original meaning of a theme, our final example illustrates how Harmonic Corruption can have specific connotations. During Act I of *Götterdämmerung*, Brünnhilde's sister valkyrie Waltraute visits her in the hope that Brünnhilde will relinquish the Ring. While Waltraute relays the tale of Wotan's defeat, the felling of the world ash tree, and the imminent transformation of Valhalla into the gods' funeral pyre, the dotted rising thirds of the "Valhalla" theme, appropriately enough, are corrupted. The chromatic harmonies Wagner chooses, however, put a subtle spin on our hearing of "Valhalla" (Gd/101/3/1);[51] the harmonic motion from i to ♭vi suggesting the sinister "Tarnhelm" progression.[52] The allusion is confirmed when "Valhalla" ends with the "Tarnhelm" theme's characteristic cadence on an open fifth in the upper voices. Melodic contour and rhythm, however, remain true to the "Valhalla" prototype (see Example 7.12a). A few moments later (Gd/104/1/3) "Valhalla" is further corrupted, this time by the harmonies that comprise the "Magic Potion" theme (see Example 7.12b). The music shown here is the second of two such

---

[49] Wagner goes on to continue his parody of the "Volsungs' Bond of Sympathy" by adding the aforementioned "Love" theme reharmonized with the "Misfortune" (half-diminished seventh) chord.

[50] Wagner 1881–83, v. 6: 135.

[51] This corrupted version of "Valhalla" appears many times in the Waltraute/Brünnhilde scene. The occurrence cited here is but one iteration. See also Wk/129/4/3–130/2/2 when this same corrupted version plays a role in "Wotan's Blessing upon the Nibelung's Son," a composite theme discussed later in this chapter.

[52] This example is not unlike the moment in *Otello* when Iago's poison motive actually "infects" Otello's music. See Noske 1994: 42–44.

(a)

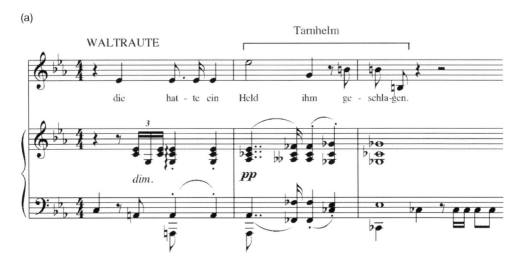

(b)

Example 7.12 Harmonic Corruption of one theme by another

a. "Valhalla" corrupted by "Tarnhelm" progression, Gd/101/3/1
b. "Valhalla" corrupted by "Magic Potion" progression, Gd/104/1/3

statements. The first, ending on V of C minor, is transposed down a half-step to the version shown, which ends on V of B minor, a key associated with the Tarnhelm and the Potion throughout *Götterdämmerung*.

While Brünnhilde may be deaf to her sister's words and the orchestra's commentary, we, the audience, are not.[53] It is at this moment that we realize, on a visceral level, just how far Wotan has fallen when we hear the

---

[53] Abbate 1991: 214–19 suggests Brünnhilde's heroism stems from her preternatural auditory prowess; Brünnhilde as sibyl hears things that others do not. Abbate also remarks on Brünnhilde's obvious "deaf spot" as well (*ibid.*, 229, 234–35): her confrontation with Waltraute. This deafness is just one of the many insidious ramifications of Alberich's Curse.

Example 7.13 Thematic Truncation of "Spear," Sg/279/3/1

musical marker of his divine hubris corrupted by the dark forces of magic
embraced by the drama's most nefarious villains.

Thematic Truncation

At certain key points in *The Ring*, Wagner abruptly cuts off an associative
theme mid-way through its appearance. These Thematic Truncations can
have great dramatic significance, and are especially powerful from the
listener's point of view; the abrupt cessation of familiar thematic material
is phenomenologically marked. Caution must be exercised in identifying
Thematic Truncations, though; many of the longer leitmotifs comprise an
entire musical phrase or period, and Wagner often restates these themes at
later points in the opera in abbreviated versions. These "abbreviations," as
we might call them, usually sound relatively complete, however, since they
contain more-or-less finished melodic and/or harmonic motions.[54] In
contrast, true Thematic Truncations produce a jarring effect by ending in
the middle of melodic and/or harmonic motions. Two examples will suffice
as illustrations.

The first example is perhaps the most graphic. On his way to wake the
sleeping Brünnhilde, Siegfried encounters the Wanderer. Following a
lengthy dialogue with him, Siegfried loses his patience and snaps the
Wanderer's spear on Siegmund's sword (the reversal of the last time these
weapons clashed, in *Die Walküre*). As the spear falls to pieces, so too does
the "Spear" theme (Sg/279/3/1) (see Example 7.13).[55] Rests inserted after
each of the last six pitches of the theme depict the weapon's dissolution; the

---

[54] For an example of this abbreviation technique, see Sg/164/4/2 and 164/4/4, which present
instances of the first sub-phrase of "The Volsungs' Bond of Sympathy."
[55] A premonition of this truncation occurs in Wk/107/2/4–6 when Wotan's will is broken at the
end of his argument with Fricka.

Example 7.14 Thematic Truncation of "Curse," Gd/337/5/3

inexorable rhythmic momentum of the "Spear" theme shatters.[56] Because
the "Spear" had been one of the most powerful and prevalent themes in
The Ring, its destruction in performance is one of *Siegfried*'s most intensely
felt moments.

During the final moments of *The Ring*, an instance of Thematic Truncation announces the spiritual salvation of the world. We hear the "Curse"
is heard one final time at the end of *Götterdämmerung* (Gd/337/5/3)
following immediately on the heels of Brünnhilde's immolation.[57] The
diatonic water of the Rhine extinguishes the chromatic fire of the apoca-
lypse and, as the Rhinedaughters reclaim the Ring (gold) that is rightfully
theirs, the power of the Curse breaks.[58] The orchestra reflects this dramatic
moment with a truncated version of the "Curse" (see Example 7.14). Not
only is the "Curse" theme itself cut short (Gd/338/1/1) but, as Robert
Gauldin notes, the C–F$\sharp$ tritone inherent in the Curse – a seminal idea
that has influenced any number of Wagner's themes and larger-scale
compositional decisions in *The Ring* – also breaks, resolving into the D$\flat$
major that closes the entire *Ring* cycle.[59]

Thematic Fragmentation

Some of the more inspired uses of Thematic Mutation occur in the
extended instrumental passages that serve as preludes, postludes, and

[56] Cf. the similar technique used by Beethoven at the end of the Funeral March that comprises the
second movement of the *Eroica* symphony.
[57] For analyses of this scene that contextualize this moment within a rotational formal scheme and
an extended reprise, see Darcy 1994 and Daverio 1991, respectively.
[58] Floros, 1983: 10 also notes the fragmentation of the "Curse" theme at the end of *Götterdämmerung*.

[59] Gauldin, *Analytical Studies in Wagner's Music* (unpublished manuscript), chapter 15: 14–15.

segues between various scenes and acts in *The Ring*. It is at these moments
that one hears Wagner's development of thematic material at its most
"symphonic" wherein he employs a technique characteristic of the Classic-
and Romantic-era sonata development: Thematic Fragmentation. Fragmentation occurs when a composer breaks a theme into its component
motives. The process is akin to Schoenberg's description of "liquidation,"
though Wagner's fragments usually retain an audible vestige of their
original thematic identity. Consequently, these thematic fragments are
often further developed and recombined to form discrete entities, resulting
in new associative themes and thematic combinations. Often, though, the
fragments themselves serve a dramatic function, representing the coming
or going of a character or an influence.

When Wotan robs Alberich of the Tarnhelm and Ring in Scene 4 of *Das
Rheingold*, Thematic Fragmentation marks the final passing of these items
from Alberich's clutches. The "Tarnhelm" theme's first cadential gesture
sounds in modified form in Rg/167/4/1–3 when Alberich asks Loge to
return the Tarnhelm to him. After Wotan decides to keep it for himself, the
same cadential gesture returns (Rg/168/3/3–4), this time true to the original (see Example 7.15a). Likewise, when Wotan tears the ring from
Alberich's finger, fragments of the "Ring" theme occur. The pairs of thirds,
descending by third, are reminiscent of the "Ring" prototype and are
broken up by Alberich's echoing thirds on "*Zertrümmert! Zerknickt!*"
(Rg/173/4/3–6) (see Example 7.15b). In both cases, fragmentation of these
themes creates an effective musical analogy – we can actually hear Alberich's power slipping through his fingers.

A beautifully fluid example of Thematic Fragmentation takes place in
the first act of *Götterdämmerung*. While Brünnhilde sits atop her mountain
amidst a circle of flame and contemplates the ring Siegfried gave her, her
sister, Waltraute, draws near. Hints of Waltraute's approach are first given
in the orchestra. The three-note dotted figure that comprises the main
rhythmic motive of the "Valkyries" occurs in the lower orchestral voices
(Gd/90/1/4), first in brief snippets and then in increasingly longer passages.
As Waltraute draws nigh, the fragments of the "Valkyries" theme draw
closer together and the "War Cry of the Valkyries" is heard as well. Most
effective is the manner in which Wagner intersperses the nascent "Valkyries" theme into the fabric of the music expressing Brünnhilde's contemplation of Siegfried.[60] The "Valkyries" fragment overlaps the end of the

[60] See also the fragmentation of "Valkyries" in Wk/263/4/1–264/2/2 when the Valkyries depart,
leaving Wotan and Brünnhilde alone.

(a)

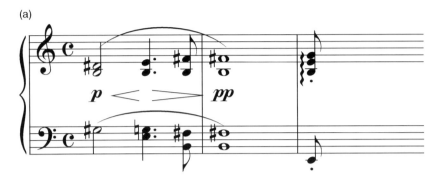

(b)

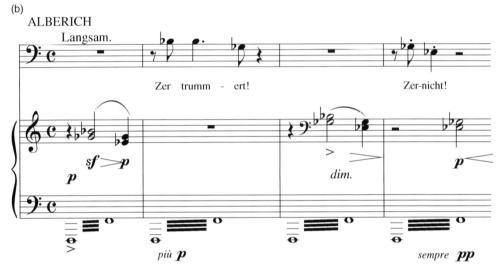

Example 7.15 Fragmentation of "Tarnhelm" and "Ring"

a. Rg/168/3/3
b. Rg/173/4/3

"World Treasure" theme (Gd/90/1/4 and 90/2/7), gradually displacing it until Waltraute finally bursts in upon the scene (see Example 7.16).[61]

Change of Texture

The final form of Thematic Mutation to be explored in this study is Change of Texture. This is meant to be an inclusive category that provides

---

[61] Incidentally, this example illustrates Wagner's use of associative themes to suggest two events presented separately in real time that actually occur simultaneously in dramatic time. While Brünnhilde contemplates the Ring, the "Magic Potion" informs the audience of Siegfried's simultaneous bewitching. See Gleaves 1988: 140.

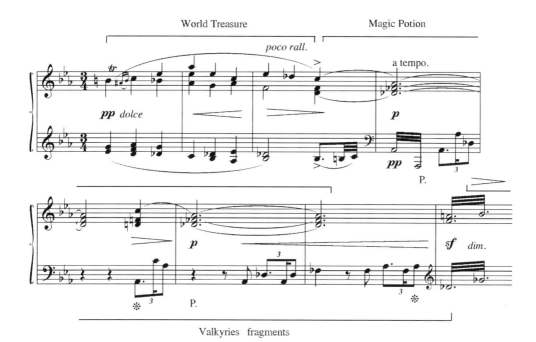

Example 7.16 Fragmentation of "Valkyries," Gd/90/1/1

for changes in register, orchestration, tempo, textural density, dynamic level, and/or articulation. In short, Change of Texture occurs when a theme's association is qualified by musical developments other than harmonic, melodic, or rhythmic alterations. In many instances, Changes of Texture are the most subtle of any of the Thematic Mutations in that they indicate a modified dramatic meaning but rarely signal, specifically, the nature of the modification. Thus, Change of Texture is often strengthened by other forms of Thematic Mutation. Two examples follow.

The first, a development of the "Love" theme in *Die Walküre*, occurs during the high point of the long scene between Siegfried and Sieglinde when the protagonists finally recognize one another and acknowledge their sibling bond. At this moment they are overcome by both erotic and familial love and the "Love" theme, a brief, protean motive, overwhelms the musical fabric.[62] The clarinet, flute, oboe, and horn (instruments often used in *The Ring* to denote tenderness and warmth) play this motive three times at the same pitch level while Sieglinde recalls Siegmund's voice (Wk/66/2/4). Siegmund remains steadfast for the winds' three iterations of the

---

[62] "Love" appears in many guises; two are marked on the example. All versions, however, share the melodic shape of a fourth descent followed by an immediate third ascent.

"Love" theme but is finally overcome and cries out the theme himself, pulling it, in his excitement, upwards in pitch.

The appearance of the "Love" theme in a purely instrumental context later in the opera is quite different. "Love" basically saturates the musical fabric of the Act II instrumental *Vorspiel*, shifting gradually from the sexual passion of the two lovers to the war-like frenzy of the Valkyries. The setting of the "Love" motive reflects this dramatic shift. No longer tender and noble, the motive is sequenced pervasively throughout the prelude, appearing in the violins and flutes in their upper registers. The sequential use of the theme might suggest physical motion and energy (in opposition to the earlier appearance of the "Love" theme, which symbolized steadfastness and an emotional outpouring). The high-register orchestration also lends energy to the theme and, coupled with the fast tempo and *fortissimo* dynamics, suggests the sexual desperation of the lovers. Note that the Harmonic Corruption of the theme contributes to its anxious quality: rhythmically accented augmented triads – forerunners of the Valkyries' music – harmonize the "Love" theme.

Our second illustration targets the "Wanderer" theme in *Siegfried*. Its first appearance, which coincides with the Wanderer's entrance, is full of broad, noble brass textures (Sg/50/3/1ff). The idiosyncratic harmonic progression of rising major thirds sequenced down by half-step reflects the Wanderer's enigmatic aura. When Wagner returned to *The Ring* after his twelve-year hiatus to write *Tristan* and *Die Meistersinger*, he applied his compositional maturity to the "Wanderer" theme in the Act III *Vorspiel* to *Siegfried*. While the tempo (*Lebhaft, doch gewichtig* rather than the earlier *Mässig und etwas feierlich*), layered orchestration, and rhythmic drive contribute to the depiction of the Wanderer's frantic mission, it is the polyphonic thematic texture that is the most impressive aspect of the *Vorspiel*. The "Riding" rhythm, "Erda," and "Twilight of the Gods" themes foreshadow the upcoming Wotan/Erda confrontation, and underneath them all, the harmony moves through the "Wanderer" theme's unique progression, signaling that the drama here is driven by Wotan's will.[63]

The many examples above have demonstrated that the process of Thematic Mutation is a powerful tool for both subtle and drastic musical-dramatic expression, effectively blending the old with the new. Enough elements of a theme are retained for the listener to grasp its associational significance, while the theme is altered to fit a new musical

---

[63] This is possible since "Wanderer" really has no distinct rhythmic profile. Its identity rests on the unique harmonic progression, in this case a backdrop for the other themes.

and dramatic context. Many of the compositional techniques used in Thematic Mutation also occur in Thematic Transformation, the topic of our next section. The distinction between the two, as in so many things Wagnerian, comes down to a question of degree.

Thematic Evolution

As any orchestral musician, and most concertgoers, would lead us to believe, Wagner's best moments are purely instrumental – the brief spans between scenes and acts of his music dramas. Without words to constrain it, the sheer expressive power of music becomes so forceful we as listeners can do nothing but allow ourselves to be swept away. Who could argue that the descent into Nibelheim, the Ride of the Valkyries, and Siegfried's Funeral March aren't among the most gripping moments in *The Ring*? When the orchestra takes over, the leitmotifs, having no singers with whom to compete, issue forth to tell the story in their own fashion.

These transitional moments are so compelling in part because they contain the life cycles of the themes. Thematic birth, growth, and decay all exist in their most explicit forms, as pure sounding drama. That these transitions facilitate scene changes is almost incidental; it is easy to forget that the thematic developments serve the needs of an unfolding storyline and not vice versa. The first transition in *Das Rheingold* is a case in point. The evolution from "Ring" to "Valhalla" at the end of Scene 1 is so subtle, so natural, that were it not for the visual cues on stage, we might miss our transportation altogether. But more importantly, *because* the transition is so smooth and natural we begin to suspect that the music on either side of it must be very closely related. With our analytic hindsight we recognize that the "Ring" and "Valhalla" themes are musically linked by their chains of falling thirds and dramatically linked by their positions as icons of power in the story.[64] But even without such hindsight, there can be little doubt that Wagner has forged a powerful bond between these two ideas – two ideas distinct enough to be considered independent associative signs, but musically and dramatically bound together nonetheless.

There is ample evidence to assert that Wagner consciously manipulated these thematic relationships in order to serve the larger purpose of

---

[64] Donington 1974: 280, and Gauldin, *Analytical Studies in Wagner's Music* (unpublished manuscript): A1–2 include these themes within a larger family of themes based on chains of thirds.

dramatic unity. A comparison of various *Ring* sketches demonstrates that musical gestures originally conceived in connection with the Norns for *Siegfrieds Tod*, for example, were altered to fit the Rhinedaughters' scenes in *Das Rheingold*. Doubtless, Wagner's strategy was to musically underscore the dramatic parallels between the two female trios. When he composed the Erda scene in *Das Rheingold*, Wagner crafted new music for the Norns and their mother (the ascending minor triad of "Erda"), and subsequently felt compelled to return to the Rhinedaughters' scene to include this new music (as the "Nature" theme, a major-mode version of "Erda"). Thus the evolution of the thematic content in *Das Rheingold*, Scene 1, owes much to the Erda scene and the original sketches for *Siegfrieds Tod*.[65] Even without knowing this compositional background, though, the audience should be able to perceive the musical relationship between "Nature" and "Erda."

These Thematic Evolutions, as I call them, bear close relation to the Thematic Mutations explored earlier. Since we likened the process of Thematic Mutation unto a biological process, we retain the metaphor here: The theory of evolution states that distinct, but related, species evolve out of shared genetic materials. In *The Ring*, distinct, but related, *themes* evolve out of shared *musical* materials. Each theme has an independent dramatic association, however, and a large number of musical disparities distinguish this relationship from Thematic Mutation. Thus, while Thematic Mutation concerns itself with musical-dramatic differences between variations of the same theme, Thematic Evolution seeks to find musical-dramatic similarities between different themes. In cases of Thematic Evolution we shall note that increased musical development and greater dramatic distinction result in a greater intensity of thematic development than in cases of Thematic Mutation, effectively elevating the mutative technique to a higher order of magnitude. For that reason, we will use different names for the themes involved in Thematic Evolution.

In extended cases of Thematic Evolution, large numbers of themes may be musically and dramatically connected, resulting in what Deryck Cooke calls "thematic families."[66] This notion arises in Wagner's own writings:

This [symphonic] unity then provides the entire work with a continuous web of fundamental themes [*Grundthemen*] which are contrasted, supplemented, re-formed, separated, and linked together again, just as in a symphonic movement;

---

[65] Darcy, 1989: 82 presents this evidence for the evolving "Erda" and "Nature" themes.
[66] Cooke 1995.

only here the dramatic action as executed-performed dictates the rules of parting and combination.[67]

The "Ring" theme is a model example of this phenomenon, begetting: "Scheming," "Curse," "Resentment," "Power of the Ring," and "Murder" (all of which feature the "Ring" theme's half-diminished seventh harmony), as well as "Valhalla," "Hunding's Rights," "Vow of Atonement," "Rising Hoard," and "Fafner as Dragon" (all of which bear a melodic relationship to the "Ring").[68]

Inspired by Wagner's nomenclature, Robert Gauldin defines these fundamental units as "*Grundmotive*" to distinguish them from the themes (*Themen*) of which they are a part.[69] *Grundmotive* are, by nature, extremely abstract and simple (e.g., arpeggiations, neighbors, and the like) and conform to the rules of strict counterpoint while surface-level themes may not.[70] The elementary nature of the materials comprising the *Grundmotive* no doubt eased Wagner's process of transforming the resultant themes.[71]

While Cooke's families and Gauldin's *Grundmotive* stress relationships between melodic and harmonic aspects of themes, in theory any musical parameter can be used to relate two or more themes, orchestration and rhythmic cells being obvious possibilities. Due to the complex interactions of all these parameters, it is conceivable, even likely, that any given theme will belong to more than one family. Thematic families, like human ones, are often fuzzy and ill-defined. Just as people recognize family ties based on blood, legal arrangements, shared cultures, and emotional bonds, so too do Wagner's themes exhibit groupings whose intersections and overlappings make drawing strict familial boundaries impractical.

Example 7.17 provides an instance of Thematic Evolution based on a surface-level motivic cell shared by the "Feminine Allure" and "Scheming" themes; note the falling minor seventh motive in both, and the harmonic similarities. In Example 7.17a Fricka mentions the Rhinedaughters'

---

[67] This statement can be found in Wagner's essay, "On the Application of Music to the Drama," which professes to be about *Holländer*, but is more reflective of Wagner's work on *The Ring* and his efforts to depict himself as Beethoven's heir apparent in the symphonic realm. See both Deathridge and Dahlhaus 1984: 72–73 and McClatchie 1998: 64.

[68] Cooke 1995.

[69] Gauldin posits eleven *Grundmotive*, all of which are strongly differentiated and transformed throughout *The Ring* to create the myriad themes. See Gauldin, *Analytical Studies in Wagner's Music* (unpublished manuscript): chapter 14, 11.

[70] Thus, the *Grundmotive* are contrapuntal cells – cells that bear a strong resemblance to high-level motives in earlier tonal music. See Cadwallader and Pastille 1992: 128.

[71] Müller and Wapnewski 1992: 448.

Example 7.17 Thematic evolution of "Feminine Allure" to "Scheming"

a. "Feminine Allure," Rg/96/4/1
b. "Scheming" Sg/1/1/1

tendency to lure men to their deaths and "Feminine Allure" sounds in its typical texture: female voice accompanied by upper winds over a bass pedal. It is important to understand, however, that this theme refers not only to the Rhinedaughters, but also to Fricka's artful plotting in this scene. She is attempting to influence Wotan to remain faithful to her by making appeals to Freia, goddess of love, and the allure of hearth and home.[72]

The transformation of "Feminine Allure" at the beginning of *Siegfried* (see Example 7.17b) casts a dark shadow over the glowing and sensuous upper winds used earlier. The new "Scheming" theme now appears in the bassoons and suggests harmonies related to B♭ minor, contrasting with the earlier major-key context.[73] It is also fragmented and subjected to rhythmic augmentation, the slower harmonic rhythm contributing to the sense of a lugubrious tempo. Even so, its relationship to "Feminine Allure" remains audible in the shared falling-seventh motive and the bass pedal.

This motivic connection suggests a dramatic connection. In most of its appearances, "Feminine Allure" accompanies the machinations of a female character whose plotting is disguised by seductive beauty or seeming innocence. When Mime and the Nibelungs formulate their nefarious plans, however, these illusions are absent and the sinister "Scheming" motive sounds instead. Example 7.17b, from the *Vorspiel* to Act I of *Siegfried*, foreshadows Mime's evil intentions for his ward, Siegfried. (Though there is no text or staged drama during the *Vorspiel*, the associations of its music are clarified moments later when the audience hears this music again during a brief monologue by Mime in which he articulates his scheme to pit Siegfried against the dragon.)

The attentive listener may recognize the use of melodic sevenths in other themes as well, like the "Ring" and "Valhalla."[74] The musical connection between all these themes ("Feminine Allure," "Scheming," the "Ring," and "Valhalla," among others) makes sense when one considers that they are all

---

[72] This theme is transformed yet again in *Götterdämmerung* when Gutrune seduces Siegfried. The "Seduction" theme (Gd/53/2/5–53/3/2) also features woodwinds and the opening descending minor seventh interval.

[73] B♭ minor serves an associative function here since it is the key of the Nibelungs.

[74] It was mentioned earlier in this chapter that Wagner sometimes illustrates Thematic Evolution relationships on the musical surface. With respect to the "Scheming" motive, its (and the "Feminine Allure" theme's) motivic relation to the "Ring" is made musically clear in an interlude (Sg/136/6/1–136/6/4) that provides a musical illustration of Mime's plans to use Siegfried to wrest the Ring away from Fafner.

tools used by various characters in *The Ring* to achieve power. Given their musical and dramatic connections, they could be considered part of a thematic family.[75]

In cases of Thematic Evolution, it is difficult to generalize the dramatic significance of a specific technique (like Change of Mode or Thematic Truncation) since almost all transformations involve many simultaneous developments. Some exceptions do occur, however. At times, when a technique more often used to enact Thematic Mutation changes the parent theme enough musically, the relationship between the two themes is best expressed via Thematic Evolution. Such a dramatic transformation parallels a significant change in meaning, requiring the new theme be given its own name. Harmonic Corruption is a case in point. Other authors have used various analytic tools to invoke Harmonic Corruption as a vehicle for Thematic Evolution. David Lewin, for one, provides a fascinating account of how the "Valhalla" theme's harmonic progression contains the theme's "seeds of its own destruction." When applied to the theme as a whole, the transformational pathway of the "Valhalla" theme's middle section produces the harmonic progression of the "Tarnhelm."[76]

Additionally, some specific techniques of thematic development introduce musical changes too radical to be considered Thematic Mutations, thus comprising effective catalysts for Thematic Evolution. One, Thematic Inversion, is often used by Wagner as a musical linking relationship implying dramatic opposition.[77] Melodic inversion had already enjoyed a long history of extra-musical association before Wagner began using it, allowing him to exploit a pre-extant cultural trope.[78] Some examples in *The Ring* described in earlier writing include: the "Curse" as an inversion of the "Ring,"[79] the

---

[75] "Feminine Allure" and "Scheming" are not mentioned in conjunction with the "Ring" and "Valhalla" in Cooke's studies. His thematic families are, however, models and are not intended to be either exclusive or exhaustive.

[76] Lewin 1992: 53–55. A close look at this analysis, however, reveals arbitrary decisions Lewin made to get the analysis to work.

[77] Dahlhaus 1979: 154 discusses two periods in *Parsifal* that feature "Yearning" and its inversion, "Suffering." The use of inversion, according to Dahlhaus, "means both derivation and contrast, association and distinction."

[78] See Elders 1991: 64 who describes the use of ascending (scalar) passages in fifteenth-century music as symbolic of the ladder to heaven (*scala regni coelesti*). While Elders does not specify the meaning of a descending scale, the lament bass and other madrigalisms make clear its negative implication. From the opposing meanings of these inversionally related gestures, we can extrapolate a generic inversion-as-opposite symbolism in Western art music from the Renaissance forward.

[79] See Gauldin, *Analytical Studies in Wagner's Music* (unpublished manuscript), Appendix 1: *Grundmotive* of the *Ring* and Their Derived Motifs: 3.

(a)

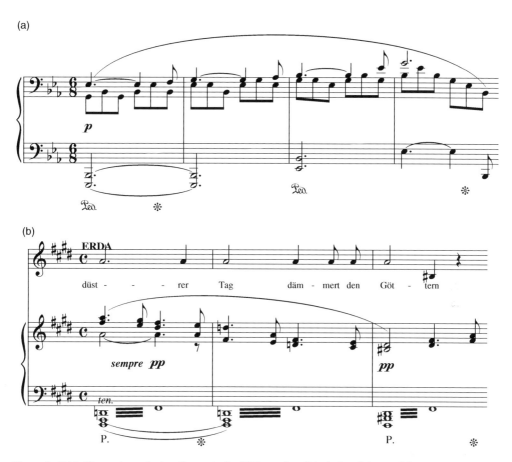

(b)

Example 7.18 Thematic evolution (inversion) of "Nature" to "Twilight of the Gods"

a. "Rhine," Rg/2/3/4
b. "Twilight of the Gods," Rg/194/2/1

retrograde inversion of "Rhine" (itself an elaboration of "Nature," Example 7.18a) to form the "Twilight of the Gods" (Example 7.18b), and a number of themes related by inversion to the "Spear" (including "Arrogance of Power," "Wotan's Revolt," and "World Inheritance").[80] Despite citing compelling examples, no earlier authors generalize about Thematic Inversion as a hermeneutic of opposition across all *The Ring* dramas. The interpretive force of such a reading becomes clear, however, as we examine the aforementioned

---

[80] Darcy's discussion of these themes can be found both in Darcy 1994: 18, and the appendix to Bribitzer-Stull 2001.

themes' dramatic relationships: The Curse is the Ring's dramatic counter-part, a dark side to complement the glory and power bestowed upon its owner. The twilight of the gods is the decay necessary to balance nature's (i.e., the Rhine's) potential for growth and life. And, finally, the arrogance of power, Wotan's revolt, and the idea of world inheritance all run counter to the rule-bound, willful, patriarchal authority of Wotan's spear: Alberich's aspirations flout Wotan's authority, Wotan's revolt is an emotional rebellion against the constraints of the laws engraved upon the shaft of the spear, and the world inheritance represents Wotan's Schopenhauerian denial of his will to power.[81]

Since the spear is a physical manifestation of Wotan's will to power, it figures prominently in the conflict between love and power that lies at the heart of *The Ring* drama.[82] Its goal-directed scalar descent is an emblem central to the entire cycle and one Wagner intended his audience to hear.[83] Many of the related themes attempt to brook the power of the spear via Thematic Evolutions that musically block or reverse the theme's directed line and, by extension, its semantic content. Themes related to "Spear" include: "Irrevocable Law," "Treaty," "Power of the Gods," "Sieglinde," "Wotan's Frustration," "Brünnhilde's Reproach," "Brünnhilde's Compassionate Love," "Drink," "Wotan's Compassionate Love for Brünnhilde," and "Blood Brotherhood," in addition to those already mentioned. Through the use of these techniques, Wagner implies that the characters are not the only ones who must overcome the will to power. The music, too, faces a Schopenhauerian moral imperative: deny the will or suffer the consequences.

Contextual Reinterpretation

Instances of Contextual Reinterpretation may seem simple at first. A second look, however, suggests that these are the most subtle and dramatically intricate of all thematic developments in *The Ring*. Unlike the other types discussed, *musical* alterations of the themes are not of

---

[81] Darcy 1987: 54. These themes related to "Spear" are cited in both Cooke 1995 and Fox 1993: 67.

[82] Darcy 1987: 53 "Brünnhilde's Reproach" also shows a musical relationship to "Spear" as a metaphor for love denying will in the Schopenhauerian sense.

[83] See Porges 1983: 41 who notes that Wagner very much wanted the "Spear"-like bass to be audible in the *Vorspiel* to Act I of *Die Walküre* since it generates the "Thunderstorm" and "Siegmund" themes.

primary concern here. Rather, a *dramatic* recontextualization bears the onus of qualifying the theme's association. Often small changes in the music highlight this dramatic shift, but the analytic process attempts to describe *dramatic* developments in terms of *musical* rationales rather than vice versa (as in the other three techniques). If one considers thematic prototypes to be tokens of an associative type, Robert Hatten's comments on context set the stage for our exploration of this topic:

> Tokens have a range of allowable variation, constrained to the extent that such variation does not obscure the identification of their type. Thus, contextual interpretation of variation in a token can lead to more individuated and less general expressive meanings than are offered by the expressive correlation of its type. Despite the constraint of remaining "true to type," tokens allow for growth of meaning, and may lead to the creation of new types in the style.[84]

That is, as we have noted many times before, leitmotifs are mutable entities; Wagner can and does modify them without destroying their sense of identity and relationship to other themes. By placing themes in new dramatic contexts, Wagner is able to construct the "more individuated ... expressive meanings" mentioned by Hatten, above. Examples of these propounded by earlier authors include Warren Darcy's conception of "thematic complexes" and Carolyn Abbate's striking claim that music in *The Ring* has the capacity to lie.[85]

Associative Transposition

Associative tonality in *The Ring* received its first detailed description in Lorenz's *Das Geheimnis der Form bei Richard Wagner,* but modern scholars are perhaps more familiar with its presentation in works by Robert Bailey and his students.[86] In short, the concept allows for extra-musical associations to be linked to keys. C minor, for example, often serves to recall the emotions surrounding the "Renunciation of Love" theme as Woglinde first sang it in Scene 1 of *Das Rheingold.* Associative tonal considerations, Bailey argues, played a central role for Wagner in *The*

---

[84] Hatten 1994: 30. See also Sayrs 2006 who takes a linguistic approach toward framing musical data and the implications that arise from context.

[85] For Carolyn Abbate's discussion of musical falsehoods in Wagner, see Abbate 1991: 19. See also the discussion in Blasius 2001: esp. 99–100.

[86] See Bailey 1977; McCreless 1982: 88–95; and Stein 1985: 43–44 and 141–87. Some aspects of Bailey's original conception have fallen out of favor, such as his assertion that keys tonally halfway between two associative tonalities are likewise dramatically halfway between these tonalities in meaning.

Ring from the sketching stage onward.[87] Tonal decisions Wagner made early in the compositional process had a causal relationship with those made later, eventually resulting in a harmonic network for the entire cycle. Thus, Wagner's choice of Bb minor for "Nibelungs," for example, probably led to his use of the relative major, Db major, for "Valhalla."[88] Even though *The Ring* evolved greatly from *Siegfrieds Tod* to the final work we know today, the tonality of many themes and larger sections was fixed from the start.[89] Evidence also indicates that once Wagner made an associative tonal decision, he remained committed to it. The sketches reveal Wagner's frequent attempts to bring back themes in their original (associative) key; when this proved too difficult in a given tonal context, he often omitted the theme altogether rather than state it in a new tonal context.[90]

Throughout Wagner's *oeuvre*, associative tonalities applied to onstage instruments as well Siegfried's horn is always in F major; the shepherd's "*alte Weise*" English horn solo in *Tristan* is in F minor; the watchman's horn in *Meistersinger* constantly sounds Gb; and the castle bells in *Parsifal* remain on C, G, A, and E.[91] Since most instruments have extra-musical connotations as well, we could even begin crafting an argument for Wagnerian associative orchestration.[92] It is tempting to wonder if there are *any* aspects of musical composition Wagner was incapable of linking to extra-musical associations, but such extended speculation must remain the province of future investigations.

[87] While *The Ring* contains Wagner's most famous and advanced uses of associative tonality, it was – like many of his compositional devices – first developed in the earlier works. In *Lohengrin* we hear Wagner beginning to link themes with tonalities and to play on the interaction between thematic and tonal association. The "Grail" theme, for instance, is associated with the key of A major. When Elsa dreams of the Grail (Lg/26/3/1–4/1), its theme appears as bII within her tonal purview, the key of Ab major. In fact, all the non-developed themes in *Lohengrin* ("Grail," "Forbidden Question," and "Elsa") occur, without exception, in one of the four associative keys (A (associated with Lohengrin and the grail), Ab (Elsa's key), F♯ minor (associated with the dark forces at work in the drama), or C (the key of the common people)). See Gauldin, *Analytical Studies in Wagner's Music* (unpublished manuscript), chapter 10: 17.

[88] See Bailey 1977: 53–54. In the sketches, Db is noted as the key for "Valhalla" twenty-five measures before the beginning of Scene 2, suggesting that Wagner had a specific pitch level in mind he wanted to reach by the end of the transition from Scene 1.

[89] Bailey 1968: 469 (e.g., Eb minor for the Norns and B minor for the Valkyries).

[90] Millington 1992: 199.

[91] Bailey 1977: 52. Instruments in the pit playing related material, however, are not limited to one key.

[92] Instrumental associations were common in the nineteenth century. The pastoral nature of the oboe, the heroism of the trumpet, and the sinister qualities of the bass clarinet were explored in a variety of musical contexts.

New to Wagner's practice in *The Ring*, themes associated with central characters are rarely tied to one key.[93] The rationale behind this decision was, no doubt, to allow associative transposition to reflect the characters in changing dramatic contexts. Themes associated with objects, concepts, and forces, however, do have associative tonalities and often direct large chunks of the music into these keys.[94] We might extrapolate from this usage of associative tonality in *The Ring* that the inanimate and intangible (e.g., the Ring, the Curse, Fate, etc.) are the driving forces behind the drama in this work. The characters themselves have little influence over events and are rather guided along their respective paths by forces they cannot control.

While Wagner's associative tonal techniques are highly advanced, they did not spring fully formed like Athena from Zeus's head. Rather, Wagner built upon associative baggage already inherent in the traditional tonal system of the late eighteenth and nineteenth centuries. By the time Wagner had begun work on *The Ring*, most tonalities carried some sort of extra-musical association; even accidentals could be suggestive (e.g., ♯ = bright versus ♭ = dark symbolism).[95] There is also some evidence that earlier German opera composers like Weber used associative keys in a manner that influenced Wagner.[96] Wagner's usage, though, is considerably more intricate than his predecessors'. Extra-musical associations in *The Ring* can be linked not only to keys, but also to chords, harmonic functions, and harmonic pathways. This, in turn, suggests that associative tonality is capable of functioning on a variety of tonal levels, from surface-level notes or chords, to background-level tonic *Stufen*.[97]

Many instances of associative tonality cited in the scholarly literature point not to *keys*, but rather to *chords* that are prolonged or expanded in some way on the musical surface – chords that play only a minor role in the unfolding of a background tonic. McCreless, for one, makes an argument for reading "harmonic problems" (the working out of a chromatic detail on fore- and deep middleground levels) as associative in absolute music.[98] The distinction is best stated by Wintle, who separates *motivic*

[93] Millington 1992: 218–19.   [94] Bailey 1977: 53.

[95] Many eighteenth-century theorists compiled lists of tonal associations. For a sample, see Wheelock 1993: 208. See also Steblin 1983. McCreless 1990: 228 mentions the flat/sharp symbolism.

[96] See Gauldin's comments on *Euryanthe* and *Der Freischütz* in Gauldin, *Analytical Studies in Wagner's Music* (unpublished manuscript), chapter 6: 3–4, and chapter 10: 13–14.

[97] For a more detailed look at the intersections and cognitive dissonances between Schenker's and Bailey's understandings of tonality, see Bribitzer-Stull 2006b: 322–23.

[98] McCreless 1982: 92–93. *Tannhäuser* presents an interesting example of such a harmonic problem. The tonal tension in the opera is expressed by conflicts between the keys of E and E♭.

tonality (hearing associative pitch-class function on the surface) from *governing tonality* (large, form-defining spans in one key).[99] Wagner's operas thrive on the tensions inherent between these.

If surface-level chords can be associative stand-ins for keys, why can't distinctive harmonic functions play a similar role?[100] Carolyn Abbate cites the D♭ major $^6_3$ chord as an associative motive of the second Norn ("*der Weltesche welkes Geäst?*" Gd/8/1/1), Hagen ("*Noth ist da*," Gd/151/4/4–152/1/2), and Brünnhilde ("*weiset Loge nach Walhall. Denn der Götter Ende dämmert nun auf,*" Gd/330/4/2–3).[101] The sound of this chord (but not its specific pitch-class level), says Abbate, is drawn from Erda's "*All was ist, endet* (Rg/194/1/5–6)." Abbate misses the point here: the association is not with the D♭ chord itself, but rather its *harmonic function* as a *Neapolitan* in the context of C. In fact, throughout *The Ring*, the Neapolitan in any key context suggests the world's end. This is why the "Twilight of the Gods" theme appears again and again, not in an associative key, but as an associative *harmonic function* – the Neapolitan chord.[102]

Like many of the other thematic developments covered in this study, caution must be exercised in identifying Associative Transpositions. Thematic transposition serves a number of musical purposes that have nothing to do with extra-musical association: shaping or elucidating musical form, for one.[103] In a work like *The Ring*, though, the level of thematic transposition often places a theme within the boundaries of an established associative tonality. If some dramatic sense can be made of the relationship between the leitmotif and its new tonality, then an argument for Associative Transposition is possible. While the paragraphs above indicate the

These keys often control large middleground spans of music. But a similar tension manifests itself between the E minor triad and the E♭ major triad (enharmonically D♯–G–A♯), which comprise the surface-level dissonance in the first iteration of the Sirens' song. See Tn/23/6/5–24/1/1.

[99] Wintle 1988: 221.

[100] Abbate 1989b discusses harmonies as *keys* and Wagner's small-scale conception of modulation (in contradistinction to a Schenkerian monotonal understanding of this music) but she neglects to discuss harmonies as *functions* (within a larger tonal context).

[101] Abbate 1989a: 112.

[102] Note that this theme appears in conjunction with two of Abbate's D♭ chords (Hagen's and Brünnhilde's). While the appearance in Brünnhilde's immolation scene doesn't, strictly speaking, *function* as a Neapolitan, I hear a strong residue of this functionality because the "Twilight of the Gods" theme has conditioned me to expect this function when it appears.

[103] In Verdi's *Aida*, for example, the only real recurring theme is one first heard in the overture and later associated with Aida and her love for Rhadames. It does not undergo any thematic transformations to speak of, though it does occur at different pitch levels. These transpositions, however, seem motivated by the exigencies of the local tonal context rather than by any associative logic.

breadth of possibilities that associative tonality embraces, we pause here for but two examples of transposition to illustrate the dramatic implications of this technique.

The first involves the "Valhalla" theme. In its original appearance (Rg/55/1/1) it appears in D♭ major, a key that maintains its association with the magical fortress (and Wotan as its lord) for the remainder of *The Ring*. "Valhalla" does not always return in D♭, however. A convincing case can be made for its Associative Transposition in *Die Walküre*. Near the beginning of Act I, "Valhalla" appears in the key of E major (Wk/26/2/3) and returns in the same key three times later in the act (Wk/44/4/2, Wk/64/2/2, and Wk/67/1/6).[104] In all cases, references are made to Wotan (in his role as the Wanderer, or as Wälse, father of the Wälsungs). The relationship between Wotan and the "Valhalla" music is clear, but why is the theme transposed to E major? Associative tonality presents the answer. Throughout *Die Walküre*, E major is associated with Wotan's love for his children (most obviously at the end of Act III when Wotan bids farewell to his daughter Brünnhilde). Since Siegmund and Sieglinde are both Wotan's children, his dramatic background presence as the benevolent patriarch is felt in the E major "Valhalla" music. One can almost sense the god, in a rare moment of tenderness, smiling down on the children he hopes will fulfill his "great idea."

The second example comprises a unique appearance by the "Sword" theme in D♭ major. The "Sword" is most often associated with C major (and later, D major) but it sounds in D♭ only once during the entire cycle.[105] This D♭ statement occurs during the final bars of *Das Rheingold*, as the gods make their triumphant entrance into "Valhalla." As noted above, D♭ is most often a marker for Valhalla and Wotan in his role as glorified ruler of the gods. The statement of the "Sword" in this key seems to indicate Wotan's self-assuredness in his plan; the first and last time in *The Ring* that we see the god so confident. The majority of "Sword" statements, however, are in C and D major. While they still convey the hopeful enthusiasm surrounding Wotan's original conception of his plan (Rg/213/1/3–3/2), they miss D♭ by a half-step on either side; in the end, it

---

[104] Like the original "Valhalla" statement, this one modulates, often to the subdominant A major. While these modulations might suggest further Associative Transpositions, I hear them as ramifications of the E major tonic, parallels of the plagal meanderings in the original D♭ statement.

[105] Note that Wagner's choice of keys (C and D major) is consistent with already-present tonal associations. Because the most common keys for eighteenth-century trumpets were C and D, these tonalities accrued associations with grandeur, pomp, celebration, and the like.

is not the sword, but rather Brünnhilde who returns the world of *The Ring* to its ultimate tonal resting point.[106]

Thematic Complexes

Composers of Western art music have combined themes for hundreds of years. The unification of discrete melodic lines occurs in the Medieval motet, the Renaissance mass, and the Baroque fugue, to name but a few. Of these, the motet most closely resembles Wagner's adoption of this technique. While the successful integration of lines by way of counterpoint guided composers of the Renaissance and Baroque, Medieval (and twentieth-century, e.g., Stravinsky) composers favored a more layered technique in which discrete lines or ideas remained distinct rather than interdependent. Like them, Wagnerian thematic combinations sound less like true counterpoint and more like vertical superimpositions.[107]

Thematic combination in Western music serves a number of artistic purposes. It can be used for economy of means (like the early eighteenth century's *Fortspinnung*) to make explicit a relationship between two themes, or to unify or summarize a work.[108] While examples of each of these appear in *The Ring*, the Thematic Complex concept refers to a specialized form of thematic *combination*. The term is one I have borrowed from Warren Darcy, and it refers to the *linear and/or vertical* fusion of two or more previously distinct leitmotifs. In addition, this new combination of themes must function like a leitmotif itself. That is, it must have a more or less specific association (often based on the associations of the component themes) and it must recur at least once after its first presentation.[109] I provide two examples below.

---

[106] This is accomplished when Brünnhilde breaks the "Curse," causing its C–F♯ tritone to resolve to D♭. See Example 7.14, above.

[107] Müller and Wapnewski 1992: 314. Though themes were grafted together, Wagner obviously intended that the constituent parts still be audible. He states, for instance, that "Siegmund" (bass) and "Sieglinde" (treble) in the "Volsungs' Bond of Sympathy" must be contrasted in performance so that each is heard. See Porges 1983: 45. See also Jackson 1975: 45 who suggests that Wagner rearranges motives to form unifying complexes. The instances he cites in *Tristan*, though, are only thematic components, not full-fledged associative themes.

[108] Brahms, for instance, conjoins previously autonomous thematic segments linearly in the codas of many of his movements. These summarizing and/or concluding themes serve to unify the melodic content of the piece and bring it closure. See Scott 1995: 182ff.

[109] To the best of my knowledge, Darcy's understanding of Thematic Complexes has never been formally defined and does not require the musical-dramatic repetition of the complex. The term is used loosely in his guides to the themes of *The Ring* (see the appendix to Bribitzer-Stull) and was also explained in his course on Wagner's *Ring* given at the Oberlin Conservatory of Music.

Example 7.19 Thematic Complex, "Wotan's Rebellion against his Destiny," Wk/109/1/1

In Act II of *Die Walküre*, Wotan reaches a crisis point. As his plans come crashing down around him, he struggles vainly against an inexorable fate. His willful spirit is associated with a new theme, a quickly rising line whose inversion of the "Spear" theme's descending scale suggests a rebellion against authority. This theme, "Wotan's Revolt," appears alone later in *The Ring*. Here, however, it bleeds into an iteration of the "Curse." These two themes are sounded again, transposed up a perfect fourth, and a third statement of "Wotan's Revolt" is, fittingly enough, cut off by the first two chords of "The Power of the Ring" and "Fricka's Wrath," the two main forces opposing Wotan. While Wotan sings a corrupted version of the "Love" theme, "Wotan's Revolt" rises one last time, only to expire with the pathetic cadence used in the "Renunciation of Love" (second form). This complex and the themes it subsumes appear in Example 7.19.

Example 7.19 (*cont.*)

Wagner combines the themes – both linearly and harmonically – to depict the powerful mixed feelings Wotan is experiencing, the forces against which he strives, and his bleak outlook on the situation. Appropriately enough, this same complex returns when Brünnhilde rebels against Waltraute's impassioned pleas (Gd/112/4/2–113/3/4).

Another complex, cited by Wagner in his own writings, accompanies Wotan's rage in the *Die Walküre* Act II monologue. After Fricka thwarts Wotan's plans to redeem the world from Alberich's Curse, Wotan's despair builds to a powerful anticlimax punctuated by "Wotan's Blessing Upon the Nibelung's Son." Though Alberich (i.e., the Nibelung) renounced compassionate love, he did not renounce the sex act itself. Thus, through the corrupted gold, he was able to purchase the affections of a mortal woman and beget a son upon her. This son is the recipient of Wotan's ironic beneficence. The music appears in Example 7.20.

This excerpt provides an example of different methods of thematic development working in conjunction to create a new association. The recontextualized use of fragments from the "Valhalla" and "Gold" themes twists their associations to fit the new, bitter dramatic context. Though the themes combine to form a complex, "Wotan's Blessing Upon the Nibelung's Son," it is important that the listener be able to distinguish the parent themes. According to Porges, Wagner stressed making a performance distinction between these conjoined themes so as to aid the listener's understanding of this moment.[110]

In addition to being combined and recontextualized, the source themes have also been subjected to Thematic Mutation.[111] The "Valhalla" theme is fragmented and harmonically corrupted. The pure major triads have decayed into fully and half-diminished seventh chords, and the root position cadential dominant in the original has been replaced by a ii

---

[110] Porges 1983: 58. The "Valhalla" corruption also bears a curious rhythmic relationship to "Hunding" and a melodic relationship to the falling thirds of "Hunding's Rights."

[111] "[E]ach of these motives had undergone mutations in closest sympathy with the rising passions of the plot – with the help of a digression in the harmony I would present them in such a way that, more than Wotan's words, this tone-figure should give to us a picture of the fearful gloom in the soul of the suffering god." These words are excerpted from Wagner 1966b: 186 in which they form part of a discussion of the harmonic changes Wagner made to these two themes in uniting them to express Wotan's emotions at this moment. Wagner also addressed this moment in his essay "On the Application of Music to the Drama": when he notes that "Wotan's Blessing Upon the Nibelung's Son" would have been nonsensical if used in an overture; it derives its meaning from the earlier Valhalla and Nature (i.e., "Gold") themes, which it distorts. See Wagner 1966g: 185–86.

Example 7.20 Thematic Complex, "Wotan's Blessing upon the Nibelung's Son," Wk/129/4/1

half-diminished seventh chord.[112] The authentic cadence of the original is weakened by the very sonority (i.e., the half-diminished seventh) that serves as an associative marker for the benighted world of *The Ring*. The "Gold" theme, too, has been mutated, darkening its major triad to minor. Together, these developments twist the meaning of the original themes to depict the legacy of despair Wotan leaves to Alberich's son. The fact that the musical symbol of Valhalla, Wotan's pride and joy, forms the heart of the musical symbol for his blackest hour evokes a sense of musical irony, our third and final form of Contextual Reinterpretation.

Thematic Irony

In this section[113] I introduce this discussion with a case in point, embracing the spirit of irony by opening with a farewell scene. The music in Example 7.21a occurs during the final act of Wagner's *Die Walküre*. A tender theme sung to Wotan's words "*zum letzten Mal . . . letztem Kuss!*" accompanies the moment of sublime poignancy as the god bids farewell to his daughter Brünnhilde while kissing away her immortality. Coincidental association of this music with the dramatic moment results in a leitmotif often referred to as the "Parting Kiss."[114]

Compare Example 7.21a with Example 7.21b, an excerpt from the second act of *Siegfried*. After a long altercation near Fafner's cave, Wotan (as the Wanderer) takes his final leave of the nefarious dwarf, Alberich. Wotan has just tricked Alberich into making a fool of himself by manipulating him into asking the dragon to give him the Ring. The dragon predictably denies Alberich's request, to Wotan's great delight. Wotan then leaves Alberich in shame, adding the parting shot that Siegfried is coming to claim the dragon's Ring and hoard for himself. Alberich acknowledges his shame, singing "*Da reitet hin auf lichtem Ross'; mich lässt in Sorg und Spott,*" as Wotan rides off in a clap of thunder. Strangely, the "Parting Kiss" theme wells up just then in the orchestra.[115] Bitter irony

---

[112] This ii chord can be heard as part of a plagal motion, or as one of Eytan Agmon's weak dominants. See Agmon 1995.

[113] This section is an abbreviated version of a more protracted discussion on Thematic Irony in Bribitzer-Stull 2004. I encourage interested readers to consult that publication for a more detailed investigation of irony, more citations, and more examples from Wagner's *Ring*.

[114] Darcy (see the appendix to Bribitzer-Stull 2001) refers to it as "Wotan's Love for Brünnhilde," but to clarify the ironic usage I cite, I will use "Parting Kiss."

[115] Note that this theme is also truncated and transposed to a new pitch level. While the truncation may be reflective of Wotan's unwillingness to linger at the scene, the transposed pitch level is due to the fact that the "Parting Kiss" grows out of the "Wanderer" theme, beginning on the correct pitch to continue the upper-voice sequence in "Wanderer."

Example 7.21 Thematic Irony, "Parting Kiss"

a. Wk/296/4/1
b. Sg/159/1/1

manifests when this once-tender theme accompanies Wotan's final dis-
missal of his hated enemy. (One might say that Alberich has been "kissed
off.") Even though the emotions between Wotan and Brünnhilde and those
between Wotan and Alberich could not be less alike (except perhaps in
their level of personal intensity), the dramatic situations have much in
common. In both, Wotan leaves another character for the last time, having
shamed him or her. The music surrounding Wotan's heartfelt farewell to
the most beautiful character in *The Ring* also accompanies his "good
riddance" to the most hideous.

Many authors have attempted to explain the unexpected use of "Parting
Kiss" at this point in the drama, but none does justice to the subtle artistry
of the moment. McCreless reads it as a "reminder that Wotan's renunciation of power does not signal a total victory for Alberich and his values,"
while Stein says that "there has not been the remotest suggestion of
anything that could call forth the motive at this moment."[116] Stein goes
on to other commentators' bungling attempts to explain this theme's
appearance and eventually concludes that this instance points to Wagner's
changing leitmotivic technique in which meaning is less important than
giving the musical dimension of the *Gesamtkunstwerk* more freedom.
While multiple interpretations are one of the beauties of Wagnerian
exegesis, I find it surprising that, in this case, none of the previous
interpretations consider the possibility of irony. The use of Thematic
Irony here actually points to the dramatic parallel between Brünnhilde
and Alberich. Since each is an aspect of Wotan (Brünnhilde as his will,
Alberich as the dark side of his lust for power), the use of the "Parting Kiss"
theme seems fitting since, in each case, Wotan is bidding farewell to a
portion of himself.[117]

Musical irony is well treated in the scholarly literature.[118] Like the other
techniques treated in this study, it lacks a formal definition and is therefore
subject to the same sorts of messiness found throughout in interpretive
work. The danger inherent in Thematic Irony is allowing Wagner's

---

[116] See McCreless 1982: 164 and Stein 1973: 129–30.

[117] These relationships are made explicit in the text. See Wagner 1881–83, v.6: 52 with
Brünnhilde's lines "*Zu Wotan's Willen sprichtest du, sagst du mir, was du willst; wer bin ich,
wär' ich dein Wille nicht?*" Also, 146 when Wotan says "*Auf wolkigen Höhn wohnen die Götter:
Walhall heißt ihr Sall. Lichtalben sind sie; Licht-Alberich Wotan, waltet der Schar.*"

[118] For some intriguing examples see Buller 1995: 63; Darcy 1987: 55; Stein 1973: 124–25; and
Dahlhaus 1979: 112–13. One of Dahlhaus's observations is particularly subtle. He maintains
that the purity and light of the "Sword" theme's C major is ironic since it functions as an
ominous ♭II in B minor (the key of the "Curse"), an example of Thematic Irony and
Associative Transposition working in tandem.

associative system to be too open so that themes can mean *anything* and, therefore, *nothing*. We have established that Wagner's themes are associated with emotions and these emotions usually have some sort of relevance to the dramatic situation at hand. Just like language then, opposite meanings must be considered a viable possibility.

Musical events can (and, in *The Ring*, often do) serve as metaphors for psychological states or processes.[119] As such, they can embody different forms of irony. Thematic Irony occurs when a leitmotif appears in a dramatic environment that creates some contradiction between the meaning of the theme and the dramatic context.[120] This incongruity results in an accumulation of associations that forces the listener to reapprehend the theme's meaning. Robert Hatten enumerates three forms of irony, all of which occur in *The Ring*: Sarcasm, Dramatic Irony (when a character does not realize the double meaning inherent in an utterance or situation), and Romantic Irony (a higher level of irony in which the author or composer as commentator invokes ironic cultural criticism or satire).[121] In fact, Wagner's use of leitmotifs is particularly suited to expressions of irony.[122] By presuming the entire *Ring* drama as past tense, these themes function like a Greek chorus, commenting upon or even foreshadowing dramatic events.[123]

One of the first instances of Thematic Irony in *The Ring* involves Wotan's noble Scene 2 aria in *Das Rheingold*, "Vollendet das ewige Werk." Here, the god first sets eyes upon Valhalla and hails its glory in the morning light (Rg/57/1/1ff). Later in the same scene, "Valhalla" is reprised, but in a new dramatic context (Rg/79/1/1ff).[124] During the gods' argument with the giants over the wage for the building of Valhalla, Wotan eagerly awaits Loge's appearance with the hopes that the eternal trickster can

---

[119] See Wintle 1992.

[120] Knowledge of associative themes and attention to their meanings is imperative to a full understanding of the music drama, creating the "discursive community" Hutcheon says is necessary for irony to function. See Hutcheon 1994: 80–101.

[121] Hatten 1994: 172–74.

[122] Dyson 1987 studies the dualistic nature of dramatic irony and how it is underscored by repetitions of musical materials. For Dyson, irony is ubiquitous in the first of *The Ring* operas: "The dualism of Wagner's imagination in *Das Rheingold*, however, is so comprehensive that under its impulse both music and drama exhibit a tendency to divide into something more, revealing new levels of significance. Indeed, virtually every dramatic situation, every important piece of dialogue, every musical episode in the work moves with an irresistible thrust toward its opposite." *Ibid.*: 33.

[123] Abbate 1991: 169–70.

[124] Darcy 1993: 148 reads this second appearance of the "Valhalla" music as a recapitulation or reprise.

weasel the gods out of their bargain. When Loge finally does appear, he is accompanied by his own slippery, chromatic music, symbolizing by its tonal ambiguity and instability that Loge is not to be trusted. The "Valhalla" theme, *The Ring*'s paradigm of diatonic tonality, is placed in close conjunction with Loge's sliding chromatic $^6_3$ chords and the "Magic Fire" music. The two themes alternate briefly while Loge sarcastically mocks the gods' wish for the perfect domicile and fortress. Then, Loge briefly recapitulates Wotan's "Valhalla" music to and including the final "Valhalla cadence" (Rg/80/3/3 – 4/1).[125] All the while Loge praises the might of the fortress with tongue firmly in cheek.[126]

If there is any confusion regarding Loge's feelings toward Valhalla, it is clarified at the end of *Das Rheingold* when he reveals his desire to consume the loathsome gods and their castle in a fiery conflagration.[127] Surely, Loge's praise of Valhalla in the second scene is completely sarcastic, and this is reflected in his presentation of the "Valhalla" music. The associative key (D♭) is kept the same (relating as an enharmonic dominant of Loge's F♯) but the tempo is light-hearted and the noble brass orchestration is replaced by the effete sounds of piano strings. In addition, the final "Valhalla cadence," used throughout *The Ring* as a symbol of might and grandeur, is undercut by Loge's slippery chromaticism. The music itself mocks the "Valhalla" theme, using the orchestration, tempo, and proximity to Loge's theme to create a sort of sarcastic tone of voice.[128]

A third, and final, example of Thematic Irony occurs in the first act of *Götterdämmerung*. In a final attempt to turn events from their cataclysmic ending, Waltraute approaches her sister Brünnhilde and asks her to fling the Ring into the Rhine, thereby returning it to its rightful owners and

---

[125] Wintle 1985 traces the appearance and dramatic association of the "Valhalla cadence" through later portions of *The Ring*.

[126] Warren Darcy calls this statement of "Valhalla" "flippant." See Darcy 1993: 149.

[127] "[Z]ur lockende Lohe mich wieder zu wandeln, spür ich lockenden Lust. Sie aufzuzehren, die einst mich gezähmt statt mit den Blinden blöd zu vergehn." See Wagner 1881–83, v. 6: 267. Often, as with Loge, the appearance of restraint in those using irony masks strong feelings (see Hutcheon 1994: 41). The final irony is that Loge eventually *does* burn up Valhalla at the end of *Götterdämmerung* but his key (spelled as G♭) is then subordinated as IV to Valhalla's D♭ (Gd/340/1/3ff). Even in death, Wotan has the last word.

[128] The musical disjunctions creating this "sarcastic tone of voice" are reminiscent of those identified in Carolyn Abbate's definition of musical narrative. See Abbate 1991: 26–27. Hatten's dramatic irony plays a role in another ironic statement of "Valhalla," cited in Buller 1995: 63. When Siegmund recounts his personal history to Hunding and Sieglinde in the first act of *Die Walküre*, he mentions returning home to find his father missing. Though Siegmund does not know what befell his father, the appearance of "Valhalla" at this moment (Wk/26/2/3–26/2/5) leaves us little doubt as to his father's identity and whereabouts.

Example 7.22 Thematic Irony, "Renunciation of Love"

a. Rg/43/1/1
b. Gd/112/1/1

vitiating the effects of the Curse. Brünnhilde replies with righteous indignation, announcing that she will never forsake Siegfried's love gift. The theme she sings presents a chilling instance of Thematic Irony.

This melody is none other than the baleful "Renunciation of Love" first sung by Woglinde when she informed Alberich of the horrible sacrifice needed to shape the Rhinegold into the ring of power. The first appearance of this theme signaled the beginning of an inevitable sequence of events that ultimately corrupts the natural world of love and beauty into one of power and death (see Example 7.22a).

Always a harbinger of doom, the "Renunciation of Love" reaches its nadir in *Götterdämmerung*. As Michael Tanner states:

It is a hideous irony that the Ring, which is the symbol of the renunciation of love, is here treated as love's guarantee, especially in the light of what will soon be happening.[129]

Example 7.22b provides Brünnhilde's statement of the "Renunciation of Love"; note the similarities in scoring, rhythm, associative key, and harmonic support between it and Example 7.22a.

Brünnhilde's recontextualized singing of this theme is ironic in three ways. First, the theme's association directly contradicts her words – a promise never to forswear love. Second, it foreshadows her betrayal of Siegfried in the following act when she serves as a conspirator in his murder (Hatten's Dramatic Irony). Third, the very fact that Brünnhilde does not heed her sister's advice and cast off the Ring forces her into the terrible evils committed in Act II. Ironically, Brünnhilde can only save Siegfried and their love by throwing away the symbol of that love. Since she does not, her life, Siegfried's life, and the world in which they live all pay the ultimate price (Hatten's Cultural Irony).

In Wagner's own words:

But the life-need of man's life-needs is the *need of Love* ... But man can only gain the stilling of his life-needs through *giving*, through *giving* of himself to other men, and in its highest climax, to *all the world of human beings*.[130]

Frits Noske states that dramatic irony in music contradicts the sense of the words, entrusting music with true expression.[131] Certainly, this is true of most of the examples treated in this chapter. Loge's music shows his words to be false, "Wotan's Blessing upon the Nibelung's Son" illustrates the

---

[129] Tanner 1996: 176.   [130] Wagner 1966a: 96–97[emphasis in original].
[131] See Noske 1994.

sarcastic vitriol behind Wotan's benison, and the "Renunciation of Love" belies Brünnhilde's promise. Consider, once more, however, Example 7.21b, the appearance of "Parting Kiss" when Wotan takes his leave of Alberich. This example is striking for achieving the opposite effect. Rather than altering our understanding of the text, it is the music itself that is contradicted – an event Dyson refers to as "parodic echo."[132] Instances such as these support Abbate's claim that particular to Wagner's works is the music's capacity for deception.

Wagner's work has been characterized as "dangerous," and rightly so. In a musical world so richly endowed with semantic fluency, Wagner's art speaks to us with an uncanny similarity to language with its capability for irony, sarcasm, *double entendre*, and falsehood. If the pen is truly mightier than the sword, *The Ring* gives us pause for thought; in Wagner's case the power inscribed with ink and quill is not confined to words alone. Like Associative Transposition and Thematic Complexes, Thematic Irony illustrates a new manner of extracting meaning from Wagner's *music*, one in which the shifting nuances of the drama and concomitant thematic development complement the mapping of theme to dramatic associate.[133] Contextual Reinterpretation provides mechanisms for classifying these techniques that go above and beyond the standard thematic transformations.

[132] Dyson 1987: 33.   [133] See Darcy 1987: 55.

Music reacted to it [Wagner's *Tristan*] as a human body to an injected serum, which it at first strives to exclude as a poison, and only afterwards learns to accept as necessary and even wholesome.

Paul Hindemith[1]

As Hindemith observed, Wagner's influence was both long-lived and mutable. In this chapter, we explore the ramifications of Wagner's thematic technique among composers of art music working during the late nineteenth and early twentieth centuries. After the 1876 premier of *Der Ring des Nibelungen*, the leitmotif concept spread like wildfire through the musical communities of Europe, with composers adapting it to numerous musicodramatic genres both old and new. This chapter aims to provide a synoptic overview of both earlier German works that inspired Wagner's thematic practice and works across Europe whose dicent (again, reviving Peirce from Chapter 4) thematic transformative meanings stem clearly from Wagnerian practice. The breadth of my search for such citations was, if not exhaustive, at least copious, and it is my hope that the range of examples will strongly suggest the pervasiveness of Wagner's influence over *fin-de-siècle* (and later) European musical composition. Before turning to the works of other composers, though, we would be remiss not to investigate briefly Wagner's own evolving thematic practice after *The Ring*.

The leitmotif in Wagner's later works

The *Ring* was the most complex of Wagner's leitmotivic works, but it was not his last. The psychological drama of *Tristan*, the self-awareness of *Die Meistersinger von Nürnberg*, and the transcendence of *Parsifal* – alongside the works of so many other composers – all pointed to the inherent flexibility and lasting appeal of the leitmotif idea. Wagner's theories and his initial attempts at putting these theories into practice

---

[1] Hindemith 1945: 50.

in the first two-and-a-half works of *The Ring* evolve further in the concluding acts of *The Ring* and in *Tristan und Isolde, Die Meistersinger von Nürnberg,* and *Parsifal.* Because examples from *Siegfried* Act III and *Götterdämmerung* were included in the previous chapter, we will focus here only on the three operas Wagner composed after he began work on *The Ring.* Our aim will be, by necessity, exemplary rather than exhaustive, and will center on the differences in thematic technique these works exhibit in comparison to *The Ring.*

Tristan und Isolde, the first drama completed after Wagner began work on *The Ring,* poses something of a leitmotivic conundrum. There is no doubt that *Tristan* contains recurrent thematic materials intimately bound up with the drama, but the themes' identities and meanings are abstruse in comparison with those in *The Ring.* The difficulty stems, in no small part, from two compositional circumstances: first, that Wagner adapted for *Tristan* materials he had originally written for *Siegfried* and, second, that he wrote the Prelude to *Tristan* Act I before penning the remainder of the opera. In both cases this resulted in the composer sometimes conceiving themes in a musical context devoid of the stage drama specific to *Tristan.*[2] Even that stage drama is problematic since action in *Tristan* is largely absent, replaced instead with complex emotional situations comprising an internal drama for one or two characters at a time. These factors make it troublesome, if not entirely inappropriate, to supply a concrete designation – for example, "Gold" – to the various themes.

Thematic obscurity in *Tristan* can also be a function of harmony. As Ernst Kurth first remarked, the core thematic innovation in *Tristan* is that its themes stress the interdependence of chord and line by comprising "non-self-justifying" harmonies formed by the intersection of two or more separate gestures (i.e., themes in polyphony).[3] For Kurth, this hegemony of theme over tonal structure created a new – at times non-functional – tonal language perfectly suited to Wagner's ineffable, Schopenhauerian dramatic aims, but also one that foreshadowed the eventual dissolution of tonality in Western art music.

Enough commentators have agreed with Kurth on this last point that it would be a small overstatement, if one at all, to claim that more analytic ink has been spilled in an attempt to understand the opening chord of the *Tristan* prelude than any other musical excerpt composed by man. It serves

---

[2] See Bailey 1985: 4–9 for an overview of Wagner's compositional process for *Tristan.*
[3] Kurth 1920: 353. For an English-language introduction to Kurth's ideas on harmony, see McCreless 1983.

Example 8.1 *Tristan und Isolde*, Act I, mm. 1–11

our purposes as exemplary of the new type of leitmotivic treatment
Wagner employed in *Tristan*. The first vertical sonority sounds like
a half-diminished seventh chord, functions retrospectively like a
predominant-functioning augmented sixth chord, and is spelled like neither (see Example 8.1, mm. 1–3).[4] The sonority is a part of a larger
leitmotif, often named "Desire," but is itself also thematic in nature,
emblematic of the unresolved longing present throughout *Tristan*. Despite
small alternations in the lines and voice leading of the next two phrases
(each a near-transposition of the first), the so-called "Tristan chord"
returns in both, its half-diminished seventh and predominant augmented
sixth harmonic function intact. In fact, it seems Wagner was more willing
to alter other elements of the theme in order to achieve his V-of-A, V-of-C,
V-of-E transposition scheme, than he was to tinker with the Tristan chord
(see Example. 8.1).[5]

The Tristan chord returns at the same pitch level throughout the opera,
with the same scoring and predominant function. It also recurs in other
guises. The opening of Act III is one example, diatonic – but no less
enigmatic – in nature (see Example 8.2). Again Wagner opens the act with
an inscrutable sonority. Again, it sounds like a half-diminished seventh
chord. Again, its function is clarified retrospectively. This time, the chord

---

[4] See Harrison 1995: 183–84 for a thorough treatment of the "Tristan" chord as one of a number
of "new" augmented sixth sonorities.

[5] Gauldin, *Analytical Studies in Wagner's Music* (unpublished manuscript) chapter 25 speculates
on the reasons for the difference between the third "Tristan" chord and the first two.

Mässig langsam.
Lento moderato.

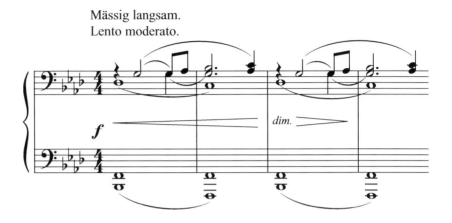

Example 8.2 *Tristan und Isolde*, Act III, mm. 1–4

can be characterized as a plagal supertonic seventh, resolving to a tonic
F minor. The reason, however, that this functional label (not to mention
the label of augmented sixth for the first Tristan chord) seems an imperfect
fit is that there is a sense when listening to these passages that normative
harmonic syntax is suspended, trumped, even determined, by the thematic
importance of the central sonority. Whatever else one may say of Wagner's
Tristan, its thematic technique is apposite beyond reproach, rife with
musical gestures full of implication and ambiguity that provide a perfect
metaphor for the play of emotions and psychological states that comprise
the drama. Thus, we see in this work and its opening sonority evidence not
only that Wagner's themes post-*Ring* cycle continued to evolve in conjunction with the drama, but also that the thematic technique itself did.

A thematic technique driven by the drama would demand that themes
in *Die Meistersinger von Nürnberg* function quite differently from those in
Tristan. Such is the case: both the libretto and the stage action are considerably more transparent in *Meistersinger*, and Wagner's attempts at a
musical evocation of the past result in thematic identities that tend to
evolve contrapuntally over time in a sort of Romantic-era *Fortspinnung*.[6]
An obvious example occurs with the "Mastersingers" theme at the opening
of the *Vorspiel* (see Example 8.3). The opening melodic fourth (x) is
inverted and filled with stepwise motion (y). This motive is then subjected
to various contrapuntal techniques (sequence, inversion, augmentation,
and fragmentation), forming a highly unified musical surface. In addition,

---

[6] Dahlhaus 1979: 77–78.

Example 8.3 Vorspiel to Act I of *Die Meistersinger von Nürnberg*, mm. 1–14

Wagner spins out this perfect fourth *Urmotiv* in other musical contexts central to the work: the chorale that opens Act I, Walther's Act III Dream Song, and the tonal motion by fourth from C to F across bars 1–14 of the *Vorspiel* comprising but a few examples.

We find in *Meistersinger* yet another Wagnerian thematic technique: inter-opus quotation. There is, of course, no question as to why Wagner quotes music from the sound world of *Tristan* during *Meistersinger* Act III, Scene 4 – the characters themselves mention the sad tale of the doomed lovers. Nevertheless, that Wagner should not only mention another opus by name, but also quote its music is a significant addition to his repertory of thematic developments, a new type of Contextual Reinterpretation based on intertextuality. The quotation in *Meistersinger* achieves the requisite dramatic association, but it is an association coated with a patina of satire, evoking a sense of Thematic Irony, as well. As we saw in Chapter 5, Wagner's music is a favorite choice for inter-opus quotation in the works of other composers who use it to signal their adoption or parody of Wagnerian leitmotivic techniques.

In *Parsifal*, Wagner's use of associative themes drifts away from the norms established in the earlier operas. For one thing, all of the themes (with one exception) originate in the orchestra. More radically, the themes tend to function more as purely musical entities and less as vessels for extra-musical association.[7] Barry Millington argues that there is only one true leitmotif in *Parsifal* – the "Wise Fool" – though even this one is unorthodox in that Gurnemanz sings its first complete presentation in a sort of dramatic foreshadowing.[8] Other commentators disagree, citing "Feast of Grace," the *Schmerzenmotiv*, "Kundry's Scream," and "Amfortas's Wounds," among others.[9] Millington's point is well taken, though; thematic development in *Parsifal* is less easily explained by reference to specific dramatic contexts, seemingly motivated more by musical than dramatic logic. There is, however, at least one instance of Thematic Evolution that recalls Wagner's leitmotivic technique in *The Ring*.

The theme associated with Amfortas's unholy wound comprises an arpeggiation of the unstable augmented triad "resolving" into a half-diminished seventh chord (see Example 8.4a). Doubtless, Wagner chose this progression as emblematic of the opera's central obstacle: the Grail Knights' state of fallen grace, literally embodied in Amfortas's wound.[10] With Parsifal's reclamation of the Spear that caused the wound, and his exhortation to Amfortas to be healed and absolved (*Sei heil, entsündigt, und entsühnt!*), Amfortas *is* healed and the theme's augmented triad resolves into a major triad, a Harmonic Redemption fitting for *Parsifal*'s tale of salvation (see Example 8.4b). The technique here is a reversal of the Harmonic Corruption technique found throughout *The Ring*; salvation, rather than decay, lies at the heart of Wagner's last work. This moment also serves as a microcosm of the principal musical binarism in the drama, namely the distinction between chromaticism (for Klingsor, magic, the unnatural, and the unholy) and diatonicism (for innocence, purity, and piety).[11]

Wagner's thematic technique in these three operas extends and problematizes the leitmotivic paradigm set out in *The Ring*. Or, perhaps it is more accurate to say that the last three operas demonstrate how Wagner tailored his thematic technique to the dramas and sound worlds at hand. As we turn to the works of other composers, this is an important point to

---

[7] Millington 1992: 259.   [8] *Ibid.*: 260.

[9] For some sources listing leitmotifs in *Parsifal*, see Bauer 1977: 8–95; Whittall 1981; and Dahlhaus 1979: 148–55.

[10] The augmented triad – and major third relations in general – pervade the score. Kinderman 2005: 150–51 shows that Wagner considered the Ab–C major third central to the entire opera. Darcy 2005 (especially 219) notes the use of third cycles on multiple levels throughout Act II. And Gauldin, *Analytical Studies in Wagner's Music* (unpublished manuscript), chapter 34, lays out the argument for the Act I *Prelude* serving as a model for the third chains throughout the work.

[11] Dahlhaus 1979: 151 mentions this binary.

(a)

(b)

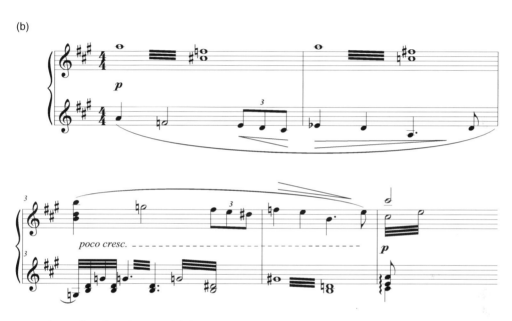

Example 8.4 "Amfortas's Wounds" from *Parsifal*

a. Ps/17/2/3–5
b. Harmonic Redemption, Ps/267/4/3–268/1/4

remember; because the thematic technique in *The Ring* is largely patent,
concrete, and pervasive, it is that approach to the leitmotif – rather than
those in *Tristan*, *Meistersinger*, or *Parsifal* – that ramifies in musics written
after Wagner. Without question, numerous works allude to, quote, parody,
or otherwise derive inspiration from Wagner's other operas, but those we
can most confidently call "leitmotivic" adopt *The Ring* as their paradigm.

Before turning to these, it will be helpful to clarify the focused nature
of our inquiry. First, we shall content ourselves here with the segment of
the repertory that arguably comprises the richest outpouring of Wagner-
inspired leitmotivic technique: dramatic Western art music of the decades

after the premiere of *Der Ring des Nibelungen*. (There are other repertories worthy of study for their leitmotivic content, one of which – film music – we turn to in Chapter 9.) Surprisingly few of these works have enjoyed thorough leitmotivic analysis; thus in the absence of theme names provided by the composers or by other analysts, I have assigned names of my own.

Second, by including a given work in this discussion, we are not concluding beyond a doubt that the composer of said work knowingly adopted a Wagnerian leitmotivic technique. It would be hard to imagine that any of the composers treated herein were unaware of Wagner's experiments (and in most cases we know they were aware), but establishing a conscious or unconscious Wagnerian influence in a given work without documentary evidence is a treacherous task. In general, it will be our aim to describe a leitmotivic technique that can be analyzed with the same language established in the previous chapter rather than to prove the direct influence of Wagner, whose leitmotivic practice was sometimes received by later composers via the intermediary of Wagner's contemporaries or close successors anyway. That said, there are obvious examples of Wagnerian quotation, parody, or allusion, and it will at times be helpful for us to point to these examples because from them we can intuit an explicitly Wagnerian influence. (As a rule, the more overt the reference, the more farcical the composer's intent.)[12]

Finally, given the breadth of this repertory, our investigations cannot hope to survey the entire body of post-Wagnerian art music, nor to provide in-depth analysis of any one work. Rather, we will investigate specific instances of Wagnerian thematic development as exemplars to show how the techniques in *The Ring* continued to operate in later works. There is a real danger in this type of survey that our attempts at establishing a common practice will be achieved at the expense of what some might say are more interesting and nuanced piece-specific thematic meanings and relationships. Fortunately, for many of the works considered herein, there exist just such detailed studies and these will be cited as necessary.

---

[12] While the works of *fin-de-siècle* French composers quickly spring to mind when considering Wagnerian parody (e.g., "Golliwog's Cakewalk" from Debussy's *Children's Corner Suite* and Fauré's *Souvenirs de Bayreuth*), obvious parody by Germans also exists (e.g., Richard Strauss's *Variationen über 'Das Dirndl is harb auf mi'* and *Le Bourgeois Gentilhomme*, among others. See Bribitzer-Stull and Gauldin 2007: 34–35). Wagner today remains a favorite for both serious imitation (e.g., Christopher Rouse's fantasy for solo percussion and orchestra on themes from *The Ring*, *Der gerettete Alberich*) and farce (e.g., Peter Schikele's bassoon quartet, *Last Tango in Bayreuth*, not to mention the Looney Tunes episode "What's Opera, Doc?").

For those lacking in-depth analytic treatment, we may hope that our survey will whet the appetites of scholars eager to peek under the many stones we leave unturned.

Leitmotif in the operas of other composers

European opera composers at the end of the nineteenth century found it difficult to escape the Wagnerian leitmotif, though each reacted to Wagner's practice in his own way. In general, leitmotivic practice in the years after Wagner's death ramified along geographic lines, with significant strains occurring around Germany, France, and Eastern Europe, though individual composers often reveal marked differences in practice from their fellow countrymen. In separating my discussion of this repertory geographically, I don't mean to imply an essentialist view of national practice, rather to admit that, for linguistic, historical, and cultural reasons, opera repertory before the twentieth century tends to exhibit a similarity of practice that runs along shared cultural-linguistic lines.

Germany and Austria

Ironically, the Beethovenian symphonic impulse that inspired so many of Wagner's musical ideas seemed to reclaim them after Wagner's death: leitmotif in German music after Wagner found its way more often into the symphonic repertory than it did the operatic. The glaring exception is, of course, the operatic output of Richard Strauss (or Richard III as he was once crowned, there being, of course, no possibility of an actual Richard II succeeding Richard I (i.e., Wagner)).[13] Before turning to Strauss, however, we must first stop to correct an oversight. The discussion in Chapter 1 cited Carl Maria von Weber among Wagner's leitmotivic forerunners. The details of Weber's thematic technique – specifically developmental practices like those outlined in Chapter 7 – however, remained by necessity unexplored since we had first to detail the many techniques in the context of *The Ring* (see Chapter 7). These techniques – employed by later

---

[13] Hans von Bülow and Alexander Ritter bestowed the Richard III moniker upon Strauss. Hans von Bülow needs no introduction to readers of this book, though Alexander Ritter may be less familiar. Ritter was a German violinist, conductor, and Wagnerian protégé. It was Ritter, in part, who convinced Strauss to abandon his early, conservative style in favor of dramatic music, and his influence on the composer is clear – Ritter's poem *Tod und Verklärung*, for example, appears as part of the published score of Strauss's work by the same name.

Germans like Strauss – are adumbrated in Weber's operas; thus we turn first to his oeuvre.

The operas of Carl Maria von Weber – operas Wagner knew well – call into question Wagner's contention that his thematic developmental techniques were symphonically inspired, for it is most likely from Weber's operas that Wagner's concept of associativity emerged. *Der Freischütz* is an obvious example, rich with associative orchestration throughout. Weber himself stated that the work contrasts two dramatic elements through timbre: hunting, represented by horns and folk-like melodies; and the dark forces of Samiel, represented by low registers, especially lower clarinet.[14] In the same opera we note an oft-cited structural usage of associativity in the Wolf's Glen music. The diminished seventh sonority associated with the eerie forces of the Wolf's Glen forms the basis of the modulatory scheme for the entire scene, which begins and ends in F♯ minor, but modulates to C and A minor for much of the intervening music.[15] Associative tonality is also obvious in uses of B major and minor, which seem to be linked with moonlight, as in Agatha's recitative No. 8 and Max's C♭ in No. 9. Associative tonality is perhaps most obvious, though, in *Euryanthe* (with forerunners found in the music of Beethoven and Schubert).[16] Weber and earlier composers stop short, however, of the sorts of "Associative Transposition" of themes as musico-dramatic developments that we find in Wagner's *Lohengrin* and throughout *The Ring* (detailed in Chapter 7).

---

[14] Weber made very clear in his prose that the drama was predicated on a struggle between good and evil. The associative key scheme and the instrumentation bear this out, and were given a great deal of detailed consideration by the composer. See the quotation of Weber's comments on *Der Freischütz* and the discussion thereof in Warrack 1976: 220–22.

[15] Wagner's most obvious use of diminished seventh chords occurs in the stormy sea passages throughout *Der fliegende Holländer*, likely modeled on Weber's diminished seventh-rich Act II storm at sea in *Oberon*. Weber's use of association (be it themes, chords, or other musical entities) came largely from Méhul and Dalayrac, though thorough tonal plans like the use of diminished seventh chords and minor third relations in the Wolf's Glen scene of *Der Freischütz* were wholly his own creation. See Warrack 2001: 305 and 309.

[16] Beethoven's *Fidelio* makes use of associative keys (A♭ for death in the F major trio "Gut, Söhnchen, gut" and later in the opera when Florestan welcomes death; C for hopeful love as in Marcellina's opening aria; and E major for beneficent spirituality, as in Leonora's hopeful hymn to the star to keep her hope alive for Florestan in her "Abscheulicher" aria) and sonorities (diminished seventh chords appear frequently at dramatically appropriate points like Pizarro's "death to Florestan" aria, the guards' wariness at the released prisoners, and Florestan's first aria). Schubert's "Erlkönig" uses expressive transposition for the ever-rising child's cry of "Mein Vater, mein Vater!" Of all composers who used associative tonality, though, it was probably Weber (especially in *Euryanthe* where E♭ is the key of divinity, E Eglantine's key, and B the key of Emma's ghost) that served as a model. See Gauldin, *Analytical Studies in Wagner's Music* (unpublished manuscript), chapter 6: 3–4, and chapter 10: 13–14.

In addition to associative sonorities, Weber's three mature operas also employ associative themes. Most of these eventually succumb to musical gravity. Stripped of their dramatic specificity, they participate in musical textures as symphonic, rather than associative, statements.[17] The horn call at the opening of *Oberon* is a good example. Its appearance at the beginning of the Act I overture primes us to hear it again in the first number where its representational quality (as the magic horn Oberon grants Sir Huon) causes its subsequent appearances to evoke its spellbinding powers. The developments it undergoes (sequence, inversion, transposition, and so forth both at the opening of the first number and at the end of Act III), however, bear no special associative meaning but rather resemble *Fortspinnung*, largely unmotivated by the dramatic context at hand.

There are, however, exceptions that prove the rule, suggesting an embryonic form of Wagner's mature technique. The "Fairies" music in *Oberon* is exemplary. It first appears in the overture and is immediately wedded to the fairy-garden choir in No. 1, played, *pianissimo*, by the strings (see Example 8.5a and note the anacrusis leading-tone figures circled throughout). This theme is then subjected to Thematic Evolution when Huon first gazes upon Babylon as Oberon encourages him to enter. The Change of Texture from quick upper-register string chords to a slower, solo bassoon alters the playful tone of the original appearance to evoke a more solemn setting appropriate to the dramatic magnitude of the quest Oberon is setting upon the knight (see Example 8.5b).[18] The "Fairies" music is also subjected to Thematic Transformation when it becomes "Oberon's Grief" in the second number of Act I. The rising, applied-leading-tone figure from the original points to the connection between these two themes, but the extreme textural changes (slow, bassoon

---

[17] See Abbate 1991: 168 who argues that it is natural in Wagnerian opera for associative themes to lose their dramatic significance and succumb to a musical gravity that pulls them back toward functioning simply as musical motives.

   An example of this in Weber occurs with "Caspar's Flip Arrogance" a trilled piccolo motive first heard in Caspar's Act I drinking song. It later appears in his vengeance aria at the end of Act I and again when he takes a drink after speaking with Samiel. When it recurs during the Act II Wolf's Glen scene, Max is looking into the Wolf's Glen noticing the night birds. While Caspar does appear in the scene, the original association with drinking is lost at this point, and the motive seems only vaguely associative.

[18] Similar statements occur also at the beginning of Rezia's Act I aria (No. 6) and, in varied form, in Rezia's Act II aria when, abandoned on an island, she sights a ship. In these, and the earlier cited instance concerning Sir Huon, the solemn texture better fits the fate Oberon has laid upon the hapless mortals than did the original, light-hearted statement.

(a)

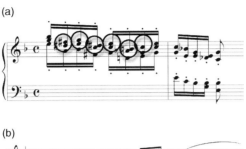

(b)

(c)

Example 8.5 "The Fairies" from Weber's *Oberon*

a. Act I, No. 1, mm. 8–9
b. Change of Texture, Act I, No. 4, mm. 88–89
c. "Oberon's Grief," Act I, No. 2, mm. 2–3

and cello line) and Change of Mode result in a different associative theme
(see Example 8.5c).

Another suggestive example, a forerunner of the "Amfortas's Wounds"
Harmonic Redemption, is the moment in *Euryanthe* when the "Ghost" theme
is finally laid to rest. Except for the last, every statement of "Ghost" from the
overture onward features pervasive chromaticism and a series of tonicized
chords, many of them minor, closing on what sounds like a dominant in B
(see Example 8.6a). By contrast, when the innocent Euryanthe's tears
upon her ring finally exorcize Emma's spirit, the "Ghost" appears in an
unambiguous C major, closing on a conclusive tonic (see Example 8.6b).

While Weber's themes were capable of development – clear harbingers
of the Wagnerian leitmotif – the structural networks of musico-dramatic
themes we find in *The Ring* exist only in nascent form in the music of
Wagner's German predecessors. Once developed by Wagner, though, the
leitmotif concept was quick to find its way into the works of his successors.

In *Guntram*, Richard Strauss used Wagnerian structural leitmotifs – a
web of musical ideas bound by "symphonic" developments – and, like
Wagner, he did so for formal reasons, groping for a method of achieving

Example 8.6 Change of Mode in "Ghost" from Weber's *Euryanthe*

A. Typical presentation: Overture mm. 129–43 (see also Act I, No. 6 mm. 100–21; etc.)
B. Final presentation: Act III, No. 25, mm. 216–23

musico-dramatic cohesion.[19] The leitmotif is hardly the only Wagnerian allusion in this opera; the medieval plot line, orchestral textures, self-quotation, and use of pre-existing materials are all examples.[20] These, though, are best read not as a callow and eclectic assembly of Wagnerian imitations, but rather as a *critical reception*, a younger composer attempting to remake the work of his predecessor.[21] Nevertheless, Wagnerian thematic developments abound, the largest number by far involving two central themes associated with the title character: "Guntram's Compassion," and "Ardor" (a theme clearly inspired by the opening "Desire" theme of Wagner's *Tristan und Isolde*, which captures Guntram's love for Freihild and his desire for peace) (see Examples 8.7a and b). The most common developments are corruptive in nature, with the vast majority of these occurring in Act III, though earlier examples are not difficult to find. "Guntram's Shame" for instance, comprises a new theme whose Thematic Transformation results from corruption of the "Ardor" theme's falling fifth (bar 2) and inversion of its ensuing rising seconds into a tritone followed by falling seconds (see Example 8.7c). "Guntram's Compassion" is likewise corrupted (see Example 8.7d).

Strauss's later operas also betray the influence of Wagnerian thematic techniques. "Octavian's Bravado" from *Der Rosenkavalier* is a particularly plastic example. Its original presentation comprises a virile horn lick appropriate to Octavian's Siegfried-like adolescent exuberance (see Example 8.8a).[22] (It's hard not to hear a relationship between this theme and the obbligato horn theme from the third movement of Mahler's Fifth Symphony, written about ten years earlier; both feature a prominent major-mode $\hat{6}$–$\hat{5}$ motive.) "Octavian's Bravado" is later subjected to Harmonic Corruption when the Marschallin chastises Octavian for leaving his sword lying around (see Example 8.8b). It also appears under Change of Mode when the Baron recognizes Octavian's face in his transvestite disguise as "Mariandel" (see Example 8.8c). It is even subject to Fragmentation and Associative Transposition when the rising three-note figure that

---

[19] Youmans 1996: 277–78.

[20] See Schmitz 1907 for a list of Wagnerian allusions in this opera. Of course Wagnerisms occur throughout Strauss's oeuvre. (See Bribitzer-Stull and Gauldin 2007: 2–3.) Strauss also uses allusions in *Guntram* that stem from other sources ranging from the cultural commonplace (e.g., the "Dresden Amen," is evoked in the theme of "Brotherhood's Judgment") to his own symphonic poems (e.g., the *Tod und Verklärung* quote, for the "Suicide" theme at Gt/30/3/3–4/ 4 (score references refer to the Boosey & Hawkes piano-vocal score)).

[21] See Youmans 1996: 289–303.

[22] Score references are to the Boosey & Hawkes piano-vocal score.

(a)

(b)

(c)

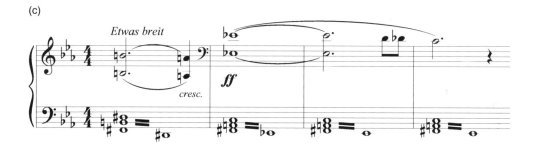

(d)

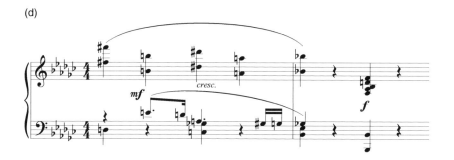

Example 8.7 Thematic developments in Richard Strauss's *Guntram*

a. "Guntram's Compassion," Gt/13/4/4–5
b. "Ardor," Gt/68/3/4–69/1/2ff
c. "Guntram's Shame," Gt/89/4/5–90/1
d. "Guntram's Compassion," subject to Harmonic Corruption and Fragmentation, Gt/93/5/2–3

(a)

(b)

Example 8.8 Thematic developments in Richard Strauss's *Der Rosenkavalier*

a. "Octavian's Bravado," Rk/1/1/1–2
b. "Octavian's Bravado," Harmonic Corruption, Rk/22/3/3–4/1
c. "Octavian's Bravado," Change of Mode, Rk/347/3/1–3
d. "Octavian's Bravado," Fragmentation and Associative Transposition, Rk/254/2/1

opens the theme is sung by Sophia in F♯ major, the key of her love duet with Octavian earlier in the act (see Example 8.8d).

Among all of Strauss's operas it is *Salome* that most obviously employs associative tonality (C major for Jochanaan, C♯ minor for Salome, and A♭ major for Christ), though, strangely, Associative Transposition is rare. Among the other forms of Wagnerian thematic development, a particularly effective example occurs with "Jochanaan's Holiness," a theme first appearing near the beginning of the opera when Salome encounters the holy man (see Example 8.9a). "Jochanaan's Holiness" is subjected to Harmonic Corruption and Thematic Fragmentation throughout his execution (see Example 8.9b for one instance). Immediately thereafter Salome repeatedly asks for Jochanaan's head with a figure that devolves from his literal and Thematic Fragmentation.

Repeated speech mannerisms like Salome's occur as well in the slightly later *Wozzeck* by Austrian composer Alban Berg. Numerous themes in this opera accompany repetitions of the same text; Wozzeck's "Wir arme Leut!" is a good example.[23] This theme recurs in purely instrumental contexts as well; a verticalization of the [0148] "Wir arme Leut!" tetrachord – an

[23] Perle 1980: 94.

Example 8.8 (*cont.*)

(a)

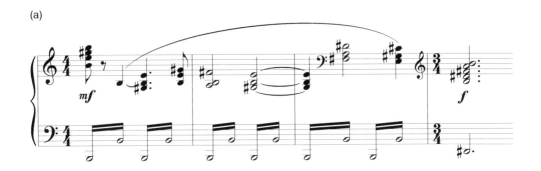

(b)

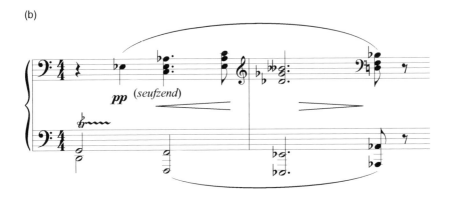

Example 8.9 Thematic development in Richard Strauss's *Salome*

a. "Jochanaan's Holiness," Sl/34/1/4–2/2
b. "Jochanaan's Holiness," subjected to Harmonic Corruption and Fragmentation, Sl/175/5/1–2 *et al.*

augmented triad with chromatic hanger-on – appears a number of times at dramatically appropriate points in the opera.[24]

Conventional wisdom tends to forget that non-tonal works like *Wozzeck* can be intensely thematic.[25] George Perle, in fact, notes many associative themes in *Wozzeck*, defining them as "any characteristic musical idea that occurs in more than one scene and that acquires an explicit referential function in the drama through its consistent association with an

---

[24] *Ibid.*: 1980, 98. See also Schmalfeldt 1983, 85–93 for an extended discussion of this tetrachord in Perle's analysis and throughout *Wozzeck*.

[25] See Perle 1980: 93–117 for an overview of what Perle calls "leitmotifs" as well as their transformations. Schoenberg's *Moses und Aron* is another post-tonal opera rich with associative themes. Their developments, however, occur more often via row partitions than the types of dramatic thematic developments treated in this book. That said, contrapuntal thematic layering, canonic operators (T and I), and even good-old-fashioned Harmonic Corruption are also present. I wish to thank Michael Cherlin for his personal correspondence on this point.

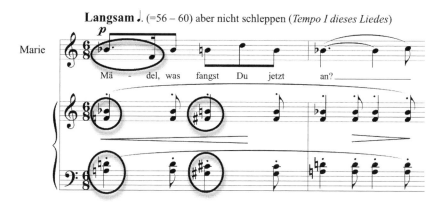

Example 8.10 "Cradle Song" in Berg's *Wozzeck*, typical presentation, Act I, mm. 371–72 (Scene 3)

extra-musical element."[26] Nor are Wagnerian leitmotivic developments absent from this work.[27] Thematic Mutation occurs with elements of the "Cradle Song" (see the perfect fourths circled in Example 8.10). This theme's perfect fourths open the children's song "Ringle Ringle, Rosen-kranz," and the Fragmentation of this motive becomes poignantly clear as Marie's orphan sings the perfect fourth interval to his "Hopp, hopp!" while he plays alone at the opera's conclusion. We also see many instances of Thematic Transformation operative in networks of related themes. One example is the "Folk Song" dotted-rhythm fourth appearing as a compon-ent of both the "Cradle Song" and Andres's Hunting Song.[28] Another is the transformation of "Earrings," appropriately enough, into "Marie's Guilt" (see Example 8.11). The melodies for these two themes are members of the same PC-set. Moreover, later in the same scene, Marie sings "Ich bin doch ein schlecht Mensch" to the tune of "Bin ich ein schlecht Mensch?" retrograded (or inverted) and transposed up a step, confirming her guilt over having accepted the Drum Major's love gift. As a final example of a loose transformation, note that even Wozzeck's vocal Db notes at the opening of the opera seemingly arise from the "Drum Major" theme tail, as if Wozzeck were nothing more than the Drum Major's afterthought.

---

[26] *Ibid.* 1980: 97.

[27] Maisel 1999: 161 argues that Berg's use of leitmotif is qualitatively different from Wagner's in that Berg structurally embodies the qualities he wants a theme to express, rather than relying so heavily on association. His example of the Wozzeck chord expressing Wozzeck's misfit status by comprising four pitch classes (PCs) from one whole-tone collection and one from another has a certain poetry about it, but strikes me as analytically dubious.

[28] Perle 1980: 111 and 113.

(a)

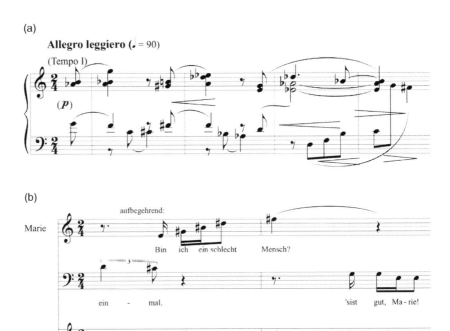

(b)

(c)

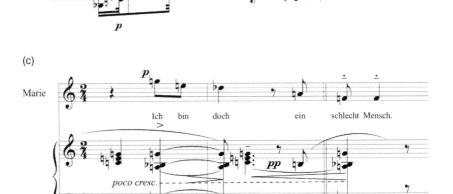

Example 8.11 Thematic transformation of "Earrings" into "Marie's Guilt" in Berg's *Wozzeck*

a. "Earrings" Act II, mm. 7–10 (Scene 1)
b. "Marie's Guilt" Act II, mm. 105–06 (Scene 1)
c. "Marie's Guilt" retrograde, Act II, mm. 126–28

France and England

Oddly, it was in France, rather than Germany, that the most immediate diaspora of Wagnerian thematic technique occurred.[29] Examples range from composers who remained more or less faithful to Wagner's practice, like Massenet (*Esclarmonde*) and Saint-Saëns (*Ascanio*),[30] to deeply ambivalent usages by composers like Debussy (*Pelléas et Mélisande*), to non-developmental associative themes in the works of the French naturalists like Charpentier, Bruneau, and Lalo that relate strongly to eighteenth-century reminiscence themes, as if Wagner's *Ring* had never existed at all.[31] The French naturalists used primarily a non-developmental leitmotif – their main difference from Wagner. Chausson was originally very impressed with Wagner (especially his *Der fliegende Holländer* and *Tristan und Isolde*) but, like many French composers, later rejected him, stating that Western music needed to "de-Wagnerify."[32] His *Le Roi Arthus*, a tale that would seem at first glance to be a prime suspect for leitmotivic treatment, rather eschews the technique.

Massenet is typical of thematic practices common in French opera at the turn of the century.[33] In *Werther*, thematic recall tends to be of wholesale sections of music, almost verbatim (though with different text, of course). The Act I F major "Clair de Lune" love duet returns in the final tableau. Its cyclicism is reminiscent of *The Ring* (and much nineteenth-century music in general) in one sense – musical materials from the opening return to round off the form at the end.[34] There is no sense, however, that *the materials themselves* have developed or recombined in the manner of *Götterdämmerung*. They exist instead to contrast the tragic events of the opera's conclusion with the halcyon beginnings of the tale. Massenet might be more often cited in Wagnerian reception history if his *Esclarmonde*

---

[29] See Berlioz's *La Damnation de Faust* for a forerunner of Wagner's Thematic Complex technique as the composer combines the previously separately stated students' and soldiers' choruses together in the "Chœur de soldats et chanson des étudiants *ensemble*." The composer uses a similar quodlibet technique in his *Romeo and Juliet*, contrapuntally combining the "Sighing Romeo" and "Party" themes during the party scene, and lovers' themes during their love scene.

[30] Kelkel 1984: 279.

[31] One might also lump Jánaček into this naturalist group, though he was Czech, not French. For more discussion of the non-developmental themes of the French naturalists, see Kelkel 1984: 284 and 286–340.

[32] Gallois 2001: 540.   [33] For more on this topic, see Huebner 1999 and 2004.

[34] This is probably at least part of the reason that Massenet introduced the children rehearsing their Christmas song into Goethe's story: their singing during the opening summer scene sets up a powerful cyclic effect when they are heard on Christmas Eve at the end of the opera.

were performed more often.[35] The work's mythic, magic-oriented libretto seems a good fit for Wagnerian pastiche, and Massenet obliges. Expressive and associative tonality abound, and despite the texture lacking the subcutaneous motivic play and thematic recombinations one finds in Wagnerian opera, there *are* a number of recurring themes. If Wagnerian-style developments are rare, they are not absent altogether: the title character's theme returns, harmonically corrupted, at appropriate points, and a number of themes group into families bound together by neighbor motives and augmented triads.

In general, French associative themes tend toward the Tristanesque, psychological type rather than being overtly dramatic or emotional, a trait often characterized as an early modernist reaction to romanticism.[36] Debussy expresses this sentiment forcefully in a letter written to his English friend, Edwin Evans, Jr. and published in the *New York Times* and the London *Daily Telegraph*:

> If in "Pelléas" the symphonic development has, on the whole, small importance, it is to react against the pernicious neo-Wagnerian aesthetic which presumes to render, at the same time, the sentiment expressed by the characters and the inner thoughts which impel its actions. In my opinion, these are two contradictory operations, from a lyrical point of view, and, when united, can only weaken each other. Perhaps it is better that music should by simple means – a chord? a curve? – endeavor to render the successive impulses and moods as they are produced, without making laborious efforts to follow a symphonic development, foreseen, and always arbitrary, to which one will necessarily be tempted to sacrifice the emotional development. That is why there is no "guiding thread" in "Pelléas," and its characters are not subjected to the slavery of "Leit-motive." Take note that the motive which accompanies "Mélisande" is never altered. It returns in the fifth act unchanged at any point, because, in reality, Mélisande is always unchanged in herself, and dies without any one – or, perhaps, only old Arkel – ever having understood her.[37]

Note Debussy's stipulation that the motive "accompanies" Mélisande; there is no mention of expression, association, or emotion.

---

[35] *Esclarmonde*, like many works of Rachmaninov and Mendelssohn, likely would have been taken more seriously by analysts if it had been written fifty years earlier. Nevertheless, there is powerful music and drama here, and the concept of voice (both the power of Esclarmonde's and the identity of Roland's) feature prominently – always an appropriate operatic trope. In my estimation, this is an unsung hero (with apologies for the play on words) of the French operatic repertory, worthy of more attention from scholars and performers alike.

[36] Kelkel 1984: 340.   [37] This letter is quoted in Grayson 1986: 231.

This might explain why early commentators detected no leitmotifs in *Pelléas*.[38] (Debussy's later revisions to *Pelléas* also added more thematic statements than were present in the original sketches and manuscript.)[39] There are, in fact, quite a few themes we can call leitmotifs, but their usage lies much closer to the technique found in Wagner's *Tristan und Isolde* – Debussy's favorite work of Wagner's – than in *The Ring* (which Debussy reviled). No doubt, the drama has much to do with it since, like *Tristan*, Debussy's *Pelléas* is largely a drama of the psyche, one that occurs in the realm of psychology and emotion; as such, blatant and active thematic presentations and developments would make little artistic sense.

Perhaps the largest deviation from Wagnerian practice in Debussy's *Pelléas* is that the leitmotifs seem to apply only to the current scene, rather than bearing the rich sense of emotion remembered from earlier scenes that they do in Wagner's works. Like those in *The Ring* though, themes through-out the opera can be grouped into families. The "Mélisande," "Pelléas," and "Golaud's Anxiety" themes, for example, all open with a melodic rising second.[40] Thematic development also differs from Wagner's practice in that these developments conform not so much to the types laid out in Chapter 7, but rather tend to be subtle and intervallic in nature; contour and rhythm remain recognizable, but specific intervals are altered in the style of the "signature transformation" described by Jay Hook.[41] Nevertheless, there are examples of Thematic Transformations, such as the oft-cited morphing of the "Golaud's Anxiety" theme into both "Mélisande's Wedding Ring" and the "Grotto" (see Example 8.12).[42] Other examples that seem influenced by Wagnerian technique include the Thematic Fragmentation of "Pellèas" at rehearsal 39 in Act I, Scene 3 as he tentatively approaches Geneviève and Mélisande (thus, as in Wagner, using fragmentation to indicate the emerging or passing away of a character, object, or influence). In Act V after rehearsal 38, the theme associated with "Golaud's Anxiety" reappears for a final time, instantiating a bitter form of Thematic Irony as the music contradicts the Doctor's reassurance that Golaud is not respon-sible for Melisande's death; Golaud and the audience know that he is.

More than a generation after Wagner, French opera composers still turned to his works for inspiration. Lili Boulanger's *Faust et Hélène* is full of Wagnerian allusions (especially to *Tristan* and *Parsifal*). The Tarnhelm progression Boulanger uses for Mephistopheles and the ghost of Paris, and associative usage of the tritone for the appearance of

---

[38] See *ibid.*: 229–30.   [39] *Ibid.*: 225–75.   [40] *Ibid.*, 261.   [41] Hook 2008.
[42] Grayson 1986: 265.

(a)

(b)

Example 8.12 Transformation of "Golaud's Anxiety" into "Melisande's Wedding Ring" in Debussy's *Pelléas et Mélisande*

a. "Golaud's Anxiety," Act I, Scene 1, mm. 5–6
b. "Melisande's Wedding Ring," Act II, Scene 1, mm. 76–77

the spirits and Faust's cry of "Hélène!" also suggest Wagnerian practice. The most prevalent leitmotif is "Faust's Doomed Longing for Hélène," and it is, appropriately, subjected to Thematic Fragmentation when the ingénue is drawn away at the opera's conclusion.

Across the Channel, British audiences developed a passion for Wagner not found outside of Germany. British opera composers, however, seemed to have little use for the Wagnerian leitmotif. While Britten and Delius employ associative themes in their operas, these lack the sense of emotion, memory, and development necessary to make them true leitmotifs. For instance, Delius's *A Village Romeo and Juliet* employs Wagnerian half-diminished seventh harmonies and recurring motives but nothing that could rightly be called a leitmotif. Benjamin Britten has few Wagnerian moments in his operas either. Of course the citation of the "Tristan" Chord and "Desire" motive in *Albert Herring* is a famous example, a fitting parody for the moment in Britten's opera when Sid and Nancy spike the lemonade (cf. the magic potion the lovers consume in *Tristan*). As for

Example 8.13 "My Mind Beats On" from Britten's *Death in Venice*

a. Original statement, mm. 1–2
b. Thematic Inversion, mm. 10–11

thematic developments in the Wagnerian style, one has to search carefully to find any. One brief example occurs at the opening of *Death in Venice,* in which the chromatic vocal line for "my mind beats on" is inverted immediately after its first statement to depict weariness, an example of Thematic Inversion as associational opposition (see Example 8.13).

Italy

There is not much to say about Wagnerian thematic technique in Italian opera. Not because thematic recall – even developmental thematic recall – doesn't exist in this repertory, but rather because there is little Italian opera after Wagner that has survived into the modern-day performance repertory; Puccini's *Turandot* is, more or less, the end of the line. Verdi perhaps comes closest to Wagner in the thematic practice of his late operas: *Otello and Falstaff.*[43] The artistic orientation of *verismo* composers virtually obviates something like leitmotif – a conventional and artificial vehicle for establishing meaning – because it stands at odds with *verismo* composers' attempts at clarity and directness of expression. While the textures of Puccini, Leoncavallo, and Mascagni operas avoid the dense contrapuntal weaving together of thematic materials one finds in Wagner, one need look no further than Act IV of *La Bohème* to find pervasive thematicism. Here, however, there is little of musical interest in terms of thematic *development*. Rather, the emotional residue the themes carry serves a purpose similar to that of Massenet's *Werther* – they set the present-day

---

[43] See Brown and Parker 1985 for an investigation of one such theme in *Otello*.

tragedy in relief by comparison to the burgeoning love story of Act I, and they serve a cyclic formal function, rounding off the work. Only in *Tosca* do we find explicit Wagnerism: form-defining themes that control large spans of music. Examples include: Harmonic Corruption of the Act I falling-thirds motive associated with Cavaradossi and Tosca's narrative imagining of a night-time tryst, and a recurring B♭–E detail that functions as something more than a Verdian *tinta*, but less than a Wagnerian *Hauptmotiv*, along the lines of *The Ring*'s pervasive C–F♯ detail that links the "Curse" theme to many of the themes associated with Hagen.

Eastern Europe

Despite lying on the outskirts of mainstream European musical practice, Russian, Czech, and neighboring cultures lost no time in adopting Wagnerian leitmotivic practice. Opera composers in the lands to the east and south of Germany were occasionally dismissive (Tchaikovsky remarked that he felt as if he had been let out of prison after the final bars of *Götterdämmerung*, and that he had never been quite so bored as with *Tristan und Isolde*) but Wagner was largely accepted with enthusiasm.[44] Even Tchaikovsky himself seems not to have been immune. In *Eugene Onegin* the "Tatyana's Wistful Longing" theme that opens the opera appears throughout in typically Wagnerian fashion. Specifically, it is associated with an aspect of Tatyana's character, rather than as a "calling card" for the character, and appears only when dramatically appropriate (e.g., not at all in Act III when Tatyana's character and her feelings for Onegin have matured).

Tchaikovsky's contemporary Nikolai Rimsky-Korsakov first encountered *The Ring* in 1888–89. The work had an immense impression on the young composer, but it was Wagner's orchestration rather than his thematic technique that Rimsky-Korsakov imitated in his next operatic project, *Mlada*, an opera-ballet whose libretto wasn't particularly suitable for leitmotivic treatment. Rimsky-Korsakov did, however, come eventually to experiment with Wagnerian thematic techniques.[45] Among the works in which he invoked them is *The Golden Cockerel*. While many recurring themes in this work fall into the hackneyed, non-developmental "calling card" type (e.g., horn fifths and dotted scalar passages for the king, a simple folk-like tune for the female servant; chromatic flourishes, diminished seventh and augmented chords for the astronomer; an arpeggio-and-scale figure repeated every time

---

[44] Tchaikovsky 1970: 184 and 431.   [45] See Frolova-Walker 2001: 404ff.

the cockerel sings), there are a few notable examples suggestive of Wagnerian influence. Some themes – "Head Servant" and "Parrot," for instance – are used in the Wagnerian style to unify a given scene. And one, "Cockerel," contains a scale motive that permeates much of the score, unifying the entire work. The common folk sing the "Cockerel" theme and the orchestra takes it up repetitively during the sleeping scene; the king sings the theme at the end of Act I (in response to the bird); and at least one thematic development of it has dramatic implications: When the scalar portion of "Cockerel" opens with a falling third incipit and then rises, the dramatic moment is invariably peaceful. When, however, the incipit comprises a rising third followed by a falling scale, danger is nigh (see Example 8.14). Thematic Inversion here, as in Wagner, highlights dramatic opposition.

In fact, Thematic Inversion is almost a leitmotif itself in *The Golden Cockerel*, since many other notable themes turn upside-down at appropriate dramatic points. Another example is the inversion of the "King's Power" theme's dotted rhythm to form the "King's Impotence" at the opening of Act II. Rimsky-Korsakov seems also to have adopted Wagner's motives of pre-sentiment – musico-dramatic bits of foreshadowing. The grace-note–turn-ornamented syncopated octaves at the end of Act I, when the people set off to confront the enemy, anticipates the mature thematic statement sounded when the king meets the enemy queen in Act II. And we catch a preview of the queen's "eastern scale" music when the head servant describes the king's erotic dream about her.

Of all Eastern European operas in the generation after Wagner, Dvořák's *Rusalka* is among the most faithful to the leitmotivic technique of *The Ring*. Given the benighted tale, it is not surprising that a large number of its thematic developments include Harmonic Corruption. The title character's theme itself appears harmonically corrupted and fragmented often; two of many instances include when the Ježibaba casts her spell on Rusalka in the middle of Act I, and when Rusalka's sisters mourn her at the end of the same act. An even more dramatic corruption of the theme occurs at the opening of Act II when Turnspit questions where Rusalka comes from and whether or not she's human (see Example 8.15). The four-note "Foreboding" motive (first stated in the melody just after the Water Gnome asks Rusalka if she loves a man, Act I, m. 360) is similarly corrupted at dramatically appropriate points (especially in Act III) and reaches an apotheosis with a form of Thematic Inversion (as "Longing") when the prince dies, and when Rusalka disappears below the water. Other developments too numerous to list also surround others of the work's main leitmotifs, among them "Ježibaba," "Nature Spirits," and the "Rusalka's Woe" tetrachord.

(a)

(b)

Example 8.14 "Cockerel" from Rimsky-Korsakov's *The Golden Cockerel*

a. Original statement, Act I, rehearsal 88

b. Thematic Inversion, Act II, six bars before rehearsal 111

If it seems that many of the operas cited in the survey above – operas not only from Germany and Austria, but also from France, Italy, England, and Eastern Europe – stand outside the usual repertory of most opera houses, we might pause and question that fact. Why do we, today, know so few of the post-Wagnerian leitmotivic operas? Did others, in emulating Wagner,

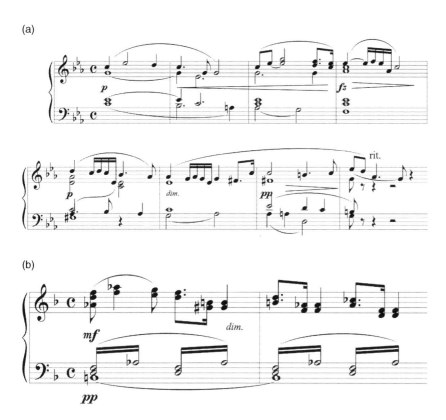

Example 8.15 "Rusalka" theme from Dvořák's *Rusalka*

a. Original statement, Act I, mm. 4–11
b. Harmonic Corruption and Truncation, Act II, rehearsal 7

fail to uncover their own unique compositional voices, thus constructing knock-offs of dubious quality? Or was the leitmotif after Wagner considered passé, unworthy of the critical attention so often necessary in canonizing a work of music? These same questions could be asked as well of the symphonic repertory we turn to next, since leitmotivic examples of these works, too, lie largely outside the common concert repertory.

Leitmotif in symphonic literature

After his death, Wagner's experiments with musical drama opened the door for leitmotivic compositions of all stripes. European composers increasingly exploited the technique in cantata, oratorio, ballet, symphonic song cycle, symphonic poem, and theatrical incidental music – virtually anything that could be construed to have a text and/or programme.[46] By and large, composers embraced the use of Wagnerian leitmotifs in these other genres, perhaps because their sense of anxiety over the composer's influence dwindled when applying the techniques outside of opera, the genre so dominated by Wagner.

Cantata and oratorio

Over the course of the nineteenth century, the popularity of both oratorio and cantata had waned; their heyday was really the early eighteenth century. Given these genres' Baroque-era origins, Christian (if not explicitly biblical) texts, and unstaged dramatic presentation, leitmotivic treatment in the few works written in the years after Wagner's death seems unlikely. Nevertheless, examples occur in the works of at least one composer: Englishman Edward Elgar.

In the nineteenth and early twentieth centuries, the oratorio (by then nearly indistinguishable from the contemporary cantata) was largely the province of English composers. A sense of nationalistic pride may thus explain Sir Edward Elgar's bizarre claim that his thematic technique in the four choral/orchestral works of the 1890s (*The Light of Life, Scenes from the Saga of King Olav, Caractacus*, and *The Dream of Gerontius*) devolved from Mendelssohn's English-language oratorio, *Elijah*, rather than from the über-Teutonic Wagner.[47] Elgar's distancing of himself from Wagner at this time stands in line with public statements made by other contemporaneous composers who eschewed Wagner's *Ring* and *Tristan* despite the obvious influence of these works (cf. Debussy and Tchaikovsky). One need turn only to Elgar's *Scenes from the Saga of King Olav* to be given pause to reconsider the composer's claims of Mendelssohnian influence.[48] In addition to the evocative Norse historico-mythic text, Wagnerian allusions in *King Olav* are not difficult to find. Thor's music, for example, references the storm music of *Die Walküre* with the sextuplet figurations recalling Donner's summoning of the storm in *Das Rheingold*, and the use of B♭ major and minor, keys associated with Donner's power over the storm. Allusions to the "Loge" (or "Magic Fire") music from *The Ring* occur at another appropriate spot in

---

[46] The post-Wagner diaspora of the leitmotif is largely grounded in symphonic works (with or without voices), though exceptions do occur. Note, for instance, the reworking of "Brünnhilde's Compassionate Love" from *Die Walküre* in the second movement of Eduard Tubin's *Sonatina for Piano*.

[47] By 1892–93 Elgar had heard *The Ring, Tristan und Isolde, Die Meistersinger von Nürnberg*, and *Parsifal* (McVeagh 2001: 123).

[48] For more on this topic, see Meadows 2008, esp. 47–66 and 100–79.

King Olav, namely at the words "Harness gold inlaid and burnished Mantle like a flame," in No. 3, "King Olaf's Return." Nor are Wagnerian allusions in Elgar's choral/symphonic works limited to *King Olav.* The slightly later (1902–03) oratorio cycle of *The Apostles* and *The Kingdom* contains the "Judas" theme from *The Apostles* (I.II, mm. 55–56 (two bars before rehearsal number 65)). It is a barely altered statement of "Magic Potion" from *The Ring.* And an obvious reference to the "Heilandsklage" from *Parsifal* occurs in the same work (*Apostles* I, R19/6–7).

It would be fair to say that, as Brahms channeled his symphonic aspirations into composing his first piano concerto, so too did Elgar focus his operatic impulses into writing cantatas and oratorios. Certainly, associative musical materials of the operatic type abound in these works. Few, however, exhibit the sense of musico-dramatic coalescence or development to qualify as leitmotifs. Among Elgar's choral/symphonic compositions, *The Apostles* and *The Kingdom* are the best examples of a post-Wagnerian thematic technique. They contain recurring themes that are, for the most part, short and harmonically ambiguous, along with self-quotations of music from the composer's earlier works, *The Light of Life* and *The Dream of Gerontius.*[49] While there is little to cite in the way of thematic development in these works, they contain at least one important thematic family: the chromatic neighbor figure at the core of the three-chord "Christ's Loneliness" theme features prominently in much of the score, and the ensuing chromatic descent is recalled in a Thematic Transformation in the "Lament of Mary Magdalene" (see Example 8.16). The shared musical material here highlights the pitiable aspect of both Jesus's and Mary's characters.

Ballet

Marian Smith makes the invidious, but difficult to disprove, claim that recurring melody as a dramatic device occurs more frequently in the ballet repertory of 1830s and 1840s France and Germany than it does in the operatic canon of the same time.[50] One sees proto-Wagnerian techniques in ballet music before 1850; a Change of Mode thematic development, for instance, occurs with the "Harvest Festival" theme in *Giselle,* a work Wagner attended in 1841.[51] It seems one could argue that ballet, as much as opera, shaped Wagner's leitmotivic technique. One could also argue that

---

[49] See Boult 2006, an audio analysis based on the careful tallying of motifs by Elgar's friend and colleague A.J. Jaeger.

[50] Smith 2000: 13.   [51] *Ibid.:* 14. See also Wagner's review of *Giselle* in Wagner 1966f.

Example 8.16 Thematic transformation between two themes in Elgar's *The Apostles*

a. "Christ's Loneliness" Part I. I. The Calling of the Apostles, rehearsal 24
b. "Lament of Mary Magdalene" Part I. III. By the Sea of Galilee, second bar of rehearsal 79

thematic development in later nineteenth-century ballet developed independent of Wagner's musico-dramatic experiments, but a look at Tchaikovsky's ballets suggests otherwise.

Though Tchaikovsky derided *The Ring*, both his *Sleeping Beauty* (Acts I and II in particular) and *Swan Lake* (Acts II–IV, in particular) betray a symphonic mode of composition based on thematic unity and development, atypical of ballet. Just as Wagner strove to do away with discrete operatic numbers and the divide between aria, ensemble, and recitative, so too did Tchaikovsky work to do away with discrete, musically unrelated dance numbers in these two ballets. In *Sleeping Beauty*, the most obvious of the leitmotifs – and leitmotifs they are, for they carry emotional residue from their instantiation, and modify their associations in tandem with the development of the drama – are those of the "Lilac Fairy," "Fairy Magic," and "Carabosse." A characteristic use of Wagnerian thematic development occurs in the final tableau of Act II, in which "Lilac Fairy" is subjected to Harmonic Corruption when her power is set against that of the evil Carabosse, whose theme is fragmented (see Example 8.17). This is followed by an apotheotic Change of Texture when the magic of the Lilac Fairy wins out.[52] Fittingly, the first three chords of "Carabosse" are stretched out and reharmonized to create the music for "Magic Spell," a form of Thematic Transformation linking the evil fairy with the dark enchantment she has wrought. A similar apotheosis transfigures the "Swan" theme at the conclusion of *Swan Lake* when Change of Mode, Change of Texture, and Harmonic Redemption sublimate the dolorous, Tarnhelm-esque theme into a glorious climax (see Example 8.18).

Song cycle

Song cycles have long employed associations with recurrent musical figures to create a sense of continuity between the various lieder they contain – think, for instance, of the arpeggiated piano accompaniments that symbolize the brook throughout Schubert's *Die Schöne Müllerin*. Few song cycles, however, are orchestral. The enormous added textural potential of a full orchestra allows for a wider range of associative

---

[52] Apotheosis is a special type of Change of Texture, mentioned by a number of authors. See, for instance, Cone 1968: 84 and Klein 2004: 31–32. The *locus classicus* in the Wagnerian repertory is the sublime statement of "Brünnhilde's Compassionate Love" in *Die Walküre* (Wk/294/2/1–295/1/2). In the Tchaikovsky example, note that melodic imitation (in the horns) during the second half of the theme adds complexity to the texture (see Act I, No. 4, mm. 272–76).

Example 8.17 "Lilac Fairy" theme from Tchaikovsky's *Sleeping Beauty*

a. Original statement, Act I, No. 4, mm. 232–38
b. Harmonic Corruption and Change of Texture, Act II, No. 19, mm. 19–22

possibilities – possibilities well realized in Schoenberg's *Gurrelieder*. Like Strauss, Schoenberg lived at a time and place when it was impossible to ignore the legacy of Wagner; not surprisingly, the composer's early dramatic works are undeniably Wagnerian in nature. *Gurrelieder*'s focus on nature as a character, doomed and forbidden love, and fairy-tale chivalry is a natural fit for Wagnerian techniques, and the composer includes plenty

(a)

(b)

Example 8.18 "Swan" theme from Tchaikovsky's *Swan Lake*

a. Original statement, Act II, No. 9, mm. 1–5
b. Harmonic Redemption and apotheosis, Act IV, No. 36, *Meno mosso*

of allusions to *The Ring* and *Tristan* in the cycle.[53] The orchestral introduction is itself thick with Wagnerian allusions, including echoes of the pastoral Forest Murmurs from *Siegfried*, the flickering light of the "Magic Fire" and the "Magic Sleep" music from the end of *Die Walküre*, and the striking sonority heard underneath the Sirens' "Naht euch dem Strande!" in the Act I *Venusberg* scene from *Tannhäuser*. An allusion to *Tristan* finds its way into the beginning of song No. 8 for the fitting text, *Du sendest mir einen Liebesblick.*

Even more than *The Ring*, *Gurrelieder* embodies a deep sense of memory and the weight of the past, a component of the work created in part by the proliferation of Wagnerian-style leitmotifs throughout.[54] Thus, it is only natural that we find thematic recall operating more in conglomerations of previously stated themes than in thematic developments that parallel the drama. A good example occurs just before rehearsal 82 in the Song of the Wood Dove when the themes from "so reich durch dich nun bin ich," "Sterne jubeln," "Ersten mal," "So tanzen die Engel," and "je meinen Kuss dir geschenkt" all occur within a few bars. This kind of saturation continues in the music that follows.

We can, however, point to a few thematic transformations that parallel the type Wagner used in *The Ring*. Among the most obvious is the Thematic Inversion of the "Sunset" theme (a falling sixth followed by a falling fourth and rising step, first played by the trumpet) in the orchestral introduction, to the "Sunrise" theme at the conclusion (heard in the low brass and the soprano choral part), a Thematic Transformation based on clear dramatic opposition (see Example 8.19).

The work's main "Love" theme appears in song 6, both in the orchestral lines and in Tove's vocal line (see especially her words, *Nun sag ich dir zum ersten Mal: "König Volmer, ich liebe dich!"* comprising a neighbor figure followed by a rising seventh and closing with a falling tenth). This theme is especially prone to thematic development for dramatic reasons. As but one example, see the Harmonic Corruption and Fragmentation of its falling

---

[53] See Cherlin 2007: 21, 22, 34, and 39–40; and Campbell 1997: 1–30, 44–46, and 62–70 who both comment on Wagnerian aspects of the composition (including the use of the love/death binary, the importance of nature as a dramatic force, the use of associative themes as memories, and the use of folk stories in the forging of the drama).

[54] This use of thematic-recall-as-memory is particularly obvious in the orchestral interludes. See, for instance, the music immediately preceding the Wood Dove's song. This piling up of memory can be used to create a "neuronal avalanche" as it does here, or to evoke irony as it does in Summer Wind's music just after rehearsal number 84, at his loaded statement, recalling the words of Tove and Waldemar from Part I: "Nun sag ich dir zum ersten Mal."

(a)

(b)

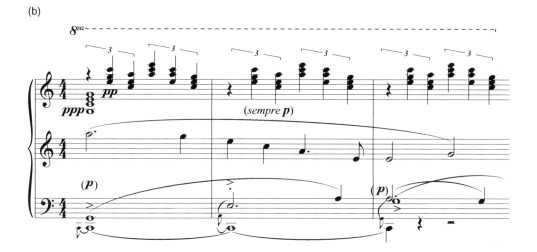

Example 8.19 Inversion of "Sunset" into "Sunrise" in Schoenberg's *Gurrelieder*

a. "Sunset," Part I, orchestral prelude, mm. 9–10
b. "Sunrise," Part III, two bars before rehearsal 102

half-step motive at rehearsal 95 shortly before the Wood Dove intones her dismal news – that Tove is dead (see Example 8.20).

Note that "Love" belongs to a family of themes with prominent neighbor figures presented in dotted rhythms. One, "Waldemar's Frantic Riding" (between rehearsal numbers 26 and 27 at *Belebt, nach und nach lebhafter und anschwellend*), is transformed into the "Love Waltz" (just before Tove's *Sterne jubeln*, i.e., seven bars before rehearsal number 35). The "Love Waltz" neighbor figure returns, rhythmically altered, in the seventh song (*Mitternacht*) when Waldemar, pretending to be a corpse remembering its earlier life, speaks of *Liebeslieder* one bar before rehearsal

(a)

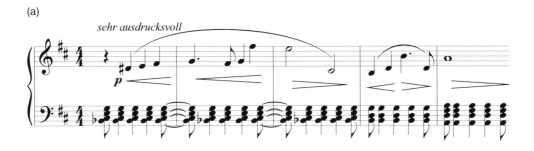

(b)

Example 8.20 "Love" theme in Schoenberg's *Gurrelieder*

a. Original statement, Part I, two bars before rehearsal 50
b. Harmonic Corruption and Fragmentation, Part I, one bar after rehearsal 95

number 57.[55] Corruptions of this figure and transformations of it into a descending chromatic motive unfold between rehearsal numbers 62 and 64 as Waldemar speaks of his time with Tove being over.

The opening neighbor motive of the "Love Waltz" appears in inversion one bar before rehearsal number 96 as the Wood Dove begins to sing, and this motive is then composed out in the Song of the Wood Dove as the song's refrain (*Weit flog ich, Klage sucht' ich, fand gar viel!* four bars before rehearsal number 102) repeats up a half-step (four bars before rehearsal number 104) and then back down again (five bars before rehearsal 107). The same motive returns for the Wood Dove's final words at the end of Part I.

Theater music

Though there are rarely singing parts in theater music, this genre would seem to be a natural fit for the leitmotif as there is a visible stage drama – be it live,

---

[55] One can't help but hear an allusion to Brahms at the return of the waltz figure coupled with the text "Liebeslieder."

or on film – with which musical ideas can be associated. Perhaps because most scores for incidental film music are limited in scope, however, leitmo-tivic treatments are rare – at least until the era of the Hollywood film score. Because the final chapter of this book deals exclusively with the theatrical music of film, we will content ourselves here with one example intended for live theater from the incidental music Edvard Grieg penned for *Peer Gynt*. Like Elgar's choral-symphonic works, Grieg's music contains a number of associative themes – "Peer Gynt," "Solveig's Song," and "Asa's Death" among them – though there are relatively few thematic developments. One, the Harmonic Corruption of the "Peer Gynt" theme by half-diminished seventh chords when the title character abducts Ingrid, makes perfect dramatic sense; the protagonist's character is corrupted and so is his music (see Example 8.21). The Thematic Transformation of the "Woman in Green"

(a)

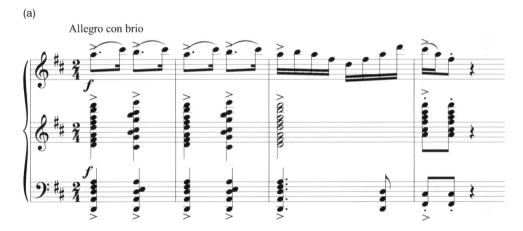

(b)

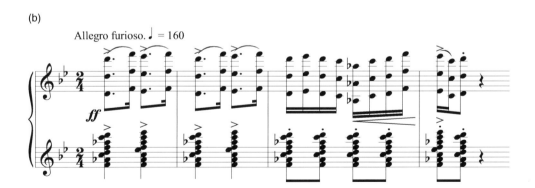

Example 8.21 "Peer Gynt" theme from Grieg's *Peer Gynt*

a. Original statement, Act I, No. 1, mm. 1–4
b. Harmonic Corruption, Act II, No. 4, mm. 1–4

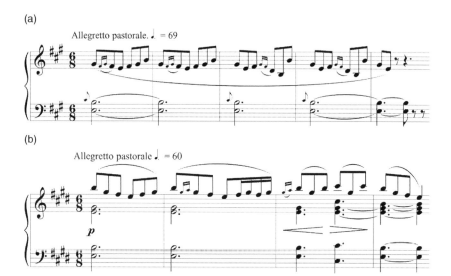

Example 8.22 Thematic transformation in Grieg's *Peer Gynt* of "Woman in Green" into "Morning"

a. "Woman in Green," Act II, No. 6, mm. 23–27
b. "Morning," Act IV, No. 13, mm 1–4

music into "Morning," however, is puzzling (see Example 8.22). Apart from the scenes' shared pastoral settings, it's difficult to know what dramatic import to make of this musical connection.

Symphonic poem

Wagner's influence on Schoenberg, Strauss, and Rimsky-Korsakov is well known, exemplified, in part, in some of the operatic excerpts discussed above. Opera isn't the only genre, however, in which the debt these composers owe Wagner is obvious. Symphonic poems like *Don Juan, Till Eulenspiegels lustige Streiche, Pelleas und Melisande,* and *Scheherazade* all feature prominent associative themes, some of which rise to the level of leitmotifs. Of course, symphonic poems have a special leitmotif obstacle to overcome: dramatic associations with musical themes must arise lacking both a text and a staged drama. In many cases, a programme, narrative cues written into the score by the composer (sometimes unpublished), and/or archival evidence of specific correspondences between music and narrative provided by the composer allow for the establishment of clear associative themes.[56] This is the case not only in

---

[56] One possible test case would be Schoenberg's *Verklärte Nacht*, which certainly sounds like it has leitmotifs. It would be difficult, however, to achieve the same level of associative precision one could manage in a staged and/or texted work. Even with Schoenberg's program notes of August

(a)

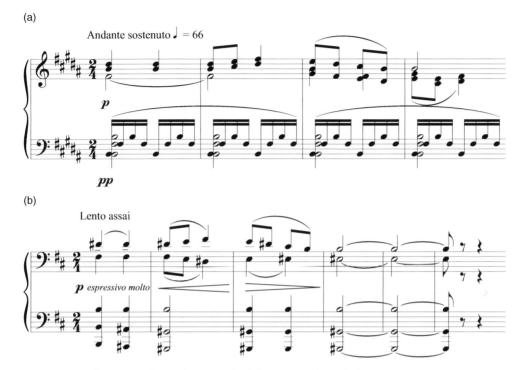

(b)

Example 8.23 "Mother and Daughter Together" from Dvořák's *Vodník*

a. Original statement, mm. 128–31
b. Harmonic Corruption and Change of Texture, mm. 549–54

works like *Till Eulenspiegel* or Berlioz's *Symphonie Fantastique*, but also in some less well-known symphonic poems.[57] Dvořák's 1896 efforts, for instance, are exemplary in this regard. *Vodník* ("The Water Goblin"), *Polednice* ("The Noon Witch") and *Holoubek* ("The Wild Dove") are three of the four works inspired by the ballads of Dvořák's fellow-countryman Karel Jaromír Erben. In them, Dvořák unfurls symphonic forms based largely on developments of

1950 (Schoenberg 1988), which give some indications, the nature of the drama is so internal and psychological that the sorts of thematic identification problems once faced in *Tristan* return here, but without the benefit of a visual stage action or a sung text to cement associations. That said, a study of how contrapuntal thematic combinations communicate complex psychological states is a project worth undertaking.

[57] Among these is Schoenberg's *Pelleas und Melisande*. In this work we enjoy the benefits of Schoenberg's thematic designations in a 1918 letter from the composer. See Cherlin 2007: 68–154 for a thorough thematic analysis. Particularly interesting to note is the use of Wagnerian developmental techniques to portray Melisande's own pathological self-reflection through the creation of a Thematic Complex built out of recursive structural combinations of Melisande's themes.

associative themes, with the composer's programme notes providing specific locations in the music that correspond to the work's narrative.

In *Vodník* we find that the theme "Mother and Daughter Together" returns during the section in which the two women are reunited after the daughter escapes from the water goblin. The theme is subjected to Change of Texture and Harmonic Corruption at this point to reflect the unhappy circumstances of the reunion: the daughter's child is being held ransom against her pledge of return to the lair of the water goblin (see Example 8.23). In the work's coda, the mother's and water goblin's themes are subjected to Fragmentation and are combined, appropriate given that everyone in the story succumbs to loss at its conclusion – the water goblin has lost his wife, and the daughter and mother have lost their son and grandson respectively, a casualty of the daughter's failure to return to the water goblin. Dvořák uses similar tactics in the other two works cited. In *Polednice*, Thematic Fragmentation of the witch's and mother's themes in the scherzo depicts their conflict. Because evil triumphs in this symphonic poem, "Noon Witch" closes the work with a Change of Texture effecting a dark apotheosis of the theme as the child's spirit is snatched away by the creature. And, in *Holoubek* the Fragmentation of the "Wife's Sorrow" theme at the end of the work illustrates the woman's passing.

∗∗∗

The examples above provide but a smattering of the great leitmotivic diaspora in dramatic art music after Wagner. The diversity of genres and of points across Europe in which Wagner's musico-dramatic ideas persisted, though, bears testament to their potency. Interestingly, of all the various dramatic genres to exhibit leitmotivic tendencies, it was theater music that most lastingly adopted Wagner's thematic technique. Composers of art music from the early mid-twentieth century onward no longer felt the shadow of Wagner looming over them quite so strongly as did their predecessors a generation earlier.[58] But – for reasons to be explored in the next chapter – as the use of the Wagnerian leitmotif waned in concert music, it found a new and natural home in the emerging genre of the film score.

---

[58] Stravinsky, for instance, did not regularly employ Wagnerian-style leitmotifs. Though some of the ballets and the works on Greek subjects do have associative themes, these are largely symbolic in nature rather than functioning as Wagnerian bearers of emotional significance to be recalled later. Among them, *Persephone* comes closest to containing what we have described in this study as a leitmotif since the "Persephone's Immortality" theme undergoes musical transformations inspired by the drama. See Carr 2002: 188–92.

9 | The modern-day leitmotif: associative themes in contemporary film music

> Every character should have a theme.
>
> Max Steiner

Recorded music does us a disservice. Or, rather, it presents a different type of experience than music with an attendant visual spectacle. As any concert-goer knows, listening to a recording of an orchestral performance is not the same as experiencing it live; there's a feeling of something missing. To be sure, there is a stage drama of sorts in any live performance, but in opera this visible drama is generally more central to the work's artistic conception than it is for purely instrumental compositions. Thus, our sense of incompleteness increases when listening to recordings of opera or musical theater. Of course, for film music, the problem is even more acute: How many of us can hear the score to a film we have seen without images and emotions flooding our consciousness?

There exists here a continuum of visual/auditory multi-media relationships; the auditory realm clearly dominates the visual in instrumental music performances (at least for most Western art music composed before the mid-twentieth century); the visual achieves greater importance in relation to the auditory for vocal performance, especially opera and other forms of musical theater; and the visual trumps the auditory in most films. After all, the filmic medium – though almost from its inception juxtaposed with sound accompaniment – originated as a purely visual art form. Even after a century of advances in filmic audio culture and technology, we still go to *see* a movie, not to *hear* it. Most movie-goers pay little to no *conscious* attention to a film's soundtrack (particularly the musical underscoring). It would be hard to argue the converse: that the majority attend a movie and devote scant attention to the on-screen images.

Over the history of film, there have been, however, at least some directors, composers, and audiences who have increasingly focused on the role of musical sound in the filmic experience. Along the way, a significant number of composers – from Max Steiner to Howard Shore – have clearly understood the dramatic and emotional power of associative themes. These themes serve various functions throughout the history of film,

255

augmenting images and myriad aspects of the drama, including those unseen, like the psychological aspects of a character's state of mind.[1] While the modern-day orchestral sonorities of a John Williams score for a special-effects-laden film rich with fantastical scenes may appear to have little to do with early silent films, in fact both share a form of musical association that has remained, in some ways, surprisingly unchanged over the past century. Since thematic composition for films emerged from the art music tradition, we shall begin our foray into the topic of leitmotif in film music with a brief overview of this historical development, exploring thereafter its intimate – some would say inevitable – relationship to the Wagnerian *Gesamtkunstwerk*.

The emergence of the leitmotivic film score

It is common knowledge that music has accompanied drama in the West at least since the time of Ancient Greece. For obvious reasons, a history of such interaction lies well outside the scope of this book. Even tracing the comparatively recent origins of film music constitutes a topic worthy of book-length treatment. Fortunately, this is a tale well treated in the extant literature, allowing us the luxury of summarizing.[2] Musical accompaniment so quickly became an expected component of filmic experience because it served a number of crucial purposes. Among them: music masked extraneous noises (like that of the projector); music provided continuity between discontinuous shots; music directed audience attention to important components of the visual narrative; music induced mood; music guided the pacing and outlines of a given scene; music communicated meaning and clarified narrative, especially in ambiguous or unseen psychological contexts; music heightened the sense of reality, time, place, and context (thus, encouraging audience absorption in the film); and music added an artistic, aesthetic legitimacy and sensibility to the nascent filmic art form.[3]

Early on, organists and orchestras accompanying silent films gravitated toward playing well-known excerpts of extant concert music (drawn largely from nineteenth-century dramatic genres) because of their pre-existing associations and familiar cultural tropes. It is well known that

---

[1] Prendergast 1992: 231–33.
[2] For a succinct history of the origins of film music, see MacDonald 1998: 1–4.
[3] This list is culled from Cohen 2001: 258 and Prendergast 1992: 213–26.

these musical selections were often anthologized so that performing forces could easily access a variety of excerpts complementary to common filmic dramatic-emotional contexts.[4] Less well known is that in 1915, S.M. Berg, an employee of New York music publisher G. Schirmer's Photoplay Department, began preparing cue sheets that designated a "theme" for a given film, an approach that was broadly accepted a couple years later, due in large part to the efforts of Samuel L. Rothapfel (better known as "Roxy"), an impresario and exhibitor who apostrophized Wagner's leitmotivic technique. Despite criticisms leveled at its banality, the thematic approach remained viable for decades, most likely because of the 1920s film industry's wild success. (As sequel- and remake-weary audiences today know all too well, Hollywood's mindset has changed little in the intervening years. After all, why change a winning formula if it's making money?)

In many cases, thematic cues *were* banal, the pairing of a particular musical theme with a character or event such that the theme could later serve as a stand-in for an absent image.[5] The use of familiar, Western art music favorites drawn from existing repertory – and popular newly composed themes – as recurring ideas achieved powerful effects by exploiting the power of memory. That is, thematic film scores cultivated an audience's perception of *déjà entendu*; the sense of re-hearing familiar music mitigated the unfamiliarity that many audiences experienced with the new, disjunct medium. Over time, newly composed themes proliferated to refresh the worn-out and overused classics. This new music quickly became "commodified," creating a cottage industry for the composition, marketing, and sale of sheet music (and eventually, recorded soundtracks as well).[6]

With the advent of "talkies" in the late 1920s came the assumption that the soundtrack would obviate the need for a score – a score whose only contribution to the genre would be a confusing aural competition with the actual soundtrack. In fact, audiences and film-makers long accustomed to musical accompaniment to film felt something was missing.[7] Film music's many functions had become integral to the experience, and had forever

---

[4] Cohen 2001: 251.

[5] Butler 2013: 168–69 discusses how much early film music used simple thematic recall rather than leitmotif. Cohen 2001: 258 calls these leitmotifs, though they hardly fit the specific definitions for "leitmotif" proposed by this book. This more restrictive usage of "leitmotif" is echoed by Altan who argues against the populist conflation of the Wagnerian leitmotif with early silent film themes. See Altman 2007: 222.

[6] See Altman 2007. For a brief history of the release of commercial soundtracks for sale, see Pool and Wright 2010: 71–74.

[7] Kracauer 1960: 138.

cemented in the minds of movie-goers the concept of filmic art as a work of multi-media. Certainly, aspects of the musical accompaniment to the moving image had to change (the advent of underscoring to make dialogue audible above the music is one), but the film score was here to stay.

As in art music, the presence of thematic material in the film score asserts itself in a variety of ways. While our main concern in this chapter will be with the so-called "leitmotivic" score ("associative thematic" score may be a better label), which features a variety of associative themes, other models proliferated as well. Some scores tended toward the monothematic (Maurice Jarre's score to *Lawrence of Arabia* is a good example), others to the developmental – in which thematic material(s) is/are subject to a sort of developing variations (as in David Raskin's score to *Laura*) – or the atmospheric (i.e., a largely athematic score in which recurrent thematic materials are not central to the musical structure, such as Howard Shore's score to *The Fly*).[8] In all cases, the music is intimately tied to the drama, just as it is in the art music genres of opera, lieder, ballet, and programme symphony.

The parallels between film music and art music are understandable when one learns that early film composers like Sergei Prokofiev, William Walton, Max Steiner, Erich Korngold, Hanns Eisler, and Franz Waxman emerged from the professional art music world. That said, all too often commentators indulge in facile but misleading equivalences between art and film music, implying that some sort of universal "nineteenth-century" style of composition undergirds both genres. Predictably, this unfortunate state of affairs is pandemic in descriptions of leitmotif, and in comparisons of film to Richard Wagner's operas. Thus, it behooves us to engage in a brief comparison of art and film music, with special attention paid to opera and to Wagner in particular.

Art music and film music

It is unsurprising that so many liken film music to the music of nineteenth-century Europe. Modern-day film composers and music scholars share the responsibility for purveying this notion. Composer Howard Shore, for instance, often cites the influence of Wagner and Mahler on his music,[9] mentions in interviews that Hollywood film music came from the European concert world,[10] admits that he himself took up composing for films

---

[8] Prendergast 1992: 227–45.   [9] Schelle 1999: 356.   [10] *Ibid.*: 334.

as a venue to get his concert music performed,[11] and draws parallels between musical functions in film and concert music.[12] Music scholars paint a similar picture.[13] Kathryn Kalinak details romantic aspects of film scoring (including its preponderance of melody, lush orchestral textures, and so forth).[14] Caryl Flinn's *Strains of Utopia* portrays film composition as an attempt to recapture the halcyon days of earlier (i.e., Romantic-era) Western art music.[15] Susan McClary points to aspects of the nineteenth-century symphony that made its discontinuous musical language a natural fit for the narrative multi-media genre of film.[16] And Rebecca Leydon goes a step further to say that filmic techniques may have inspired compositional techniques used by Claude Debussy.[17]

These connections are all worth noting, but any implication that Romantic-era concert music and modern-day film music are somehow isomorphic is an overgeneralization.[18] When people compare the two genres, they usually refer to specific composers (Wagner, Mahler, and Strauss, for instance, rather than Brahms, Scriabin, or Saint-Saëns). And they refer to specific styles of dramatic or programme music (opera, lieder, and programme symphony rather than string quartet, concerto, or etude). This is most likely because the idiosyncrasies of tonality, form, and thematic treatment in dramatic concert works of music bear a special set of artistic challenges and rewards; they stand apart from so-called absolute music because they are works of multi-media.

Most germane to our undertaking here are those genres that include both a visual, staged drama (opera, melodrama, and ballet) and a performed text and/or dialogue (opera, lieder, melodrama, oratorio, cantata, and some symphonies); the vast majority of films include both. Of these, only opera and melodrama have both a visible, staged drama *and* a performed text. Melodrama never really emerged as a genre to challenge

---

[11] *Ibid.*

[12] See Schelle 1999: 328 in which the author quotes Shore as saying that film music accomplishes what the piano accompaniment in Schubert lieder does.

[13] Adorno and Eisler 1994: xx–xxi state that a working knowledge of the classics formed the basis of the typical Hollywood composer's career, as early film composers often borrowed from the classics when creating film scores.

[14] Kalinak 1992: 100–102.   [15] Flinn 1992.   [16] McClary 2007: 50–51.

[17] See Leydon 2001, whose arguments in this regard are predicated on a nationalist rationale for Debussy's compositional choices. Her study raises the obvious question: Do modern-day film composers continue to be influenced by visual techniques in the films they write for?

[18] Even implying that nineteenth-century European practice was a unary one seems to be a misapprehension, at least according to the many scholars who believe in the emergence of a "second practice" of nineteenth-century tonality that emerged from and co-existed with earlier techniques during the Romantic era. See, for instance, Kinderman and Krebs 1996.

opera in the history of Western music, though its influences are obvious from the eighteenth century's accompanied recitative and *Singspiel* to the modern-day soap opera.

And here we must pause, because the genre of melodrama shines a light on the shadowy underside of this tale. A great body of music fell to the wayside of the grand historical narrative we like to tell, not just melodrama, but also operetta, incidental music, and salon music (among others). The origins of this music in the eighteenth century led to its heyday in the early nineteenth, and composers we often associate with loftier genres wrote in these as well; Schubert's *Die Zauberharfe* is but one example. While incidental music remains in the performance repertory today (think Mendelssohn's *Midsummer Night's Dream* or Grieg's *Peer Gynt*), melodrama, operetta, and salon music were, by the end of the nineteenth century, relegated to a tawdry, populist second-class of music, at least by self-defined musical elites. And they remain there today, largely ignored as they stand on the street corners outside the concert halls where we house our most cherished masterpieces. The traditions of these genres, however, lie closer to film than any so-called "art" music. That is because they involved spoken dialogue, acting, and musical "underscoring."[19] The over-acting and heightened emotionality we associate with melodrama in particular contribute to the misconception that melodrama and associated genres influenced only the *theatrical* side of early film. These theatrical characteristics remain in today's film (at least some film, not to mention in television). They also, however, linger as a component of film *music*, not only its practice of pairing background music with spoken dialogue, but also the overblown, bombastic, and highly emotional scores that contribute to today's blockbusters and sentimental tear-jerkers.

The fact of the matter, though, is that there is a deep-seated point of view that has persisted in Western musical culture for well over a hundred years that makes the adjective *theatrical* a pejorative. Neither scholarship nor performance has made available to us anywhere near the wealth of knowledge about melodrama that it has about opera, which, despite being a theatrical genre, finds itself firmly entrenched in high society even if it can't aspire to the Hanslickian purity of something like the string quartet or the symphony. For that reason, then, it makes sense to evaluate the claims of similarity between art and film music by circumscribing the comparison to focus on tonal, thematic film scores and Romantic-era opera, at least until

---

[19] And melodrama's thematic recall arguably flowed directly into the appearance of cue sheets for silent cinema.

there is considerably more analytic work completed on the neglected dramatic music of the nineteenth-century theater and salon.

Opera and film music

It is not difficult to find comparisons between film music and opera on record. Again, Howard Shore: "I think opera *is* film music";[20] "It [the *Silence of the Lambs* score] is not really scored like a horror movie or a thriller – the music is operatic, dark, but very beautiful . . . it's actually not a very dissonant score, it's more of a dread tonality";[21] and

The *Lord of the Rings* is an opera in concept. And what I mean is, it's three acts. It's three films. And it has the complexity and the relationships of what we think of as opera music, because it so goes beyond what you think of as a film score. A film score you think of as having just a few characters and it doesn't always have the scope of what you think of as opera music. I don't know if it has to do with drama. I think it's an emotional thing.[22]

When pressed by the interviewer "In what sense do you mean operatic?" Shore responded, "A certain kind of emotional writing that could have been Puccini if you take away the vocals. They used to put out records of opera without the singing. That's film music of the purest form. It's dramatic underscoring."[23]

Shore has a point; opera and film music share a number of characteristics. Both typically involve characters engaged in a drama the audience witnesses visually; both engage narrative storytelling practices; both include dialogue; and both demand that composers create music to fit the characters, drama, narrative, and dialogue. That is, both have a pre-existing non-musical structure that serves to shape and inspire the music that must be composed for it.[24] In addition, film music also adopts many musical characteristics native to nineteenth-century European opera.

---

[20] Schelle 1999: 341(italics in the original).

[21] Schelle 1999: 347. When asked how he creates tonal dread, Shore's reply was as follows: "Working in fourths, fifths, a lot of ninths and sevenths, a lot of seconds – but not necessarily in a functional way, more in a way of overlapping and playing them against each other – as opposed to triads. It's unsteady – the tonality is insecure, but I'm not creating a great deal of dissonance." *Ibid.*: 348.

[22] It almost sounds like Shore equates *opera* with *epic* in the quotation above, evoking no other operatic work so much as Wagner's epic *Ring* cycle. Karlin and Wright 2004: 141–42.

[23] Brown 1994: 336.

[24] In fact, one could argue that opera and film stand in opposition to the conception of "absolute" musical traditions like symphony or concerto because constellations of leitmotifs and tonal areas form a coherent plan for dramatic works in these genres distinct from the way keys and

Among them are orchestrations typical of Weber, Wagner, Strauss, Rimksy-Korsakov, and other opera composers; tonally ambiguous harmonies rich with chromaticism and chordal dissonance; melodic and motivic structures common to art music from western Europe; and musical topics that preserve a code of meaning established in nineteenth-century opera.[25] One might argue that much film even maintains the musical distinction between recitative, aria, and incidental music, using non-thematic underscoring to accompany dialogue and some action sequences, and reserving rich moments of heightened thematicism for those highly charged moments or scenes when time seems to stretch out (and for transitional moments when the filmic narrative changes time or place). This is certainly true in John Williams's score to *Harry Potter and the Sorcerer's Stone*. In it, associative themes are largely absent from action sequences, reserved instead for moments of narrative import, especially those of a magical or stygian nature. Overtures rich in thematic presentation and development, too, appear in films, sometimes over the opening credits or – more often in recent years – as "aftertures" over the closing credits.[26]

Despite the similarities, however, there are a number of important differences between film and opera. For one, musical composition intended for a specific dramatic moment in a given film virtually never predates the existence of the film. Such is not the case in opera, where some composers – like Wagner, who wrote his own libretti – conceived of musical and dramatic ideas simultaneously.[27] Opera composers also have a great deal

---

themes function in (monotonal) instrumental forms. That is, music in opera and film serves the drama rather than creating its own internal logic and coherence. See Rodman 2011b.

[25] Huckvale 1988: 52.

[26] By way of another example, consider the citation below, which enumerates one author's view of the ways film music engages with the earlier operatic tradition: 1) a reconsideration of the question of how several different arts could be combined into one unified artistic production, 2) a reapplication of the Wagnerian techniques of leitmotif and continuous melody, 3) the provision of a vast repertoire of dramatic music which was freely used, 4) filmed operas which caused more serious probes into the question of how to provide appropriate musical accompaniments, 5) the use of music on the set as an aid for helping actors emote, and 6) an updating of the structural principle of the pasticcio opera, i.e., compilation. See Berg 1976: 93. This list raises important points (among them many – like filmed opera – that we will not have the opportunity to explore here).

[27] Or even, in some cases, of music first. See, for example, Wagner's sketches of the "Brangäne's Consolation" theme (also referred to as *Freundesliebe*) in *Tristan und Isolde* and his initial uncertainty as to where this music belonged. See Dreyfus 2010: 205–06. That said, trusting Wagner's recollections is a dicey proposition at best. Confident statements of when the composer's musical ideas emerged vis-à-vis his operatic texts are best corroborated by careful sketch study.

more control over the length of their music; in film, composers are often asked to write music that fits a given length of time, measured down to the second. Most importantly, it is a myth to think of the film score as a composer's medium. Setting aside the exigencies of team composition, the director has ultimate say over the final product, including the music, and can choose to be intimately involved in the compositional process or not.

The upshot of these differences is a real impact in terms of musical form, tonality, and thematic development. Extended or deep-level formal, tonal, and thematic processes are almost impossible to achieve in film music. The sort of motivic, harmonic, and tonal parallelisms centered on minor thirds in Weber's Wolf's Glen scene from *Der Freischütz* or the multi-layered, nested bar forms of Act II, Scene 4 from Wagner's *Die Walküre*, for instance, would be almost unthinkable in a film score. Likewise, the complex network of leitmotifs or of associative tonality that exist in Wagner's *Ring* would require a film series of mammoth proportions; *The Ring* is over fifteen hours long, and those fifteen-plus hours all include musical sound. The same is not true in film where musical sound can occupy less than half the total time of the completed work.

Adorno and Eisler reach a similar conclusion, criticizing tonality (more accurately, its lack) in film music. In short, they believe traditional tonality is an impossibility in a filmic context because the art form demands musical brevity and discontinuity; there simply isn't the breadth of canvas necessary to unfold more than a tonal snippet.[28] Consequently, film composers elevate harmony and harmonic progression at the expense of tonality.[29] And the harmonies film composers prefer – according to Adorno and Eisler – are modern, tension-filled, complex cliché sonorities rather than simpler, tried-and-true patterns, because traditional harmony is often inadequate to express the blockbuster, epic sense of emotionality that film attempts to produce.[30] (Admittedly, Adorno's characterization of film music as a formless, non-autonomous commodity rife with cliché sounds suspiciously like what he had to say about the music in the Wagnerian *Gesamtkunstwerk*.)[31]

These distinctions between opera and film music are, however, often conveniently ignored. And when they are ignored, when Richard

---

[28] Adorno and Eisler 1994: 41–2, n. 2. One can argue, though, that the Wagnerian corpus creates an opportunity for the rare narrative "down-conversion"; if one knows the Wagnerian repertory, it is easy enough to bottle the epic impulse through references to Wagner's works into a much smaller package, a point made by Metz 2013.

[29] Adorno and Eisler 1994: 42.   [30] *Ibid.*: 37.

[31] This is the overarching sentiment one gleans from Adorno and Eisler 1994.

Wagner – the composer to whom the origins of contemporary film music's language is most often attributed – is evoked, rarely is it acknowledged that he never even wrote for the movies. Prokofiev, Ibert, Satie, Walton (none of them a strong Wagnerian cultural descendant) and a host of other well-known composers of concert music wrote early film scores, so why is it to *Der Ring des Nibelungen* that scholars and commentators turn for comparison with the modern-day genre?[32] Why is it musical prose, leitmotif, associative tonality, and endless melody that get dragged out time and again to explain the structure and function of film music?[33] In short, "Why Wagner?"

Wagner and film music

The most facile answer to the above question is, of course, *Gesamtkunstwerk*. As the progenitor of an artistic philosophy that relegated music to a collaborative, rather than a central, role, Wagner paved the way for a similar treatment in film.[34] Film composer Miklós Rózsa once said, "Filmmaking is a composite art, a Wagnerian *Gesamtkunstwerk*, and film music should be written in this way."[35] Even Wagner's idealized setting for the performance of *Musikdrama* at Bayreuth resembles the modern-day film experience: the auditorium is darkened (not true of many concert settings before the twentieth century), the orchestra is invisible, and the seats are uncomfortable.

Wagner's *Musikdrama* practice and his theories in *Oper und Drama* comprise forerunners for film music.[36] There are clear examples of "Mickey Mousing" in Wagner's score to *The Ring* (Alberich's scrabbling

---

[32] This is not to imply that film composers all, or even mostly, modeled themselves after Wagner. David Raskin's developmental, monothematic score to *Laura* seems more reminiscent of an opera like *Eugene Onegin* than it does *Götterdämmerung*. But even a quick perusal of the published work on film music will show that references to Wagner far outnumber those to, say, Tchaikovsky.
Moreover, many composers after Wagner (Walton, in his film music, for one – see Lloyd 1999: 112–13, 120, and 127) were clearly influenced by his music, but that hardly makes a case for Wagner being the one who fathered the genre.

[33] See, for instance, Berg 1976: 70–83 who relates the history of film music to opera in just such a manner. The definition of leitmotif, *ibid.*: 76, explicitly mentions thematic development but not emotional association.

[34] Wagner, of course, didn't always adhere to this philosophy in practice. As Jean-Jacques Nattiez makes clear throughout his monograph, however, Wagner's gendered metaphor of music as the feminine help-mate to the gendered-masculine poetry is a pervasive one in the composer's writings. See Nattiez 1997.

[35] Flinn 1992: 13.

[36] Huckvale 1988 compares a number of moments from Wagner's *Ring* with moments in cinema, citing the parallel functions music plays in both.

over rocks and sneezing in scene 1 of *Das Rheingold* is but one) and his use of prelude-as-drama is a precursor to the use of title-music-as-drama in film.[37] Perhaps most compelling is the distinction between recitative-type "underscoring" in *The Ring*[38] – lengthy passages where the music qua music is less than compelling (no doubt, the passages that inspired Rossini to state that "Wagner has wonderful moments and dreadful quarters of an hour").[39] The same is true of film; the bits that make it onto soundtrack releases aren't usually the underscoring passages, but rather the moments of melodic and dramatic intensity. Wagner himself wrote of "melodic moments of feeling" when drama and music reach a focal point together;[40] these are – at least in theory – the birthplaces of the leitmotifs – the points of thematic and associative fixity described in Chapters 2–5 – and, one presumes, Rossini's "wonderful moments" that break up the tedium of the "dreadful quarters of an hour."

We might admit, then, that at least some film music returned to the earlier aesthetic of the nineteenth century, an aesthetic that can be traced back to the Romantic symphony, whose developments were, by his own admission, what Wagner was trying to emulate in the composition of *The Ring*.[41] The visual imagery Wagner uses in his essay on Beethoven's Ninth, and the contemporary audience accounts of symphonies by the likes of Schumann, Tchaikovsky, Rachmaninov, and Mahler, to name but a few, were often narratively based in a schematic way rather than unified by an internal musical coherence in the manner of, say, Beethoven or Mozart.[42]

And it is not just in Hollywood film music that Wagner's legacy looms large. Caryl Flinn's study of new German cinema makes an example of Peer Raben's score for the fourteen-hour serial *Berlin Alexanderplatz*, which uses character calling-card-type themes – themes that, rather than being a hackneyed throwback to a bygone era, accomplish much in terms of characterization: painting musical portraits of the characters, reminding the audience of the characters and their natures (important in this long, complex, serialized art form), and using the blending of themes and structural relationships between themes to illustrate how characters inter-act with and get inside each other.[43] This is but one of Flinn's examples of

[37] This is a point made by Franklin 2010: 55 and 57–58.
[38] Note that film composer Max Steiner was influenced by the operas of Wagner and other art music composers; he even christened Wagner the first underscorer. Neumeyer 2010: 116–18.
[39] Naumann 1876: IV, 5.
[40] Wagner discusses this idea repeatedly in *Oper und Drama*. See Wagner 1966b: 233, 249, 256, and 347, among others.
[41] See Millington 1992: 84.   [42] Franklin 2007: 13–18.   [43] Flinn 2004: 83–84.

Wagnerian influence on New German Cinema, not just as a musical presence (i.e., using Wagner's music in film) or influence (on texture, thematic usage, and so forth) but as an ambivalent cultural icon, one that can symbolize both Germany's benighted past as well as its lasting legacy of artistic greatness.

Not everyone, however, accepts the claim that film music owes the bulk of its substance to Wagnerian opera. Christoph Henzel finds underscoring to be a very different animal from foreground operatic music, and argues that mood music and Mickey Mousing have nothing to do with tonal structure.[44] And Scott Paulin arrived at the conclusion that the invocation of *Gesamtkunstwerk* in the history of film-music composition was largely employed as a sleight-of-hand – a connection fabricated to create the illusion of conceptual unity in film music belying its synthetic and multiple-author nature. In essence, Wagner's name was used as a fetishistic talisman to create a patina of nineteenth-century, unary artistic genius for the mass-produced, entertainment-function industry of film.[45]

Paulin's assertion of Wagner's name as fetishistic talisman has the ring of truth to it. But there is more to the story. Wagner's legacy in Western music is one that glorifies his ability to use music to capture the ineffable residue of emotion in a dramatic scene, and whatever else can be said of Wagner, it would be hard to argue that he did not possess an innate sense of drama. Modern-day composers recognize that in his music. Howard Shore acknowledges it when he says that Wagner's music "speaks the unspeakable," referring at many points to music expressing the emotions of the scene at hand.[46] This mode of expression seems to be especially true in fantasy, science-fiction, and horror genres where Wagner's model of engaging directly with the numinous (cf. Schopenhauer) works well for such otherworldly settings.[47] This merger of myth and music links Romantic-era operas like *Der fliegende Holländer*, *Lohengrin*, or *The Ring* with modern-day films that treat similar subjects. Fantasy and horror genres, with their elements of the supernatural, are metaphors for the Jungian collective unconscious and thus invite a union of myth and music.[48] (It is perhaps no coincidence that among the most famous film and television motives are three drawn from the horror genre: the opening motive of the music for *The Twilight Zone*, the screeching string figure from *Psycho*'s shower scene, and the rising half-step from *Jaws*.)[49] One turns easily to examples from Wagner – say, the musical depiction of the

[44] Henzel 2004: 91–92.   [45] Paulin 2000.   [46] Schelle 1999: 349.   [47] Rosar 2010.
[48] Huckvale 1988: 49.   [49] Karlin 1994: 26.

dragon, Fafner, in the prelude to Act II of *Siegfried* – when seeking forerunners of twentieth-century horror-film music.[50]

So, it should be no surprise that Wagner's name arises so frequently in discussions of film music. For those who care about the legitimization of the art form, a Wagnerian association accomplishes much. Among other things, it conjures the illusion of musical unity, it conveys a sense of artistic legitimacy through a link to the past, it suggests film music's prodigious ability to manipulate emotions, and it links the film score to a mythic cultural collective unconscious. But the central component of Wagner's influence on film music is considerably more concise and concrete than all of these. The single most powerful thing Wagner had to offer film music was the leitmotif.

Leitmotif, in Wagner's hands, had the power to conflate all of the above: musical coherence, history, dramatic emotionality, myth, and ineffability – that elusive mélange film-makers so desperately sought to capture in their new medium. Leitmotif also handed composers a ready-made, concise, and easily recognizable nugget of form, tonality, and thematic content; its ability to unite these things made it invaluable as a tool for reinforcing narrative across disjunct scenic cuts in space and time.[51] Moreover, Wagner's technique appealed to film composers because it divorced the orchestra from the sung (or in film, spoken) self-expression of onstage characters, allowing it to serve instead as a narrator,[52] even an unreliable one.[53]

Naturally, then, references to leitmotifs in film-music commentary are pandemic. Unfortunately, they suffer even more than does Wagner scholarship from the "calling-card mentality."[54] Since many were laid out in Chapter 1, we consider here but one more: Theodor Adorno's more nuanced attack. He argues that filmic leitmotifs are derivative – not derivative in the way one might think, that is based on a nineteenth-century *semantic code*, but rather derivative in that they draw much of their identity and meaning from nineteenth- and late eighteenth-century

---

[50] See Darby and DuBois 1990: 364, who cite this prelude inspiring many subsequent movie-monster musical passages, particularly those composed by Bernard Hermann.

[51] The Wagnerian leitmotif as accompaniment to silent film emerged strongly in response to film editing in order to establish continuity, creating this continuity through recurring thematic/dramatic material. See Kalinak 1992: 61–64.

[52] Buhler 2010: 37–38.

[53] As Carolyn Abbate so eloquently points out, Wagner's music can lie. See Abbate 1991: 19.

[54] See, for one, Sinn 1911: 135, an early commentator who basically defines leitmotifs as musical calling cards.

formal functions. Expository thematic statements, closing themes, transitional or developmental themes, and so forth, all have a semantic and functional residue drawn from common-practice music.[55] Moreover, Adorno argues that the filmic leitmotif is musically simple and repetitive – like an advertising jingle[56] – for the benefit of the musical tyro – worse even than Wagner's efforts in that film lacks the enormity and continuity of Wagnerian opera. Film's discontinuous modernity obviates its leitmotifs' symbolic value and relegates them to the populist calling-card stereotype.[57]

There is plenty of evidence, however, that many scholars and composers understand the leitmotif as a more subtle and powerful tool than its stereotype would imply. Royal Brown echoes Wagner when he says vis-à-vis the function of the leitmotif: "it creates a kind of *mémoire involontaire* and a sense of active expectation within the filmic context by linking characters and situations from the filmic past to those of the filmic present while also, at certain points, paving the way for the filmic future."[58] Film composer Franz Waxman also describes them in a way consistent with our conclusions in Chapter 1:

> The leitmotif technique is common in film scoring. That is, the attaching of themes to characters and then varying them as the situations change, and I have found this very practical in writing film music. It is an aid to composition and an aid to listening. Motifs should be characteristically brief, with sharp profiles. If they are easily recognizable, they permit repetition in varying forms and textures, and they help musical continuity.[59]

Waxman also notes that the layering of associations throughout a film makes themes more powerful at the film's conclusion (cf. the end of *Götterdämmerung*).[60] It is thus the musical development of themes rather than the crafting of the themes themselves that should comprise the bulk of a film composer's work.[61] Christoph Henzel provides a specific example; namely, the development of a pervasive half-step motive he hears permeating a number of themes in Howard Shore's score to *The Lord of the Rings* films.[62] Likewise, film composer Danny Elfman evokes the Wagnerian developmental ideal when he speaks of the torturous experience of crafting

---

[55] Adorno and Eisler 1994: 60–61.   [56] *Ibid.*: 99.   [57] *Ibid.*: 4–6.   [58] Brown 1988: 201.
[59] Karlin 1994: 73.   [60] *Ibid.*: 73.   [61] *Ibid.*: 76–7 cites Danny Elfman on this point.
[62] See Henzel 2004: 102–08. His analysis of this music is largely concerned with thematic development and connection, and he notes that, at least in these films, there is a strong similarity to Wagnerian practice. Henzel also notes the use of associative keys, like D minor for Mordor and Isengard, the realms of the film's primary antagonists.

themes for an original movie and how it's much more fun to write for a sequel in which he can compose variations on the original themes. Tellingly, he also mentions beginning composition with emotional, dramatic scenes rather than action sequences – sequences he implies are more complicated to coordinate but which require less artistry than the emotional, dramatic scenes.[63]

If it is, in fact, the Wagnerian leitmotif that lies at the center of comparisons between film music and Wagner, film music and opera, and even film music and art music, what remains to be done is to investigate the uses of associative themes in film. Did some composers effectively emulate Wagner? That is, do filmic leitmotifs ever conform to the precepts of the Wagnerian exemplar we sketched out in Chapters 1 and 7, or are they all more akin to earlier, non-developmental examples of associative themes that fit the calling-card model? In short, did any film composers get it right in imitating Wagner, or did they fall prey, *en masse*, to stereotype?

Thematic practice in the Hollywood film score

While the bulk of our ensuing investigation will focus on film music post-1970, we will pause briefly to consider the first period of leitmotivic composition during Hollywood's so-called "Golden Age" of the 1930s and 1940s, when composers who trained in Europe (or at least in the European tradition) began producing what we regard today as the first examples of great film music.

The first period of leitmotivic composition

Many of these men were clearly influenced by Wagner and conceived of Wagnerian-style leitmotifs in their film scores. The best known to concert audiences is doubtless Arnold Schoenberg, who seems to have regarded film composition first from a *thematic* standpoint. During negotiations to score the film version of Pearl S. Buck's novel *The Good Earth* (a contract eventually given to Herbert Stothart and Edward Ward), Schoenberg made a number of sketches comprising various themes and motives to which he gave vague titles like "funeral/death," "pearl/wealth," and "fear of the Wang

---

[63] See the video interviews with Elfman included on the DVD releases of *Spiderman* and *Spiderman 2*.

family because of the soldiers."[64] Rather than associating themes simply with characters or things, Schoenberg's titles suggest that he – like Wagner – imagined concepts and emotions lying at the heart of themes' projected semantic functions.

Max Steiner, an Austrian trained by Brahms and Mahler who later emigrated to the United States, adopted a similar compositional approach, a fact that emerges from Charles Leinberger's analytic studies of the composer's film scores. While Leinberger's early work on Steiner's score to *Now, Voyager* cites examples of the score's seven leitmotifs and examines each with regard to the corresponding drama, it does not suggest intimate connections to Wagnerian practice. Leinberger engages no overarching discussion of the exact thematic transformative techniques Steiner uses, nor mentions any consistently associative qualities of these transformations. Despite Steiner's themes' harmonic open-endedness and his predilection for Neapolitan-to-dominant progressions (tritone root movement) – both Wagnerian characteristics[65] – Leinberger understands the themes as assigned to the main characters and situations rather than associated with emotions.[66]

Leinberger's later work on *Now, Voyager*, however, treats thematic variation in relation to the drama much the way this book does.[67] The analysis of associative tonality is also augmented considerably in relation to Leinberger's earlier work.[68] Charlotte in *Now, Voyager*, for instance, has an associative key (G) and her theme is not associated with her *character* but rather with her *feelings of gratitude toward Jerry and her transformation into a beautiful young woman*. Another associative key is B♭, the goodbye key; Charlotte's theme modulates there when she and Jerry say good-night.[69] Most interesting is Leinberger's observation that thematic statements ending with perfect authentic cadences match with visual fades to black, both lending such moments a sense of finality.[70] Thematic transformation, even in early film scores, then, was capable of meshing with film editing techniques to enhance the sense of associativity. Having located Wagner-style leitmotif in *Now, Voyager*, Leinberger distinguishes between the "Charlotte" and "Mother and Daughter" themes, which are truly developed and others that are mere stage props whose function is to preserve a musical simplicity appropriate for a two-hour film.[71] Thus we see that both sides of the film-leitmotif commentary can claim validation. It would appear that two types of associative thematic practice existed side

---

[64] Feisst 1999: 93.   [65] Leinberger 1996: 291.   [66] Leinberger 1996.   [67] Leinberger 2002.
[68] Leinberger 1996: 295 includes only a cursory overview of associative tonality.
[69] Leinberger 2002: 64.   [70] *Ibid.*: 70.   [71] *Ibid.*: 76.

by side, not only within the "Golden Age" of film composition at large, but even within the same soundtrack.

The use of associative themes in film is only natural given the operatic experience of composers like Schoenberg and Steiner (not to mention others like Erich Korngold). As we have seen, however, the technique suffered from harsh criticism in the mid-twentieth century, not only by Adorno and Eisler, but also by many others – among them Aaron Copland – for being used too frequently and heavy-handedly due to a lack of the massive dramatic proportions and uninterrupted spans of music native to Wagnerian musical drama that was necessary for sufficient thematic development.[72] Film composers retaliated by stating that no other form of musical expression was developable in such a short span of time as a film.[73] Nevertheless, the middle of the twentieth century saw film music largely turning away from the associative theme.

By the 1950s, mainstream film scoring had largely strayed from the leitmotif model in favor of more pop-inspired, atmospheric, or monothematic scores. That said, echoes of the technique persisted even in these formats. The 1962 film *Lawrence of Arabia* features a monothematic soundtrack by Maurice Jarre (see Example 9.1 for the prototypic statement of the main theme). The score's one main theme, however, is often subjected to developments that parallel the drama.[74] These include: a military march setting when Lawrence and Ali ride out for Aqaba with fifty of Feisel's men; the arpeggiation of the main theme in a repeated, disorienting, lick-like texture to accompany the disorienting sameness of the landscape as Lawrence crosses the desert; and a fragmentation of the theme built up to a full statement when Lawrence appears out of the desert after having gone back for his fallen comrade (cf. the use of Thematic Fragmentation described in Wagner's *Ring* in Chapter 7).

Certainly, there are dozens more leitmotivic film scores one could point to by composers like Steiner, Korngold, and their contemporaries. Space prevents us here from investigating more of them. Nevertheless, these European-born and -trained composers provide a crucial link between the legacy of Wagner and the second period of leitmotivic composition in Hollywood (which had become, by then, wholly American in flavor) ushered in by John Williams's music for *Star Wars*.

---

[72] Flinn 1992: 27.   [73] Kalinak 1992: 103–05.

[74] This is also the case with David Raskin's score to the 1944 film *Laura*; it is essentially monothematic, but the main leitmotif develops in a number of ways to parallel the drama. See Kalinak 1992: 170–71.

Example 9.1 The central theme in Maurice Jarre's monothematic score to *Lawrence of Arabia*

The second period of leitmotivic composition

The classical Hollywood film score evolved, in no small part, to serve the narrative, with associative themes inserted to reinforce the establishment and development of characters.[75] But, from the late 1950s until *Jaws* in 1975, composers diverged so much from the classical, leitmotivic, film-score model that the European orchestral version virtually disappeared (the American "pop score" arose as its main challenger, though the synth score and the jazz score were also fashionable).[76] Why film composers largely abandoned leitmotivic scoring techniques in the mid-twentieth century may never be fully explained. Certainly, criticism alone couldn't bear all the blame. TV's increasing market share and the 1958 musicians' union strike likely produced contributing effects.[77] But, while its lapse may be open to interpretation, the revival of leitmotivic film scoring in the 1970s is not; commentators are in near perfect agreement that it was John Williams who revolutionized film scoring by harking back to the "glory days" of composers like Steiner and Korngold from the 1930s, 1940s, and 1950s.[78] And, while early scores of Williams – like *Jaws* and *The Cowboys* – employed thematic techniques to reflect the vicissitudes of the drama, the sea change came with the score to *Star Wars*.[79]

One can debate the chicken-and-egg question of whether it was director George Lucas or composer John Williams who was ultimately responsible for the leitmotivic ethos of the *Star Wars* soundtrack. Certainly, Lucas knew he wanted an orchestral, nineteenth-century style for *Star Wars*, something similar to what Erich Korngold and Max Steiner had written for earlier films.[80] But then, he was most likely drawn to Williams because

---

[75] Kalinak 1992: xv and 31.   [76] *Ibid.*: 184–87.   [77] Cooke 2001: 800.

[78] See, for instance, Scheurer 1997 and MacDonald 1998: 261.

[79] See Darby and Du Bois 1990: 525 for an overview of Williams's musical manipulation of a single theme in *The Cowboys* (1972) to reflect the drama.

[80] See MacDonald 1998: 260. Karlin and Wright remark that space and/or action films call for this type of heroic, orchestral scoring growing out of Maurice Jarre's *Lawrence of Arabia* (1962) and Korngold's *The Sea Hawk* (1940) and *Captain Blood* (1935). Karlin and Wright 2004: 320.

he was familiar with the composer's earlier work and knew Williams was capable of writing engaging thematic scores. We know that Korngold and Steiner had used a leitmotivic film-scoring technique that devolved from Wagner;[81] how much of their approach Lucas and Williams attributed to Wagner in the mid-1970s is not clear,[82] but much of the language both men used to describe the music of the *Star Wars* film (not to mention the music itself) is strongly suggestive of Wagnerian influence, in particular, its ineffable, mythic quality.[83]

Williams remarks that the opening sequence of *Star Wars* – a sequence that unites text-image and sound over a panoramic space backdrop – speaks to "some collective memory of a mythic past."[84] Another moment – one cited by *Star Wars* scholar James Buhler – is perhaps a better example. Buhler correctly explains leitmotif as an emotional vessel when he describes the "Two Suns" cue in *Star Wars*. This scene, occurring just after Luke returns to find his home and family destroyed, features the film's protagonist standing atop a sand dune at evening, gazing pensively toward the horizon where can be seen the setting of the two suns that light Luke's desert planet of Tatooine. Just then, the audience hears the "Force" theme. At this moment in the filmic narrative, we have no idea of what this musical signifier actually signifies, but we know it means *something important*. For Buhler this moment approaches Wagner's mythic use of music.[85] Buhler also notes an association of genre with elements of the drama. Specifically, he contrasts the natural musical sounds of the Force and the rebels with the "technological" sounds of the Dark Side. Moreover, Williams uses functionally tonal music for protagonists and tonal, but non-functional, music for antagonists, resisting the then-cliché use of *atonal*

[81] MacDonald 1998: 261. In fact, Max Steiner himself praised Wagner as the model for movie music. See Max Steiner Society 2002.

[82] See Evensen 2008. Though not a scholarly article, the author traces a number of viable intervallic, rhythmic, and harmonic similarities between musical themes of related dramatic content in *Star Wars* and *The Ring*. Despite failing to address these themes' instrumentation or texture, the author convincingly suggests that Williams and Wagner were at least composing from a shared collection of associative gestures (some of which were created by Wagner) even if Williams was not directly influenced by Wagner's music. Given the mythic tropes Evensen illustrates operating in both works, it is not inconceivable that such ideas might lead to a similar musical setting even in the absence of direct influence.

[83] See Kulezik 1997. The entirety of the article argues that music in film eventually achieved a role similar to myth in that both comprise unconsummated symbols capable of multiple meanings. This was an attempt by film-makers to "mythologize" the visual and narrative aspects of film.

[84] Buhler 2000: 34, but see also Byrd 1997.

[85] Buhler 2000: 44. Note that the use of the "Force" theme at this moment was Lucas's idea, not Williams's (*ibid.*: 56, n. 20).

music for antagonists, instead reserving this type of music for accompanying exotic landscapes and fight or action scenes.[86]

As for a Wagnerian approach to thematic development motivated by
explicit dramatic purposes (e.g., Harmonic Corruption for a twisted dramatic circumstance), the scholarly reaction to *Star Wars* is mixed. Buhler
argues that Williams's themes never really develop consequentially – they
are cast in new keys to sound fresh and are developed to reflect different
semantics, but these developments seem untethered to any overarching
musico-dramatic logic. This may be due, in part, to the *Star Wars* plot.
Buhler argues that the audience longs for primal statements of themes –
themes that are recapitulated to mark a return to the past (the idyllic days
of yore for which the Rebellion is fighting) rather than those subjected to
any kind of true thematic development. Or, put more succinctly, the
themes have no "meaningful history."[87] In Buhler's words, "The closest
any of the scores comes to thematic transformation is the derivation of the
Imperial March from the falling third of the Storm Trooper music and the
Han and Leia theme from Leia's theme."[88] Kathryn Kalinak notes the lack
of thematic continuity between the films as well; the only musical ideas *The
Empire Strikes Back* reprises from *Star Wars* are the main title (with its
"Star Wars" theme), the "Force" theme, and the opening of Leia's theme,
which becomes the Han and Leia love theme.[89] Kalinak, however, does cite
developments in instrumentation for dramatic purposes. Specifically, a
softened "Empire" theme near the end of *Return of the Jedi* suggests to
the audience that they feel sympathy with the repentant Vader.[90] (Applying the parlance introduced in Chapter 7 of this book, we would say the
theme was subjected to a Change of Texture to reflect new dramatic
circumstances.)

Star Wars may be a problematic example, but others by John Williams
and his contemporaries clearly indicate a Wagnerian thematic heritage. As
a brief example, we might pause to consider Williams's score to *E.T.* Like
the falling half-step *Urmotiv* of Wagner's *Ring*, the *E.T.* score features a
rising fifth as a motive common to all of its themes.[91] Many other scores –
penned by Williams and his contemporaries – employ thematic developmental techniques with the same associations established in Wagner's

---

[86] *Ibid.*: 44–49.   [87] *Ibid.*: 51–54.   [88] Buhler 2000: 57, n. 39, cites Kalinak 1992: 194.
[89] Kalinak 1992: 192.
[90] *Ibid.*: 198. Kalinak also provides a quick listing of leitmotivic developments that parallel
      narrative developments in *The Empire Strikes Back* ice-battle scene, though there is no musical
      analysis of these per se. *Ibid.*: 200–201.
[91] MacDonald 1998: 294–95.

Ring. And audiences have noticed, as do Karlin and Wright: "Changing any compositional element at a dramatic moment in the film can shift the emotional emphasis or affect its intensity."[92] The remainder of this book aims to demonstrate just such a Wagnerian influence upon filmic leitmotif. As in the previous chapter, analysis of specific examples bolsters the argument that Peircian dicent meanings for specific thematic transformations indicate a link to Wagnerian practice.

Analyzing the film score

The act of analysis comprises breaking an object down into its constituent parts to see how each functions independently and within the whole. Film music poses a specific set of analytic challenges. Many were adumbrated in the Preface, but we pause briefly here to consider others and their attendant analytic approaches.

Music in general – and associative themes specifically – is not properly perceived in film unless it is "foregrounded." Thus, certain types of musical ideas (brief, pithy, distinguished from stock musical gestures, connotatively correct, etc.) are more suitable than others for leitmotivic treatment.[93] And, repetition or variation of these may help foreground them – not to mention granting them thematic status as noted in Chapter 2.[94] Moreover, musical themes may comprise a set of premises leading to conclusions; that is, some thematic presentations can't necessarily be properly comprehended in isolation and must rather be perceived in context as part of a teleological musico-dramatic span.[95] Analysis can help explain how this process works.[96]

Analyzing film music in context means analyzing it as one component of a multi-media form. Nicholas Cook's comments on multi-media are helpful here: Cook lays out a collection of similarity and difference tests for considering two media together. Specifically, he defines three possibilities: conformance (in which the two media accomplish the same objective – one might even question the sense of *multi* here), complementation (the most common arrangement, in which the whole is greater than the sum of its parts), and contest (in which what each medium achieves on its own

---

[92] Karlin and Wright 2004: 299.   [93] London 2000.
[94] Nasta 1991: 47. See also the "leitmotif" chapter in Comuzio 1980.   [95] *Ibid.*: 48.
[96] In fact, Howard Shore stressed the importance of analyzing his own music after he writes it. See Schelle 1999: 339 and 350.

contends with the other(s)).[97] In film, of course, there are more than two media. We have not only image to match to music, but also the larger soundtrack (including dialogue, sound effects, ambient scenic noise, and so forth), and the overarching sense of narrative or drama.[98]

In terms of reference to image, it is difficult to analyze film music without mentioning it, since even a black screen is noteworthy for its absence of image if concurrent music provides a sense of narrative. Music and image have a tendency to fuse together in meaning. A perceptual study by Marshall and Cohen supports this claim of a conjoined perceptual and mnemonic union of music and image if the two are in conformance or complementation with one another (to use Cook's terminology).[99] That is, in Example 9.2a , if element "a" of the film occurs during music "x," the two have a tendency to unite in perception and memory as "ax."[100] Later work by Cohen significantly enriches this simplistic view to accommodate the interaction of numerous stimuli in a back-and-forth relationship with long-term memory that more accurately captures the cognitive process of audience members viewing a film (see Example 9.2b).[101]

This implies that associative themes that work in conformance or complementation with the visual stimulus comprise a sort of "parallel" narrative in which both image and music alone function in parallel and non-hierarchical interpretive streams that together mime the collective, overarching narrative.[102] Thus, Marshall and Cohen suggest that auditory structures in film can direct the encoding of coincidental visual features. That is, music generates associations that contextualize the interpretation of actions in the film.[103] Numerous other studies support this assertion.[104] Among them, one suggests that the level of musical closure impacts the perception of narrative closure in film (though visual cues usually trump auditory ones).[105] Another demonstrates that music colored audiences' real-time reactions to film scenes that were ambiguous (i.e., scenes that

---

[97] Cook 1998.

[98] This is hardly the place to broach the competing definitions of musical narrative, of musical drama, and their contradistinctions. For an introduction to these topics, see: Maus 1988, Maus 1991, Abbate 1991, and Almén 2003.

[99] Marshall and Cohen 1988.   [100] Marshall and Cohen 1988: 110, Fig. 8b (109).

[101] Cohen 2013: 39, Fig. 2.7.

[102] This notion of parallel, non-hierarchical streams comes from Schubert 1997: 34.

[103] A separate study by Cohen corroborates these findings. In it, Cohen asserts that both musical and visual information "independently activate associations of both affect and denotation" and that meaning in film is dependent upon the interaction of the two at any given moment. See Cohen 1993.

[104] See, for example, Lipscomb and Kendall, 1994.   [105] Thompson et al. 1994.

(a)

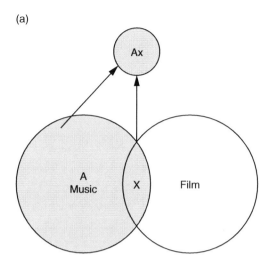

(b)

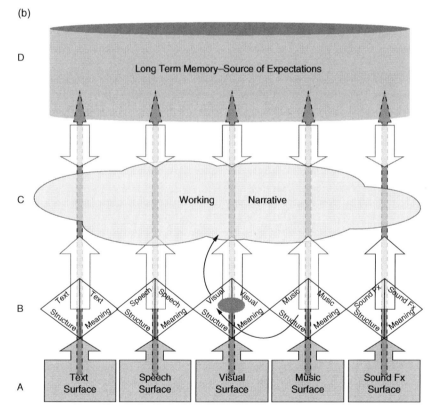

Example 9.2 Marshall and Cohen's model for the union of music and image in memory of film

a. Preliminary model
b. Enrichment of preliminary model

could be interpreted as either positive or negative). It also had an effect on their memories of scenic elements one week later, cementing memories of scenic details reinforced by mood-consistent musical information and weakening those with mood-inconsistent musical information.[106] This brings us to music that acts in contest (to use Cook's third term) with image. It seems that examples of music and image in contest have a striking effect on the audience's overall impression of narrative as a whole. Audiences remember film scenes better if the music *foreshadowing* the scene is *incongruent* with what actually occurs (i.e., the audience is set up to expect one thing and is then surprised).[107] These studies suggest that Cook's category of music in contest with visual drama functions differently depending on whether or not the music accompanies or precedes the dramatic activity in question.

Film music interacts not only with visual cues, but also with outside auditory stimuli. That is, the music in film often has the added burden of competing with dialogue and sound effects with which it may or may not be coordinated. Annabel Cohen has much to say on this topic as well. In short, she describes four psychological effects of combining music with sound:

1. Meaning and Associationism – things happen at the same time and, because of connotative overlap (as in metaphor), one can evoke the other even when it is absent (i.e., music can recall emotion of previous scene it was linked to – just as Wagner theorized).
2. Structure and Organization – when both auditory and visual stimuli exhibit similar "structures" (in a Gestalt sense), as when they both change at the same time (the music imitates a character's actions), facilitating information-processing tasks.
3. Memory and Awareness – musical soundtracks are popular in part because they evoke memories of the movie (often implying subjectivity). Such memories are often visual (Cohen's study suggests that people are very good at recalling if a scene was included in the movie or not), less often auditory (one can't always tell if a specific clip of music was part of a film or not).
4. Experimental Aesthetics – audiences like it best if music and voice are not sounded simultaneously and when the music is congruent with the effect of scene. Gripping music, however, may sometimes overshadow the content of information (as in educational documentaries).[108]

---

[106] Boltz 2001.   [107] Boltz *et al.* 1991.   [108] Cohen 1990.

Of course, whether the music complements or acts in contest with the visual drama really isn't up to the composer, who rarely has the final say on it, since an array of directors, producers, and editors usually have input on the soundtrack.[109] Moreover, orchestration is often left up to a team of composers who take over when the lead composer has sketched out the pitch and rhythmic details of the musical material.[110] Since musical styles of these various composers on the team have to be standardized as much as possible, this is sometimes accomplished by asking all of them to work with the same thematic material,[111] a frenetic, chaotic arrangement that makes "sketch study" or any kind of analysis of the musical decision-making process nigh unto impossible.[112] The end result is that music as conceived by the composer for the film is often not exactly what ends up in the final product. Associative aspects of, say, orchestration, or Thematic Truncation, are ultimately subject to the whims of many contributors. This raises special concerns for analysts, who must choose whether to attempt to delve into the mind of the lead composer (poietic analysis), simply describe the musical materials that appear in the film (neutral-level analysis), or assess the impact of the end product upon movie-goers (esthesic analysis).[113] This book tilts toward the latter two approaches. That is, analysis herein relies on the musical materials *as heard* in the DVD release of the motion picture, taking this in the context of the filmic totality as a sort of "neutral" level suitable for hermeneutic interpretation. Hypotheses as to esthesic response are sometimes included, but – for obvious reasons – poietic musings are kept to a minimum. Finally, examples and figures are used liberally in the text that follows, though usually only to establish what music corresponds to a given theme name by reminding the reader with musical notation rather than providing notation for every thematic development cited.

Wagnerian thematic techniques in recent film music

We lack from film composers the reams of theorizing that we find in Wagner's prose, but interviews and liner notes often provide details about

---

[109] Karlin and Wright 2004.

[110] Howard Shore describes this process in Karlin and Wright 2004: 325–26.

[111] Raskin 1989: 174.

[112] See Raskin 1989. See also Wright 1989. The whole article lays out the history and status of bibliographic and source-material study problems associated with film music as of late 1980s.

[113] This threefold division of analytic attention will be familiar to scholars of semiotics. See Nattiez 1990, Monelle 1992, and Monelle 2000 for examples of the application of semiotics to musical analysis.

film-composition technique that echo those in Wagner's writings.[114] It is my hope that the musical analyses that close this chapter will speak for themselves concerning the immense influence Wagnerian leitmotivic practice still has on the film score. Above and beyond that, however, we know it weighs heavily on the minds of film composers. By way of example, consider the bonus material included on the DVD release of Peter Jackson's *The Fellowship of the Ring*. In it, Howard Shore makes comments that, *mutatis mutandis*, would be at home in any number of Wagner's treatises and open letters. Shore mentions the "fully-formed" version of the "Fellowship" theme and how it occurs when Elrond proclaims the Fellowship in Rivendell about halfway through the film. After Gandalf, the leader of the Fellowship, falls in Moria, Shore remarks that the score never includes "that heroic version" of the theme again. Shore also notes the first time the score presents the nascent form of the "Fellowship" theme, namely when the hobbits are in a cornfield on the boundary of the Shire, preparing to leave their homeland.[115]

You'll first hear the Fellowship theme forming in the film when Frodo leaves Hobbiton with Sam on his way to Bree – but it's just a fragment of the theme. Later on, after they meet up with Merry and Pippin in the cornfield, you hear a more developed version of the theme – it's growing. Then they get to Bree and they meet Strider, and it develops even further as they leave Bree. Once in Rivendell, when they meet Gimli and Legolas and Gandalf arrives, the Fellowship is now in its full orchestrated form. At the end of "The Council of Elrond" cue, you hear the full, grand statement of the Fellowship Theme. So the two and a half hours of score is very carefully shaped in terms of the thematic material – how it's introduced and developed throughout the whole film.[116]

This admission of conscious thematic development – from emergent forerunners, to fully formed statements, to thematic dissolution – lines up strongly not only with Wagner's description of motives of precognition and reminiscence but also with his practice as analyzed in Chapter 7.

Another practice noted in film also derives from Wagner. This is the so-called "leitmotif" song – diegetic song that returns either diegetically or

---

[114] There is no question that developmental leitmotifs occur in multi-media art forms apart from film (science-fiction, fantasy, and horror television is a good example). See Haskins 2010. While the comments that follow will also apply to such non-filmic art forms, it is the film score we are focused upon here.

[115] This is true for the original theatrical presentation, but new music composed for the extended DVD release presents this theme, appropriately enough, when the title (*The Fellowship of the Ring*) rolls in the opening credits.

[116] See Goldwasser 2001. This is an excerpt of an interview with Howard Shore available at www.soundtrack.net/content/article/?id=89 (accessed October 1, 2012).

Example 9.3 First phrase of the "Harry Potter" theme from John Williams's score to *Harry Potter and the Sorcerer's Stone*

non-diegetically as part of the soundtrack to mark or foreshadow import-ant moments in a film. Classic examples include: "Mrs. Robinson" in *The Graduate*, "Underneath the Mango Tree" in *Dr. No*, "As Time Goes By" in *Casablanca*, and "Something Wicked This Way Comes!" from *Harry Potter and the Prisoner of Azkaban*.[117] One needn't look hard to find the same technique in Wagner. Perhaps the best example is Senta's ballad in *Der fliegende Holländer*, though certainly Tannhäuser's hymn to Venus, Siegmund's spring song, and Mime's Starling song would all qualify.[118]

Likewise, the use of non-diegetic music as narrative commentary devolves from Wagnerian practice (and its antecedents).[119] Its use with leitmotif in sci-fi, fantasy, and horror films is common. For instance, in *Harry Potter and the Sorcerer's Stone*, caretaker Filch is searching Hogwarts late at night. When he asks, "Anyone here?" we hear the first phrase of the "Harry Potter" music (see Example 9.3). Filch, deaf to this non-diegetic musical information, can't pick up the clue that Harry is hiding just out of sight – a clue intended to reinforce the audience's experience of the narrative. But audiences should be warned against naively believing every non-diegetic musical reference. Leitmotifs in film, as in Wagner, can lie.[120]

The absence of a given leitmotif can be as meaningful a clue to audiences as its presence. A good example occurs in John Williams's score to *Jaws* when the expected "Jaws" motive is missing while a shark fin approaches a beach full of people at a publicity event. The fin is soon revealed to be a

---

[117] Nasta 1991: 84–86. Rodman 2006 explores the use of popular song (specifically in compilation soundtracks) for connotative/denotative meaning based on musical style and social practice, that is, style itself having something of an associative function.

[118] See Abbate 1991: 85–87 for a discussion of Senta's narrative as a special type of narrative song, one that Abbate refers to as "reflexive," that is, both self-referential and deterministic of the operatic plot outside of the song narrative.

[119] Transgressions of the diegetic/non-diegetic boundary are largely used for humorous effect in modern scores. See, for instance, the seemingly non-diegetic foreboding orchestra music that wells up during a car trip in Mel Brooks's *High Anxiety* and turns out to be a diegetic symphony orchestra rehearsing on a passing bus.

[120] As in Tannhäuser's Act III Rome narrative or Wotan's Act II monologue in *Die Walküre*. See Abbate 1991: 98–117 and 223–29. These lies, however, are, in film, often used for dramatic effect rather than, as in Wagner, to depict the subjectivity of a given character's reminiscence.

Example 9.4 The "Voldemort" theme prototype in *Harry Potter and the Sorcerer's Stone*

fake, propelled by a couple of children swimming underwater. Darth Vader's appearance in the cave scene on Dagobah in *The Empire Strikes Back* comprises another example. It is not accompanied by the "Imperial March" theme as one might expect because the image of Vader is a projection of Luke's fear; the villain is not physically present. Likewise, the "Isengard" music that accompanies Saruman through much of *The Lord of the Rings* score does not play during scenes with the mysterious White Wizard in *The Two Towers* since he is, in actuality, the benevolent Gandalf, remade.

One finds Wagner's dramatic tonal techniques in film scores, too. In *Harry Potter and the Sorcerer's Stone* there is a nascent statement of the "Voldemort" theme when Ollivander gives Harry the wand that will be his, saying "when its brother gave you that scar" (see Example 9.4).[121] The musical statement is then repeated up a half-step under Ollivander's words, "he who must not be named," an example of both thematic presentiment and of expressive tonality reflecting rising dramatic tension. Similarly, associative tonality looms large in some film scores. *The Lord of the Rings* is a good example, including D major for the hobbits, the Shire, and forces of goodness; D minor for the forces of darkness (particularly Mordor and Isengard); B♭ minor for the sorrow of the elves; and A major for the Fellowship of the Ring.[122]

Scholars often draw distinctions between Wagnerian and filmic leitmotivic practice. For instance, Carolyn Abbate notes that leitmotifs in most Wagnerian opera (*The Ring* excepted) have a tendency to succumb to musical gravity, losing their specific associations and becoming more generic musical objects. Film music, however – at least according to Michael Matessino's liner notes for *The Star Wars*

---

[121] The prototypic statement of the "Voldemort" theme occurs when Harry encounters Voldemort in the Dark Forest.

[122] See Halfyard 2004: 151–52 for an example of associative tonality in John Williams's scores to *Batman* and *Batman Returns*, namely that the "Batman" and "Love" themes occur most often in C minor/major (the duality of mode representing the duality of Batman vs. Bruce Wayne).

Trilogy: A New Hope – can't work the same way.[123] Because it lacks the extended musical canvas necessary for leitmotifs to revert to serving motivic or thematic functions characteristic of "absolute music," Matessino argues that film music instead "secularizes" the leitmotif – granting it extra-musical meaning by removing it from the extended musical canvas it requires to revert into being pure music, and turning it into a stage prop instead.[124] This "demythologizes" the musical ideas, making of them associative themes – hackneyed, simplified varieties that can only pretend toward being true leitmotifs. Stated *in music*, these stage-prop themes serve as entertainment, but pose as art, lending the audience a false sense of depth and clarity.[125]

This distinction is a sensible one, appropriate in many cases. Nevertheless, further consideration often reveals a thematic practice in these scores that remains closer to the Wagnerian model. One might argue, for instance, that Matessino's "secularization" process unfolds across Danny Elfman's score to *Sleepy Hollow*. Here, themes originally associated with Ichabod Crane's disturbing memories of childhood and with the Headless Horseman later seem to be used irrespective of dramatic context. Janet Halfyard suggests that this may be a kind of unconscious dramatic genius on Elfman's part, since both themes link aspects of the drama that deal with the mysterious,[126] but it seems more likely that this is just another Wagnerian thematic behavior, likely one Elfman learned from his predecessors.[127] In this case, applying Matessino's critique would miss the point; Wagner's themes aren't simply "calling cards" or a musical component that lends a mythic aura to the work, but are rather *bearers of emotional significance, intimately tied to memory*, something filmic leitmotifs can also achieve. Elfman's themes in *Sleepy Hollow* attempt to capture the surreal and ineffable side of memory, and, for that reason, might be granted a hermeneutic value that rises above the banal.

---

[123] Lucasfilm, Ltd. CD 09026-68746-2, 1997.

[124] Matessino's point is weakened by the five other *Star Wars* film scores subsequently penned by Williams – scores that, when taken together, extend the entire musical canvas to operatic lengths.

[125] In this view, Matessino concurs with Adorno. See the latter's comments on leitmotif and phantasmagoria in Adorno 1991: 43–61 and 85–96; and in Adorno and Eisler 1994: 4–6 and 60–61.

[126] Halfyard 2004: 28–29.

[127] Elfman, like Wagner, plays up his self-proclaimed identity as musical autodidact, stating that he watched lots of horror, sci-fi, and fantasy films during his adolescence in Los Angeles. Elfman maintains that this experience comprised his training in film music composition. See Halfyard 2004: 21.

The true test of Wagnerian leitmotivic composition in any genre is, however, evidence that thematic development occurs to match changing dramatic contexts and to achieve a concomitant layering of emotional associations.[128] Thus, we conclude with a series of examples that follow both the Wagnerian model's transformation types and their dicent associations. Apart from the absence of leitmotivic combinations in counterpoint – true counterpoint based on dissonance treatment being, perhaps, the most significant distinction between the bulk of tonal popular music of the last few decades and the concert music of the common-practice period – all of the typical Wagnerian developmental techniques are found readily throughout the film-score repertory.

Change of Mode

Change of Mode as a semantic device is as common today as it was in Wagner's time. Examples range from the trite to the nuanced. Among the former is John Williams's darkening of the "Heroism" theme to minor. This occurs in *Star Wars* when the last member of Luke Skywalker's team is killed, leaving Luke the only remaining X-wing fighter to finish off the Death Star. A similar musical statement in the sequel, *The Empire Strikes Back*, accompanies Luke crash-landing on Dagobah (see Example 9.5 for the thematic prototype). (Cf. the "Indy's Feelings for Marion" Change of Mode example cited in Chapter 1.) Likewise, James Horner's title music for *The Wrath of Khan* recasts the main theme in minor at many salient points: one occurs when Uhura says (of Khan to Kirk), after the Reliant attacks the Enterprise, "He wishes to discuss terms of our surrender." Another appears in the next film – *Star Trek III: The Search for Spock* – when the Klingon ship attacks the Enterprise. Example 9.6 presents the prototypical main theme.

Of course, minor gives way to major as well. The example of Howard Shore's "Ring" theme that opened this book is one such instance. Others occur in Danny Elfman's score to Tim Burton's *Nightmare Before Christmas*. The refrain to the song, "This is Halloween," sounds in major when Jack returns, triumphant, after rescuing Santa Claus. Moreover, the cadence to "Sally's Lament" occurs in major when she and Jack are

---

[128] For a study that does this, though without relating the thematic developments to Wagnerian practice, see London 2000, who discusses semantically and musically altered themes in Max Steiner's score to *Mildred Pierce*.

Example 9.5 Prototypic major-mode version of the "Heroism" main-title theme from John Williams's scores to the *Star Wars* films (this theme occurs with a number of different bass lines, but the overarching sense is almost always of the major mode)

Example 9.6 Prototypic major-mode title theme from James Horner's *Star Trek* films

reunited at the end of the film.[129] John Williams's score to *Harry Potter and the Prisoner of Azkaban* presents a more nuanced example. The theme associated with "Harry's Longing for Familial Love" becomes major when, at the climactic moment of the film, Harry thwarts the dementors by summoning a Patronus inspired by thoughts of his parents. Rather than altering the melody by simply changing the mode of the third (and possibly the sixth and seventh) scale degrees, Williams here keeps the melody itself in the same mode (albeit with a raised leading tone), but adds a bass pedal and vocal accompaniment that cause the ear to reinterpret the melody as outlining the supertonic within a major-mode context. Because the melody doesn't change, this example might rightly be considered a blending of Change of Mode and Contextual Reinterpretation (see Ex. 9.7).

Harmonic Corruption

Just as Wagner treats the central "Gold" theme in *Das Rheingold* Scene 1 (refer back to Examples 7.6 and 7.9), John Williams subjects the central "Heroism" theme in *Star Wars* not only to Change of Mode, but also to Harmonic Corruption. One example sounds when Luke and Han take Chewie to the detention block in the Death Star and Han says, "This isn't

[129] The cadence in question features a ♭II to V^{6-5}_{4-3} progression in minor, being originally sung to Sally's words "and will he see how much he means to me? I think it's not to be," during the self-pitying solo she performs while Jack is on his Christmas flight taking over for Santa Claus.

(a)

(b)

Example 9.7 "Harry's Longing for Familial Love" from John Williams's score to *Harry Potter and the Prisoner of Azkaban*

a. Prototypic statement when Harry speaks of his feelings to Remus Lupin during the covered bridge scene
b. Change of Mode/Contextual Reinterpretation: major-mode harmonization with melody beginning on $\hat{2}$ rather than $\hat{1}$

going to work." The melody remains largely the same, but its harmonization becomes dissonant (see Example 9.8). Similar moments occur in other Williams scores. There is a corruption of the "Will of the Hindu Gods" theme in *Indiana Jones and the Temple of Doom* when Short Round and the other children working in the mines are whipped. Example 9.9 presents the thematic prototype. And, in *Indiana Jones and the Last Crusade* the "Grail" theme is corrupted after Donovan shoots Indy's father and says to Indy, "It's time to ask yourself what you believe." (The Grail is the only object capable of healing the elder Jones's wounds.) The "Grail" theme

D: I⁶   ♭II   I   ♭II   iv   V

Example 9.8 Harmonic Corruption of the "Heroism" theme in *Star Wars*

Example 9.9 Prototypic statement of "Will of the Hindu Gods" from John Williams's score to *Indiana Jones and the Temple of Doom*

b♭:   i   v   i   VI   V♮   i   III   i   V⁶₄ − +⁶   − ⁵₃

Example 9.10 "Grail" theme prototype from John Williams's score to *Indiana Jones and the Last Crusade*

prototype appears in Example 9.10. Finally, the "Ring" theme in Howard Shore's score to *The Return of the King* is corrupted when Denethor contradicts the Fellowship's mission to destroy it, arguing instead that the Ring of Power be brought to Gondor and used in its last defense.

Harmonic Redemption

As in Wagner's oeuvre, this reversal of Harmonic Corruption is comparatively rare. A strikingly powerful example is one described in more detail at the end of this chapter. In brief, the many themes that feature ♯$\hat{4}$ throughout the three *Lord of the Rings* films – themes of the supernatural – are resolved

Example 9.11 Thematic Complex in *The Fellowship of the Ring*

a. "Forces of Darkness" motive
b. "Urgency" motive
c. "Running" motive
d. "Battle" rhythm

into the surpassingly diatonic, ♮$\hat{4}$, plagal "Into the West" music at the end to symbolize the return to normalcy (i.e., the simple life of the Shire).

Thematic Complex

It is difficult, in the limited time span of the average film score, to establish a number of distinct leitmotifs and then combine them into a new associative entity. Lengthy films and film series seem the most natural place to look for such Thematic Complexes, and we find one in Howard Shore's score to *The Fellowship of the Ring*. The motives associated with "Forces of Darkness," "Urgency," and "Running," superimposed onto the "Battle" rhythm, comprise a new theme, "Weathertop," to capture the emotions and sense of drama surrounding the scene where Aragorn and the hobbits encounter the Ringwraiths at the ruined tower of Weathertop (see Example 9. 11).[130]

[130] Shore casts the "Forces of Darkness," "Urgency," and "Running" motives in D minor, putting them into the tonal purview of Mordor. Earlier occurrences in the film certainly involve the

Thematic Truncation

Truncation stands as one of the most common Wagnerian thematic techniques used by film composers. The emotional effect created by the passing away of an important component of the drama remains as powerful in film as it was in *Musikdrama*. Examples from the works of John Williams include the truncation of the "Force" theme in *Star Wars* when Ben (Obi Wan) Kenobi is cut down by Vader's light saber; the truncation of the "Yoda" theme when Luke's tutor passes on near the beginning of *Return of the Jedi*; and the truncation of the "Voldemort" theme in *Harry Potter and the Sorcerer's Stone* when Professor Quirrell (Voldemort's host) collapses near the end of the film.

Thematic Fragmentation

We will recall that in Wagner's *Ring*, the composer used Thematic Fragmentation to capture the sense of emotion associated with the emergence or departure of an important dramatic element (including a character). Similar usage occurs in two John Williams scores. First, near the beginning of *Star Wars*, the audience hears a fragment of the "Leia" theme during the princess's first brief appearance before we understand her importance to the tale at hand. (The prototypic statement of the Leia theme occurs on the planet Tatooine during R2D2's playback of Leia's plea for help (see Example 9.12).) A better example sounds near the beginning of *Indiana Jones and the Last Crusade* when the young Indy, having liberated the Cross of Coronado from a band of ruffians, attempts to escape them by boarding a moving train. On the train, the young Indy finds a whip; viewers familiar with the first two *Indiana Jones* films will understand this object's iconic significance to the title character and the music sounds a fragmented version of the "Adventure" theme as a marker that it is at this moment that the young hero's adult persona begins to emerge (see Example 9.13 for the prototype).

dark forces of Mordor – these motives are pervasive during the hobbits' flight from the Ringwraiths in the Shire and also during Gandalf's journey to Minas Tirith for information – but I hesitate to call them "Mordor" motives per se. The "Battle" rhythm is also associated with the forces of darkness, specifically physical combat with them. Its first appearance occurs during the Last Alliance of Men and Elves against Sauron at the beginning of *The Fellowship of the Ring*. Finally, note that the "Forces of Darkness" motive comprises falling thirds moving down by step and can begin on any note of the scale, most often $\hat{5}$ or $\hat{3}$.

Example 9.12 "Leia" theme prototype from John Williams's score to *Star Wars*

Example 9.13 First phrase of "Adventure" theme prototype from John Williams's score to *Raiders of the Lost Ark*

Thematic Evolution

The shorter genre of film allows fewer opportunities for one theme to emerge from another. Nevertheless, there are many examples to choose from. Janet Halfyard has noted the relationship between the "Catwoman" and "Penguin" themes in *Batman Forever*. The dramatic resonance of these themes' musical relationships is obvious since each is associated with a villain who possesses both animalistic traits and freakish, super-human abilities.[131] Another is the growth of the "Marauders' Map" theme (for the

---

[131] See Halfyard 2004: 30. The author also notes differences in orchestration for the three dualistic, animal characters (brass for Batman, strings for Catwoman, and organ and full symphonic textures for Penguin).

Example 9.14 Thematic evolution in John Williams's score to *Harry Potter and the Prisoner of Azkaban*

a. "Mischief"
b. "Weasleys"
c. "The Marauders' Map"

magical map that allows the protagonists to get up to all kinds of shenanigans) and the "Weasleys" music (many of the Weasleys are inherently mischievous) from the more generically associative "Mischief" theme in *Harry Potter and the Prisoner of Azkaban* (see Example 9.14). Note how the later themes make use of the "Mischief" theme's repeated-note figure and chromatic double neighbors. A second John Williams score, to *Superman*, includes the "Parting" theme growing out of the title character's theme, as if to suggest that Superman's very identity damns him to an existence in which he can never truly maintain a relationship with another being. "Parting," like the main "Superman" theme, opens with a rising perfect fifth and features diatonic double-neighbor motion around $\hat{5}$ (see Example 9.15).

Associative Transposition

This is another comparatively rare technique in film music.[132] Its relative scarcity is perhaps best explained as due to the local nature of film music,

---

[132] Key center is, of course, but one of many musical characteristics capable of bearing extra-musical associations. Howard Shore mentions the associative potential of different types of

Example 9.15 Thematic evolution in John Williams's score to *Superman*

a. Main theme ("Superman")
b. "Parting"

in which brief thematic statements must be able to occur in almost any tonal context at any time. This quickly transitional medium does not have the same sense of tonality as much art music, particularly the lengthy *Auskomponierung* spans that compose out a given tonic over the course of a number or entire scene in opera. That said, there are a few examples to point to. One is the transposition of "Heroism" into G Phrygian when Luke's speeder is hit by fire from Imperial walkers in *The Empire Strikes Back*. The combination of Harmonic Corruption with the statement in the key of the Empire (i.e., G minor) is particularly effective. In James Horner's score to *Krull*, the "Love" theme associated with Lyssa and Colwyn returns in E major (the key of adventuring) when Lyssa gives Colwyn the fire he needs to destroy the Beast, simultaneously reuniting the lovers and bringing the adventure to a joyful conclusion. Finally, in *The Fellowship of the Ring*, the "Shire" theme (usually in D major) sounds in C when Bilbo says he will finish his book with the line "and he lived happily ever after until the end of his days." C major is the key Shore uses for happy endings; we hear it (among other places)

harmony (*sic*) like modality, serialism, diatonic vs. chromatic harmony, etc. including harmony-as-theme. See Karlin and Wright 2004: 223–78, especially 266–67.

after the conclusion of the filmic narrative when Annie Lenox performs the "Into the West" music over the end credits.

Change of Texture

As in opera, Change of Texture remains a common technique for modifying thematic association in film music. It is most often used to show a change in character, as in *Return of the Jedi* when a plaintive, monophonic version of the "Imperial March" accompanies Darth Vader's repentant death.[133] (The prototypic statement of this theme was shown in Example 6.9.) More uplifting transformations occur in *The Lord of the Rings* films. There is a muscular version of the "Shire" theme in *Fellowship of the Ring* for the hobbits' new-found heroism when they set forth from Rivendell (mentioned by Shore in the extended quotation earlier in this chapter). And, the "Sorrow of the Elves" takes on a martial quality in *The Two Towers* when the elvish forces arrive to assist in the battle at Helm's Deep.[134]

Thematic Irony

The subtlety of Thematic Irony is such that one might suspect it to be absent from a popular genre like the film score, especially films of a sci-fi, fantasy, or horror bent. While examples of Thematic Irony in film scores are few and far between, their potential has been realized for some years. In *Star Wars Episode 3: Revenge of the Sith* when Anakin and Padme are reunited, Padme tells Anakin she is pregnant and Anakin says "This is a happy moment – the happiest of my life!" At that moment the audience hears the "Doomed Love" theme, a clear case of romantic irony since the audience knows what horrible fate lies in store for the two characters, though the characters themselves do not (see Example 9.16). A curious cross-diegetic case occurs in Harry Gregson-Williams's score to *The Lion, the Witch, and the Wardrobe*. Mr. Tumnus's diegetic flute melody – the modal melody used to put Lucy to sleep near the beginning of the film – returns non-diegetically when Aslan and Lucy awaken Mr. Tumnus from his stone-statue slumber near the film's end.

---

[133] Kalinak 1992: 198 notes this moment as well and says that the rescored theme "activates celestial associations" that prompt the audience to forgive Vader.

[134] Howard Shore comments on this thematic development in his interview included on the DVD release of *The Two Towers*.

f: i   ii°⁷ i   VII   VI   v   III   ♮⁶₄   i

Example 9.16 "Doomed Love" thematic prototype from John Williams's score to *Star Wars Episode 3: Revenge of the Sith*

Long-range processes: a brief case study of Howard Shore's music for Peter Jackson's *The Lord of the Rings* films

It is difficult to resist the temptation to round off our exploration of the leitmotif by returning, here at the end, to the materials mentioned at the opening. Thus, we conclude our analytic survey of Wagnerian thematic developmental techniques in film music with an extended analysis of music from Howard Shore's scores to Peter Jackson's *The Lord of the Rings* trilogy.[135] Shore's comments on *The Fellowship of the Ring* set the stage appropriately:

I thought of it as Act One of an opera. When you go to the opera, you quite often may have a symphony orchestra in the pit, a sixty-person choir on stage, and soloists. You could make the argument that all film music is operatic, but this is different. Between the orchestra and the choir, I had 200 pieces at my disposal, as part of my palette to work from. There are also some North African instruments, and an Indian bowed lute, which I used in "Lothlórien."[136]

Shore's concentration on large and varied orchestral forces is fitting for a narrative of epic proportions. In modern-day parlance, "epic" has come to mean anything particularly large or grand. Its original meaning, of course, derives from narrative poetry, particular that which comes in multiple parts or installments and/or covers a lengthy period of time. The poem for Wagner's *Ring* cycle is a perfect example. And, while not a poem per se, the narrative covered in Peter Jackson's *The Lord of the Rings* trilogy fits

---

[135] Howard Shore was not the only musician to contribute to the *Lord of the Rings* soundtrack. A number of cues, for instance, were written and performed by Enya. An examination of the interaction between Shore's and Enya's musics is a worthwhile endeavor, but, alas, one that lies outside the scope of this book.

[136] See www.soundtrack.net.

the bill as well.[137] Both works embody a sense of mythic hugeness, and that patina of epicness that clings to the Wagnerian leitmotif is an important reason that composers use them when working with such narratives. *The Lord of the Rings, Star Wars*, and the *Harry Potter* films are probably the most akin to the epic quality of *The Ring*, though the *Batman, Indiana Jones*, and *Star Trek* movies are also candidates (changing composers midstream hampered the musical connections between early and later films in some of these series).

Of course the reason the Wagnerian leitmotif fits the epic narrative so well is its embodiment of time. Simply by virtue of being developed, thematic statements need time to reach the status of the true leitmotif. Moreover, Wagnerian techniques of foreshadowing and reminiscence can alert the listener consciously (or subconsciously) to the passage of time in the narrative. Finally, an enormity of motivic connections between themes carves out a motivic space that is itself epic in nature. Such is the case with Wagner's *Ring*, though it rarely happens to anywhere near the same degree in film music.[138] The simple reason for this is that a ninety-minute film provides too brief a temporal and dramatic span to introduce and develop a legion of leitmotifs bound by motivic relationships to one another. An epic film series, however – like *The Lord of the Rings* – makes such a thing conceivable.

Though our focus will be on one motivic process, it is important to note that Shore's Wagnerian approach links themes by other means as well. The themes of men and hobbits are singable melodies, but ones that remain unsung, featuring solo melodic instruments rather than human voices. Themes of elves and other elder races (like the ents, dwarves, and Nazgûl), however, often comprise disembodied vocal sounds.[139] Likewise, specific instruments or instrumental families evoke elements of the drama regardless of their thematic content (if any); solo flute and clarinet conjure up the Shire, while the Norwegian fiddle is emblematic of Rohan.

Among all film composers, Shore is perhaps the most Wagnerian when it comes to form. Like Wagner, many of his scenes are unified by one central theme or motive – a theme or motive that serves as a refrain, alternating with contrasting material.[140] Examples from Wagner's *Ring*

---

[137] For a brief overview of music associated with various tellings of these tales both before and after the Peter Jackson trilogy, see Donnelly 2006.

[138] There are many studies of long-range, multi-level motivic continuity in Wagner's *Ring*. For one on the half-step "Anguish" motive in *Das Rheingold* Scenes 3 and 4, see Bribitzer-Stull 2008.

[139] Buhler 2006: 243–44.   [140] For more on the Wagnerian refrain form, see Newcomb 1989.

include the Alberich/Loge battle of wits from Scene 3 of *Das Rheingold*, the opening of *Die Walküre* Act III ("Ride of the Valkyries"), and the Wanderer/Mime riddle game and Siegfried's forging scenes from Act I of *Siegfried*, among others. In *The Fellowship of the Ring*, one hears a similar formal structure in the opening Shire scene, where the "Shire" theme and a chaconne I–V–vi–IV–V–I progression serve as the refrain. Another refrain form follows shortly thereafter, where the "Gollum" theme (refer back to Example 6.11) unites the entire "Riddles in the Dark" scene.

Throughout Shore's scores to Peter Jackson's films, however, there is one motivic detail that returns time and again, ultimately cinching the dramatic power of the penultimate scene when many of the tale's protagonists board the elvish boats that will bear them away from Middle Earth forever. This detail is the use of $\hat{4}$. Recall from our first citation of Shore's music in Chapter 1 that the "Ring" theme develops into a climactic version near the end of the last film in which scale degree $\sharp\hat{4}$ features prominently in the melody as a reworking of the rising half-step of the original version of this theme.[141] (Note that the addition of the untexted voices for this climactic citation of "Ring" also lends it a supernatural quality, given how untexted voices have been used throughout the trilogy for supernatural races.)

This is not the first time we have heard a prominent $\sharp\hat{4}$ in a leitmotif within Shore's score. Others include "Sorrow of the Elves," "Dwarves of Yore," "Lothlórien," and "Andúril, Flame of the West." See Example 9.17 in which the scale degree in question is circled. Each theme is associated with a more-than-human race (elves, dwarves, or the work of the Númenoreans) and stands in sharp distinction to the music of the Shire and its residents, the hobbits, who are the true protagonists of the trilogy and who are meant as stand-ins for the common folk – ordinary mankind.

Note that the "Shire" theme assiduously avoids the use of $\hat{4}$ in the melody, except for a brief embellishment (see Example 9.18). Since the narrative proper of the trilogy (i.e., the "real time" story that commences after Galadriel's prologue of events long past) begins and ends in the Shire, the relationship of the "Shire" music to other themes in the score is of paramount importance. All this comes out in the final denouement to *The*

---

[141] One instance of the "Ring" theme may seem puzzling, namely its statement when the Fellowship passes through the twin statues of the Argonath on the river Anduin. One of the statues is, however, of Isildur, the Númenorean whom the Ring betrayed to his death, when it slipped from his finger in the same river. Shore's usage of the "Ring" theme here indicates both his deep understanding of Tolkien's tale and a Wagnerian sensitivity to leitmotivic flexibility. Note that Henzel 2004: 104 explains the appearance of the "Ring" theme in this scene similarly, though I had drawn the same conclusion (with the help of my husband) before reading Henzel.

Example 9.17 Themes from Howard Shore's scores to Peter Jackson's *The Lord of the Rings* trilogy that feature ♯4̂

a. "Sorrow of the Elves"
b. "Dwarves of Yore"
c. "Lothlórien"
d. "Andúril, Flame of the West"

Example 9.18 The "Shire" theme from Howard Shore's score to *The Fellowship of the Ring*

Example 9.19 "Into the West" from Howard Shore's score to *The Return of the King*

Return of the King, when Frodo, Bilbo, Gandalf, and the elves depart for the blessed realms of the West.

At this point in the filmic narrative, we have heard numerous magical and supernatural themes that feature ♯$\hat{4}$. In order to reach the ♯$\hat{4}$-less normalcy of the natural world when Sam returns to it in the final scene of the film, Shore brilliantly decides to saturate the final leitmotif of the trilogy, "Into the West," with ♮$\hat{4}$–$\hat{3}$ melodic motion and 4–3 suspensions (see Example 9.19).[142] After ten-plus hours of filmic narrative, the plagal, ♮$\hat{4}$, downward-resolving half-step comes as a benediction and a completion, inverting the earlier ♯$\hat{4}$–$\hat{5}$ motive and filling in the "Shire" theme's missing $\hat{4}$. Moreover, the special status of the "Into the West" theme has been prepared, "saved" one might say, in a specifically Wagnerian manner. Just as Wagner introduced the "Glorification of Brunnhilde" theme in Act III, Scene 1 of *Die Walküre* and then saved any further repetition for the end of *Götterdämmerung*, so too does Shore allow "Into the West" to sound just twice before we hear its full expression near the end of the film.

---

[142] Note that Fran Walsh and Annie Lenox collaborated with Shore on the "Into the West" song the audience hears over the final credits, largely by writing the text. Fran Walsh served a similar role in writing the text for "Gollum's Song" at the end of *The Two Towers*.

The first time occurs when Gandalf speaks to Pippin in Minas Tirith of what happens after death (appropriate, since the journey to the West represents a kind of heavenly ascension). The second foreshadowing occurs on the slopes of Mount Doom as Sam picks up Frodo and begins carrying him toward the Cracks of Doom. Sam's support is what ultimately makes the entire Ring quest successful and we hear hints of that successful-but-bittersweet conclusion at the moment when Sam's support of Frodo becomes most tangible. (One might also hear this latter statement as something of an irony, since the theme is about the sweet sorrow of parting; and Sam picking up Frodo comprises the hobbits' moment of greatest union.)

"Into the West" also occurs as the refrain of a texted song performed over the closing credits. Thus it and "Gollum's Song" (which is performed with sung text over *The Two Towers* credits) comprise a sort of reverse leitmotif song, in which a texted song appears *non-diegetically, after* being heard as an orchestral leitmotif.[143] This is a notable involution of operatic practice, since such a process works opposite to the more usual arrangement, and contrary to Wagner's theories concerning thematic origination with text followed later by orchestral statements.

Connections to *The Lord of the Rings* scores from *The Hobbit*

Any doubt about Howard Shore's desire to create an interconnected musical epic to accompany the drama of Tolkien's story must be dispelled by listening to the music of *The Hobbit*. Many themes from *The Lord of the Rings* recur, among them: "Gollum," "Ring," "Lothlórien," "Sorrow of the Elves," "Rivendell," "Hope,"[144] and "Nazgûl."[145] There are also allusions to others. The rising scale from "Dwarves of Yore" makes an appearance when Gandalf gives Thorin the key and map that are the tangible markers

---

[143] In the song version, an accompanimental, interstitial horn motive during the refrain *descends* $\hat{1}-\hat{7}-\hat{6}$, reversing the minor-third *ascent* of the accompanimental, interstitial horn motive heard at the very opening of the trilogy as part of the "Ring" theme (see Example 1.2A). This is a nice orchestrational highlighting of the dramatically appropriate Thematic Inversion that occurs between the "Ring" and "Into the West" themes.

[144] This theme comprises music featuring a 5–6 shift, variants of which occur during Arwen's rescue of Frodo in *The Fellowship of the Ring*, the moth as messenger to the Eagle when Gandalf sits atop Orthanc in *The Fellowship of the Ring*, Galadriel's gifting scene in *The Fellowship of the Ring*, and the Ents' decision to attack Isengard in *The Two Towers*. Perhaps a better name for it is "Rescue."

[145] The music accompanying the Ringwraiths exiting Minas Morgul in *The Fellowship of the Ring* returns in *The Hobbit* during the White Council's discussion of Angmar and the morgul blade.

of his heritage (this theme was sounded only once in *The Lord of the Rings*, when the Fellowship experiences Dwarrowdelf in Moria); fragments of it occur in appropriate places later in *The Hobbit* as well. The opening I–♭VII progression of "Fellowship" sounds as Bilbo begins to narrate his adventures and we see the map of Middle Earth. Of course this theme doesn't manifest, being inappropriate for this movie. Its function, though, as a transitional theme often used for journeys and scene changes is taken over by the "Muster of the Dwarves" theme, a leitmotif song whose first appearance the dwarves sing diegetically in Bilbo's hobbit hole ("Far over the Misty Mountains old, in caverns deep and dungeons cold") and which appears later, non-diegetically, as a stand-in for "Fellowship."

There are other connections as well. The underscoring in general (featuring Shore's $\hat{1}$–$\hat{2}$–$\hat{3}$ in minor piling-up-tone-cluster, and the sonority of mixed, textless voices over strings) indicates to the listener that we inhabit the same sound universe as *The Lord of the Rings*. Likewise, thematic connections persist as well. Two new themes are linked by their usage of stepwise major-third melody lines: "Smaug" ($\hat{1}$–$\hat{2}$–$\hat{3}$ in major, though harmonized beginning with the submediant) and "Erebor," the Lonely Mountain that the dragon, Smaug, attacks, each note of whose minor-mode $\hat{3}$–$\hat{4}$–$\hat{5}$ is preceded by a brief anacrusis $\hat{1}$.

Finally, both the "Shire" and the supernatural ♯$\hat{4}$ recur as well. "Shire" is subjected to a notable Change of Texture featuring a faster tempo and more active scoring when Bilbo runs after the dwarves to leave the Shire and join their company. Likewise, the supernatural ♯$\hat{4}$ returns in scenes with the mythic Arkenstone and Elrond's readings of the magical moon runes. Moreover, the minor-mode $\hat{5}$–$\hat{3}$–$\hat{4}$–$\hat{2}$ "Forces of Darkness" motive (used in *The Hobbit* for spiders, orcs, Dol Guldur, and so forth) from *The Lord of the Rings* recurs at appropriate dramatic points in *The Hobbit* with ♯$\hat{4}$ substituting for ♮$\hat{4}$ seemingly indiscriminately.

The release of *The Hobbit* was a boon to leitmotif enthusiasts everywhere, promising more of the music Howard Shore wrote for the original trilogy. While the number and nature of Wagner's music dramas remains fixed, with virtually no prospect of uncovering heretofore unknown works or revisions, the leitmotivic style of composing that arose with Wagner remains alive and well in the scores of Shore, Williams, and many others. How long this second period of filmic leitmotivic composition will last is uncertain, but so long as it does, the thematic techniques Wagner honed will continue to delight audiences who enjoy modern versions of musical drama. This book has endeavored to serve those audiences, and the analysts among them, in better understanding the leitmotif wherever it may appear.

Works cited

Abbate, Carolyn. 1988. "Orpheus in the Underworld." In *Tannhäuser, Opera Guide Series* 39. Edited by John Nicholas. London: Calder. 33–50.

    1989a. "Opera as Symphony: A Wagnerian Myth." In *Analyzing Opera: Verdi and Wagner*. Edited by Carolyn Abbate and Roger Parker. Berkeley: University of California Press. 92–124.

    1989b. "Wagner, 'On Modulation,' and *Tristan*." *Cambridge Opera Journal* 1/1: 33–58.

    1991. *Unsung Voices: Opera and Musical Narrative in the Nineteenth Century*. Princeton University Press.

Abbate, Carolyn and Roger Parker. 1989. "Introduction: On Analyzing Opera." In *Analyzing Opera: Verdi and Wagner*. Edited by Carolyn Abbate and Roger Parker. Berkeley: University of California Press.

Adorno, Theodor. 1982. "On the Problem of Musical Analysis." Translated by Max Paddison. *Music Analysis* 1/2: 169–87.

    1991. *In Search of Wagner*. Translated by Rodney Livingstone. London: Verso.

Adorno, Theodor and Hanns Eisler. 1994. *Composing for the Films*. New York: The Athlone Press.

Agawu, Kofi. 1991. *Playing with Signs: A Semiotic Interpretation of Classic Music*. Princeton University Press.

Agmon, Eytan. 1995. "Functional Harmony Revisited: A Prototype-Theoretic Approach." *Music Theory Spectrum* 17/2: 196–214.

Aldritch, Richard. 1905. *A Guide to The Ring of the Nibelung*. Boston: Oliver Ditson Company.

Allen, Graham. 2000. *Intertextuality*. London and New York: Routledge.

Almén, Byron. 2003. "Narrative Archetypes: A Critique, Theory, and Method of Narrative Analysis." *Journal of Music Theory* 47: 1–39.

Altman, Rick. 2007. "Early Film Themes: Roxy, Adorno, and the Problem of Cultural Capital." In *Beyond the Soundtrack*. Edited by Daniel Goldmark, Lawrence Kramer, and Richard Leppert. Berkeley: University of California Press. 205–24.

Anderson, Lyle John. 1977. "Motivic and Thematic Transformation in Selected Works of Liszt." Ph.D. diss., Ohio State University.

Anson-Cartwright, Mark. 1996. "Chord as Motive: The Augmented-Triad Matrix in Wagner's *Siegfried Idyll*." *Music Analysis* 15: 57–71.

Babbitt, Milton. 1961. "Set Structure as a Compositional Determinant." *Journal of Music Theory* 5/1: 72–94.

Bach, Carl Philipp Emanuel. 1949. *Essay on the True Art of Playing Keyboard Instruments.* Translated by William J. Mitchell. New York: W.W. Norton.

Bailey, Robert. 1968. "Wagner's Musical Sketches for *Siegfrieds Tod.*" In *Studies in Music History: Essays for Oliver Strunk.* Edited by Harold Powers. Princeton University Press. 459–94.

1972. "The Evolution of Wagner's Compositional Procedure After Lohengrin." In *International Musicological Society Report 1972.* New Haven: Yale University Press. 240–42.

1977. "The Structure of the *Ring* and its Evolution." *19th-Century Music* 1/1: 48–61.

1985. *Wagner: Prelude and Transfiguration from Tristan and Isolde.* New York: W.W. Norton.

Barthes, Roland. 1974. *S/Z.* Trans. Richard Miller. New York: Hill and Wang.

1977. "Introduction to the Structural Analysis of Narratives." In *Music, Image, Text.* Trans. Stephen Heath. New York: Hill and Wang. 79–124.

Bass, Richard. 2001. "Half-diminished Functions and Transformations in Late Romantic Music." *Music Theory Spectrum* 23/1: 41–60.

Bauer, Hans Joachim. 1977. *Wagners Parsifal: Kriterien der Kompositionstechnik. Vol. 15 of Berliner Musikwissenschaftlich Arbeiten.* Edited by Carl Dahlhaus and Rudolph Stephan. Munich-Salzburg: Emil Katzbichler.

Beggs, John M. and Dietmar Plenz. 2004. "Neuronal Avalanches are Diverse and Precise Activity Patterns that are Stable for Many Hours in Cortical Slice Cultures." *The Journal of Neuroscience* 24/22: 5216–29.

Berg, Charles Merrell. 1976. *An Investigation of the Motives and Realization of Music to Accompany the American Silent Film, 1896–1927.* New York: Arno.

Berger, Anna Maria Busse. 2005. *Medieval Music and the Art of Memory.* Berkeley: University of California Press.

Bernstein, Fred. 2007. "The Smartest Man in the World is Gay." *The Advocate.* June 19: 44–53.

Berry, Wallace. 1966. *Form in Music.* Englewood Cliffs, NJ: Prentice-Hall.

Blasius, Leslie. 2001. "Nietzsche, Riemann, Wagner: When Music Lies." In *Music Theory and Natural Order from the Renaissance to the Early Twentieth Century.* Edited by Suzannah Clark and Alexander Rehding. Cambridge University Press. 93–107.

Bloom, Harold. 1973. *The Anxiety of Influence: A Theory of Poetry.* Oxford University Press.

1975. *A Map of Misreading.* New York: Oxford University Press.

Bolen, Jean Shinoda. 1992. *Ring of Power: The Abandoned Child, the Authoritarian Father, and the Disempowered Feminine – A Jungian Understanding of Wagner's Ring Cycle.* San Francisco: HarperCollins.

Boltz, Marilyn G. 2001. "Musical Soundtracks as a Schematic Influence on the Cognitive Processing of Filmed Events." *Music Perception* 18/4: 427–54.

Boltz, Marilyn, Matthew Schulkind, and Suzanne Kantra. 1991. "Effects of Background Music on the Remembering of Filmed Events." *Memory & Cognition* 19/6: 593–606.

Boretz, Benjamin. 1969. "Meta-Variations Part I: Studies in the Foundations of Musical Thought." *Perspectives of New Music* 8/1: 1–74.

1970a. "Meta-Variations Part II: Sketch of a Musical System." *Perspectives of New Music* 8/2: 49–111.

1970b. "Meta-Variations Part IIIA: The Construction of Musical Syntax." *Perspectives of New Music* 9/1: 23–42.

1971. "Meta-Variations Part IIIB: The Construction of Musical Syntax." *Perspectives of New Music* 10/1: 232–70.

1972. "Meta-Variations Part IVA: Analytic Fallout." *Perspectives of New Music* 11/1: 146–223.

1973. "Meta-Variations Part IVB: Analytic Fallout." *Perspectives of New Music* 11/2: 156–203.

Boult, Adrian. 2006. *The Apostles* and *The Kingdom*: An Illustrated Introduction by Adrian Boult." Tracks included in CD 4 from *Elgar: Choral Works* box set. EMI.

Breig, Werner. 1992. "The Musical Works." Translated by Paul Knight and Horst Loeschmann. In *Wagner Handbook*. Edited by Ulrich Müller and Peter Wapnewski. English translation edited by John Deathridge. Cambridge, MA: Harvard University Press. 397–482.

Bribitzer-Stull, Matthew. 2001. "Thematic Development and Dramatic Association in Wagner's *Der Ring des Nibelungen*." Ph.D. diss., Eastman School of Music.

2004. "'Did You Hear Love's Fond Farewell?' Thematic Irony in Wagner's *Ring*." *Journal of Musicological Research* 23/2: 123–57.

2007. "Naming Wagner's Themes." In *New Millennium Wagner Studies: Essays on Music and Culture*. Edited by Matthew Bribitzer-Stull *et al.* New York: Palgrave. 91–110.

2006a. "The A♭ – C – E Complex: The Origin and Function of Chromatic Major Third Collections in Nineteenth-Century Music." *Music Theory Spectrum* 28/2: 167–90.

2006b. "The End of *Die Feen* and Wagner's Beginnings: Multiple Approaches to an Early Example of Double-Tonic Complex, Associative Theme, and Wagnerian Form." *Music Analysis* 25/3: 315–40.

2008. "Echoes of Alberich's Anguish: Compositional Unity, Analytic Plurality, and Wagner's *Das Rheingold*." *Journal of Schenkerian Studies* 3: 59–91.

Bribitzer-Stull, Matthew and Robert Gauldin. 2007. "Hearing Wagner in *Till Eulenspiegel*: Strauss's Merry Pranks Reconsidered." *Intégral* 21: 1–39.

Bribitzer-Stull, Matthew, Alex Lubet, and Gottfried Wagner. 2007. *New Millennium Wagner Studies*. New York: Palgrave.

Brown, Hilda Meldrum. 1991. *Leitmotif and Drama: Wagner, Brecht, and the Limits of Epic Theatre*. Oxford: Clarendon.

Brown, Kristi. 2002. "Perfectly Executed: Bach's Music, Violence, and Technology in Film." Paper presented to the American Musicological Society, Columbus, OH.

Brown, Matthew. 1989. "Isolde's narrative: From *Hauptmotive* to Tonal Model." In *Analyzing Opera: Verdi and Wagner*. Edited by Carolyn Abbate and Roger Parker. Berkeley: University of California Press. 180–201.

2005. *Explaining Tonality: Schenkerian Theory and Beyond*. Rochester: University of Rochester Press.

Brown, Matthew and Roger Parker. 1985. "Ancora un Bacio: Three Scenes from Verdi's *Otello*." *19th-Century Music* 9/1: 50–62.

Brown, Matthew, Douglas Dempster, and David Headlam. 1997. "The ♯IV(♭V) Hypothesis: Testing the Limits of Schenker's Theory of Tonality." *Music Theory Spectrum* 19/2: 155–83.

Brown, Royal S. 1988. "Film and Classical Music." In *Film and the Arts in Symbiosis: A Resource Guide*. Edited by Gary R. Edgerton. New York: Greenwood. 165–215.

1994. *Overtones and Undertones: Reading Film Music*. Berkeley: University of California Press.

Brown, Stephen. 2006. "Tracing the Origins of Shostakovich's Musical Motto." *Intégral* 20: 69–103.

Buhler, James. 2000. "*Star Wars*, Music, and Myth." In *Music and Cinema*. Edited by James Buhler, Caryl Flinn, and David Neumeyer. Hanover: Wesleyan University Press. 33–57.

2006. "Enchantments of *Lord of the Rings*: Soundtrack, Myth, Language, and Modernity." In *From Hobbits to Hollywood: Essays on Peter Jackson's Lord of the Rings*. Edited by Ernst Mathijs and Murray Pomerance. Amsterdam: Rodopi. 231–48.

2010. "Wagnerian Motives: Narrative Integration and the Development of Silent Film Accompaniment, 1908–1913." In *Wagner and Cinema*. Edited by Jeongwon Joe and Sander Gilman. Bloomington: Indiana University Press. 27–45.

Buller, Jeffrey L. 1995. "The Thematic Role of *Stabreim* in Richard Wagner's *Der Ring des Nibelungen*." *The Opera Quarterly* 11/4: 59–76.

Burke, Kenneth. 1945. *A Grammar of Motives*. New York: Prentice-Hall, Inc.

Burkhart, Charles. 1978. "Schenker's 'Motivic Parallelisms.'" *Journal of Music Theory* 22/2: 145–75.

Burkholder, J. Peter. 2006. "A Simple Model for Associative Musical Meaning." In *Approaches to Meaning in Music*. Edited by Byron Almén and Edward Pearsall. Bloomington: Indiana University Press.

Burnham, Scott. 1995. *Beethoven Hero*. Princeton University Press.

Busoni, Ferruccio. 1957. *The Essence of Music and Other Papers*. Translated by Rosamund Ley. London: Rockliff.

Butler, David. 2013. "The Work of Music in the Age of Steel: Themes, Leitmotifs, and Stock Music in the New *Doctor Who*." In *Music in Science Fiction*

Television. Edited by K.J. Donnelly and Philip Hayward. New York: Routledge. 163–78.

Byrd, Craig L. 1997. "Interview with John Williams." *Film Score Monthly* 2/1. www.filmscoremonthly.com/features/williams.asp (accessed October 1, 2012).

Cadwallader, Allen. 1988. "Prolegomena to a General Description of Motivic Relationships in Tonal Music." *Intégral* 2: 1–35.

Cadwallader, Allen and William Pastille. 1992. "Schenker's High-Level Motives." *Journal of Music Theory* 36/1: 119–48.

Campbell, Brian. 1997. "Text and Phrase Rhythm in *Gurrelieder*: Schoenberg's Reception of Tradition." Ph.D. dissertation, University of Minnesota.

Caplin, William. 1998. *Classical Form: A Theory of Formal Functions for the Instrumental Music of Haydn, Mozart, and Beethoven.* Oxford University Press.

Carpenter, Patricia. 1983. "*Grundgestalt* as Tonal Function." *Music Theory Spectrum* 5: 15–38.

Carr, Maureen. 2002. *Multiple Masks: Neoclassicism in Stravinsky's Works on Greek Subjects.* Lincoln: University of Nebraska Press.

Cenciarelli, Carlo. 2012. "Dr. Lecter's Taste for 'Goldberg', or: The Horror of Bach in the Hannibal Franchise." *Journal of the Royal Musical Association* 137/1: 107–34.

Cherlin, Michael. 2007. *Schoenberg's Musical Imagination.* Cambridge University Press.

    2012. "'Pierrot Lunaire' as Lunar Nexus." *Musical Analysis* 31/2: 176–215.

Chion, Michel. 2009. *Film, A Sound Art.* Translated by Claudia Gorbman. New York: Columbia University Press.

Chomsky, Noam. 1957. *Syntactic Structures.* The Hague: Mouton & Co.

Cohen, Annabel. J. 1990. "Understanding Musical Soundtracks." *Empirical Studies of the Arts* 8/2: 111–24.

    1993. "Associationism and Musical Soundtrack Phenomena." *Contemporary Music Review* 9: 163–78.

    2001. "Music as a Source of Emotion in Film." In *Music and Emotion.* Edited by Patrik N. Juslin and John A. Sloboda. Oxford University Press. 249–74.

    2013. "Congruence-Association Model of Music and Multimedia." In *The Psychology of Music in Multimedia.* Edited by Siu-Lan Tan *et al.* Oxford University Press. 17–47.

Cohn, Richard. 2004. "Uncanny Resemblances. Tonal Signification in the Freudian Age." *Journal of the American Musicological Society* 57/2: 285–323.

Columbia Pictures Industries, Inc. 2002. "Composer Profile: Danny Elfman." *On Spider-Man, Widescreen Special Edition.* Culver City, CA: Columbia Pictures Industries, Inc.

    2004. "Sound & Music." *On Spider-Man 2: Widescreen Special Edition.* Culver City, CA: Columbia Pictures Industries, Inc.

Comuzio, Ermanno. 1980. *Colonna Sonora: dialoghi, musiche, rumori dietro lo schermo*. Milan: Edizione il Fornichiere.

Cone, Edward. 1968. *Musical Form and Musical Performance*. New York: W.W. Norton.

Cook, Nicholas. 1998. *Analyzing Musical Multimedia*. Oxford University Press.

Cooke, Deryck. 1979. *I Saw the World End: A Study of Wagner's Ring*. London: Oxford University Press.

1990. *The Language of Music*. New York: Oxford University Press.

1995. *An Introduction to* Der Ring des Nibelungen. London Records, CD 443 581–2 (rerelease of 1969 recording).

Cooke, Mervyn. 2001. "Film Music." In *The New Grove Dictionary of Music and Musicians*. Edited by Stanley Sadie. London: Macmillan. 797–810.

Cord, William O. 1995. *An Introduction to Richard Wagner's* Der Ring des Nibelungen. Athens: Ohio University Press.

Corse, Sandra. 1990. *Wagner and the New Consciousness: Language and Love in the Ring*. Rutherford: Fairleigh Dickinson University Press.

Cumming, Naomi. 1999. "The Subjectivities of *Erbarme Dich*." *Music Analysis* 16/1: 5–44.

2000. *The Sonic Self: Musical Subjectivity and Signification*. Bloomington: Indiana University Press.

Dahlhaus, Carl. 1974. *Between Romanticism and Modernism*. Translated by Mary Whittall. Berkeley: University of California Press.

1979. *Richard Wagner's Music Dramas*. Translated by Mary Whittall. Cambridge University Press.

1989. "What is a Musical Drama?" *Cambridge Opera Journal* 1/1: 95–111.

1992. "The Music." Translated by Spencer Stewart. In *Wagner Handbook*. Edited by Ulrich Müller; and Peter Wapnewski. English edition edited by John Deathridge. Cambridge, MA: Harvard University Press. 297–314.

Darby, William and Jack Du Bois. 1990. *American Film Music: Major Composers, Techniques, Trends, 1915–90*. Jefferson, NC: McFarland.

Darcy, Warren. 1987. "Redeemed from Rebirth: The Evolving Meaning of Wagner's *Ring*." In *Wagner in Retrospect: A Centennial Reappraisal*. Edited by Leroy R. Shaw *et al*. Amsterdam: Rodopi. 50–61.

1989. "Creatio ex Nihilo: The Genesis, Structure, and Meaning of the *Rheingold* Prelude." *19th-Century Music* 13/2: 79–100.

1993. *Wagner's Das Rheingold*. New York: Oxford University Press.

1994. "The Metaphysics of Annihilation: Wagner, Schopenhauer, and the Ending of the Ring." *Music Theory Spectrum* 16/1: 1–40.

2001. "Appendix" to Matthew Bribitzer-Stull, "Thematic Development and Dramatic Association in Wagner's *Der Ring des Nibelungen*." Ph.D. dissertation, Eastman School of Music.

2005. "'Die Zeit ist da:' Rotational Form and Hexatonic Magic in Act 2, Scene 1 of *Parsifal*." In *A Companion to Richard Wagner's Parsifal*. Edited by William Kinderman and Katherine R. Syer. Rochester, NY: Camden House. 215–44.

Darrow, A. 2006. "The Role of Music in Deaf Culture: Deaf Students' Perception of Emotion in Music." *Journal of Music Therapy* 43/1: 2–15.

Daverio, John Joseph. 1991. "Brünnhilde's Immolation Scene and Wagner's 'Conquest of the Reprise.'" *Journal of Musicological Research* 11/1–2: 33–66.

1993. *19th-Century Music and the German Romantic Ideology*. New York: Macmillan.

Deathridge, John. 1981. "Review of *Richard Wagner and the English, et al.*" *19th-Century Music* 5/1: 81–89.

Deathridge, John and Carl Dahlhaus. 1984. *Wagner*. New York: Norton.

Debussy, Claude. 1977. *Debussy on Music*. Edited and translated by Richard Langham Smith. New York: Knopf.

Deliège, Irene. 1992. "Recognition of the Wagnerian *Leitmotife*: Experimental Study Based on an Excerpt from *Das Rheingold*." Translated by Craig Douglas. *Musikpsychologie: Jahrbuch der Deutschen Gesellschaft fur Musikpsychologie* 9: 25–54.

Dennison, Peter. 1985. "Musical Structuring and its Evolution in Wagner's *Ring*." *Miscellanea Musicologica* 14: 29–56.

Donington, Robert. 1974. *Wagner's Ring and its Symbols*. New York: St. Martin's Press.

Donnelly, K.J. 2006. "Musical Middle Earth." In *The Lord of the Rings: Popular Culture in Global Context*. Edited by Ernest Mathijs. London: Wallflower Press. 301–16.

Drabkin, William. n.d. "Theme." In *Grove Music Online*. Edited by Deana Root. www.oxfordmusiconline.com (accessed June 9, 2014).

Drake, Warren. 1985. "The Norns' Scene in *Götterdämmerung*: A Cycle within a Cycle." *Miscellanea Musicologica* 14: 57–77.

Dreyfus, Laurence. 2010. *Wagner and the Erotic Impulse*. Cambridge, MA: Harvard University Press.

Dyson, J. Peter. 1987. "Ironic Dualities in *Das Rheingold*." *Current Musicology* 43: 33–50.

Elders, Willem. 1991. *Composers of the Low Countries*. Translated by Graham Dixon. Oxford: Clarendon Press.

Ellinwood, Leonard. 1962. "Introduction to Tallis's Tunes for Archbishop Parker's Psalter (1567)." In Thomas Tallis, *Early English Church Music: English Sacred Music II: Service Music, vol. XIII*. Transcribed and edited by Leonard Ellinwood. London: Stainer and Bell, for the British Academy. vii–xiii.

Evensen, Kristian. 2008. *"The Star Wars Series and Wagner's Ring: Structural, Thematic, and Musical Connections*. www.trell.org/wagner/starwars.html (accessed October 1, 2012).

Feisst, Sabine M. 1999. "Arnold Schoenberg and the Cinematic Art." *The Musical Quarterly* 83/1: 93–113.

Flinn, Caryl. 1992. *Strains of Utopia: Gender, Nostalgia, and Hollywood Film Music*. Princeton University Press.

   2004. *The New German Cinema: Music, History, and the Matter of Style*. Berkeley: University of California Press.

Floros, Constantin. 1983. "Der 'Beziehungszauber' der Musik im 'Ring des Nibelungen' von Richard Wagner." *Neue Zeitschrift für Musik* 144/7–8: 8–14.

Fox, Malcolm. 1993. "Wotan's Spear." *Wagner* 14/2: 56–70.

Franklin, Peter. 2007. "The Boy on the Train, or Bad Symphonies and Good Movies." In *Beyond the Soundtrack*. Edited by Daniel Goldmark, Lawrence Kramer, and Richard Leppert. Berkeley: University of California Press. 13–26.

   2010. "Underscoring Drama – Picturing Music." In *Wagner and Cinema*. Edited by Jeongwon Joe and Sander Gilman. Bloomington: Indiana University. 46–64.

Frolova-Walker, Marina. 2001. "Nikolay Andreyevich Rimsky-Korsakov." In *The New Grove Dictionary of Music and Musicians*. Edited by Stanley Sadie. 400–22.

Gabrielsson, A. and E.N. Juslin. 1996. "Emotional Expression in Music Performance: Between the Performer's Intention and the Listener's Experience." *Psychology of Music* 24: 68–91.

Gallois, Jean. 2001. "(Amédée-) Ernest Chausson." In *The New Grove Dictionary of Music and Musicians*. Edited by Stanley Sadie. 538–42.

Gauldin, Robert. 1991. "Beethoven's Interrupted Tetrachord and the Seventh Symphony." *Intégral* 5: 77–100.

   2013. *A Practical Approach to 18th-Century Counterpoint*. Long Grove, IL: Waveland Press, Inc.

Gjerdingen, Robert. 2007. *Music in the Galant Style*. New York: Oxford University Press.

Gleaves, Ian Beresford. 1988. "Wagner and Time." *Wagner* 9/4: 126–46.

Goldwasser, Dan. 2001. "Interview: And in the Darkness Bind Them." www.soundtrack.net/content/article/?id=89.

Gopinath, Sumanth. 2013. *The Ringtone Dialectic: Economy and Cultural Form*. Cambridge, MA: MIT Press.

Gorbman, Claudia. 1987. *Unheard Melodies*. Bloomington: Indiana University Press.

Goslich, Siegfried. 1975. *Die deutsche romantische Oper*. Tutzing: Hans Schneider.

Grayson, David. 1986. *The Genesis of Debussy's* Pelléas et Mélisande. Ann Arbor: University of Michigan Press.

Grey, Thomas. 1992. "The Music Drama and its Antecedents." In *The Wagner Compendium*. Edited by Barry Millington. New York: Schirmer Books. 79–92.

1993. "Wagner's Lohengrin: Between Grand Opera and Musikdrama." In *Lohengrin, Opera Guide Series 47*. Edited by Nicholas John. London: Calder. 15–31.

1995. *Wagner's Musical Prose: Texts and Contexts*. Cambridge University Press.

1998. "Leading Motives and Narrative Threads: Notes on the Leitfaden Metaphor and the Critical Pre-History of the Wagnerian Leitmotif." In *Musik als Text, v. II*. Edited by Hermann Danuser and Tobias Plebuch. Basel: Bärenreiter-Kasssel. 352–58.

2008. "Leitmotif, Temporality, and Musical Design in the Ring." In *The Cambridge Companion to Wagner*. Cambridge University Press. 85–114.

Hacohen, Ruth and Naphtali Wagner. 1997. "The Communicative Force of Wagner's *Leitmotifes*: Complement Relations Between Their Connotations and Denotations." *Music Perception* 14/4: 445–76.

Halfyard, Janet K. 2004. *Danny Elfman's Batman*. Lanham, MD: Scarecrow Press, Inc.

Harrison, Daniel. 1994. *Harmonic Function in Chromatic Music: A Renewed Dualist Theory and an Account of Its Precedents*. University of Chicago Press.

1995. "Supplement to the Theory of Augmented-Sixth Chords." *Music Theory Spectrum* 17/2: 170–95.

2002. "Non-conformist Notions of Nineteenth-Century Enharmonicism." *Music Analysis* 22/2: 115–60.

Haskins, Rob. 2010. "Variations on Themes for Greeks and Heroes: Leitmotif, Style, and the Musico-dramatic Moment." In *Music, Sound, and Silence in Buffy the Vampire Slayer*. Edited by Paul Attinello, Janet K. Halfyard, and Vanessa Knights. Surrey: Ashgate. 45–60.

Hatten, Robert. 1994. *Musical Meaning in Beethoven: Markedness, Correlation, and Interpretation*. Bloomington: Indiana University Press.

2004. *Interpreting Musical Gestures, Topics, and Tropes: Mozart, Beethoven, and Schubert*. Bloomington: Indiana University Press.

Henzel, Christoph. 2004. "Wagner und die Filmmusik." *Acta Musicologica* 76/1: 89–115.

Hepokoski, James and Warren Darcy. 2006. *Elements of Sonata Theory: Norms, Types, and Deformations in the Late-Eighteenth-Century Sonata*. Oxford University Press.

Herder, Johann Gottfried. 2006. *Selected Writings on Aesthetics*. Translated and edited by Gregory Moore. Princeton University Press.

Hindemith, Paul. 1945. *The Craft of Musical Composition, v. 1*. Translated by Arthur Mendel. London: Schott.

Hoeckner, Bertold and Howard C. Nusbaum. 2013. "Music and Memory in Film and Other Multimedia: The Casablanca Effect." In *The Psychology of Music in Multimedia*. Edited by Sui-Lan Tan *et al*. Oxford University Press. 235–66.

Holloway, Robin. 1985. "Motif, Memory, and Meaning in *Twilight of the Gods*." In *Götterdämmerung, Opera Guide Series 31*. Edited by Nicholas John. London: Calder.

Holman, J.K. 1996. *Wagner's Ring: A Listener's Companion and Concordance*. Portland: Amadeus Press.

Hook, Julian. 2008. "Signature Transformations." In *Music Theory and Mathematics: Chords' Collections and Transformations*. Edited by Charles Smith, Martha Hyde, and Jack Douthett. University of Rochester Press. 137–60.

Hooper, Jason. 2011. "Heinrich Schenker's Early Conception of Form, 1895–1914." *Theory and Practice* 36: 35–64.

Huckvale, David. 1988. "Wagner and the Mythology of Film Music." *Wagner* 9/2: 46–67.

Huebner, Steven. 1999. *French Opera at the Fin de Siècle: Wagnerism, Nationalism, and Style*. Oxford University Press.

  2004. "Thematic Recall in Late Nineteenth-Century Opera." In *"L'insolita forma:" Strutture e processi analitici per l'opera italiana nell' epoca di Puccini*. Edited by Virgilio Bernadoni. Lucca: Centro Studi Giacomo Puccini. 77–104.

Hunt, Graham. 2007. "David Lewin and Valhalla Revisited: New Approaches to Motivic Corruption in Wagner's *Ring* Cycle." *Music Theory Spectrum* 29/2: 177–96.

Hutcheon, Linda. 1994. *Irony's Edge: The Theory and Politics of Irony*. London: Routledge.

Hutcheson, Ernest. 1940. *A Musical Guide to the Richard Wagner* Ring of the Nibelung. New York: Simon and Schuster.

Hyer, Brian. 1995. "Reimag(in)ing Riemann." *Journal of Music Theory* 39: 101–38.
  2006. "*Parsifal* hystérique." *Opera Quarterly* 22/2: 269–320.

Iwamiya, Shinichiro. 2013. "Perceived Congruence Between Auditory and Visual Elements in Multimedia." In *The Psychology of Music in Multimedia*. Edited by Sui-Lan Tan *et al.* Oxford University Press. 141–64.

Jackson, Roland. 1975. "*Leitmotife* and Form in the *Tristan* Prelude." *Music Review* 36/1: 42–53.

Jakobson, Roman. 1959. "Linguistics and Poetics." In *Style and Language*. Edited by Thomas Sebeok. Cambridge, MA: MIT Press. 350–77.
  1973. *Questions de poétique*. Paris: Seuil.

Jenkins, John Edward. 1978. "The Leitmotife 'Sword' in *Die Walküre*." Ph.D. diss., University of Southern Mississippi.

Joe, Jeongwon and Sander Gilman, eds. 2010. *Wagner and Cinema*. Bloomington: Indiana University Press.

Kalinak, Kathryn. 1992. *Settling the Score: Music and the Classical Hollywood Film*. Madison: University of Wisconsin Press.

Karlin, Fred. 1994. *Listening to Movies: The Film Lover's Guide to Film Music*. New York: Schirmer.

Karlin, Fred and Rayburn Wright. 2004. *On the Track: A Guide to Contemporary Film Scoring*. New York: Routledge.

Kassabian, Anahid. 1994. "Songs of Subjectivities: Theorizing Hollywood Film Music of the 80s and 90s." Ph.D. diss., Stanford University.

Katz, Adele T. 1972. *The Challenge to Musical Tradition: A New Concept of Tonality*. New York: Da Capo Press.

Kaufman, J.B. 2002. Liner notes to the recording produced by the Max Steiner Society, *The RKO Years, 1929–1936*, No. 25781.

Keiler, Allan. 1978a. "The Empiricist Illusion: Narmour's *Beyond Schenkerism*." *Perspectives of New Music* 17/1: 161–95.

  1978b. "Bernstein's 'The Unanswered Question' and the Problem of Musical Competence." *The Musical Quarterly* 64/2: 195–222.

Kelkel, Manfred. 1984. *Naturalisme, Vérisme et Réalisme dans l'Opéra de 1890 à 1930*. Paris: Librairie Philosophique J. Vrin.

Kendall, Roger A. and Scott D. Lipscomb. 2013. "Experimental Semiotics Applied to Visual, Sound, and Musical Structures." In *The Psychology of Music in Multimedia*. Edited by Sui-Lan Tan *et al.* Oxford University Press. 48–65.

Kinderman, William. 2005. "The Genesis of the Music." In *A Companion to Richard Wagner's* Parsifal. Edited by William Kinderman and Katherine R. Syer. Rochester, NY: Camden House. 133–76.

Kinderman, William and Harald Krebs. 1996. "Introduction." In *The Second Practice of Nineteenth-Century Tonality*. Edited by William Kinderman and Harald Krebs. Lincoln: University of Nebraska Press. 1–14.

Kirby, F.E. 2004. *Wagner's Themes: A Study in Musical Expression*. Warren, MI: Harmonie Park Press.

Kivy, Peter. 1980. *The Corded Shell: Reflections on Musical Expression*. Princeton University Press.

  1984. *Sound and Semblance: Reflections on Musical Representation*. Princeton University Press.

  1989. *Sound Sentiment: An Essay on the Musical Emotion, Including the Complete Text of* The Corded Shell. Philadelphia: Temple University Press.

  1990. *Music Alone: Reflections on the Purely Musical Experience*. Ithaca: Cornell University Press.

Klein, Michael. 2004. "Chopin's Fourth Ballade as Musical Narrative." *Music Theory Spectrum* 26: 23–55.

  2005. *Intertextuality in Western Art Music*. Bloomington: Indiana University Press.

Kobbé, Gustav. 1916. *How to Understand Wagner's* Ring of the Nibelungs. London: William Reeves.

Kopp, David. 2002. *Chromatic Transformations in Nineteenth-Century Music*. Cambridge University Press.

Korsyn, Kevin. 1993. "Schenker's Organicism Reexamined." *Intégral* 7: 82–118.

Kracauer, Siegfried. 1960. *Theory of Film: The Redemption of Physical Reality.* New York: Oxford University Press.

Kramer, Lawrence. 2002. *Musical Meaning: Toward a Critical History.* Berkeley: University of Calfornia Press.

Krebs, Harald. 1988. "Dramatic Functions of Metrical Consonance and Dissonance in *Das Rheingold.*" *In Theory Only* 10/5: 5–21.

Krims, Adam. 1998. "Disciplining Deconstruction (for Music Analysis)." *19th-Century Music* 21/3: 297–324.

Kulezik, Danijela. 1997. "The Audio-Visual Structure of Film and the Influence of the Poetics of Myth on its Maturing." *New Sound* 9: 59–64.

Kundera, Milan. 1984. *The Unbearable Lightness of Being.* Translated by Michael Henry Heim. New York: Harper & Row.

Kurth, Ernst. 1920. *Romantische Harmonik und ihre Krise in Wagners "Tristan."* Bern: P. Haupt.

Laufer, Edward. 1971. "Analysis Symposium: Brahms Op. 105/1." *Journal of Music Theory* 15/1–2: 34–57.

Lavignac, Albert. 1926. *The Music Dramas of Richard Wagner and His Festival Theatre in Bayreuth.* Translated by Esther Singleton. New York: Dodd and Mead Company.

LeGuin, Ursula K. 1975. *The Tombs of Atuan.* New York: Bantam Books.

Leinberger, Charles. 1996. "An Austrian in Hollywood: Leitmotifs, Thematic Transformation, and Key Relationships in Max Steiner's 1942 Film Score, *Now, Voyager.*" Ph.D. diss., University of Arizona.

   2002. "Thematic Variation and Key Relationships: Charlotte's Theme in Max Steiner's Score for *Now, Voyager.*" *The Journal of Film Music* 1/1: 63–77.

Lerdahl, Fred. 1994. "Tonal and Narrative Paths in Parsifal." In *Eleven Essays in Honor of David Lewin.* Edited by Raphael Atlas and Michael Cherlin. Roxbury: Ovenbird. 121–46.

Lévi-Strauss, Claude. 1963. *Structural Anthropology.* Garden City: Basic Books.

Lewin, David. 1962. "A Theory of Segmental Association in Twelve-Tone Music." *Perspectives of New Music* 1: 89–116.

   1984. "Amfortas's Prayer to Titurel and the Role of D in *Parsifal*: The Tonal Spaces of the Drama and the Enharmonic Cb/B." *19th-Century Music* 7/3: 336–49.

   1992. "Some Notes on Analyzing Wagner: The *Ring* and *Parsifal.*" *19th-Century Music* 16/1: 49–58.

Leydon, Rebecca. 2001. "Debussy's Late Style and the Devices of the Early Silent Cinema." *Music Theory Spectrum* 23/2: 217–41.

Lidov, David. 2005. *Is Language a Music?* Bloomington: Indiana University Press.

Lipscomb, Scott D. 2013. "Cross-modal Alignment of Accent Structures in Multimedia." In *The Psychology of Music in Multimedia.* Edited by Sui-Lan Tan *et al.* Oxford University Press. 192–216.

Lipscomb, Scott D. and Roger A. Kendall. 1994. "Perceptual Judgment of the
     Relationship between and Audio and Visual Components of Film."
     Psychomusicology 13: 60–98.

Lloyd, Steven. 1999. "Film Music." In *William Walton: Music and Literature*.
     Edited by Stewart R. Craggs. Aldershot: Ashgate. 109–31.

London, Justin. 2000. "Leitmotifs and Musical Reference in the Classical Film
     Score." In *Music and Cinema*. Edited by James Buhler, Caryl Flinn, and David
     Neumeyer. Hanover: Wesleyan University Press. 85–96.

  2007. "Review of *Conceptualizing Music: Cognitive Structure, Theory,
     and Analysis* by Lawrence M. Zbikowski." *Music Theory Spectrum* 29/1:
     115–25.

MacDonald, Laurence. 1998. *The Invisible Art of Film Music*. New York: Ardsley
     House Publishers, Inc.

Maisel, Arthur. 1999. "Voice Leading as Drama in Wozzeck." In *Schenker Studies
     2*. Edited by Carl Schachter and Hedi Siegel. Cambridge University Press.
     160–91.

Margulis, Elizabeth Hellmuth. 2014. *On Repeat: How Music Plays the Mind*.
     New York: Oxford University Press.

Marshall, Sandra K. and Annabel J. Cohen. 1988. "Effects of Musical Soundtracks
     on Attitudes to Animated Geometric Figures." *Music Perception* 6/1: 95–112.

Marvin, William. 2001. "Tonality in Selected Set Pieces from Wagner's *Die
     Meistersinger von Nürnberg*: A Schenkerian Approach." Ph.D. diss.,
     Eastman School of Music.

  2007. "Subverting the Conventions of Number Opera from Within: Hierarchical
     and Associational Uses of Tonality in Act I of *Der fliegende Holländer*." In
     Richard Wagner for the New Millennium. Edited by Matthew Bribitzer-Stull,
     Alex Lubet, and Gottfried Wagner. New York: Palgrave. 71–90.

Maus, Fred. 1988. "Music as Drama." *Music Theory Spectrum* 10: 56–73.

  1991. "Music as Narrative." *Indiana Theory Review* 12: 1–34.

Max Steiner Society. 2002. Liner notes to Audio CD, *The RKO Years: 1929–1936*.

McClary, Susan. 1991. *Feminine Endings: Music, Gender, and Sexuality*.
     Minneapolis: University of Minnesota Press.

  2007. "Minima Romantica." In *Beyond the Soundtrack*. Edited by Daniel
     Goldmark, Lawrence Kramer, and Richard Leppert. Berkeley: University of
     California Press. 48–65.

McClatchie, Stephen. 1998. *Analyzing Wagner's Operas: Alfred Lorenz and
     German Nationalist Ideology*. University of Rochester Press.

McClelland, Clive. 2012. *Ombra: Supernatural Music in the Eighteenth Century*.
     Lanham: Lexington Books.

McCredie, Andrew. 1985. "Leitmotife: Wagner's Points of Departure and Their
     Antecedents." *Miscellanea Musicologica* 14: 1–28.

McCreless, Patrick. 1982. *Wagner's* Siegfried: *Its Drama, History, and its Music*.
     Ann Arbor: University of Michigan Press.

1983. "Ernest Kurth and the Analysis of the Chromatic Music of the Late Nineteenth Century." *Music Theory Spectrum* 5: 56–75.

1990. "Motive and Magic: A Referential Dyad in Parsifal." *Music Analysis* 9/3: 227–65.

1991. "Syntagmatics and Paradigmatics: Some Implications for the Analysis of Chromaticism in Tonal Music." *Music Theory Spectrum* 13: 147–78.

McGuire, Charles. 2002. *Elgar's Oratorios: The Creation of an Epic Narrative.* Aldershot: Ashgate.

McVeagh, Diana. 2001. "Edward Elgar." In *The New Grove Dictionary of Music and Musicians.* Edited by Stanley Sadie. 8: 115–37.

Meadows, Laura. 2008. "Elgar as Post-Wagnerian: A Study of Elgar's Assimilation of Wagner's Music and Methodology." Ph.D. diss., Durham University.

Metz, Walter C. 2013. "What's Wagner, Doc?" Paper presented at the Wagner WorldWide Conference. Columbia: University of South Carolina.

Millington, Barry. 1992a. *Wagner.* Princeton University Press.

ed. 1992b. *The Wagner Compendium: A Guide to Wagner's Life and Music.* New York: Schirmer.

Monelle, Raymond. 1992. *Linguistics and Semiotics in Music.* London: Routledge.

2000. *The Sense of Music: Semiotic Essays.* Princeton University Press.

2006. *The Musical Topic: Hunt, Military, Pastoral.* Bloomington: Indiana University Press.

Morgan, Catherine. 2011. "Good vs. Evil: The Role of the Soundtrack in Developing a Dichotomy in *Harry Potter and the Sorcerer's Stone.*" M.M. thesis, University of North Carolina–Greensboro.

Morgan, Robert. 1976. "Dissonant Prolongations: Theoretical and Compositional Precedents." *Journal of Music Theory* 20/1: 49–91.

Morris, Charles. 1946. *Signs, Language, and Behavior.* New York: Prentice-Hall.

Müller, Ulrich and Peter Wapnewski, eds. 1992. *Wagner Handbook.* Translated by John Deathridge. Cambridge, MA: Harvard University Press.

Murphy, Scott. 2000. "Chromatic Neighbor-Note Motions, Absolute Progressions, and an Assessment of One Dialect from the Polyglot of Recent American Film Music." Paper delivered to the Music Theory Society of New York State, New York University.

2006. "The Major Tritone Progression in Recent Hollywood Science Fiction Films." *Music Theory Online* 12/2.

Murray, David. 1978. "Major Analytical Approaches to Wagner's Musical Style: A Critique." *Music Review* 39/3–4: 211–22.

Narum, Jessica. 2013. "Sound and Semantics: Topics in the Music of Arnold Schoenberg." Ph.D. diss., University of Minnesota.

Nasta, Dominique. 1991. *Meaning in Film: Relevant Structures in Soundtrack and Narrative.* Berne: Peter Lang.

Nattiez, Jean-Jacques. 1990. *Music and Discourse.* Translated by Carolyn Abbate. Princeton University Press.

1997. *Wagner Androgyne*. Princeton University Press.

Naumann, Emil. 1876. *Italienische Tondichter, von Palestrina bis auf die Gegenwart*. Berlin: R. Oppenheim.

Nelson, Robert. 1962. "Stravinsky's Concept of Variations." *The Musical Quarterly* 48/3: 327–39.

Neumeyer, David. 1997. "Source Music, Background Music, Fantasy, and Reality in Early Sound Film." *College Music Symposium* 37: 13–20.

2000. "Performances in Early Hollywood Sound Films: Source Music, Background Music, and the Integrated Sound Track." *Contemporary Music Review* 19: 37–62.

2010. "Wagnerian Opera and Nineteenth-Century Melodrama in the Film Scores of Max Steiner." In *Wagner and Cinema*. Edited by Jeongwon Joe and Sander Gilman. Bloomington: Indiana University Press. 111–30.

New Line Productions, Inc. 2001. "Music for Middle Earth." On *The Fellowship of the Ring*, Special Extended Edition. New Line Productions, Inc. DVD N5549D.

Newcomb, Anthony. 1981. "The Birth of Music out of the Spirit of the Drama." *19th-Century Music* 5/1: 33–66.

1989. "Ritornello Ritornato: A Variety of Wagnerian Refrain Form." In *Analyzing Opera: Wagner and Verdi*. Edited by Carolyn Abbate and Roger Parker. Berkeley: University of California Press. 202–21.

Newman, Ernest. 1989. *The Wagner Operas*. Princeton University Press.

Noske, Frits. 1994. "Verbal and Musical Semantics in Opera: Denotation and Connotation." In *Die Semantik der musiko-literarischen Gattungen: Methodik und Analyse – Eine Festgabe für Ulrich Weisstein zum 65. Geburtstag*. Edited by Walter Bernhart. Tübingen: Narr. 35–50.

Orosz, Jeremy. 2013. "Translating Music Intelligibly: Musical Paraphrase in the Long 20th Century." Ph.D. diss., University of Minnesota.

Osborne, Charles. 1993. *The Complete Operas of Richard Wagner*. New York: Da Capo Press.

Parry, Sir C. Hubert H. 1889. "Leit-Motif." In *Grove's Dictionary of Music and Musicians, v. II*. Edited by J.A. Fuller Maitland. London: Macmillan & Co. 115–18.

Patterson, Franklin P. 1896. *The Leitmotives of* Der Ring des Nibelungen. Leipzig: Breitköpf & Härtel.

Paulin, Scott. D. 2000. "Richard Wagner and the Fantasy of Cinematic Unity: The Idea of the *Gesamtkunstwerk* in the History and Theory of Film Music." In *Music and Cinema*. Edited by James Buhler, Caryl Flinn, and David Neumeyer. Hanover: Wesleyan University Press. 58–84.

Peirce, Charles Sanders. 1960. *Collected Papers of Charles Sanders Pierce, vol. II, "Elements of Logic."* Edited by Charles Hartshorne and Paul Weiss. Cambridge, MA: Harvard University Press.

Perle, George. 1980. *The Operas of Alban Berg, vol. I.* Berkeley: University of California Press.

Pinker, Steven. 1999. *Words and Rules.* New York: Basic Books.

Pool, Jeannie Gayle and Stephen H. Wright. 2010. *A Research Guide to Film and Television Music in the United States.* Lanham, MD: Scarecrow Press.

Porges, Heinrich. 1983. *Wagner Rehearsing the Ring: An Eyewitness Account of the Stage Rehearsals of the First Bayreuth Festival.* Translated by Robert L. Jacobs. Cambridge University Press.

Prendergast, Roy M. 1992. *Film Music: A Neglected Art.* New York: W.W. Norton.

Proctor, Gregory. 1978. "Technical Bases of Nineteenth-Century Chromatic Tonality: A Study in Chromaticism." Ph.D. diss., Princeton University.

Propp, Vladimir. 1968. *Morphology of the Folktale.* Austin: University of Texas Press.

Puri, Michael. 2011. *Ravel the Decadent: Memory, Sublimation, and Desire.* Oxford Univerity Press.

Raskin, David. 1989. "Holding a Nineteenth-Century Pedal at Twentieth-Century Fox." In *Film Music I.* Edited by Clifford McCarty. New York: Garland. 167–82.

Ratner, Leonard. 1980. *Classic Music.* New York: Schirmer.

Reale, Paul. 1970. "The Process of Multivalent Thematic Transformation." Ph.D. diss., University of Pennsylvania.

Reti, Rudolph. 1978. *The Thematic Process in Music.* Westport: Greenwood.

Rieger, Eva. 2010. "Wagner's Role on Gender Roles in Early Hollywood." In *Wagner and Cinema.* Edited by Jeongwon Joe and Sander Gilman. Bloomington: Indiana University Press. 131–51.

Ringer, Alexander L. n.d. "Melody." In *Grove Music Online.* Edited by Deane Root. www.oxfordmusiconline.com (accessed June 9, 2014).

Rodman, Rod. 2006. "The Popular Song as Leitmotif in 1990s Film." In *Changing Tunes: The Use of Pre-existing Music in Film.* Edited by Phil Powrie and Robyn Stilwell. Burlington, VT: Ashgate. 119–36.

Rosar, William H. 2010. "The Penumbra of Wagner's Ombra in Two Science-Fiction Films from 1951: *The Thing from Another World* and *The Day the Earth Stood Still.*" In *Wagner and Cinema.* Edited by Jeongwon Joe and Sander Gilman. Bloomington: Indiana University Press. 152–66.

Rose, Paul Lawrence. 1990. *Revolutionary Antisemitism in Germany from Kant to Wagner.* Princeton University Press.

1992. *Wagner, Race, and Revolution.* New Haven: Yale University Press.

Rosen, Charles. 1980. *Sonata Forms.* New York: W.W. Norton.

2011a. "Dallas Redux: The Death and Re-birth of the Auteur in American Narrative Television Music." Paper presented to the University of Minnesota Musicology and Music Theory Colloquium Series.

2011b. "The Operatic Stothard: Leitmotifs and Tonal Organization in Two Versions of *Rose-Marie.*" *Journal of Film Music* 4/1: 5–19.

Ross, Alex. 2003. "The Ring and the Rings." *The New Yorker* Dec. 22 & 29:
    161–65.
Rothgeb, John. 1983. "Thematic Content: A Schenkerian View." In *Aspects of
    Schenkerian Theory.* Edited by David Beach. New Haven: Yale University
    Press.
Rothstein, William. 1989. *Phrase Rhythm in Tonal Music.* New York: Schirmer.
Rushton, Julian. 1971. "An Early Essay in Leitmotif: J.B. Lemoyne's *Électre.*" *Music
    & Letters* 52/4: 387–401.
Santa, Matthew. 1999. "Defining Modular Transformations." *Music Theory
    Spectrum* 21/2: 200–29.
Saussure, Ferdinand de. 1959. *Course in General Linguistics.* Trans. Wade Baskin.
    New York: Philosophical Library.
Sayrs, Elizabeth. 2006. "Frame-Shifting as a General Process in Tonal
    Music." Paper presented to Music Theory Midwest Conference. Ball State
    University.
Schelle, Michael. 1999. *The Score: Interviews with Film Composers.* Los Angeles:
    Silman-James Press.
Schenker, Heinrich. 1906. *Neue musikalische Theorien und Phantasien, vol. I:
    Harmonielehre.* Stuttgart: Cotta.
    1979. *New Musical Theories and Phantasies: Part Three, Free Composition.*
    Translated and edited by Ernest Oster. New York: Longman.
    1992. *Beethoven's Ninth Symphony.* Edited and translated by John Rothgeb. New
    Haven: Yale University Press.
    1994. "On Organicism in Sonata Form." In *The Masterwork in Music,* vol. 2.
    Edited by William Drabkin. Translated by Ian Bent *et al.* Cambridge
    University Press. 23–30.
Scheurer, Timothy A. 1997. "John Williams and Film Music Since 1971." *Popular
    Music and Society* 21/1: 59–72.
Schmalfeldt, Janet. 1983. *Berg's* Wozzeck: *Harmonic Language and Dramatic
    Design.* New Haven: Yale University Press.
Schmitz, Eugen. 1907. *Richard Strauss als Musikdramatiker.* Munich: Dr. Heinrich
    Lewy.
Schoenberg, Arnold. 1967. *Fundamentals of Musical Composition.* Edited by
    G. Strang and L. Stein. Oxford University Press.
    1988. "Program Notes to a Recording of *Verklärte Nacht.*" In *Arnold Schoenberg:
    Self-Portrait.* Edited by Nuria Schoenberg Nono. Pacific Palisades, CA:
    Belmont. 119–23.
    1995. *The Musical Idea and the Logic, Technique, and Art of Its Presentation.*
    Edited and translated by Patricia Carpenter and Severine Neff. New York:
    Columbia University Press.
Schubert, Linda. 1997. "Bringing the Dead to Life: Scores for Romantic
    Supernatural Films of the 1940s." *The Sonneck Society for American Music
    Bulletin* 23/2: 33–37.

Scott, Anna Besser. 1995. "Thematic Transmutation in the Music of Brahms: A Matter of Musical Alchemy." *The Journal of Musicological Research* 15/3: 177–206.

Sessions, Roger. 1979. "The New Musical Horizon." In *Roger Sessions on Music, Collected Essays*. Edited by Edward T. Cone. Princeton University Press. 45–52.

Shaw, Bernard. 1898. *The Perfect Wagnerite: A Commentary on* The Ring of the Nibelungs. London: G. Richards.

Sinn, Clarence E. 1911. "Music for the Pictures." *Moving Picture World* 8/3: 135.

Skelton, Geoffrey. 1991. *Wagner in Thought and Practice*. London: Lime Tree.

Smith, Charles. 1986. "The Functional Extravagance of Chromatic Chords." *Music Theory Spectrum* 8: 94–139.

Smith, Marian. 2000. *Ballet and Opera in the Age of* Giselle. Princeton University Press.

Sobaskie, James. 1985. "A Theory of Associative Harmony for Tonal Music." Ph.D. diss., University of Wisconsin.
    1987. "Associative Harmony: The Reciprocity of Ideas in Musical Space." *In Theory Only* 10/1–2: 31–64.

Solie, Ruth. 1977. "Metaphor and Model in the Analysis of Melody." Ph.D. diss., University of Chicago.

Spencer, Stewart and Barry Millington, eds. and trans. 1987. *Selected Letters of Richard Wagner*. London: J.M. Dent & Sons, Ltd.

Spencer, Stewart *et al.* 1993. *Wagner's* Ring of the Nibelung: *A Companion*. London: Thames & Hudson.

Steblin, Rita. 1983. *A History of Key Characteristics in the Eighteenth and Early Nineteenth Centuries*. Ann Arbor: University of Michigan Press.

Stein, Deborah. 1989. "Schubert's 'Erlkönig': Motivic Parallelism and Motivic Transformation." *19th-Century Music* 13/2: 145–58
    1985. *Hugo Wolf's Lieder and Extensions to Tonality*. Ann Arbor: UMI Research Press.

Stein, Jack Madison. 1973. *Richard Wagner and the Synthesis of the Arts*. Westport: Greenwood.

Stokes, Jeffrey Lewis. 1984. "Contour and Motive: A Study of 'Flight' and 'Love' in Wagner's *Ring*, *Tristan*, and *Meistersinger*." Ph.D. diss., State University of New York.

Stravinsky, Igor. 1970. *Poetics of Music*. Cambridge, MA: Harvard University Press.

Stuckenschmidt, H.H. 1969. *Maurice Ravel: Variations on His Life and Work*. Translated by Samuel R. Rosenbaum. London: Calder and Boyars.

Swinden, Kevin. 2005. "When Functions Collide: Aspects of Plural Function in Chromatic Music." *Music Theory Spectrum* 27/2: 249–82.

Tanner, Michael. 1996. *Wagner*. Princeton University Press.

Tarasti, Eero. 1979. *Myth and Music: A Semiotic Approach to the Aesthetics of Myth in Music, Especially That of Wagner, Sibelius, and Stravinsky*. Gravenhage: Mouton.

Taruskin, Richard. 2010. *Music in the Seventeenth and Eighteenth Centuries*. Oxford University Press.

Tchaikovsky, Modeste. 1970. *The Life and Letters of Peter Ilich Tchaikovsky*. Edited and translated by Rosa Newmarch. New York: Haskell House.

Thompson, William Forde, Frank A. Rosa, and Dan Sinclair. 1994. "Effects of Underscoring on the Perception of Closure in Filmed Events." *Psychomusicology* 13: 9–27.

Thorau, Christian. 2003. *Semantisierte Sinnlichkeit: Studien zu Rezeption und Zeichenstruktur der Leitmotiftechnik Richard Wagners*. Stuttgart: Franz Steiner Verlag.

Tolkien, J.R.R. 1981. *The Letters of J.R.R. Tolkien*. Edited by Humphrey Carpenter. Boston: Houghton Mifflin.

Tovey, Donald Francis. 1949. "Tonality in Schubert." In *The Main Stream of Music and other Essays*. New York: Oxford University Press. 134–59.

Treitler, Leo. 1997. "Language and the Interpretation of Music." In *Music & Meaning*. Edited by Jenefer Robinson. Ithaca: Cornell University Press. 23–56.

Turino, Thomas. 1999. "Signs of Imagination, Identity, and Experience: A Peircian Semiotic Theory for Music." *Ethnomusicology* 43/2: 221–55.

Twain, Mark. 1996. *The Complete Humorous Sketches and Tales of Mark Twain*. Edited by Charles Neider. Cambridge, MA: Da Capo Press.

Wagner, Cosima. 1978. *Diaries*. Translated by Geoffrey Skelton, vol. I. New York: Harcourt, Brace, Jovanovich.

   1994. *Cosima Wagner's Diaries: An Abridgement*. Edited and translated by Geoffrey Skelton. New Haven: Yale University Press.

Wagner, Gottfried. 1999. *Twilight of the Wagners: The Unveiling of a Family's Legacy*. New York: Picador.

Wagner, Richard. 1881–83. *Gesammelte Schriften und Dichtungen von Richard Wagner*. Leipzig: E.W. Fritzsch.

   1966a. "The Artwork of the Future." In *Richard Wagner's Prose Works*, vol. 1. Translated by William Ashton Ellis. New York: Broude Brothers. 69–213.

   1966b. "Opera and Drama." In *Richard Wagner's Prose Works*, vol. 2. Translated by William Ashton Ellis. New York: Broude Brothers. 3–376.

   1966c. "A Communication to My Friends." In *Richard Wagner's Prose Works*, vol. 1. Translated by William Ashton Ellis. New York: Broude Brothers. 269–392.

   1966d. "On Franz Liszt's Symphonic Poems." In *Richard Wagner's Prose Works*, vol. 3. Translated by William Ashton Ellis. New York: Broude Brothers. 237–54.

1966e. "Zukunfstmusik." In *Richard Wagner's Prose Works*, vol. 3. Translated by William Ashton Ellis. New York: Broude Brothers. 293–346.

1966f. Review of Giselle. In *Richard Wagner's Prose Works*, vol. 8. Translated by William Ashton Ellis. New York: Broude Brothers. 141–48.

1966g. "On the Application of Music to the Drama." In *Richard Wagner's Prose Works*, vol. 6. Translated by William Ashton Ellis. New York: Broude Brothers. 175–91.

1966h. "Art and Religion." In *Richard Wagner's Prose Works*, vol. 6. Translated by William Ashton Ellis. New York: Broude Brothers. 211–52.

Walton, Kendall. 1997. "Listening with Imagination: Is Music Representational?" In *Music & Meaning*. Edited by Jenefer Robinson. Ithaca: Cornell University Press. 57–82.

Warrack, John. 1976. *Carl Maria von Weber*. Second edition. Cambridge University Press.

2001. *German Opera: From the Beginnings to Wagner*. Cambridge University Press.

Weiner, Marc. 1997. "Wagner and the Perils of Reading." *Wagner* 18/2: 59–82.

Weisel, Eilat Meir. 1978. "The Presence and Evaluation of Thematic Relationship and Thematic Unity." *Israel Studies in Musicology* 1: 77–91.

Weiss, Piero and Richard Taruskin. 1984. *Music in the Western World: A History in Documents*. New York: Schirmer.

Wheelock, Gretchen. 1993. "*Schwarze Gredel* and the Engendered Minor Mode in Mozart's Operas." In *Musicology and Difference*. Edited by Ruth Solie. Berkeley: University of California Press. 201–24.

White, David. 1988. *The Turning Wheel: A Study of Contracts and Oaths in Wagner's Ring*. Selinsgrove, PA: Susquehanna University Press.

Whittall, Arnold. 1981. "The Music." In *Richard Wagner: Parsifal*. Cambridge National Opera Handbook. Edited by Lucy Beckett. Cambridge University Press. 61–86.

Windsperger, Lothar. n.d. *Das Buch der Motive, Band II*. Mainz: B. Schott's Söhne.

Wintle, Christopher. 1976. "Milton Babbitt's *Semi-Simple Variations*." *Perspectives of New Music* 14/2–15/1: 111–54.

1985. "The Questionable Lightness of Being: Brünnhilde's Peroration to the Ring." In *Götterdämmerung, Opera Guide Series 31*. Edited by Nicolas John. London: Calder. 39–48.

1988. "The Numinous in *Götterdämmerung*." In *Reading Opera*. Edited by Arthur Groos and Roger Parker. Princeton University Press. 200–34.

1992. "Analysis and Psychoanalysis: Wagner's Musical Metaphors." In *Companion to Contemporary Musical Thought*, vol. 2. Edited by John Paynter *et al.* London: Routledge. 650–91.

Wolzogen, Hans von. 1876. *Thematischer Leitfaden durch die Musik zu Richard Wagners Festspiel "Der Ring des Nibelungen."* Leipzig: Feodor Reinboth.

1897. "Leitmotive." *Bayreuther Blätter* 20: 313–30.

Wörner, Karl. 1931–32. "Beiträge zur Geschichte des Leitmotifs in der Oper." *Zeitschrift für Musikwissenschaft* 14: 151–72.

Wright, H. Stephen. 1989. "The Materials of Film Music: Their Nature and Accessibility." In *Film Music I*. Edited by Clifford McCarty. New York: Garland, 3–15.

Youmans, Charles. 1996. "Richard Strauss's *Guntram* and the Dismantling of Wagnerian Musical Metaphysics." Ph.D. diss., Duke University.

Zbikowski, Lawrence. 2002. *Conceptualizing Music: Cognitive Structure, Theory and Analysis*. Oxford University Press.

Index

2001: A Space Odyssey, 123

A.I., 155
Abbate, Carolyn, 23, 26, 29, 73, 79, 98, 101,
    108, 113, 118, 121, 129, 164, 167, 180, 195,
    198, 208–9, 212, 223, 267, 276, 281–82,
    301, 304, 314–15
Adorno, Theodor, 26, 28, 56, 86, 141, 160, 259,
    263, 267, 271, 283, 301, 307
Agawu, Kofi, 3, 50, 92, 301
Agmon, Eytan, 205, 301
Aldritch, Richard, 24, 301
Allen, Graham, 124, 301
Allusion, 60, 114, 124–25, 179, 220, 226, 235,
    242, 246–48, 250, 299
Almén, Byron, 276, 301, 304
Altman, Rick, 141, 257, 301
Ambros, August Wilhelm, 22
Anderson, Lyle John, 61, 301
Anson-Cartwright, Mark, 46, 68, 70, 121, 301
Associative theme. See "Theme, associative"
Associative tonality. See "Tonality, associative"
Associative Transposition, 195–200, 207, 222,
    226, 228, 291–93
Associativity, 79–155
Atlas, Raphael, 312
Atmospheric film score. See "Film score,
    atmospheric"
Attinello, Paul, 309

Babbitt, Milton, 133, 302
Bach, Carl Philipp Emanuel, 302
Bach, Johann Christian, 21
Bach, Johann Sebastian, 37, 46, 94, 109–10,
    304–5
    "Erbarme dich", 94
    Fugue #2 in C Minor from Das
        Wohltemperierte Klavier, Book I, 48
Bailbé, J.M., 15
Bailey, Robert, 52–53, 114, 170, 195–97, 214,
    302
Bakhtin, Mikhail, 124
Ballet, 238, 241, 243–45, 254, 258–59

Barthes, Roland, 87, 112, 302
Baskin, Wade, 317
Bass, Richard, 148, 302
Batman films, 147, 151, 282, 290, 295, 309
Bauer, Hans Joachim, 218, 302
Beach, David, 317
Beckett, Lucy, 320
Beethoven, Ludwig van, 10, 28, 33, 35, 37, 43,
    49–50, 61, 94, 98–99, 117, 130–32, 160,
    162, 169, 182, 189, 222, 265, 304–5,
    308–9, 317
    An die ferne Geliebte, 98–99
    "Auf dem Hügel sitz ich, spähend", 98
    Bagatelle in G Minor, Op. 119, No. 1, 49
    Fidelio, 222
    "Nimm sie hin denn, diese Lieder", 98
    String Quartet in F Major, Op. 81, 94
    Symphony No. 3 in E-flat Major ("Eroica"),
        182
    Symphony No. 5 in C Minor, 130–31
    Symphony No. 9 in D Minor ("Choral"), 160
Beetlejuice, 152
Beggs, John M., 133, 302
Bent, Ian, 317
Berg, Alban, 100, 228, 231, 316–17
    Wozzeck, 100, 228, 231, 313, 317
Berg, Charles Merrell, 262, 264, 302
Berg, S.M., 257
Berger, Anna Maria Busse, 107, 302
Berlin Alexanderplatz, 265
Berlioz, Hector, 15–16, 81, 98, 104, 118–19,
    139, 144, 153, 233, 253
    Harold in Italy, 98, 144, 153
    La Damnation de Faust, 118–19, 139,
        153, 233
    Symphonie Fantastique, 15–16, 104, 253
Bernadoni, Virgilio, 310
Bernhart, Walter, 315
Bernstein, Fred, 98, 302
Bernstein, Leonard, 87, 107, 311
    West Side Story, 107
Berry, Wallace, 34, 302
Blasius, Leslie, 195, 302

322

Rose BRUFORD COLLEGE
LEARNING RESOURCES CENTRE

Lamorbey Park
Sidcup Kent
DA15 9DF

Printed in Great Britain
by Amazon

36100796R00203